ADVANCE PRAISE FOR

Social Justice Journalism

"Ever since Linda J. Lumsden's incisive biography of Inez Milholland, I have been reading everything she writes. *Social Justice Journalism* is no exception. Lumsden draws a clear, straight line from the social justice journals of the early twentieth century to the digital social movement advocacy of today that, like its print predecessors, often meets the high journalistic standard of verification."

—BROOKE KROEGER, NYU Arthur L. Carter Journalism Institute,
author of *The Suffragents: How Women Used Men to Get the Vote*;
Nellie Bly; and *Undercover Reporting: The Truth About Deception*

"From the abolitionist press and woman's suffrage press to the online Resistance media against POTUS45, Linda J. Lumsden brings to life in these pages the energizing history of America's social justice media. Against often daunting odds for labor, for environmentalists, for civil rights movements, for disabled activists, and others, media activism has been the heart and mind of pressure for progressive change."

—JOHN D. H. DOWNING, author of *Radical Media:
Rebellious Communication and Social Movements*

Social Justice Journalism

scholarsourcing

Jane Singer, City, University of London, *Founding Series Editor*
Carolyn Bronstein, DePaul University, *Associate Series Editor*

VOLUME 2

The AEJMC–Peter Lang Scholarsourcing Series
is part of the Peter Lang Media and Communication list.
Every volume is peer reviewed and meets
the highest quality standards for content and production.

PETER LANG
New York • Bern • Berlin
Brussels • Vienna • Oxford • Warsaw

Linda J. Lumsden

Social Justice Journalism

A Cultural History of Social Movement Media from Abolition to #womensmarch

PETER LANG
New York • Bern • Berlin
Brussels • Vienna • Oxford • Warsaw

Library of Congress Cataloging-in-Publication Control Number: 2019003103

Bibliographic information published by **Die Deutsche Nationalbibliothek**.
Die Deutsche Nationalbibliothek lists this publication in the "Deutsche
Nationalbibliografie"; detailed bibliographic data are available
on the Internet at http://dnb.d-nb.de/.

ISSN 2373-6976 (print)
ISSN 2373-6984 (online)
ISBN 978-1-4331-6505-4 (hardcover)
ISBN 978-1-4331-6506-1 (paperback)
ISBN 978-1-4331-6507-8 (ebook pdf)
ISBN 978-1-4331-6508-5 (epub)
ISBN 978-1-4331-6509-2 (mobi)
DOI 10.3726/b15024

Dedicated with much love to
Jessalee Lumsden Landfried
and
Samuel Lumsden Landfried

CONTENTS

ACKNOWLEDGMENTS

Many people lent a hand to help me complete this book. First, thanks to Beth Stahmer, director of the University of Arizona's Social & Behavioral Sciences Research Institute (SBSRI), whose enthusiasm and support always have been a boon to my research. Thanks to SBSRI as well for a 2016 grant to do research at the Sierra Club archives at The Bancroft Library, University of California, Berkeley, and for an SBSRI Research Professorship that enabled me to work on the book full-time in fall 2017. I also am grateful for a UA Udall Center for Studies in Public Policy Fellowship that allowed me to devote the 2016 spring semester to research.

Social Justice Journalism would not have been possible without the Association for Education in Journalism and Mass Communication (AEJMC). Many thanks to everyone who voted for this project in the 2016 AEJMC-Peter Lang Scholarsourcing Book Competition. Special thanks to the Editorial Committee that selected the project in the final round of judging: Jane Singer, City University, London; Carolyn Bronstein, DePaul University; David Perlmutter, Texas Tech University; Paula Poindexter, University of Texas at Austin; and Richard Waters, University of San Francisco. Carolyn Kitch, Temple University, joined the committee later and generously offered insightful notes on the original manuscript. And if that support were not enough, a 2016 AEJMC

Senior Scholar Research Grant enabled me to do archival work at the London School of Economics. I am very grateful to this excellent organization. Many thanks as well to everyone on the editorial and production teams at Peter Lang Publishing, especially former senior acquisitions editor Mary Savigar and her successors, Kathryn Harrison and Erika Hendrix.

Other organizations also provided funding for research trips. Thank you to the Sallie Bingham Center for Women's History and Culture for the Mary Lilly Research Grant for research in Robin Morgan's archival papers at Duke University. Thanks as well to the American Journalism Historians Association, of which I've been a proud member for more than twenty-five years, for awarding me a Joseph Kerns Research Grant in 2015 that funded research at Bancroft.

Researchers are dependent on the kindness of research librarians in the archives they visit, and I have been fortunate to work with excellent librarians who were generous with their time and expertise during visits to the collections of: The Bancroft Library; the Sallie Bingham Center for Women and History, Special Collections, Duke University; the Archives and Special Collections at the British Library of Political and Economic Science, London School of Economics and Public Policy; the GLBT Historical Society Archives in San Francisco; the Walter P. Reuther Library of Labor and Urban Affairs, Wayne State University, Detroit; the Sophia Smith Collection, Smith College; and the Archives of the Tamiment Library, New York University. The librarians who get the biggest shout-out, however, are located much closer to home. I never could have written the book without the expert staff of UA's Library Interlibrary Loan Office, which filled hundreds of requests for books, articles, and more. I also am indebted to the many scholars of social movements and journalism whose excellent work made my own study possible.

One of the most esteemed of those scholars, John D. H. Downing kindly read the introduction and made suggestions that reshaped the book. I appreciate his sage insights. My gratitude extends to Kathryn Abbott for her supportive comments on the final manuscript. Thanks also to graduate student Zeina Cabrera-Peterson for helping to track down citations for Chapter Five. I am obliged as well to copy editor Bridget Leahy, who deftly proofread the manuscript on short notice. Any errors or omissions, of course, are mine alone.

I also would like to thank the journalists and activists—or both!—who took time to speak with me. I am especially grateful to the staff at *Sierra* magazine, who let me follow them around for a day: *Insider* newsletter editor Tom Balton, story editor Wendy Becktold, editor-in-chief Jason Mark, and senior editor Paul Raub. In London, Jakub Sobik was a gracious and informative host at Anti-Slavery International. I also very much appreciate two enlightening telephone interviews with Carmen Rios of Ms. magazine and Marilee Adamski-Smith of ADAPT.

I work with the best colleagues in the world in the UA School of Journalism. Their devotion to our students and to the journalism profession inspires me. Thanks to former school Director Dave Cuillier for signing grant and leave applications that helped advance my research and writing of this book. Many friends in Tucson and beyond offered encouragement during the research, writing, and editing of this book—*muchas gracias por todo*!

Last but never least, I am grateful for my far-flung family's love and support: my sister, Laurie Kamuda, in Vermont; my daughter and son-in-law, Jessalee Landfried and Aaron Reuben, in North Carolina; and my son, Samuel Landfried, in Colorado.

Tucson, Arizona
November 30, 2018

INTRODUCTION

Abolition Editors, Digital Activists, and Social Justice Journalism

Florida school-shooting survivor Sarah Chadwick had no idea that the subversive YouTube video in which she mocks the National Rifle Association owed a debt to a dour nineteenth-century Scot named Zachary Macaulay.[1] Her viral video was part of the #MarchForOurLives social media campaign created by Marjory Stoneman Douglas High School students after seventeen of their classmates died in the 2018 Valentine's Day school shooting. Forty days later, some two million people marched in Washington, D.C., and 763 other locations to demand stricter gun control laws.[2] Nearly two centuries earlier, abolitionist editor Macaulay also wielded sarcasm in the pages of the *Anti-Slavery Monthly Reporter* to confront a foe even more formidable than the NRA—the proslavery establishment that ran the British Empire.[3]

Virtually every digital message made by twenty-first-century social movement media echoes strategies that Macaulay pioneered in the dense abolitionist magazine he launched in 1825. The world's first transnational social movement periodical and voice of the world's oldest social movement continues today as the London-based Anti-Slavery International's *Reporter* magazine, making it since 1840 the longest continually published social justice journal in the world.[4] Although scholars have showered attention upon social media's role in facilitating activism since the Arab Spring briefly bloomed in 2010, the

Anti-Slavery Monthly Reporter reminds us that social movement media did not originate online. Macaulay and his magazine exemplify myriad links among old and new forms of journalism for social justice, an ethic that avows that all human beings deserve equality, fairness, and dignity.

Social Justice Journalism argues that to better understand the evolution, impact, and future of digital social justice media, we need to understand their connections to a venerable print culture of dissent. *Smart Mobs* author Howard Rheingold's observation that the Internet brings together "people who are able to act in concert even if they don't know each other" could as easily apply to the abolitionist press.[5] The Internet collapses time and space to exponentially expand opportunities for what Benedict Anderson famously described as "imagined communities," but it is worth recalling that his groundbreaking work on how media can create a symbolic community is based on the invention of the newspaper.[6] Just as publishing a newspaper was the first priority of past social movement organizations, creating a Twitter hashtag is often the first task of today's social justice activists.

A social movement is "a collectivity acting with some continuity to promote or resist a change in the society or group of which it is a part," as defined by Ralph H. Turner and Lewis M. Killian in the 1950s.[7] John McCarthy and Mayer Zald in 1973 defined social movements as "voluntary collectives that people support in order to effect change in society."[8] A quarter century later, Sidney Tarrow characterized social movements as contentious "collective challenges, based on common purposes and social solidarities, in sustained interaction with elites, opponents, and authorities."[9] A social movement can be a force for good or evil, but this book examines only movements for social justice. White supremacy may be a social movement, but readers of *Social Justice Journalism* will not find a discussion of the *Fiery Cross*, a Ku Klux Klan newspaper in 1920s Indiana.[10]

This cultural history seeks to deepen and contextualize knowledge about digital activism by training the lens of social movement theory back on the nearly forgotten role of eight twentieth-century American social justice journals in effecting significant social change. The book also compares these periodicals to their counterparts online to illuminate links between print culture and digital media. The book deliberately conflates "social movement media" with newer and broader conceptions of "social justice journalism" to highlight changing definitions of journalism, an umbrella-term open to interpretation. Sociologists refer to social movement media to describe a wide range of "self-mediated" materials produced by social movement organizations to advocate for their cause. Social movement media matter because they are the "central battleground" on which movements, according to leading scholar William A. Gamson, define themselves and their issues as they challenge dominant institutions.[11]

One of those institutions is mainstream news media, which in the twentieth century worshiped at the altar of "objectivity" that has since been widely debunked as the subjective worldview of the overwhelmingly white, heterosexual, middle-class men who controlled news media.[12] They rejected the open advocacy practiced by social movement media as unprofessional, although a new ethos of transparency is overtaking objectivity as journalism's normative ideal. Historically, some of the nation's most significant journalism has been produced by social justice movement media. After a mob lynched three friends of Ida Wells-Barnett, for example, the African American publisher of *Memphis Free Speech* documented terrorism against blacks across the South in the 1890s. Wells's activist stance against lynching did not negate her investigation, which, to use Bill Kovach and Tom Rosenstiel's phrase, displayed the essence of journalism as "the discipline of verification."[13]

Despite their advocacy, many social movement media fulfill what media scholars Charlie Beckett and Robin Mansell list as the essential functions of traditional journalism: to report, analyze, and comment, filter, edit, and disseminate.[14] Further, the abolitionist press, the suffrage press, and the labor press all exemplified some of the profession's highest ideals as expressed in the Society of Professional Journalists Code of Ethics: "Be vigilant and courageous about holding those with power accountable. Give voice to the voiceless."[15] Unlike for-profit mainstream news media, social movement media publishers measure success not in circulation or advertising dollars but in effecting social change. Journalism historian Bob Ostertag observes that even some of the smallest, shortest-lived social movement journals have "played a critical role in the constant process of reinventing American society."[16] David Paul Nord's classic study of how newspapers build communities, in fact, argues that William Lloyd Garrison's fire-and-brimstone abolitionist newspaper, the *Liberator*, best embodied Alexander de Tocqueville's vision of American newspapers as the lifeblood of the young democracy.[17] Other examples include abolitionist Frederick Douglass's *North Star* newspaper (1847–1851), the gay rights magazine the *Advocate* (1967–present), and the Sierra Club's "Beyond Coal" online multimedia report in 2018, "Toxic Coal Dust Coating Homes, Playgrounds, and Lungs."

Social Justice Journalism—Disrupting the Information Model?

All three examples above also exemplify social justice journalism, a broader concept that began to gain traction among news media in the early twenty-first century. Dizzying new digital tools that facilitate collaborations between activists and journalists in what Jeff Jarvis terms "networked journalism" spurred a re-envisioning of journalism models.[18] Adrienne Russell's *Journalism as Activism*, for example, lauds a new "hybrid journalism" comprising a "news-media vanguard of political activists and innovative traditional reporters who are changing the way reporting the news works to serve the public interest."[19] Michela Ardizzoni uses "matrix activism" to explain the complex convergence of resistance enabled by digital technology that she asserts encompasses mainstream media, alternative media, social media, face-to-face communication, art, and performance.[20] Globally, a new generation of digital reporters intentionally label themselves "media activists" instead of journalists even though they practice the craft by documenting oppression with their cell phones. Pioneering radical media scholar John D. H. Downing describes a "meld of legacy and digital media activism" that challenges conventional conceptions about journalism.[21] Cultural scholar Barbie Zelizer states that journalism is inherently informed by social justice ideals. Many forms of journalism operate primarily from a critical impulse that, she writes, "draws from the oppositions and the disenfranchised. ..."[22] For that matter, she argues that definitions of journalism vary among interpretative communities: "The most recognizable terms—'journalists' and 'journalism'—are often used as generalized labels for the broadest possible range of activities associated with news making and the people who engage in them."[23]

The trend toward social justice journalism has links to such historical iterations as "civic journalism" (or "public journalism"), a popular movement in the 1990s that called for newspapers to drop their detachment, acknowledge themselves as members of the communities they cover, and use their forum to help solve problems they reported on. "Citizen journalism" (or "participation journalism") gained traction in the early 1990s to describe acts of reporting, analyzing, and disseminating news by ordinary citizens as more people got connected to the Internet.[24] Dan Gillmor traces citizen journalism back even farther to pamphleteer Tom Paine, whose self-mediated "Common Sense" persuaded American colonists in 1776 to declare their independence from their superpower Mother Country.[25] Nellie Bly's first-person "Ten Days in a

Madhouse," her undercover exposé of a women's mental institution in 1887, presaged the "immersion journalism" (or "saturation journalism" or "participatory journalism") of Barbara Ehrenreich's foray into the world of the working poor, *Nickel and Dimed: On (Not) Getting By in America* (2001).[26] Hunter S. Thompson revved this genre into high gear with his "gonzo journalism," the antithesis of detached reportage.[27]

Even if not specifically identified as its own genre, social justice journalism always has been woven into the larger field. In 2017, the Pulitzer Prizes unveiled a vast online archive called "Social Justice and Equality" to showcase the many winning works on this theme over its past century, including the *New York World's* 1923 Public Service Award for articles exposing activities of the Ku Klux Klan, Howard Van Smith's 1959 National Reporting Award for a *Miami News* series that exposed deplorable living conditions at a migrant labor camp, and the *Seattle Times* team's 1997 Investigative Reporting Award for a series on widespread corruption and inequities in a federally sponsored housing program for Native Americans. The phrase began showing up in collegiate journalism programs in the early 2010s as educators scrambled to find new ways to prepare students for a radically transforming field.

One of the earliest offerings appears to be a 2011 course titled "Civic Journalism and Social Justice" at the University of Richmond. In 2013, American University's School of Communication received a $300,000 grant to fund the Justice Project to teach students and community fellows how to produce "social justice journalism," defined as in-depth reports on societal inequities and systemic abuses that "drive collective engagement and change on those issues." The phrase was so new that a fellow who had spent his journalism career covering marginalized communities said he had not considered his reporting as social justice journalism until he was invited to apply to the project.[28] Although the program ended in 2016, the school still plugs its master's degree in journalism with the tagline, "Telling Stories to Compel Change." Northwestern University's Medill School of Journalism offers a specialization in Social Justice and Investigative Reporting that teaches students how to tell "stories of people who are disenfranchised, vulnerable or oppressed…" (although it does not mention advocacy).[29] The University of California at Berkeley in 2016 introduced a Massive Open Online Course (MOOC) in "Journalism for Social Change," described as "using solution-based journalism to drive social change."[30] The Aronson Awards for Social Justice Journalism & Cartooning with a Conscience, administered by Hunter College of the City University of New York, have championed social justice journalism since the

1990s. The 2017 winners included a *St. Louis Post-Dispatch* team that not only revealed the effects of toxic stress from violence and poverty on children in Ferguson, Missouri, but also offered resources to help families heal.

Environmental Health News, which won an Aronson Award for an in-depth investigation titled "Sacred Water: Environmental Justice in Indian Country," is representative of the new breed of digital-native news outlets whose activism is organic to their journalism. *VICE IMPACT*, for example, boosts its reporting with an "Action Button" at the end of each story that readers can use to email, call, or tweet their representatives on issues, such as a story on how legal marijuana could revolutionize PTSD treatment for veterans. ProPublica, the Pulitzer Prize–winning investigative journalism digital news outlet, acknowledges it "has quite self-consciously measured its own success by the impact of its journalism, i.e. by the change and reform that journalism has spurred."[31] The independent nonprofit newsroom lists in its annual reports all tangible impacts spurred by its reporting, such as a flurry of bills that states passed in 2018 to address rising U.S. maternal death rates revealed in "Lost Mothers," a joint ProPublica/National Public Radio investigative series.[32] Back on campus, a *College Media Review* article promoting social justice journalism suggests several forms of activism that students might incorporate in their stories. One suggestion is to accompany stories with related online petitions for readers to sign,[33] a tactic that demonstrates the ties between digital activism and the historical print culture of social justice journalism. Nineteenth-century abolitionist journals were full of petition forms and advice to readers on how to start and circulate them. Petitions remain a staple of virtual social movements, the process vastly sped up and simplified by online generators such as Change.org, which by October 2018 claimed 30,542 victories in 196 nations thanks to 253,874,085 petitioners around the world.[34]

The emerging model of journalism-activism mash-up has sparked introspection among professionals. On the heels of the March for Our Lives, an editor of the Stoneman Douglas student newspaper challenged the profession's creed of objectivity, whose origins date back to the rise of the commercial penny press in the 1830s.[35] "Journalism is a form of activism," stated Rebecca Schneid, co-editor-in-chief of the *Eagle Eye*, on CNN's *Reliable Sources*.[36] Some legacy journalists disagreed, but a surprising number concurred. "Does anybody think that even the fairest and most diligent of investigative reporters wrote their horrifying stories hoping that nothing would change?" tweeted Matt Pearce of the *Los Angeles Times*.[37] Supporters emphasized that social justice journalists revere facts and verification, differentiating their advocacy from the divisive braying of cable-TV political pundits who prize volume over veracity.[38] Its emphasis on facts and documentation also distinguishes social justice journalism from propaganda, defined as biased or misleading information used to help or injure a particular cause or point of view. Propaganda does appear in some social movement media but also, according to "propaganda model" proponents Noam Chomsky and Edward S. Herman, in mainstream media.[39]

Social Justice Journalism refers to all forms of reportorial endeavors past and present that advocate positive social change as social justice journalism, whether they appear in Environmental Justice journal or in the New York Times. Just like legacy media professionals, social justice journalists use facts, storytelling, narrative, and emotion to engage readers.

An Amalgam of Sociology, Journalism History, and Media/Communication Studies

Social Justice Journalism aims to help fill a scholarly gap between sociology, journalism history, and media/communications studies of social justice journalism.[40] Sociologists, for example, emphasize social movement activism but practically ignore movement media's role in facilitating collective action.[41] Downing notes the field's "splendidly self-confident neglect of communication and media as integral dimensions of social movements."[42] Communications scholars who study social movement rhetoric concentrate on performance or protests.[43] Communications and media studies that do address social movement media fixate on social media such as Twitter or digital activism such as culture jamming.[44] Russell's history of the rise of online "networked journalism" between 1990 and 2010, for example, barely acknowledges the existence of myriad social movements' dynamic print cultures.[45] In contrast, journalism historians delve into old social movement periodicals but generally follow a narrative approach that minimizes theoretical analysis. They treat social movement periodicals as discrete segments of a broader and vaguer "alternative press," "dissident press," or "alternative media" that obscures their central role in social change.[46] Scholars of digital activism have adopted the latter term, although even Alternative Media author Joshua Atkinson concedes it is "slippery."[47] The alternative-media label further clouds discussion of social justice journalism because beyond periodicals it encompasses a galaxy of texts including songs, murals, virtual sit-ins, street theatre, and even clothing, like the sea of pink pussy hats displayed during the 2017 Women's March in Washington, D.C., and hundreds of other cities.[48]

This study takes a cultural approach to explore the history of a single but significant star amid that media galaxy: twentieth-century social justice movement newspapers and magazines and the precedents they set for activists that migrated online in the new millennium. It uses cultural historical research methods, a loosely defined qualitative approach that involves close readings of cultural texts such as books, periodicals, and imagery to explore representations and the struggle over meaning that is at the heart of social justice journalism.[49] The book argues that while the Internet exponentially expands and speeds social justice movements' short-term ability to communicate and coordinate collective action, the five basic functions of social movement media remain much the same in 2019 as they did when Macaulay's *Anti-Slavery Monthly Reporter* debuted on June 30, 1825: (1) recruit members; (2) inform and educate their audience; (3) build and sustain a collective identity; (4) engage and counter mainstream media; and (5) mobilize collective action.

The study highlights how social movement periodicals used or transformed traditional journalism tools to fulfill those five functions. Before leaping back to the twentieth century, however, a few definitions and a brief discussion of the theoretical foundations guiding this inquiry may prove useful. The following sections address why social justice movements create their own media, explain framing theory and the importance of collective action frames, discuss the role of narrative and storytelling in journalism, and consider how both social movements and journalists employ emotion. The Introduction concludes with a brief overview of the nine chapters and conclusion that follow.

Social Movements and Mainstream Media

Numerous scholars across disciplines have demonstrated how mainstream news media historically have ignored, demonized, or denigrated social movements[50] and distorted their messages.[51] An example is Todd Gitlin's conclusion in his classic study of New Left politics that 1960s activists were "trivialized, polarized, marginalized and disparaged" by mainstream media.[52] Noted journalism historian Michael Schudson concurs: "The press is presumably the bastion of free expression in a democracy, but too often it has been one of the institutions that limits the range of expression, especially expression that is critical of leading centers of power in society."[53] Communication scholars Robert Hackett and William Carroll attribute "media's democratic deficit" to its failure to create a true "public sphere." As conceived by philosopher Jürgen Habermas, the public sphere is the dynamic space between the state and its citizens where a free exchange of ideas from all sectors identifies the "public will" that is elemental to real democracy.[54] Because mainstream media decline to give their ideas a fair hearing in the public sphere, social movements going back to the nineteenth-century abolitionists have created their own media to frame their issues.

Framing Theory

Since the 1980s, social movement scholars have treated framing as the central dynamic in the struggle over meaning between social movements and dominant powers.[55] Frames are sets of beliefs that "assign meaning to and interpret relevant events and conditions in ways that are intended to mobilize potential adherent and constituents, to garner bystander support, and to demobilize antagonists," according to David A. Snow and Robert D. Benford.[56] Editors choose words, story and image placement, headline sizes, rhetorical devices, and sources that when combined frame movement issues and events. These "media packages" give meaning to media messages, according to Gamson and Andre Modigliani.[57] Framing theory has proven effective in numerous media studies.[58] Bart Cammaerts defines social movement media framing as "strategic attempts to fix meaning, to establish ideological boundaries and to construct a 'we' that is juxtaposed to a 'them.'"[59] Framing is integral to creating the collective identity—that "we" versus "them"—that is fundamental to building a social movement. Collective identity, states Doug McAdams, comprises "the shared meanings and cultural understandings that people bring to any instance of potential mobilization."[60] "How successfully groups frame their identities for the public thus affects their ability to recruit members and supporters, gain a public hearing, make alliances with other groups, and defuse opposition," assert Francesca Polletta and James M. Jasper.[61] The framing process is dynamic and never-ending.

Framing remains fundamental for understanding social movement dynamics despite reconsiderations of social movement theory in the digital era.[62] Lance W. Bennett and Alexandra Segerberg posit a "logic of connective action" in which collective identity is not a prerequisite of what they call "connective action" online. They claim individuals identify with a social movement by adapting its ideology to their personal beliefs.[63] Others scholars, however, maintain collective identity remains integral even if its nature is transformed by social media.[64] Cammaert's study of Britain's Twitter-fueled anti-austerity movement even found more collective action frames than connective action frames: he found online discourse often evolved into offline collective action.[65] He argues that digital social movement media continue to fit into Gamson's categorization of collective action frames: they construct collective identities and ideological enemies, create solutions to problems, and issue calls to action.

Collective action frames suggest not just that "something can be done, but that *we* can do something," as Gamson put it.[66] He categorized them into injustice frames, identity frames, and agency frames: Injustice frames describe an injury as a wrong perpetrated by some identifiable actor against others. Identity frames shape an adversary based on differences in interests and values, creating an "us" versus "them." Agency frames describe actions that can be taken to solve the problem if the aggrieved act collectively.[67]

Emotions in Social Movement Frames

Early framing theory focused almost solely on cognition and ignored the role emotions play in meaning making. As more scholars began to view social movements through a cultural lens, they began to acknowledge the role of emotion in framing.[68] Gamson indirectly referenced emotion when he stated that injustice frames depend on "the righteous anger that puts fire in the belly and iron in the soul." He described injustice as "a hot cognition, not merely an abstract intellectual judgment. ..."[69] Jeff Goodwin, Jasper, and Polletta returned emotions to the center of social movements studies by the end of the twentieth century.[70] Jasper believes emotions infuse every aspect of social movements, influencing the recruitment, motivation, strategy, and sustenance of participants.[71] "It is hard to think of activities and relationships that are more overtly emotional than those associated with political protest and resistance," conclude Goodwin and associates.[72] The ring of authenticity in *Reporter* accounts engaged readers' emotion, for example, because they enabled the audience to experience the slave's mistreatment at a deeply emotional level.

Narrative and Storytelling in Social Justice Journalism

Recognizing emotion as central to the study of collective action opened the door to explorations of narrative and storytelling as part of the social movement repertoire. Narrative is any discourse designed to communicate a sense of overall meaning instead of chronicling events in the order they occurred. Narrative, declares psychology professor Donald E. Polkinghorne, is "the primary form by which human experience is made meaningful."[73] Narrative analysis is valuable when looking at social justice media because it highlights values and symbols in making meaning and sustaining collective identity. "[S]ocial movements are dominated by stories and storytelling," points out sociologist Joseph E. Davis, adding that narrative "illuminates core features of identity-building and meaning-making in social activism."[74] Polletta and Pang Ching Bobby Chen argue the study of storytelling may illuminate how narrative strategies help or hinder campaigns to elicit public interest and enlist support.[75] Activists' main motivation throughout history, according to Frederick W. Mayer, has been that "they are compelled by the dramatic imperative of a collective story in which they have come to see themselves as actors."[76]

Emotion in Journalism

Emotion always has infused the news.[77] A basic reporting technique is to focus on an individual who embodies a larger social issue to compel audiences to keep reading. Examples include John Hersey's *Hiroshima* (1946), J. Anthony Lukas's Pulitzer Prize–winning *Common Ground: A Turbulent Decade in the Lives of Three American Families* (1986), and Sonia Nazio's *Enrique's Journey* (2006). Journalism textbooks instruct students to appeal to readers' emotions to make their stories more compelling. Journalists rely on narrative techniques to make their stories stir fear or humor, love or anger, without abandoning the facts that define their craft. A 2012 study found that magazine-style pieces with a narrative focus are more effective than nonnarrative stories in establishing empathy for stigmatized groups that can lead to correcting injustice.[78]

Jacob Riis's *How the Other Half Lives* (1889), for example, has been credited with eliciting Americans' empathy toward immigrant tenement dwellers. "His stories effected real social change and helped bolster a budding movement to end poverty," states a 2015 article in the *Columbia Journalism Review*.

The authors cite considerable research that shows empathic responses in the human brain increasing as a person learns more about others. They cite the outpouring of support for a homeless girl profiled in "Invisible Child," an investigative series in the *New York Times*. Donations were extended to her school and to the Brooklyn shelter where she lived. The authors assert the story is "an example of what motivates many journalists, what we believe is possible through our narratives: to extend empathy for the individual to the group, to correct injustice and inspire change, or at least awareness."(The authors, however, are studying whether reading online reduces empathy.)[79]

These stories demonstrate storytelling's political power. Davis asserts that "stories precede frames, stories make frames compelling, and stories overshadow frames in mobilizing power and as a political resource."[80] Stories also provide "counternarratives" to institutional power, what Patricia Ewick and Susan S. Silbey call "subversive stories."[81] Facts alone can hold emotional power, an insight the muckrakers exploited in the early 1900s.

Muckraking in the Progressive Era

"Muckraking" was the derisive term a displeased President Theodore Roosevelt slapped on the popular "literature of exposure" that became popular in the Progressive Era.[82] These prototype investigative reporters appropriated the president's insult to describe their practice of collecting an arsenal of facts and wrapping them in moral outrage.[83] Muckraking combined the advocacy of collective action frames with the craft of journalism. Quintessential muckraker Ida Tarbell, for example, propelled "a battery of facts charged with rhetorical power" in *McClure's* magazine to expose oil mogul John D. Rockefeller's monopolistic malfeasance, states scholar Cecelia Tichi.[84] Public outrage stoked by Tarbell's detailed exposé is largely credited with the federal government's breakup of Standard Oil in 1911.[85] The case demonstrates the power of facts to persuade when the audience is presented with solutions to a social problem. Muckraking has thrived in the twenty-first century, beginning with Eric Schlosser's 2001 *Fast Food Nation: The Dark Side of the All-American Meal*, which wowed reviewers with its "arsenal of startling facts."[86] As rhetorician James Phelan observes, "[T]here are multiple facts and multiple ways of construing facts."[87]

No one understood that better in 1825 than abolitionist editor Macaulay, introduced in the opening paragraph. Macaulay's deadpan description of horrific slave laws compared with the #MarchForOurLives satirical NRA spoof on YouTube described above demonstrates just one link between digital activists' techniques and the world's oldest transnational social justice journal. New media scholar Roger Silverstone makes a similar observation. "Interactivity arguably offers a new hybridity," Silverstone states. "But at the same time, from the perspective of communication theory, there is not so much, arguably, that is new."[88]

Chapter One focuses on Macaulay's *Anti-Slavery Monthly Reporter* because it vividly demonstrates the parallels between old and new social justice journalism. It traces the *Reporter* to the nineteenth-century American abolitionist press that laid the foundation for all future U.S. social movements. The chapter sets the template for the others that follow: it begins with an in-depth profile of a pioneer journal, traces the emergence and functions of similar periodicals over time, and teases out their framing strategies and use of emotions before ending with a comparison to a digital descendant that highlights connections between print culture and digital iterations of social justice journalism. Chapter Two traces the role of the venerable *Sierra Club Bulletin* in sowing seeds for the environmental movement at the turn of the twentieth century. Chapter Three examines the socialist daily the [New York] *Call's* challenge to the rise of the corporate state in the 1910s. Chapter Four considers the *Suffragist*, last but not least of dozens of periodicals that worked to win votes for women in the 1910s. Chapter Five situates the *Arkansas State Press* in the vanguard of the Civil Rights Movement as it confronts police brutality during World War II. Chapter Six analyzes how Cesar Chavez's *El Malcriado* newspaper shaped the embryonic United Farm Workers movement in the 1960s. Chapter Seven focuses on *Ms.* magazine's role in the 1970s as the Women's Liberation Movement's bridge to mainstream media. Chapter Eight probes how the *Disability Rag* built a collective identity among diverse disabled people in the 1980s. Chapter Nine focuses on the *Gateway* and *FTM*, newsletters famously edited by pioneering transgender activist Lou Sullivan, a mentor and role model in the LGBTQ movement on the cusp of the 1990s. The conclusion summarizes the findings and considers what they reveal about the past, present, and future of journalism for social justice.

Notes

1. Daniel Politi, "March for Our Lives Put Sarah Chadwick's Spoof NRA Ad on the Big Screen and It Was Glorious," *Slate*, March 24, 2018, https://slate.com/news-and-politics/2018/03/march-for-our-lives-watch-sarah-chadwicks-spoof-nra-ad.html.

2. Kanisha Bond, Erica Chenaworth, and Jeremy Pressman, "Did You Attend the March for Our Lives? Here's What It Looked Like Nationwide," *Washington Post*, April 13, 2018, https://www.washingtonpost.com/news/monkey-cage/wp/2018/04/13/did-you-attend-the-march-for-our-lives-heres-what-it-looked-like-nationwide/?utm_term=.d39faa7df6cf.

3. See for example, "West Indian Controversy," *Anti-Slavery Monthly Reporter*, [hereafter called *Reporter*] November 30, 1826, 261; "W.I. *Reporter*—Answer to Challenge of W.I. *Reporter*," ibid., July 1829, 29–30; and "New Slave Code of Jamaica," ibid., February 1832, 57.

4. Charles Tilly and Lesley J. Wood, *Social Movements, 1768–2008* (Boulder, CO: Paradigm, 2009), 25, 33, 32. Tilly concedes the American Revolution is a contender for the title of first social movement. Ibid., xx.

5. Howard Rheingold, *Smart Mobs: The Next Social Revolution* (New York: Perseus Publishing, 2002), xii.

6. Benedict Anderson, *Imagined Communities: Reflections on the Origin and Spread of Nationalism* (London: Verso, 2006).

7. Ralph H. Turner and Lewis M. Killian, *Collective Behavior*, sub. ed. (London: Pearson, 1987), 223.

8. John McCarthy and Mayer Zald, *The Trend of Social Movements in America: Professionalization and Resource Mobilization* (Morristown, NJ: General Learning Press, 1973), 2.

9. Sidney Tarrow, *Power in Movement: Social Movements and Contentious Politics* (Cambridge: Cambridge University Press, 1998), 9.

10. Nor will it look at the NRA's *American Rifleman* magazine, whose increasingly "apocalyptic messaging" since its origins in 1923 offers a classic lesson of building collective identity. See Sahil Chinoy, Nicholas Kristof, and Jessa Ma, "How the N.R.A. Builds Loyalty and Fanaticism," *New York Times*, November 8, 2018, https://www.nytimes.com/interactive/2018/11/08/opinion/nra-mass-shootings-thousand-oaks.html?action=click&module=Opinion&pgtype=Homepage.

11. William A. Gamson, *The Strategy of Social Protest*, 2d ed. (Belmont, CA: Wadsworth Publishing, 1990), 147.

12. See Herbert J. Gans, *Deciding What's News: A Study of CBS Evening News, NBC Nightly News, Newsweek, and Time* (New York: Random House, 1979), xviii, 61.

13. Bill Kovach and Tom Rosenstiel, *The Elements of Journalism: What Newspeople Should Know and the Public Should Expect*, rev. 3rd ed. (New York: Three Rivers Press, 2014), 5.

14. Charlie Beckett and Robin Mansell, "Crossing Boundaries: New Media and Networked Journalism," *Communication, Culture and Critique* 1, no. 1 (March 2008): 93.

15. "Code of Ethics," Society of Professional Journalists, accessed October 22, 2018, https://www.spj.org/ethicscode.asp.

16. Bob Ostertag, *People's Movements, People's Press: The Journalism of Social Justice Movements* (Boston: Beacon Press, 2006), 2.

17. See David Paul Nord, "Tocqueville, Garrison, and the Perfection of Journalism," in *Communities of Journalism: A History of American Newspapers and Their Readers*, reprint ed. (Columbus: Ohio State Press, 2001), 92–107.

18. Jeff Jarvis, "Networked Journalism," *BuzzMachine*, July 5, 2006, https://buzzmachine.com/2006/07/05/networked-journalism/. See also David Carr, "Journalism, Even When It's Tilted," *New York Times*, June 30, 2013, http://www.nytimes.com/2013/07/01/business/media/journalism-is-still-at-work-even-when-its-practitioner-has-a-slant.html?_r=0; David Edwards, "Journalist Or Activist? Smearing Glenn Greenwald," *Media Lens*, October 23, 2013, http://medialens.org/index.php/alerts/alert-archive/alerts-2013/746-journalist-or-activist-smearing-glenn-greenwald.html; and Jeff Jarvis, "There Are No Journalists," *Buzz Machine*, June 30, 2013, http://buzzmachine.com/2013/06/30/there-are-no-journalists-there-is-only-journalism/.

19. Adrienne Russell, *Journalism as Activism: Recoding Media Power* (Cambridge: Polity Press, 2016), 8.

20. Michela Ardizzoni, *Matrix Activism: Global Practices of Resistance* (New York: Routledge, 2017), 160, 161.

21. John D. H. Downing, "Looking Back, Looking Ahead: What Has Changed In Social Movement Media Since the Internet and Social Media?," in *The Routledge Companion to Media and Activism*, ed. Graham Meikle (London: Routledge, 2018), 18.

22. Barbie Zelizer, "How Communication, Culture, and Critique Intersect in the Study of Journalism," *Communication, Culture & Critique* 1, no. 1 (March 2008): 89–91.

23. Barbie Zelizer, *Taking Journalism Seriously: News and the Academy* (Thousand Oaks, CA: Sage Publications, 2004), 21. See also Steen Steensen and Laura Ahva, "Theories of Journalism in a Digital Age," *Digital Journalism* 3, no. 1 (2015): 1–18.

24. See Shayne Bowman and Chris Willis, "We Media: How Audiences are Shaping the Future of News and Information," *Media Center*, September 21, 2003, http://www.hypergene.net/wemedia/weblog.php.

25. See Dan Gillmor, *We the Media: Grassroots Journalism by the People for the People* (Sebastopol, CA: O'Reilly Media, 2004).

26. "Participatory journalism" has been used to describe both the work of reporters who deliberately participate in activities they report on and ordinary citizens who get involved in reporting news (aka citizen journalism). Clair Hunt, "Participatory Reporting as Method Acting: The Journalism-Theatre Connection." (Thesis, University of Missouri–Columbia, 2007), 14.

27. See Jeffrey Steinbrink, "Mark Twain and Hunter Thompson: Continuity and Change in American 'Outlaw Journalism,'" *Studies in American Humor* 2, no. 3 (Winter 1983–84): 221–235.

28. Jacob L. Nelson and Dan A. Lewis, "Training Social Justice Journalists: A Case Study," *Journalism & Mass Communication Educator* 70, no. 4 (2015): 397, 401.

29. "Social Justice and Investigative Reporting," Medill School of Journalism, Media, Integrated Marketing Communication, accessed October 22, 2018, http://www.medill.northwestern.edu/journalism/graduate-journalism/specializations/social-justice-and-investigative-reporting/index.html.

30. "Press Release: Journalism for Social Change," *News Center*, February 26, 2015, https:// gspp.berkeley.edu/news/news-center/press-release-journalism-for-social-change.

31. "Nonprofit Journalism: Issues Around Impact," *ProPublica*, accessed October 22, 2018, https://www.propublica.org/impact/.

32. "ProPublica/NPR Collaboration a Finalist for the Pulitzer Prize for Explanatory Reporting," *ProPublica*, April 16, 2018, https://www.propublica.org/atpropublica/propublica-npr-collaboration-a-finalist-for-the-pulitzer-prize-for-explanatory-reporting.

33. Jeff Jeske, "Why Social Justice Journalism?," *College Media Review*, June 3, 2013, 17.

34. "Impact," *Change.org*, accessed October 22, 2018, https://www.change.org/impact.

35. See Dan Schiller, *Objectivity and the News: The Public and the Rise of Commercial Journalism* (Philadelphia: University of Pennsylvania Press, 1981).

36. Brian Stelter, "Journalism and Activism: This 'Reliable Sources' Segment Sparked a Debate," *CNN Media*, March 27, 2018, http://money.cnn.com/2018/03/27/media/journalism-activism-reliable-sources/index.html.

37. Danielle Tcholakian, "Is Journalism a Form of Activism?," *Longreads*, March 2018, https:// longreads.com/2018/03/29/is-journalism-a-form-of-activism/. For other discussions on the topic, see Deepak Adhikari, "The Case Against: Can Journalists Be Activists?," *Al Jazeera*, April 10, 2017, https://www.aljazeera.com/indepth/opinion/2017/03/case-journalists-activists-170327135341852.html; Tamar Ashuri, "Activist Journalism: Using Digital Technologies and Undermining Structures," *Communication, Culture & Critique* 5, no. 1 (March 2012): 38–56; Roy Greenslade, "What's So Wrong with Being a Journalist and an Activist?" *Guardian*, June 27, 2011, http://www.theguardian.com/media/greenslade/2011/jun/27/us-press-publishing-new-york-times; "The Line Between Journalism & Activism," *Frontline*, February 13, 2007, http://www.pbs.org/wgbh/pages/frontline/newswar/tags/activism.html; John H. McManus, "Objectivity: It's Time to Say Goodbye," *Nieman Reports* 63, no. 2 (Summer 2009), 78–79; Joel Simon, "What's the Difference Between Activism and Journalism?," *Nieman Reports*, December 11, 2014, http://niemanreports.org/articles/whats-the-difference-between-activism-and-journalism/; Terje Skjerdal, "Journalists Or Activists? Self-Identity in the Ethiopian Diaspora Online Community," *Journalism* 12, no. 6 (August 2011): 727–744; Bob Steele, "The Dangers of Activist-Driven Journalism," *CNN Opinion*, September 30, 2010, http://www.cnn.com/2010/OPINION/09/30/steele.objective.journalism/; and Melissa Wall, "Social Movements and the Net: Activist Journalism Goes Digital," in *Digital Journalism: Emerging Media and the Changing Horizons of Journalism*, ed. Kevin Kawamoto (Lanham, MD: Rowman & Littlefield, 2003), 113–22.

38. For definitions and critiques of cable TV punditry, see Paul Farhi, "Pundits—or Propaganda Pass-throughs?," *Washington Post*, August 24, 2016, https://www.washingtonpost.com/lifestyle/style/pundits--or-propaganda-pass-throughs/2016/08/24/017d32fc-696a-11e6-8225-fbb8a6fc65bc_story.html?noredirect=on&utm_term=.fde6cb0b89ea; David Folkenflik, "Donna Brazile's Resignation Illustrates Cable TV's Pundit Problem," *NPR*, November 2, 2016, https://www.npr.org/2016/11/02/500407470/donna-braziles-resignation-illustrates-cable-tvs-pundit-problem; Lynn Letukas, *Primetime Pundits: How Cable News Covers Social Issues* (Lanham, MD: Lexington Books, 2014); and Greg Satell, "The Media Is Not Solely to Blame for Bad Political Coverage, We Bear Responsibility Too," *Forbes*, November 11, 2016, https://www.forbes.com/sites/gregsatell/2016/11/11/

the-media-is-not-solely-to-blame-for-bad-political-coverage-we-bear-responsibility-too/#50e583545238.

39. Edward S. Herman and Noam Chomsky, *Manufacturing Consent: The Political Economy of the Mass Media* (New York: Pantheon, 1988), 4. See also John C. Merrill, "Propaganda and Journalism," in *Journalism Ethics: Philosophical Foundations for News Media* (New York: St. Martin's Press, 1997), 17–38.

40. See McCurdy, "Social Movements," 251.

41. Social movement periodicals are largely unexplored, for example, in Jeff Goodwin and James M. Jasper, *The Social Movements Reader: Cases and Concepts*, 3rd ed. (Hoboken, NJ: John Wiley & Sons, 2015); Suzanne Staggenborg, *Social Movements* (New York: Oxford University Press, 2015); David S. Meyer, *The Politics of Protest: Social Movements in America*, 2nd ed. (New York: Oxford University Press, 2014); and James M. Jasper, *Protest: A Cultural Introduction to Social Movements* (Cambridge: Polity Press, 2014).

42. John D. H. Downing, "Introduction," in *Encyclopedia of Social Movement Media*, ed. John D. H. Downing (Los Angeles: Sage, 2011), xxv. See also Bart Cammaerts, *The Circulation of Anti-Austerity Protest* (London: Palgrave MacMillan, 2018), 7.

43. See Barbara Warnick, *Rhetoric Online: Persuasion and Politics on the World Wide Web* (New York: Peter Lang, 2007).

44. See for example, Victoria Carty, *Social Movements and New Technology* (Boulder, CO: Westview Press, 2015); Manuel Castells, *Networks of Outrage and Hope: Social Movements in the Internet Age*, 2nd ed. (Cambridge: Polity Press, 2015); Paolo Gerbaudo, *Tweets and the Streets: Social Media and Contemporary Activism* (London: Pluto Press, 2012); Christine Harold, "Pranking Rhetoric: 'Culture Jamming,' as Media Activism," *Critical Studies in Media Communication* 21, no. 3 (September 2004): 189–211; Henry Jenkins, "The New Political Commons," *Policy Options*, November 1, 2012, 10–12; Leah Lievrouw, *Alternative and Activist New Media* (Cambridge: Polity Press, 2011); *Media Activism in the Digital Age*, ed. Victor Pickard and Guobin Yang (New York: Routledge, 2017); and Clay Shirky, "The Political Power of Social Media," *Foreign Affairs* 90, no. 1 (January/February 2011): 28–41.

45. Adrienne Russell, *Networked: A Contemporary History of News in Transition* (Cambridge: Polity Press, 2011).

46. See David Armstrong, *A Trumpet to Arms: Alternative Media in America* (Boston: South End Press, 1981); Lauren Kessler, *The Dissident Press: Alternative Journalism in American History* (Beverly Hills: Sage, 1984); John McMillian, *Smoking Typewriters: The Sixties Underground Press and the Rise of Alternative Media in America* (New York: Oxford University Press, 2011); Bob Ostertag, *People's Movements, People's Press: The Journalism of Social Justice Movements* (Boston: Beacon Press, 2006); and Rodger Streitmatter, *Voices of Revolution: The Dissident Press in America* (New York: Columbia University Press, 2001).

47. Joshua D. Atkinson, *Alternative Media and Politics of Resistance: A Communication Perspective* (New York: Peter Lang, 2009), 13. Atkinson elaborates on the varied meanings attached to the term in "Alternative Media," in *Journey into Social Activism: Qualitative Approaches* (New York: Fordham University Press, 2017), 173–96. See also Olga G. Bailey, Bart Cammaerts, and Nico Carpentier, *Understanding Alternative Media* (New York: Open University Press, 2007), 30, 20; Leah A. Lievrouw, *Alternative and Activist New Media*

(Cambridge, UK: Polity Press, 2011); and Chris Atton and James Hamilton, *Alternative Journalism* (London: Sage, 2008).

48. See "Editorial: Pussy Hats as Social Movement Symbols," *Journal of Popular Culture* 50, no. 2 (April 2017): 215–17. See also "Why You'll See a Lot of 'Evil Eye' Gloves at the March for Our Lives," *CNN*, March 24, 2018, https://www.cnn.com/2018/03/23/us/evil-eye-gloves-march-for-our-lives-trnd/index.html.

49. See Peter Burke, "Introduction," in *What Is Cultural History?* 2nd ed. (Cambridge: Polity Press, 2008), 1–5.

50. See for example, Tim Baylor, "Media Framing of Movement Protest: The Case of American Indian Protest," *Social Sciences Journal* 33, no. 3 (1996): 241–56; Stanley Cohen, *Folk Devils and Moral Panics* (London: MacGibbon and Kee, 1972); James Hertog and Douglas McLeod, "Anarchists Wreak Havoc in Downtown Minneapolis: A Multi-Level Study of Media Coverage of Radical Protests," *Journalism & Mass Communication Monographs*, Iss. 151 (June 1995): 1–48; Carolyn Martindale, "Selected Newspaper Coverage of Causes of Black Protest," *Journalism Quarterly* 66 (1989): 920–23, 964; Graham Murdock, "Political Deviance: The Press Presentation of a Militant Mass Demonstration," in *The Manufacture of News: Deviance, Social Problems and the Mass Media*, ed. Jock Young and Stanley Cohen (London: Constable, 1981), 206–25; and Daniel J. Myers and Beth Schaefer Caniglia, "All the Rioting That's Fit to Print: Rioting Effects in National Newspaper Coverage of Civil Disorders, 1968–1969," *American Sociological Review* 69, no. 4 (August 2004): 519–43.

51. Jules Boykoff, "Framing Dissent: Mass-Media Coverage of the Global Justice Movement," *New Political Science* 28, no. 2 (June 2006): 201–208; William A. Gamson and Gadi Wolfsfeld, "Movements and Media as Interacting Systems," *Annals of the American Academy of Political and Social Science* 528 (July 1993): 117; Gitlin, *The Whole World Is Watching*, 7, 27; James Halloran, Philip Elliott, and Graham Murdock, *Demonstration and Communication: A Case Study* (London: Penguin Books, 1970); Douglas M. McLeod and James K. Hertog, "Social Control and the Mass Media's Role in the Regulation of Protest Groups: The Communicative Acts Perspective," in *Mass Media, Social Control, and Social Change: A Macrosocial Perspective*, ed. David P. Demers and Kasisomayajula Viswanath (Ames: Iowa State University Press, 1999), 305–30; and Pamela Shoemaker, "Media Treatment of Deviant Political Groups," *Journalism & Mass Communication Quarterly* 61, no. 1 (Spring 1984): 66–75, 82. See also Herbert Gans, *Deciding What's News* (New York: Pantheon, 1979), 61; Robert A. Hackett and William K. Carroll, *Remaking Media: The Struggle to Democratize Public Communication* (New York: Routledge, 2006), 2–10; Frankie Hutton and Barbara Straus Reed, *Outsiders in the 19th-Century Press History: Multicultural Perspectives* (Bowling Green, OH: Popular Press, 2002), 1, 2; John Lofton, *The Press as Guardian of the First Amendment* (Columbia, SC: University of South Carolina Press, 1980), 279; Herbert Schiller, *Culture Incorporated: The Corporate Takeover of Public Expression* (New York: Oxford University Press, 1989), 163; and Mitchell Stephens, *A History of News: From the Drum to the Satellite* (New York: Penguin, 1988), 5.

52. Gitlin, *The Whole World Is Watching*, 27. See also Lance W. Bennett, "Toward a Theory of Press-State Relations," *Journal of Communication* 40, no. 2 (Spring 1990): 103–25.

53. Michael Schudson, *Why Democracies Need an Unlovable Press* (Cambridge: Polity Press, 2008), 51. See also Gans, *Democracy and the News*, 8; Stuart Hall, "Encoding/Decoding," in ed. Stuart Hall, Dorothy Hobson, Andrew Lowe, and Paul Wills, *Culture, Media and Language: Working Papers in Cultural Studies, 1972–79* (New York: Routledge, 1991), 107–16; Jay Rosen, *What Are Journalists For?* (New York: Yale University Press, 1999), 4–5; and Kovach and Rosenstiel, *Elements of Journalism*, 17, 24.

54. Hackett and Carroll, *Remaking Media*, 11. See also Jürgen Habermas, "Civil Society and the Political Public Sphere," in *Between Facts and Norms: Contributions to a Discourse Theory of Law and Democracy*, trans. William Rehg (Cambridge, MA: MIT Press, 1996), 387.

55. See Robert D. Benford and David A. Snow, "Framing Processes and Social Movements: An Overview and Assessment," *Annual Review of Sociology* 26, no. 1 (2000): 611–39. See also William A. Gamson and A. Modigliani, "Media Discourse and Public Opinion on Nuclear Power: A Constructionist Approach," *American Journal of Sociology* 95, no. 1 (July 1989): 1–37; and William A. Gamson, *Talking Politics* (New York: Cambridge University Press, 1992).

56. David A. Snow and Robert D. Benford, "Ideology, Frame Resonance, and Participant Mobilization," *International Social Movement Research*, no. 1 (1988): 198.

57. Gamson and Modigliani, "Media Discourse," 3–4.

58. See Robert M. Entman, *Projections of Power: Framing News, Public Opinion, and U.S. Foreign Policy* (Chicago: University of Chicago Press, 2009); Gitlin, *The Whole World Is Watching*; Pippa Norris, Montague Kern, and Marion Just, *Framing Terrorism: The News Media, the Government and the Public* (London: Routledge, 2003).

59. Cammaerts, *Circulation*, 33.

60. Doug McAdam, "Social Movement Theory and the Prospects for Climate Change Activism in the United States," *Annual Review of Political Science* (2017), 194. See also Scott A. Hunt, Robert D. Benford, and David A. Snow, "Identity Fields: Framing Processes and the Social Construction of Movement Identities," in *New Social Movements: From Ideology to Identity*, ed. Enrique Laraña, Hank Johnston, and Joseph R. Gusfield (Philadelphia: Temple University Press, 1994), 185–204.

61. Francesca Poletta and James M. Jasper, "Collective Identity and Social Movements," *Annual Review of Sociology* 27 (2001): 285, 295.

62. Michael A. Cacciatore, Dietram A. Scheufele, and Shanto Iyengar, "The End of Framing as We Know It … and the Future of Media Effects," *Mass Communication and Society* 19, no. 1 (2016): 7–23.

63. W. Lance Bennett and Alexandra Segerberg, *The Logic of Connective Action: Digital Media and the Personalization of Contentious Politics* (Cambridge: Cambridge University Press, 2013).

64. See Paolo Gerbaudo and Emiliano Treré, "In Search of the 'We' of Social Media Activism: Introduction to the Special Issue on Social Media and Protest Identities," *Information, Communication & Society* 18, no. 8 (2015): 865–71; and Cristina Flesher Fominaya, "Creating Cohesion from Diversity: The Challenge of Collective Identity Formation in the Global Justice Movement," *Sociological Inquiry* 80, no. 3 (August 2010): 378.

65. Cammaerts, *Anti-Austerity Protest*, 194.

66. William A. Gamson, "Constructing Social Protest," in *Social Movements and Culture*, ed. Hank Johnston and Bert Klandermans (Minneapolis: University of Minnesota Press, 1995), 90. [emphasis in original]

67. Gamson, *Talking Politics*, 7–8, 109.

68. See Tarrow, *Power in Movement*, 174; and Doug McAdam, "Culture and Social Movements," in *New Social Movements*, 36.

69. Gamson, *Talking Politics*, 32. See also Alberto Melucci, "The Process of Collective Identity," in *Social Movements and Culture*, 45.

70. See *Passionate Politics: Emotions and Social Movements*, ed. Jeff Goodwin, James M. Jasper and Francesca Polletta (Chicago: University of Chicago Press, 2001).

71. James M. Jasper, "Emotions and Social Movements: Twenty Years of Theory and Research," *Annual Review of Sociology* 37 (August 2011): 285–303. See also James M. Jasper, *The Art of Moral Protest: Culture, Biography, and Creativity in Social Movements* (Chicago: University of Chicago Press, 1997); and James M. Jasper, "The Emotions of Protest: Affective and Reactive Emotions in and Around Social Movements," *Sociological Forum* 13, no. 3 (September 1998): 397–424.

72. Jeff Goodwin, James M. Jasper, and Francesca Polletta, "The Return of The Repressed: The Fall and Rise of Emotions in Social Movement Theory," *Mobilization: An International Quarterly* 5, no. 1 (March 2000): 78.

73. Donald E. Polkinghorne, *Narrative Knowing and the Human Sciences* (Albany, NY: SUNY Press, 1988), 1.

74. Joseph E. Davis, "Narrative and Social Movements: The Power of Stories," in *Stories of Change: Narrative and Social Movements*, ed. Joseph E. Davis (Albany: State University of New York Press, 2002), 4.

75. Francesca Polletta and Pang Ching Bobby Chen, "Narrative and Social Movements," in *The Oxford Handbook of Cultural Sociology*, ed. Jeffrey C. Alexander, Ronald N. Jacobs, and Philip Smith (New York: Oxford University Press, 2012), 487–506.

76. Frederick W. Mayer, *Narrative Politics: Stories and Collective Action* (New York: Oxford University Press, 2014), 2. See also Robert D. Benford, "Controlling Narratives and Narratives as Control within Social Movements," in Davis, *Stories of Change*, 53–75; Marshall Ganz, "The Power of Story in Social Movements," in the *Proceedings of the Annual Meeting of the American Sociological Association*, Anaheim, California, August 18–21, 2001, http://nrs.harvard.edu/urn-3:HUL.InstRepos:27306251; and Gary Alan Fine, "The Storied Group: Social Movements as 'Bundles of Narratives,'" in Davis, *Stories of Change*, 229–43.

77. Charles Beckett and Mark Deuze, "On the Role of Emotion in the Future of Journalism," *Social Media + Society* 2, no. 3 (July 2016): 1–6.

78. Mary Beth Oliver, James Price Dillard, Keunmin Base, and D.J. Tamul, "The Effect of Narrative News Format on Empathy for Stigmatized Groups," *Journalism & Mass Communication Quarterly* 89, no. 2 (June 2012): 205–24.

79. Lene Bech Sillesen, Chris Ip, and David Uberti, "Journalism and the Power of Emotions," *Columbia Journalism Review*, May/June 2015, https://www.cjr.org/analysis/journalism_and_the_power_of_emotions.php. See also Andrea Elliott, "Invisible Child Part 1: Girl in the Shadows: Dasani's Homeless Life," *New York Times*, December 9, 2013, http://www.nytimes.com/projects/2013/invisible-child/index.html#/?chapt=1.

80. Davis, "Power of Stories," 25.
81. Patricia Ewick and Susan S. Sibley, "Subversive Stories and Hegemonic Tales: Toward A Sociology of Narrative," *Law & Society Review* 29, no. 2 (January 1995): 197–226.
82. George W. Alger, "The Literature of Exposure," *Atlantic Monthly* 96 (August 1905): 210–13. Lincoln Steffens traced the genre back further: "I was not the original muckraker. The prophets of the Old Testament were ahead of me." Lincoln Steffens, *The Autobiography of Lincoln Steffens* (New York: Harcourt, Brace, 1931), 357.
83. See Aileen Gallagher, *The Muckrakers: American Journalism During the Age of Reform* (New York: Rosen Publishing Group, 2006); Laurie Collier Hillstrom, *The Muckrakers and the Progressive Era* (Detroit: Omnigraphics, 2009); and Judith Serrin and William Serrin, *Muckraking! The Journalism that Changed America* (New York: The New Press, 2002).
84. Cecelia Tichi, *Exposes and Excess: Muckraking in America, 1900/2000* (Philadelphia: University of Pennsylvania Press, 2013), 91. See also Ida Minerva Tarbell, *The History of the Standard Oil Company* (New York: McClure, Phillips & Company, 1904).
85. Gilbert King, "The Woman Who Took on the Tycoon," *Smithsonian.com*, July 5, 2012, https://www.smithsonianmag.com/history/the-woman-who-took-on-the-tycoon-651396/.
86. Tom Vanderbilt, "Hold the Mayo," *Los Angeles Times*, March 11, 2001, http://articles.latimes.com/2001/mar/11/books/bk-36064/2. See also the section on "21st Century Muckrakers," *Nieman Reports* 63, no. 2 (Summer 2009): 49–77.
87. James Phelan, *Narrative as Rhetoric: Technique, Audiences, Ethics, Ideology* (Columbus: Ohio State University Press, 1996), 17.
88. Roger Silverstone, "The Sociology of Mediation and Communication," in *The Sage Handbook of Sociology*, ed. Craig Calhoun, Chris Rojek, Bryan S Turner (London: Sage, 2005), 201. See also Carolyn Marvin, *When Old Technologies Were New: Thinking About Electric Communication in the Late Nineteenth Century* (New York: Oxford University Press, 1988).

· 1 ·

JUST THE FACTS?

From the *Anti-Slavery Monthly Reporter* to William Lloyd Garrison's *Liberator*

"The man wanted money," read the account of the Jamaican plantation owner's transaction, "and, one of the female slaves having two fine children, he sold one of them, and the child was torn from her maternal affection. In the agony of her feelings she made a hideous howling, and for that crime was flogged. Soon after he sold her other child. This 'turned her heart within her,' and impelled her into a kind of madness. She howled night and day in the yard; tore her hair; ran up and down the streets and the parade, rending the heavens with her cries, and literally watering the earth with her tears."

So stated the "Brief Sketch of Colonial Slavery" in the July 1825 issue of the London-based *Anti-Slavery Monthly Reporter*. Editor Zachary Macaulay's mix of fact (he was a statistical genius) and emotion accounts for why, as Macaulay's biographer asserts, the *Anti-Slavery Monthly Reporter* did "more than anything else to provide the means by which slavery would be abolished in the British Empire."[1] This chapter explores how its social justice journalism played a leading role in what historian David Brion Davis calls the "extraordinary mobilization" of public opinion to end slavery across Britain's remote colonies.[2] It concludes with a comparison with the version of the *Reporter* still published by Anti-Slavery International in 2018.

Although Parliament prohibited the slave trade in 1807, it did not abolish the practice of slavery in its West Indies, South African, and other colonies. In 1823, Macaulay helped found the Society for the Mitigation and Gradual Abolition of Slavery Throughout the British Dominion. He created the *Monthly Reporter* as the society's forum for documenting, publicizing, and abolishing colonial slavery's unseen horrors. As Macaulay declared in 1828, the *Reporter* countered proslavery forces "by referring to the facts on record, which we undertake to prove, and by pointing out the documents which establish them all."[3]

Macaulay faced the formidable task of forging a sense of collective identity among Britons with distant, unseen, enslaved Africans by "bridging geographic, economic, political, and racial difference."[4] The first wave of abolitionists in the late 1700s relied largely on pamphlets to bridge that gap. Bound essays of as many as a hundred pages that appeared as one-time publications, pamphlets relied on sentimental rhetoric calculated to stir readers to action by exposing slavery's inhumanity.[5] One hundred antislavery pamphlets appeared at their peak in 1788, building on the tradition of the so-called "pamphlet wars" that had been tools for European political and religious debate since the sixteenth century.[6] Pamphlets were the source of the evidence and arguments in William Wilberforce's seminal speech in the House of Commons on May 12, 1789, which introduced the first bill calling for an end to the Atlantic Ocean slave trade.[7]

Macaulay's Rise in the Abolition Movement

That same year, twenty-one-year-old Macaulay arrived in England after having served six years as bookkeeper for a Jamaican sugar plantation, where the teen had quickly recognized that the whip was "the grand badge of slavery." Initially appalled at the idea of inflicting such punishment, he soon "assimilated" (as he euphemistically put it)—a process that later informed his argument that slavery degrades both blacks and whites.[8] The young Scot settled in England with his sister and brother-in-law, who introduced him to Wilberforce. They formed the core of the activist Clapham Sect, whose "practical Christianity" profoundly inspired the hardened Macaulay. He quickly adopted the Anglican Evangelicals' dichotomous worldview of civilization (embodied by Christian Britain) versus barbarism (slavery).[9] Conversely, the evangelicals appreciated Macaulay's intellect, aptitude with numbers, and managerial skills. They sent their fervent convert to Sierra Leone, the African religious colony the evangelicals had founded as a home for emancipated slaves, where he served as a rather authoritarian—and unpopular—governor from 1793 to 1799.[10]

Once back in England, Macaulay worked invisibly but closely with Wilberforce in the long campaign to abolish the slave trade. He proved an indefatigable researcher with a photographic memory. As antislavery colleague Sir George Stephen recalled, "Blue books and state papers were child's play to him, however dull or voluminous."[11] Macaulay gained journalism experience as founding editor of the Clapham Sect's dense monthly magazine, the *Christian Observer*, from 1802 to 1816.[12] Wilberforce's so-called "saints" in Parliament persevered until they abolished the Atlantic slave trade on March 25, 1807.

Instead of the occasional, one-time pamphlet, Macaulay determined to create a periodical to regularly document and publicize abuses of the hundreds of thousands of slaves that still toiled in British colonies to build a nationwide campaign. Macaulay's perspective as an eyewitness to slavery combined with his editorial experience, investigative stamina, organizational skills, powerful written rhetoric, and facility with statistics made him uniquely qualified to create a new instrument to expand the modern social movement repertoire. Thus he became first in a long line of activist editors for whom journalism was primarily a tool to serve their cause. Sir Stephen called the *Anti-Slavery Monthly Reporter* that debuted June 30, 1825, "the nucleus of a system to which, under the blessing of God, after some revolutions in its management, all the subsequent success must be ascribed."[13] The eight-page magazine eventually reached a paid circulation of twenty thousand, and pass-along readership expanded its reach much further.

Collective Action Frames in the *Reporter*

The *Reporter*'s social justice journalism created an abolitionist identity that relied on dichotomized frames of antislavery forces as good and proslavery forces as evil. The *Reporter* framed the slave-owning West Indies plantocracy as "other" to Parliament, the grand symbol of British civilization. Plantation owners provided the *Reporter* with the human adversaries that William Gamson says the public needs to identify as agents of injustice and potential targets of collective action, as abstractions fail to motivate. Macaulay helped British readers identify with slaves when he explained that plantation owners scheduled slaves' food markets on Sundays, their only day off, making it impossible for them to attend church. Under such conditions, Macaulay asked, how could slaves become Christians?[14] The de facto prohibition of religion inclined the *Reporter*'s middle-class British audience to empathize with the geographically and culturally distant slaves. The *Reporter* repeatedly allied abolitionists with Christian ideals juxtaposed against heathen slaveholders; Volume V contained fifteen essays that discussed the incompatibility of slavery with Christianity. The *Reporter*'s most pragmatic identity frame demonstrated how slavery damaged British self-interest; Macaulay once computed it cost British taxpayers four million pounds sterling annually to maintain slave labor in the Caribbean.[15] A seven-page report in 1826 detailed how bounties and duties on sugar hurt English workers.[16]

Slavery's inherent racism was the abolitionists' greatest obstacle to forging a collective antislavery identity among white British citizens.[17] Macaulay tackled the subject head on. "Nature has not given to the white men a right to the bodies of black men," the *Reporter* proclaimed.[18] Macaulay argued that slavery perverted whites as well as blacks—"not merely as it prompts the master to acts of cruelty and oppression, but as it operates to subvert and vitiate the best sympathies of our nature."[19] One "demoralizing" aspect was owners' inhumane view of other humans. "When men purchase their fellow creatures like cattle, they imperceptibly come to view them in the light of cattle," he wrote. "Slavery hardens the heart. ..."[20] Thus Macaulay performed the astounding feat of painting a picture of corrupted white virtue that won converts by framing Britons as victims of West Indies slavery. Nonetheless, he had internalized the sense of racial superiority that permeated the British Empire. Abolitionist arguments could be noble but often were condescending. Macaulay, like other first-generation abolitionists through most of the 1820s, favored gradual emancipation in the West Indies in the belief that slaves needed instruction on how to live free.

Not surprisingly, injustice frames dominated the *Anti-Slavery Monthly Reporter*. Macaulay published lists submitted to Parliament, for example, of dozens of free people of color unjustly jailed as escaped slaves but who often were sold to pay the cost of their incarceration. Macaulay reframed the practice by labeling it a felony.[21] The codification of slavery also fit the injustice frame. Dry *Reporter* accounts of slave law reforms were chilling, such as a new, supposedly improved, Mauritius ordinance that limited the weights of chains and fetters to nine pounds for a pair of men, or three pounds of chains for a single "negress" or child, neither of whom could be fettered.[22] The magazine defended slaves who revolted in Jamaica, framing the uprising as a reasonable response to owners' unjust demands that they work on what was supposed to be their weekly day off.[23]

Agency frames surfaced in the *Reporter*'s efforts to keep far-flung abolitionists apprised of the Society's numerous activities. Informing readers about antislavery activity across Britain showed them "not merely that something can be done but that 'we' can do something," as Gamson describes the agency frame.[24] Merely reading accounts of antislavery meetings, impassioned resolutions, and petitions made the audience part of the movement.[25] The magazine kept readers well apprised of lengthy Parliamentary debates on slavery. In 1833, Macaulay used his editing skills to distill evidence from 1,400 pages of testimony—"a most ponderous and unwieldy mass"—by seventeen proslavery and nine antislavery witnesses.[26]

The *Reporter*'s major appeal to agency was promoting the mammoth petition campaigns at the heart of the antislavery movement.[27] In 1830, Macaulay amplified the effect of Edmund Clarke's speech on how to organize and write abolition petitions by publishing his advice in the nationally distributed *Reporter*.[28] The monthly saw itself as the abolition newspaper of record and routinely published entire texts of innumerable petitions calling for Parliament to end slavery. The July 31, 1826, issue reported 674 petitions presented to the House of Commons in its prior session.[29] Reports on new societies also promoted agency. The September 1825 issue, for example, reported on the formation of Ladies Anti-Slavery Societies in Colchester and Wiltshire, where members pledged to use only slave-free sugar as well as to spread word among family about the evils of slavery.[30] These were acts anyone could perform.

Mobilizing Emotions in the *Reporter*

Macaulay filled the *Anti-Slavery Monthly Reporter* with subversive stories aimed at producing what sociologist Francesca Polletta characterizes as "mobilizing emotions."[31] In 1828, for example, Macaulay quoted a report to Parliament that cited eyewitness accounts of mistreated slaves. One matter-of-factly described the beating of a slave whose captors poured hot oil on his calves and set dogs on him. When the man asked for water he was given urine. The white man cut off the black's man's genitals before the victim died.[32] Macaulay, like many antislavery writers, often presented facts as melodrama, a polarized world of moral absolutes that made the genre a useful tool of the historically voiceless.[33]

Slavery's standard practices were so horrific they needed no rhetorical adornment. The *Reporter* merely had to cite a newspaper notice describing a recently sold slave to remind British readers that the barbaric practice of branding persisted: "William Nelson, alias Thomas Mole, an Eboe, 5 ft. 5 1/2 in. marked ASIA on shoulders, breasts, and cheeks, to Mr. Holmes, of Vere.— Oct. 17, 1823."[34] These accounts also helped challenge constructions of black people as less than human and thus suitable for slavery, as they required audiences to acknowledge the brutal reality of slavery. Macaulay once abstracted a 760-page report that coldly calculated the average price of slaves ranged from sixteen pounds fifteen shillings to ninety pounds.[35] A 1934 tribute to the editor praised how "month after month, year after year, he kept up a steady stream of exact analysis. No detail however horrible was spared. Every statement was documents and proved." Charles Booth continued:

> He would sit up, night after night, regardless of sleep, and insensible of fatigue, until he had waded through huge folios of officials papers, often full of arithmetical detail and dry statistics, and had weighed each fact and almost every word in the scale of truth; and the next *Anti-Slavery Monthly Reporter* was certain to contain a clear analysis of all that was important in them; and thus condensed into a pamphlet of twenty or thirty pages, a faithful journal was given to the world of all that daily passed on the subject of slave treatment.[36]

Muckraking and "Moral Shock"

An important aspect of these accounts was their ring of authenticity, which enabled readers to experience the slaves' mistreatment at an emotional level impossible to achieve other than living it. Like the muckrakers nearly a century later, Macaulay relied on documents–government reports, reports, texts of Parliamentary debates, newspaper accounts, church reports, court records, letters, and eyewitness accounts. He reframed official information as antislavery arguments by labeling as "*moral* statistics" governmental lists that enumerated marriages, schools, and religion. Antigua, he wrote, reported sixty-nine marriages among two thousand white residents, fifty-one marriages among five thousand free people of color, and a mere thirty-one marriages among thirty thousand slaves.[37] The prim editor knew his British middle-class audience would share his moral indignation that slave owners forced the vast majority of slaves to have sex outside of marriage.

The report demonstrates how his social justice journalism produced the "moral shock" that can mobilize people who share no prior common identity. Sociologists James M. Jasper, who coined the term, and Jane D. Paulsen state that moral shock occurs "when an event or situation raises such a sense of outrage in people that they become inclined toward political action, even in the absence of a network of contact."[38] Macaulay's publication of lists of South African colonial court proceedings, for instance, needed no sentimental rhetoric to inflate the moral shock they induced in readers. In one account, a slave convicted of threatening his master was "condemned to be exposed to public view, made fast by a rope under the gallows; whereupon to be flogged, branded, and confined to Robbin Island (to work in irons) for life."[39] Bishops' reports provided even more fodder, as in an 1826 account that quoted an overseer who explained women no longer were whipped but put in stocks or switched, a more humane punishment, he claimed, because switches, "do not *lacerate* the skin."[40]

Macaualay's acerbic barbs stung powerful enemies. The *Anti-Slavery Monthly Reporter* played David to a Goliath British media hegemony that largely accepted slavery as economic reality. The proslavery *John Bull* magazine falsely castigated "Saint Zachary" as a hypocritical profiteer, just one arrow slung in an "anti-Macaulay polemic" that so vexed the pious editor he eventually sued. He dropped the libel case in 1827 after accumulating some two thousand pounds in legal bills.[41] The pillorying of Macaulay is an example of cultural theorist Stuart Hall's argument that mainstream news media demonize politically deviant social movements to help preserve the dominant social order.[42]

Nonetheless, the *Reporter*'s effectiveness propelled the nationwide movement that finally resulted in the Slavery Abolition Act of 1833, which set the stage to free nearly eight hundred thousand people of color mainly in the Caribbean over the next few years.[43] Another portentous result of the British act was that it helped inspire the founding that same year of the American Anti-Slavery Society in Philadelphia. Moral shock would serve as an essential ingredient of the American abolitionist journals that followed the template Macaulay's magazine had established for social justice journalism.

The American Abolitionist Press

Among founders of the American Anti-Slavery Society was scarecrow-thin, black-frocked William Lloyd Garrison, the United States' loudest, angriest, and most radical abolitionist editor. He proclaimed in his inaugural issue of his fiery *Liberator* on January 1, 1831:

> Tell a man whose house is on fire to give a moderate alarm; tell him to moderately rescue his wife from the hands of the ravisher; tell the mother to gradually extricate her babe from the fire into which it has fallen;—but urge me not to use moderation in a cause like the present. I am in earnest—I will not equivocate—I will not excuse—I will not retreat a single inch—**AND I WILL BE HEARD.**[44]

The *Liberator* was in part a product of an active transatlantic exchange of abolitionist literature dating back to colonial America. British abolitionist texts filled columns of the first U.S. antislavery journal, the *Genius of Universal Emancipation*, which was published by Benjamin Lundy from 1822 to 1839.[45] Lundy, for example, published Elizabeth Heyrick's radical pamphlet of 1824, *Immediate, Not Gradual Abolition*. The isolated, iconoclastic editor in the slave port city of Baltimore shared the shunned abolitionists' views on the power of their press. "Types are potent implements of modern political and moral warfare," Lundy thundered. "Castles will fall before them—canons [sic] are silenced—swords and bayonets are crumbled."[46]

Despite his hubris, Lundy's unanswered call for the gradual emancipation of slaves paled in comparison to *David Walker's Appeal to the Colored Citizens of the World* in 1829. The free black Bostonian's eighty-eight-page pamphlet demanded immediate freedom for the nation's two million slaves, nearly a sixth of the U.S. population in 1830 and the backbone of the South's agrarian economy.[47] Walker squarely confronted the harsh irony and contradiction of the young democracy's slavery as he detailed its cruelty, excoriated white Christian hypocrisy and, even more brazenly, called for equal rights for black people. "*Walker's Appeal* is the first sustained written assault upon slavery and racism to come from a black man in the United States," according to historian Herbert Aptheker. "Never before or since was there a more passionate denunciation of the hypocrisy of the nation as a whole—democratic and fraternal and equalitarian and all the other words."[48] Truly a voice for the voiceless, *Walker's Appeal* established a revolutionary tone for American abolition rhetoric. Walker even obliquely suggested that slaves rebel: "[T]hey want us for their slaves and think nothing of murdering us in order to subject us to that wretched condition—therefore, if there is an *attempt* made by us, kill or be killed."[49]

Traveling preachers, sailors, laborers, and others carried Walker's contraband pamphlet into the South and passed it along through a large underground network. Literate slaves read the *Appeal* aloud to those who could not, in a merger of oral and print culture that was the predecessor of a tweet going viral. One node in the network was slave Jacob Cowan, whose owner allowed him to operate a small tavern in Wilmington, North Carolina. Cowan was jailed and sold into the Deep South after he was discovered, highlighting the risks for slaves found with abolitionist literature. Authorities blamed *Walker's Appeal* for several slave uprisings the following year and enacted new and stricter laws criminalizing antislavery material and teaching slaves to read.[50]

Walker's Appeal ignited Garrison, who in 1829 was helping Lundy edit the *Genius of Universal Emancipation* in Baltimore. The impoverished Massachusetts native's newspapering career began at thirteen, when he entered a seven-year apprenticeship as a printer's devil at the semiweekly *Newburyport Herald*. He briefly published his own failed newspaper at twenty-one and was editing a Boston journal when Lundy recruited him at the age of twenty-three. At the *Genius*, Garrison added a new "Black List" comprising brief reports on the barbarities of slavery, not unlike the accounts Macaulay published in his *Reporter*. A pair of slave traders he named on the Black List accused Garrison of libel—a crime at the time. Convicted but unable to pay the fifty-dollar fine, Garrison served seven weeks of a six-month jail sentence before abolitionist Arthur Tappan paid his fine. Once free, Garrison returned to Massachusetts to launch the *Liberator*, which, according to his biographer, "remains today a sterling and unrivaled example of personal journalism in the service of civic idealism."[51]

An Angry God and Apocalyptic Metaphors

The *Liberator*'s editor is also representative of the uncompromising zealots who risked violence and endured poverty to publish their social justice journals. Garrison's courage is undeniable, but C. Vann Woodward was not the only historian a bit troubled by his "persistent moral aggression and authoritarianism."[52] He was incapable of compromise, perhaps a requisite quality in a social revolutionary. Despite Garrison's avowed pacifism, his newspaper overflowed with references to blood and revolution. An angry God and apocalyptic metaphors animated *Liberator* collective action frames. James Darsey places Garrison at the forefront of the prophetic discourse he argues has characterized American radical movements.[53] Garrison placed the Bible by the abolitionists' side as he built an abolitionist collective identity. He cited Scripture that invoked God's wrath as a good reason to convert, as in Exodus 21:16: "He that stealeth a man and selleth him, or if he be found in his hand, he shall surely be put to death." Garrison believed "moral suasion" alone through the spoken and written word could persuade Americans of the rightness of immediate emancipation. "For Garrison public opinion was a force to be molded to conform to an uncompromising demand that slavery was an evil to be eliminated from the face of God's earth," writes scholar Horace Seldon. "He sought a revolution in that public opinion."[54]

Like Macaulay, Garrison and editors of another estimated thirty to forty abolitionist journals in antebellum America published shocking accounts of mistreatment of chattel slaves; provided moral and religious arguments against the institution of slavery; publicized abolition society rallies, meetings, and resolutions; documented the societies' growth; posted news about slave-related events around the world; kept track of political developments; and lambasted slavery's supporters. In Garrison's view, slavery's sinners included the complicit North, the institutional church, and President Lincoln, whom he scored for prioritizing preservation of the Union above emancipation.[55]

Garrision could use one collective action frame Macaulay could not in the form of the Declaration of Independence and its promise of "life, liberty, and the pursuit of happiness." The Declaration also helped legitimize the antislavery argument that "all men are created equal." Garrison, however, rejected the U.S. Constitution because he argued it legalized slavery. He made his stand clear by emblazoning on the top right-hand corner of the *Liberator* front page a line adapted from the Bible's Book of Isaiah: "NO UNION WITH SLAVEHOLDERS/ The United States Constitution is a 'covenant with death, and an agreement with hell.'" Garrison's extreme view not only opposed any political compromise to preserve the union but also urged the northern states to secede and rewrite the irredeemable Constitution.

As that slogan indicated, the *Liberator* was more apoplectic than the *Reporter*, and Garrison more a proselytizer than a journalist. Less constrained than Macaulay as an editor, Garrison raised the decibel level of *Liberator* pages with completely capitalized or italicized sentences that often ended in a string of exclamation points. His satirical critiques of the gap between Republican ideals and the reality of slavery dripped acid. His Fourth of July speeches, an annual ritual of polemical fireworks, denounced the celebration:

> [A] mingling of spurious patriotism and brazen hypocrisy, of glaring falsehood and open blasphemy, what long processions, what loud huzzas, what swaggering speeches, what sumptuous dinners, what alcoholic toasts, what drunken revels! All in grateful and honorable observance of the Fourth of July! A free country—and every sixth man on the soil a slave![56]

Amplifying the Abolition Message

Unlike Macaulay, who seldom spoke and preferred working behind the scenes, Garrison was an omnipresent and commanding presence on the abolition lecture circuit, the movement's main forum. Newspapers like the *Liberator* amplified the abolitionist message by printing entire texts of speeches delivered on the circuit. "The printed version often reached as wide, if not a wider, audience than the speech itself and thus was a more persuasive message than the original," according to rhetorician Ernest G. Bormann.[57] The practice was to take down the speech in shorthand then transcribe it in longhand, set it in type, and publish it. Speakers more cognizant of their far-flung newspaper readers often targeted their speeches for this larger imagined community instead of the crowd standing in front of them.

Historian David Paul Nord argues that Garrison's *Liberator* epitomized how American "communities of journalism" were at the "vortex of many collective efforts to build community."[58] He celebrates Garrison's impassioned community-building in the 1830s as "a lush first flowering of democratic journalism in America."

The *Liberator* Advances Women's Rights

The democratic *Liberator* also introduced its audience of two thousand subscribers (single sales and pass-along extended its reach) to the abolitionist movement's path-breaking female speakers, in an era when taking the podium was a radical act for a woman. Maria Stewart, one of the first African American women to speak publicly on slavery, was a contributor. The April 27, 1833, issue quoted her recent speech in Boston for equal rights and liberty, a truly radical concept for a group whose enslavement was justified on the grounds its members were subhuman: "We have pursued the shadow, they [whites] have obtained the substance; we have performed the labor, they have received the profits; we have planted the vines, they have eaten the fruits of them."[59] Garrison also published a South Carolina woman's letter about her troubling experiences as a member of an upper-class, slaveholding family, launching Angelina Grimké's career as an abolitionist and advocate for woman's rights, another of Garrison's social justice crusades.[60] After the Civil War broke out, he hired former slave Harriet Jacobs, author of the influential memoir, *Incidents in the Life of a Slave Girl,* to report for the *Liberator* on the condition of former slaves seeking refuge in the nation's capital. Her letter signed by the pseudonym "Linda" filled nearly three columns of the September 5, 1862, issue. "It is almost impossible to keep the building in a healthy condition," she reported. "Each day brings its fresh additions of the hungry, naked and sick."[61]

Frederick Douglass's *North Star*

Another *Liberator* reader was former escaped slave Frederick Douglass. Garrison so inspired him that Douglass began to publicly share his stories of life as a slave. Douglass's personal narrative of this unknown world galvanized northern audiences. In 1841, Garrison invited him onto the American Anti-Slavery Society lecture circuit, but after publication of his *Narrative of the Life of Frederick Douglass, an American Slave,* Douglass fled to England to avoid capture by bounty hunters. British abolitionists raised funds to buy Douglass's freedom and help him launch his own abolitionist newspaper, the *North Star* (December 3, 1847–April 17, 1851). The upstate New York weekly was one of at least forty-two black-owned newspapers published before the Civil War, beginning with the anticolonization *Freedom's Journal* in 1827.[62] Douglass believed it crucial that slaves have a voice in the abolitionist movement. "It has long been our anxious wish to see, in this slave-holding, slave-trading, and negro-hating land," Douglass wrote in the *North Star's* inaugural issue, "a printing-press and paper, permanently established, under the complete control and direction of the immediate victims of slavery and oppression. ..."[63] Despite its evocative name, Douglass's biographer describes the *North Star* as "solemnly polemical."[64] His launch of a rival newspaper also created the first cracks in his eventual split with Garrison.

Editors as Victims of Mob Violence

Garrison's aggressive agitation made him a prime target of the violence that made the campaign to end slavery so much bloodier in the United States than in Britain, even before the Civil War. Attacks on abolitionist editors foreshadowed the violence that would stalk editors of future social justice journals that challenged powerful institutions. Southerners blamed the *Liberator* for Nat Turner's slave rebellion in Virginia a few weeks after its launch, and Georgia offered a $5,000 reward to anyone who delivered Garrison to the state to face seditious libel charges.[65] In 1835, a Boston mob grabbed Garrison in front of Faneuil Hall, tied a rope around his waist and was yanking him toward the Boston Common to tar and feather him when the mayor intervened.[66] Racial intermingling among male and female abolitionists incensed many northerners. In 1838, Garrison was among speakers at the abolitionists' "mixed" Pennsylvania Hall in Philadelphia when a mob forced them out and burned down the building.[67]

Alton [Illinois] *Observer* editor Elijah Lovejoy became a martyr to abolition and to freedom of the press in 1837 when a mob stormed a warehouse, hurled his printing press into the Mississippi River—his fourth to be destroyed by a mob—and murdered him.[68] Editors seemed impervious to violence. Even after a mob held editor Gamaliel Bailey and his printers hostage for three days in 1848 in the Washington, D.C., offices of the *National Era* (1847–1860), in June 1851 Bailey began serializing *Uncle's Tom Cabin* in chapters that Harriet Beecher Stowe cranked out weekly over ten months.[69] The book, published the following year, helped move abolition into American mainstream thought over the next decade by humanizing slaves in a way the ferocious Garrison could not. But the uncompromising editor and his fearless compatriots had primed the audience for this sea change in public opinion.

Once the Civil War broke out, Garrison kept up his refrain that slavery was its root cause—and only emancipation could justify the loss of life.[70] He did, however, come around to support the war effort. In December 1861, Garrison replaced the *Liberator* motto that called the Constitution a "covenant with death" with the more amenable, "Proclaim Liberty Throughout All the Land." When Congress ratified the Thirteenth Amendment that abolished slavery at the end of 1865, Garrison shuttered the *Liberator* after 1,820 consecutive issues, declaring its work was done.[71]

Connections to Twenty-First-Century Antislavery Editors

Unfortunately, however, the abolition mandate remains unfinished. Macaulay's *Reporter* lives on in a converted stable on the south bank of the Thames River in London,[72] edited by Anti-Slavery International's Jakub Sobik in a warren-like, second-floor office suite. Despite more than two centuries of campaigns to end slavery, modern slavery in 2018 involved an estimated forty million people coerced into forced marriage or forced labor, including prostitution.[73] Sobik explains during a coffee break on a sunny afternoon that a quarter of them are children.[74] Anti-Slavery International works with forty local partner organizations in more than twenty countries to help individual victims, crack down on abusers, and enact antislavery laws. Just as during Macaulay's day, journalism remains integral to its operations. Anti-Slavery cosponsors dozens of reports with its global partners to bolster its lobbying efforts and campaigns. For example, Anti-Slavery International uncovered the issue of forced labor of Nepali migrants in the Middle East in 2011 and initiated the [London] *Guardian* newspaper's 2013 investigation into the numerous deaths of Nepali migrants in forced labor to prepare Qatar for the 2022 FIFA World Cup.

Macaulay's reporting methods also presaged the investigations that today are standard practice of nongovernmental organizations (NGOs) that defend human rights around the globe.[75] NGOs such as Human Rights Watch and Witness perform some the world's most important social justice journalism, early exemplars of the hybrid model.[76] A 2015 study, in fact, found that the leading human rights advocacy organizations' resources rival those of major news organizations that increasingly rely on the activists' reports as they shutter foreign news bureaus.[77] As far back as 1990, however, international human rights lawyer Diane Orentlicher pronounced the human rights field "has come of age," attributing its growing influence to the spotlight shone by NGOs on human rights abuses. She wrote, "The strategy—promoting change by reporting facts—is almost elegant in its simplicity."[78]

The *Reporter* also presaged the twenty-first-century emphasis on transparency by encouraging readers to go to original sources identified in copious footnotes, the nineteenth-century equivalent of ProPublica's practice of linking to original documents, as in a 2018 exposé of a child psychiatrist who endangered her young research subjects.[79] The *Reporter* used footnotes to fact-check claims in the proslavery Duke of Manchester's testimony before

Parliament, much like today's "Politifact" website checks newsmakers' claims. Macaulay even was a pioneer news aggregator, not unlike computer software that fuels Google and Facebook's newsfeeds, by republishing articles from other abolitionist periodicals and pamphlets.

Digital technology largely explains why the *Reporter*'s current print edition has slimmed down to a sixteen-page, pamphlet-sized biannual glossy. A PDF version is available on Anti-Slavery's website, the locus of the organization's mobilization efforts. Sobik says the print version of the *Reporter* is mainly a way to inform members who don't visit the website. Its blog has largely subsumed the print *Reporter* but remains surprisingly true to editor Macaulay's emphasis on practicing fact-based reporting to catalyze change. Teenaged "Catherine" in one post recounts her experiences as a domestic worker in Tanzania, where she learned about her rights through an Anti-Slavery project run by its partner, the Tanzania Domestic Workers Coalition. Catherine provides a human face for the East African nation's estimated one million child domestic workers. Following in the tradition of Macaulay, Anti-Slavery researchers have compiled shocking statistics about them: 40 percent suffer physical abuse, 17 percent suffer sexual abuse, over half receive little or no pay despite working over sixty hours a week, and as many as 30 percent are under the national working age of fourteen.[80]

While its reporting techniques are similar to those of the nineteenth-century *Reporter*, the twenty-first-century journal offers readers many more options for taking action: they can post Catherine's story on Facebook or LinkedIn or Twitter. In one click readers can sign up for the Anti-Slavery newsletter; download dozens of reports ranging from the "wahaya" practice of selling women as unofficial wives in Niger to an explanation of child laborer rights in Arabic; explore an interactive map of products produced by slave labor; or get directions on how to sponsor a fundraising event.

Another significant difference between the old and new magazines enabled by technology is the importance of imagery in today's *Reporter*. Images are crucial to stir public emotion, Sobik says, and YouTube figures prominently in Anti-Slavery International's strategy. A 2017 multimedia report on forced labor in Uzbekistan cotton fields was the centerpiece of its transnational Cotton Campaign coalition. Freelance videographers sneaked onto the fields to document abuses in a video report that Sobik posted on YouTube. Social media distributed the undercover footage among thousands of people, some of whom used www.antislavery.org's interactive features to join or donate to the organization or to protest government officials. Anti-Slavery also posted a 2:10-minute cartoon, an innovation that explained the Uzbekistan system. The global antislavery Cotton Campaign harkens back to the British consumer boycott of "blood sugar" produced by slave labor. By the end of 2017, more than twenty-five global brands had signed the online Cotton Pledge to boycott Uzbek cotton.

Unfair labor practices have provoked a host of social justice activism since even before the start of the Industrial Revolution. Chapter Two explores how a lively socialist print culture confronted the rise of industrial capitalism in the early 1900s.

Notes

1. Iain Whyte, *Zachary Macaulay, 1768–1838: The Steadfast Scot in the British Anti-Slavery Movement* (Liverpool, UK: Liverpool University Press, 2011), 111. *The Anti-Slavery Monthly Reporter* is also discussed in Catherine Hall, *Macaulay and Son: Architects of Imperial Britain* (New Haven, CT: Yale University Press, 2012), 84–86.

2. David Brion Davis, *The Problem of Slavery in the Age of Emancipation* (New York: Alfred A. Knopf, 2014), 267. For more on the British abolition movement, see Adam Hochschild, *Bury the Chains: Prophets and Rebels in the Fight to Free an Empire's Slaves* (New York: Houghton Mifflin Harcourt, 2006).

3. "The Society's General Meeting," *Reporter*, May 1828, 218.

4. Stephen Ahern, "Introduction: The Bonds of Sentiment," in *Affect and Abolition in the Anglo-Atlantic, 1770–1830*, ed. Stephen Ahern (London: Routledge, 2013), 18.

5. See Brycchan Carey, "'Read This and Blush': The Pamphlet Wars of the 1780s," in *British Abolitionism and the Rhetoric of Sensibility: Writing, Sentiment and Slavery, 1760–1807* (New York: Palgrave Macmillan, 2005), 107–43.

6. See Joad Raymond, *Pamphlets and Pamphleteering in Early Modern Britain* (Cambridge: Cambridge University Press, 2003). A pamphlet typically was one to two sheets of printing paper folded in quarto and bound into an eight-page to 96-page book. Ibid., 5.

7. See Brycchan Carey, "William Wilberforce's Sentimental Rhetoric: Parliamentary Reportage and the Abolition Speech of 1789," *The Age of Johnson: A Scholarly Annual* 14 (2003): 281–305.

8. Viscountess Knutsford [Margaret Jean Treveylan], *Life and Letters of Zachary Macaulay* (London: Arnold, 1900), 394, 7, 9.

9. Roger Fay, "The Clapham Sect and the Abolition of the Slave Trade," *Evangelical Times*, July 2012, http://www.evangelical-times.org/archive/item/5605/Historical/The-Clapham-Sect-and-the-abolition-of-the-slave-trade--3-/.

10. See Chapter 2, "Slave Traders and French Invaders," in Whyte, *Zachary Macaulay*, 28–52; Chapter 4, "The Trials of the Governor," in ibid., 72–96; and Bronwen Everill, *Abolition and Empire in Sierra Leone and Liberia* (London: Palgrave, Macmillan, 2013).

11. Sir George Stephen, *Anti-slavery Recollections: In a Series of Letters Addressed to Mrs. Beecher* (London: Thomas Hatchard, 1854), 51, 52.

12. Stephen Tomkins, *The Clapham Sect: How Wilberforce's Circle Transformed Britain* (Oxford, UK: Lion Books, 2012), 183–184. The *Christian Observer* lasted until 1877.

13. Stephen, *Anti-slavery Recollections*, 77.

14. "Report of The Incorporated Society for the Conversion and Religious Instruction and Education of the Negro Slaves in the British West India Islands," *Reporter*, October 1828, 312.

15. *Reporter*, July 31, 1825, 2.

16. "On the Bounties and Protected Duties, and the Restrictions on Trade, Intended for the Support of the Slave System," *Reporter*, October 31, 1826, 241–48.

17. "The Question Calmly Considered," *Reporter*, November 10, 1830, 3.

18. "The Society's General Meeting," *Reporter*, May 1828, 230.

19. "Case of Betto Douglas, a St. Kitts Slave," *Reporter*, June 1827, 1–7.

20. "On the Demoralizing Influence of Slavery," *Reporter*, January 1828, 167.

21. "I.—Statistics of Slave Colonies," *Reporter*, March 1833, 3.

22. See "Picture of Mauritius Vindicated," *Reporter*, July 1830, 294. See also "Progress of Reform—Berbice," *Reporter*, September 1827, 93; "Slavery in the Mauritius," *Reporter*, November 1828, 339; "Flogging of Females," *Reporter*, July 1828, 273; and "New Slave Code of Jamaica," *Reporter*, February 1832, 57.

23. "A Calm, and Authentic Review," *Reporter*, February 1832, 65–112. See also "Rebellion in Jamaica," *Reporter*, June 1832, 243.

24. William A. Gamson, *Talking Politics* (Cambridge: Cambridge University Press, 1992), 29.

25. See "Proceedings of the General Meetings of the Anti-slavery Society ... December 21, 1825," *Reporter*, January 1826; and "The Society's General Meeting," *Reporter*, May 1828, 214–18.

26. "Report of the Committee of the House of Lords," *Reporter*, February 1833, 474.

27. "On Framing Petitions to Parliament," *Reporter*, October 20, 1830, 451. See also "Anti-Slavery Petitions and Motions," *Reporter*, July 31, 1826, 197.

28. "On Framing Petitions," ibid., 451.

29. "Anti-Slavery Petitions and Motions," *Reporter*, July 31, 1826, 197.

30. *Reporter*, September 30, 1825, 32.

31. Francesca Polletta, "Plotting Protest: Mobilizing Stories in the 1960 Student Sit-Ins," in *Stories of Change: Narrative and Social Movements*, ed. Joseph E. Davis (Albany: State University of New York Press, 2002), 31–52. See also Francesca Polletta, "Contending Stories: Narrative in Social Movements," *Qualitative Sociology* 21, no. 4 (December 1998): 419–446; and Matthew Norton, "Narrative Structure and Emotional Mobilization in Humanitarian Representations: The Case of the Congo Reform Movement, 1903–1912," *Journal of Human Rights* 10, no. 3 (2011): 311–338.

32. "Cases of Cruelty at Bel Ombre," *Reporter*, January 1829, 390. See also "The Case of Felix, a Slave Boy," *Reporter*, January 1829, 398–99.

33. Ralph J. Poole and Ilka Saal, *Passionate Politics: The Cultural Work of American Melodrama from the Early Republic to the Present* (Cambridge, MA: Cambridge Scholars Publishing, 2009), 16. See also Peter Brooks, *The Melodramatic Imagination: Balzac, Henry James, Melodrama, and the Mode of Excess* (New Haven, CT: Yale University Press, 1976), 12–13.

34. Rev. R. Bicell, "The West Indies as They Are," *Reporter*, July 31, 1825, 5.

35. "Statistics of Slave Colonies," *Reporter*, December 1826, 283.
36. Charles Booth, *Zachary Macaulay: His Part in the Movement for the Abolition of the Slave Trade and of Slavery: an Appreciation* (London: Longmans, Green, 1934), 88.
37. "I.—Statistics of Slave Colonies," *Reporter*, March 1833, 5. [italics in original]
38. James M. Jasper and Jane D. Poulsen, "Recruiting Strangers and Friends: Moral Shocks and Social Networks in Animal Rights and Anti-Nuclear Protests," *Social Problems* 42, no. 4 (November 1995), 498.
39. "Slavery at the Cape of Good Hope," *Reporter*, January 1827, 294. See also "Samples of Jamaica Jurisprudence," *Reporter*, February 1826, 85.
40. "Report of the Bishops of Jamaica and Barbadoes on the State of Their Respective Dioceses," *Reporter*, June 30, 1826, 193. [italics in original] See also "New Slave Code.—Order in Council of Nov. 2, 1831," *Reporter*, January 1832, 4.
41. Knutsford, *Life and Letters*, 393; and Whyte, *Zachary Macaulay*, 208. Historian Stephen Tomkins dismisses the charges as "completely unfair." Tomkins, *Clapham Sect*, 183–184.
42. See Stuart Hall, "Encoding/Decoding," in *Culture, Media and Language: Working Papers in Cultural Studies, 1972–79*, ed., Stuart Hall, Dorothy Hobson, Andrew Lowe, and Paul Wills (New York: Routledge, 1991), 107–16.
43. Jeffrey Kerr-Ritchie, *Rites of August First: Emancipation Day in the Black Atlantic World* (Baton Rouge: Louisiana State University Press, 2007), 17. Although the act went into effect on August 1, 1834, a provision designated former slaves over the age of six years as "apprentices" who were to be officially freed in 1838 or 1840. Protests against the provision resulted in emancipation of all former slaves on August 1, 1838. The act did not apply to British India, including Ceylon (now Sri Lanka), where slaves were freed in 1843. Ibid., 16–17.
44. "To the Public," *Liberator*, January 1, 1831, 1. [capital letters, boldface in original] The newspaper's entire run is available at http://fair-use.org/the-liberator/.
45. The *Genius* evolved from Tennessean Elihu Embree's monthly *Emancipator*, which the Quaker started in April 1820 to replace his short-lived weekly newspaper, *Manumission Intelligencer*. The *Emancipator* only lasted until that October, when Embree died. Lundy took over Embree's press in 1822. *Manumission Intelligencer* and *Emancipator, The Tennessee Encyclopedia of History and Culture* are available at http://tennesseeencyclopedia.net/entry.php?rec=831.
46. "The Libel Persecution," *Genius of Universal Emancipation*, November 1830, 114.
47. U.S. Census Bureau, *1830 Census: Abstract of the Returns of the Fifth Census*, (Washington, D.C.: Duff Green, 1832), 51.
48. Herbert Aptheker, ed., *One Continual Cry: David Walker's Appeal to the Colored Citizens of the World 1829–1839: Its Setting and Its Meaning*, 1st paperback ed. (New York: Humanities Press, 1965), 54.
49. David Walker, *Walker's Appeal, in Four Articles; Together with a Preamble, to the Coloured Citizens of the World, but in Particular, and Very Expressly, to Those of the United States of America*, 29–30, Documenting the American South, accessed October 26, 2018, http://docsouth.unc.edu/nc/walker/walker.html.
50. See Bob Ostertag, *People's Movements, People's Press: The Journalism of Social Justice Movements* (Boston: Beacon Press, 2006), 33–39.

51. Henry Mayer, *All on Fire: William Lloyd Garrison and the Abolition of Slavery* (New York: St. Martin's Press 1998), xiii.

52. C. Vann Woodward, "The Crusader Finally Had Nothing to Say," *New York Times*, June 30, 1963, Sec. VII, 6.

53. See James Darsey, "Prophecy as Krisis: Wendell Phillips and the Sin of Slavery," in *The Prophetic Tradition and Radical Rhetoric in America* (New York: New York University Press, 1999), 61–84.

54. Horace Seldon, "Garrison's Political Activity, Moral Vision, Public Opinion and Lincoln," *The Liberator Files*, accessed October 26, 2018, http://theliberatorfiles.com/4-garrisons-political-activity-moral-vision-public-opinion-and-lincoln/.

55. See Ford Risley, *Abolition and the Press: The Moral Struggle Against Slavery* (Chicago: Northwestern University Press, 2008).

56. "Garrison the Perjury of July 4th," *Liberator*, July 5, 1836, http://theliberatorfiles.com/garrison-the-perjury-of-july-4th/.

57. Ernest G. Bormann, ed., *Forerunners of Black Power: The Rhetoric of Abolition* (Englewood Cliffs, NJ: Prentice-Hall, 1971), 93.

58. David Paul Nord, "Tocqueville, Garrison, and the Perfection of Journalism," in *Communities of Journalism: A History of American Newspapers and Their Readers*, reprint ed. (Urbana: University of Illinois Press, 2001), 2.

59. "Address Delivered at the African Masonic Hall in Boston, Feb 27, 1833 by Mrs. Maria W. Stewart," *Liberator*, April 27, 1833, http://theliberatorfiles.com/address-delivered-at-the-african-masonic-hall-in-boston-feb-27-1833-by-mrs-maria-w-stewart/.

60. See Gerda Lerner, *The Grimké Sisters from South Carolina: Pioneers for Women's Rights and Abolition*, 2nd ed. (Chapel Hill: University of North Carolina Press, 2004).

61. Linda, "Life Among the Contrabands," *Liberator*, September 5, 1862, 4.

62. Angela Jones, *African American Civil Rights: Early Activism and the Niagara Movement* (Santa Barbara, CA: ABC-CLIO, LLC, 2011), 158. See also Jacqueline Bacon, *Freedom's Journal: The First African-American Newspaper* (Lanham, MD: Lexington Books, 2007). The entire run of *Freedom's Journal* (1827–1829) is available at https://www.wisconsinhistory.org/Records/Article/CS4415.

63. See also Patsy Brewington Perry, "Before *The North Star*: Frederick Douglass' Early Journalistic Career," *Phylon* 35, no. 1 (1974): 96–107.

64. William McFeely, *Frederick Douglass* (New York: W.W. Norton, 1991), 166.

65. Tom Chaffin, "Disunion: The Messianic Schoolmaster," *New York Times*, December 29, 2010, https://opinionator.blogs.nytimes.com/2010/12/29/the-messianic-schoolmaster/.

66. Mayer, *All on Fire*, 204–206. City newspapers blamed Garrison for the attack. Ibid., 404.

67. See Ira V. Brown, "Racism and Sexism: The Case of Pennsylvania Hall," *Phylon* 37, no. 2 (June 1976): 126–36.

68. See Paul Simon, *Freedom's Champion: Elijah Lovejoy* (Carbondale, IL: Southern Illinois University Press, 1994).

69. See Stanley Harrold, *Gamaliel Bailey and Antislavery Union* (Kent, OH: Kent State University Press, 1986).

70. William Lloyd Garrison, "The War—Its Cause and Cure," *Liberator*, May 3, 1861.

71. "Section 1. Neither slavery nor involuntary servitude, except as a punishment for crime whereof the party shall have been duly convicted, shall exist within the United States, or any place subject to their jurisdiction," Amendment XIII, U.S. Constitution. To fill the void, abolition colleagues created *The Nation*, which continues today.

72. The *Anti-Slavery Monthly Reporter* appeared infrequently after 1833, and was absent more than a year before its 113th number appeared in July 1836. Macaulay died on May 13, 1838, a few weeks after all slaves across the British Empire were freed. The British and Foreign Anti-Slavery Society that replaced the original organization in 1839 published the journal from 1840 through 1852. In 1853, a new series appeared as volume one of the *Anti-Slavery Reporter*, which continued until 1909. That year, the Anti-Slavery Society merged with the Aboriginal Peoples Society. The *Anti-Slavery Reporter and Aborigines Friend* appeared in October 1909, a consolidation of both groups' previous periodicals into a quarterly that continued to fight new forms of slavery throughout the twentieth century, sometimes irregularly.

73. Adam Taylor, "There Are an Estimated 40 Million Slaves in the World. Where Do They Live and What Do They Do?," *Washington Post*, September 19, 2017, https://www.washingtonpost.com/news/worldviews/wp/2017/09/19/there-are-an-estimated-40-million-slaves-in-the-world-where-do-they-live-and-what-do-they-do/?utm_term=.32fc751a8929.

74. Jakub Sobik, interview by author, June 16, 2016, Anti-Slavery International, London.

75. See, for example, "Using Social Media to Promote Human Rights," Office of the High Commissioner for Human Rights, United Nations, August 10, 2011, http://www.ohchr.org/EN/NewsEvents/Pages/InternetFreedom.aspx.

76. See Sam Gregory, "Transnational Storytelling: Human Rights, Witness, and Video Advocacy," *American Anthropologist* 108, no. 1 (March 2006): 195–204.

77. Matthew Powers, "The New Boots on the Ground: NGOs in the Changing Landscape of International News," *Journalism: Theory, Practice & Criticism* 17, no. 4 (2016): 401–16. News reporting by NGOs also raises ethical issues. See Glenda Cooper, "When the Lines between NGO and News Organizations Blur," 2009 Special Report: NGOs and the News, *Nieman Journalism Lab*, December 21, 2009, http:// www.niemanlab.org/2009/12/glenda-cooper-when-lines-between-ngo-and-news-blur/; and Kate Wright, "These Grey Areas," *Journalism Studies* 17, no. 8 (2016): 989–1009.

78. Diane Orentlicher, "Bearing Witness: The Art and Science of Human Rights Fact-Finding," *Harvard Human Rights Journal* 3 (1990): 83, 84.

79. See links to documents in Jodi S. Cohen, "The $3 Million Research Breakdown," *ProPublica*, April 26, 2018, https://www.propublica.org/article/university-of-illinois-chicago-mani-pavuluri-3-million-research-breakdown.

80. Sarah Mathewson, "Unlock the Future of Tanzania's Child Domestic Workers," Anti-Slavery, November 7, 2017, https://www.antislavery.org/unlock-future-tanzanias-child-domestic-workers/.

· 2 ·

STRIKE

The New York *Call* and Socialist Print Culture

When workers at Standard Oil's refinery in Bayonne, New Jersey, went on strike for liveable wages and more humane working conditions in October 1916, editors of New York City's socialist daily newspaper, the *Call*, predicted strikers would die and the mainstream press would blame the workers for their own deaths.[1]

Call editors were correct on both counts. Police shot seven people October 12, killing four, including a new bride sitting by a window in her home, and injured dozens more in what labor historian Philip Foner called "a prime example of police mob rule."[2] New Yorkers never would glean that information, however, from browsing newspaper headlines: "New Bayonne Mob Clubbed Out of Captured R.R. Station" (*New York Mail*); "Bayonne Strikers Renew Their Threats" (*New York Evening Post*); "Oil Strikers Begin Looting; Rioting Mobs Hold Bayonne" (*New York Evening World*); "Bayonne Rioters Loot Stores" (*New York Journal*); and "Bayonne Rioters Held in Check" (*New York Times*). A *New York World* editorial proclaimed that, "Clearing the streets, entering houses forcibly, putting down all opposition by the force of arms are the only means of dealing with riotous mobs that refuse to yield to milder measures."[3] The *Call* framed the Bayonne strike differently.

A. Howland's eyewitness account appeared under the headline, "The March of the Murderers":

> I felt last night that I just got back from the trenches. The police were merciless. Again and again the shots rang out. Again and again the ambulances passed and returned. ... The strikers are utterly unorganized. Practically all of them are unarmed. I saw no evidence of either attack or even of resistance, only a desire to get out of the way of the murderous bullets.[4]

Socialists' "Print Culture of Dissent"

When it debuted on May 30, 1908, the *Call* joined hundreds of socialist newspapers and magazines that challenged the emerging corporate state in the early twentieth century.[5] They were the product of a communications revolution of technological and transportation advances that fueled astronomical newspaper and magazine growth in the late nineteenth century.[6] Socialist periodicals, along with the journals of the equally prolific anarchists and the Industrial Workers of the World, demanded the abolition of capitalism, making them more radical than the Progressive Era's reformers. The anticapitalists participated in what Jason Martinek called a rich "print culture of dissent" that protested the gaping inequity between workers and a new class of multimillionaires who controlled the monopolistic trusts epitomized by John D. Rockefeller Sr.'s Standard Oil conglomerate.[7] Such captains of industrial capitalism battled workers' attempts to organize, backed invariably by the state. As a result, claims historian Michael Cohen, American labor history is "the bloodiest of any western industrialized nation."[8]

The only solution was for workers to take over the means of production, socialist journals proclaimed, so everyone could thrive in a cooperative commonwealth. Hundreds of socialist periodicals reached a million people in 1908, a socialist journalist estimated.[9] This lively "alternative public sphere," as radical historian Paul Buhle characterized it, offered a compelling alternative vision to industrial capitalism.[10] While inspired by Karl Marx, many U.S. socialists' vision of the cooperative commonwealth was rooted in an egalitarian American ethic of social justice. Furthermore, moderate socialists like the *Call*'s publishers rejected Marx's dictum that capitalism could be vanquished only by violent revolution; they believed that electoral politics could gradually replace capitalism with a cooperative commonwealth (a view rejected by anarchists and the Industrial Workers of the World). In summer 1901, the

Socialist Party of America emerged from the union of the Social Democratic Party of America and disgruntled deserters from the Socialist Labor Party.[11]

Fractious socialists stood united in their belief that they needed their own journals to argue their cause. During the Progressive Era, mainstream news media were central in the mix of "repressive institutions and violent practices that enforced workplace and labor discipline, patrolled and surveilled subaltern racial and class groups, and punished radical dissent," according to Cohen.[12] A provision of the new Socialist Party's constitution, however, forbade the new political party from publishing its own newspaper for fear its editor would hold too much power. By 1912, the ban against an official national party newspaper had by one count helped spawn at least 323 socialist newspapers and magazines, including five English and eight foreign-language dailies, 262 English and thirty-six foreign-language weeklies, and ten English and two foreign-language monthlies.[13] Although a testament to the socialists' faith in democratic journalism, the cacophony of socialist voices hindered forging a cohesive socialist collective identity. Although socialism never triumphed as a political force in the United States for a number of reasons, socialists in the early 1900s fought for programs and policies that many Americans take for granted today, including workplace safety laws, regulation of trusts, disability insurance, and workers' right to organize.[14]

The Socialist Press in the 1900s

The granddaddy of the socialist press was Julius Wayland's folksy *Appeal to Reason*, founded six years before the Socialist Party. The homespun weekly reached a peak circulation of 750,000 in 1913, making it "the most successful institution of the socialist movement in the United States and the one national weekly newspaper that unified the movement from coast to coast," according to Wayland biographer Elliott Shore.[15] The pithy "One Hoss Philosopher" published his *Appeal* in the socialist colony he established in Girard, Kansas, centered around a 20,000-square-foot "Temple of the Revolution" that housed a state-of-the-art, three-deck color Goss cylinder press capable of running off as many as 45,000 newspapers an hour.[16] Wayland's plain-spoken satire and individualism made the *Appeal* "the most important evangelistic propaganda organ of the Left and the clearest expression of indigenous American socialism," according to Buhle.[17] Its most famous muckraking venture sent socialist writer Upton Sinclair to Chicago's brutal meatpacking district, culminating in an explosive series beginning in February 1905 that detailed appalling working conditions faced by its fictionalized protagonist, Lithuanian immigrant Jurgis Rudkus.[18] Sinclair's *The Jungle* launched a long line of sensational muckraking stories in the *Appeal*.[19] In 1914, for example, John Kenneth Turner criss-crossed the nation 12,000 miles to research his "Government by Gunmen" series on the use of state-sanctioned violence to quash strikes and unions.[20] Anonymous sources and sensational claims, however, left a question mark above much *Appeal* journalism.

Wayland's contender for title of most influential socialist publisher was fellow Midwesterner Charles Kerr, whose biographer Allen Ruff asserts was "the foremost socialist publisher of the era."[21] The mission of Charles Kerr & Company, founded in Chicago in 1893, was to introduce American workers to European radical literature. Kerr published the first English editions of *Das Capital*'s second and third volumes, and its affordable Pocket Library of Socialism published sixty volumes in the company's first decade, including works by American socialists such as Eugene Debs and Jack London. Kerr launched the *International Socialist Review* in July 1900 to Americanize socialism and raise the intellectual level of movement discourse.[22] After firing editor Algie Simons in 1908, Kerr retooled the *Review* into a vivid chronicler of the nation's labor movement with first-person accounts of strikes and lockouts, illustrated by black-and-white photos documenting the action. Reaching a national circulation of more than 40,000 by 1911, *Review* reportage from South Africa to China did more than any other periodical to educate Americans about corporate globalization.[23] Kerr's advocacy of "direct action," such as strikes, put him at odds with Wayland as well as with the *Call*'s politically active publishers, personified by New York labor lawyer and national Socialist Party leader, Morris Hillquit. Despite their differences, Hillquit, Kerr, and Wayland all believed that the socialist press was the most effective way to promote socialism across the United States.

Most socialist periodicals were local, however, like the four-page *Truth* (1912–1913) in Tacoma, Washington, or regional, like the *California Social Democrat*, the state party's official organ. "Scores of small-town Socialist weeklies appeared in Oklahoma, from the Okemah *Sledge Hammer* to the Sentinel *Sword of Truth*," recalled *Oklahoma Pioneer* publisher Oscar Ameringer.[24] Some of the nation's sizable foreign-language ethnic press advocated socialism, like the Yiddish-language *Jewish Daily Forward*, edited by Lithuanian-born Abraham Cahan.[25] Several union newspapers also endorsed socialism, such as the militant Western Federation of Miners' *Miner's Magazine*.[26] The radical-chic mix of art and satire in the Greenwich Village monthly the *Masses* (1911–1917) attracted an audience of bohemian intellectuals.[27] Other pre-war socialist journals targeted specific demographic groups, such as *Socialist Woman*, *Christian Socialist*, the *Young Socialists' Magazine*, and the *Messenger*, the only African American socialist periodical.[28]

The East's Most Important Socialist Periodical

The *Call* stood out as the most important socialist periodical in the East, one of only a handful of English-language socialist dailies, along with the *Chicago Daily Socialist* (1906–1911) and the *Milwaukee Leader* (1911–1938).[29] New York socialists in 1882 formed a Workingmen's Cooperative Publishing Association with the goal of publishing a daily socialist newspaper that spoke to Americans in English. They survived internecine socialist politics and finally raised $50,000 to launch the newspaper after twenty-six years of fund-raising fairs, picnics, and sales of $5,000 bonds. Finances remained a constant struggle, a common problem among social movement media. Even when the *Call* hit peak circulation of 32,000 in 1912, the association suffered a net loss of nearly $10,000.[30]

The newspaper sold advertising to boost revenue but never resolved the contradiction of an anticapitalist journal that sold ads.[31] Philosophically, its publishers and editors subscribed to the Marxist dictum that mass media are the enemy of the people, in part because advertising corrupted commercial media and turned them into capitalist lapdogs. The front page of the *Call's* first issue raged: "The epileptic editions of Park Row's jaundiced journals are nothing less than a criminal imposition on the reader, robbing him of valuable time which he is forced to squander in search through a wilderness of words for actual news." In 1916, the *Call* described the mainstream press as "a slimy, venomous, treacherous, lying reptile; a thing to hate and avoid; a thing worthy of no credence whatever in a life and death struggle between labor and capital."[32] Mainstream newspapers' coverage of the Bayonne strike offers insights into why the socialist daily so despised them.

The WCPA's Board of Management oversaw the *Call*, one of several ways in which the socialist daily differed from commercial newspapers.[33] The collective management structure was a deliberate strategy to avoid capitalist hierarchy, an experiment future social movement media would follow. Another difference from mainstream media was the newspaper's vocal support for labor.

A main *Call* function was to counter the mainstream press's widespread hostility to labor. As the *Call's* front-page motto stated, the six- to eight-page *Call* was "Devoted to the Interests of the Working People." Top stories of the *Call's* January 19, 1910, front page demonstrated how labor strife dominated the era: "5,000 Pants Workers Go Out on Strike," "Milk Strikers Sue Boss for Security," and "Phila. Traction Strike Probable." The *Call* also reported on the era's frequent industrial accidents, such as a factory worker crushed by an elevator or workers boiled alive in a boiler explosion.[34]

The newspaper also experimented with citizen journalism when it announced its "newsgathering machine" of correspondents, which it likened to an "Associated Press of Labor."[35] Nothing much came of the reporting corps, but the *Call* tried to enlist readers in a 1916 campaign to enforce factory fire laws.[36] Headlines and text framed subjects of its stories as victims of the capitalist system, blaming even the sinking of the *Titanic* on capitalism.[37] Perhaps as an antidote to all this bad news, the *Call* also showcased a vibrant socialist culture that produced books, poetry, plays, songs, and art.[38] This culture helped bond socialists' collective identity. Notices and ads for socialist picnics, lectures, and dances indicate socialism's social aspects, including the *Call's* annual fund-raising fair and ball.[39]

Social Justice Journalism in the *Call*

Exposés of poor labor conditions and incompetent city government became staples, however, beginning with an early series on child hunger.[40] The *Call's* first substantial scoop in 1909 revealed that New York City was renting property on the Bowery to brothels. Other newspapers picked up the story, and the city shuttered the brothels.[41] Other examples of social justice journalism ranged from a 1910 series that examined the city's "slovenly" foster care system[42] to a 1912 investigation of filthy kitchens in luxury hotels.[43] The unseemly facts presented in these investigations aimed for delivering a moral shock. Despite its antipathy toward the mainstream press, *Call* exposés emulated the crusading style of media moguls William Randolph Hearst and Joseph Pulitzer's "yellow journalism," which combined sensational headlines with shameless self-promotion.[44] The *Call* often was a main character in its own stories. "*The Call* Wins Fight on Rotten Buildings" and "*The Call* Helps Union to Get Rid of Spy" typified headlines.[45] *Call* campaigns differed from the crusading yellow press because the newspaper championed labor in contrast to mainstream media's negative view of labor actions.[46] It rejected the emerging professional ethos of objectivity embodied by the *New York Times*, bragging in 1917 that striking railroad unions viewed the *Call* as "practically their official paper."[47]

The daily did more than report sympathetically on strikers: its activism is what most distinguished the *Call* from the commercial dailies it otherwise emulated despite its invective. It published special editions like a June 12, 1912, issue that supported waiters with page-one coverage, editorials, cartoons, and photos.[48] Hotels tried to buy up the issue to try to hide the bad publicity about unsanitary conditions.[49] The *Call* even bought 5,000 "Don't Be a Scab" sashes for young women to wear to support striking trolley car conductors in 1916.[50] The *Call* also refused ads from companies whose workers were on strike.[51] *Call* coverage of "The Uprising of the Twenty Thousand" demonstrates its activist journalism on several fronts.

The *Call* Supports the Shirtwaist Workers' Strike

The unprecedented strike of women workers was sparked in October 1909 when Triangle Waist Company locked out a group of mostly Italian and Jewish immigrant teenaged girls who were trying to organize a union to help them raise their average weekly five-dollar wages and reduce their typical 66-hour workweek. They began picketing the ten-story Asch Building near Washington Square, whose top three floors housed Triangle. By November, the pickets' numbers mushroomed to 20,000 workers who shut down the entire Lower East Side garment district.[52] Socialist women joined in by helping strikers conduct shop meetings. Upper-class women in the Women's Trade Union League mobilized to provide funds and protect pickets from police assaults in a groundbreaking—if tense—cross-class alliance.[53]

While the conflict between factory owners and scrappy seamstresses captured mainstream media attention, no newspaper covered the strike more thoroughly than the *Call*. A story in its "Woman's Sphere" section traced the low pay, long hours, and poor conditions that led to the strike.[54] Stories listed strikers' names and fines, and charts tallied arrests, fines, and jail terms.[55] The newspaper reported on harassment of pickets and name-calling by police.[56] It directly aided the strikers by printing rules for pickets in three languages.[57] The *Call* appealed for financial aid for the fledgling union.[58] Former *Call* editor Algernon Lee stood next to legendary labor activist Mother Jones at a socialist rally for them and declared, "The labor movement must organize women, treat them as sisters, as comrades and equals!"[59] Editorials scored police and courts, and cartoons lampooned them in oppositional framing of them as the movement's enemy.[60] Poems like "The Ballad of the Shirt Waist Worker" romanticized strikers in a blatant pitch to emotion.[61]

The *Call*, as usual, cast itself in a leading role. The Christmas Day front-page headline read, "Waist Makers' Union Through the *Call* Denies that the Strike is About to Be Called Off." On December 29, 1909, the *Call* published a special fund-raising number for the shirtwaist strikers. All proceeds went to the strike fund, despite the newspaper's financial woes, indicative of socialist press priorities. Vassar College alumnae edited the special, which included articles in Italian, Yiddish, and English. A thousand shirtwaist workers peddled the four-page issue for a nickel each. The lead story framed the strike's significance in building collective identity: "For its deeper meaning lies in that the working class woman is feeling her identity of interests with the working class man, that she is not only feeling, but THINKING, and thinking she is becoming conscious of her power as a member of the working class." The special listed shops that settled, published portraits of key players, listed dates and fines of 653 arrests, reprinted "The History of the Strike" from the *Survey*, one example of sympathetic mainstream coverage, and admonished female readers to only wear shirtwaists bearing the union label. All 45,000 copies sold out in two hours at an average price of eight cents.[62] Hillquit, who managed the *Call* as a member of the WCPA board, represented the jailed pickets in court.[63] Many shirtwaist workers won higher wages, shorter hours, and better working conditions—but no union. Their collective action, however, laid the groundwork for the International Ladies Garment Workers Union's future success.

The tragic epilogue to the spirited strike struck on March 25, 1911, when fire engulfed the Triangle factory. Illegally blocked doors trapped more than 200 workers on the ninth floor. Smoke and flames drove workers to the windows, from which dozens jumped to the sidewalk. The final death toll was 146 people.[64] Outrage at the unnecessary loss of life triggered a new era in the fight for occupational safety, thanks to public outrage fuelled by massive media coverage and highlighted by graphic photographs of crumpled corpses that were a harbinger of imagery's ascendance in twentieth-century media.[65] Artist John Sloan's iconic political cartoon stretched across five-columns of the *Call*'s March 27, 1911, front page, conveying the larger story: a young woman's charred corpse lies inside a triangle whose three sides are labelled "Rent," "Profits," and "Interest," flanked by a skeleton and a porcine capitalist.[66] The second page displayed photographs of twenty victims, unprecedented for the *Call*, which was just beginning to experiment with new photo reproduction technology. The graphic photographs demonstrated the emotional power of a frozen image. "Murder and nothing else but murder," the *Call* editorialized.[67]

Call coverage went a step further than other newspapers by framing the lethal fire as a product of capitalist greed, condemning an entire economic system instead of just the individual factory owners.[68] *Call* reportage emphasized the factory owners' culpability more than the city's lax fire code. "WAIST SHOP OWNERS MADE MILLIONS; TRY TO PUT BLAME ON CITY OFFICIALS," screamed the March 28 lead headline.[69] Unlike many mainstream papers that were satisfied with the indictment of Triangle's owners on murder charges, the socialist newspaper campaigned for investigations in other factories. "Capitalist justice is usually satisfied if an individual is punished, but it seeks to let the class continue its former inhuman actions," it editorialized.[70] Another editorial warned that many more workers were being "slaughtered by capitalism."[71] Its critique went beyond rhetoric. When Triangle tried to buy a $250 ad, the *Call* called it a bribe, published a copy of the check, and sent it back. The factory owners' acquittal, however, revealed the immense indifference of the hegemonic forces aligned against workers, evidenced by a juror who, despite the overwhelming evidence of the owners' culpability, described the fire as "an act of God."[72]

Banned in Bayonne

Nowhere is the *Call*'s advocacy more apparent than in its response to the Standard Oil refinery strike in Bayonne, New Jersey, that began in July 1915. Most of Standard Oil's 5,000 employees were European immigrants whose average salary was $2.50 a day for a 76-hour workweek. In addition to a 15-percent raise, strike demands included dismissal of a reviled foreman. *Call* managing editor Chester Wright described conditions for 10,000 workers in the gigantic refinery on Constable Hook:

> In the Standard Oil plants the men work under terrific temperatures and in conditions that defy description. Still cleaners work in a stench that is all but unbearable. Men don't last long in those plants. That is why only the strongest of immigrant workers come to these places. But soon they find that the wages don't buy enough food and clothes, don't pay rent, don't give the workers any chance at all for anything that goes to make up life. And they revolt.[73]

During several days of unrest, police and "deputies"—in reality thugs hired off the street by Standard—shot and killed five unarmed workers and rampaged their neighborhoods. Police arrested more than a hundred workers and as many refinery guards. After reaching a fragile truce, Standard Oil fired the most active strikers but gave remaining workers raises up to 10 percent. No one ever was charged with the killings.[74] European-born paraffin workers struck again for higher wages on October 4, 1916. On October 10, management shut down the entire plant when 1,200 strikers blocked the entrance, putting nearly 5,000 men out of work. The mayor—who doubled as Standard's lawyer—announced his support for any police action his client deemed necessary. The *Call* worried the next day: "Never yet has there been a labor dispute with Rockefeller that the laborers did not furnish some corpses to grace the occasion."[75] A *Call* photographer and reporter crossed the Hudson River to watch each morning as police forced milling crowds of strikers and sympathizers back from the Standard Oil gates and into an adjacent tenement neighborhood. Police shot at people on the street and into their windows, tore up saloons that ignored an order to close, and raided homes.[76]

"Throughout the afternoon there came the sound of volley firing as the police showed no mercy to strikers or mere sympathizers," wrote the *Call's* Howland in his first-person account of police marching eight abreast upon the neighborhood on October 12, shouting at people to get off the street or be killed.[77] His narrative framed workers as victims of state violence. *Call* photographs showed police with Gatling guns and rapid-firing rifles, as did the mainstream newspapers. Once past headlines and lead sentences, the big dailies' descriptions of events were surprisingly similar to the *Call's*; their narratives differed mainly on whom they blamed the violence. Bayonne strike coverage helps explain why socialists considered hegemonic news media labor's enemy. In contrast, *Call* editors assured readers: "The *Evening Call* is the people's paper, your paper. It isn't muzzled by any trust."[78] The *New Republic* also challenged mainstream newspapers' pro-police narrative.

Virtually all of the mainstream newspapers, however, played up negative ethnic stereotypes. The *Bayonne Evening Review* blamed the alleged riots on immigrant workers' "hereditary impulse to wreck and ruin when the restraints of their native environment was [sic] changed to the wide freedom in their new homes in America."[79] A *New York Times* story headlined "Threaten Race War in Bayonne Strike" praised 300 English-speaking workers who planned to march through the strike zone to return to work.[80] Only the *Call* criticized the xenophobic nature of the assault on the immigrant workers. Editor Wright, in contrast, offered an injustice frame for the racial divide between "whites" and what he called the "others"—Bayonne's many Eastern European immigrants: "For the 'others' yesterday was a day of terror."[81] He reported seeing police bash captured strikers' skulls with clubs. After police bullets claimed a third bystander on October 13, a *Call* editorial charged that Standard Oil controlled the state of New Jersey.[82] Anarchy reigned in Bayonne, another charged.[83] The *Call* sought out quotes from strikers, like one from an anonymous worker who said, "And, let me tell you, a man can't raise a family on $1.50 a day or $2 a day. That's what this strike is all about it."[84] The *Call's* agency frames supported the strike's collective action.

Officials considered the *Call's* support for strikers so threatening that Bayonne police confiscated copies of the newspaper. Publishers continued to smuggle copies into the city.[85] The violence subsided October 14, American-born workers re-entered the plant under police guard October 18, and the remaining strikers returned to work on October 20 on the promise that federal mediators would negotiate for their demands. While the *New York Times* headline announced, "American Workers Break Oil Strike," the *Call* headline that morning framed the end of the strike differently: "Bayonne Strikers Cowed by Guns of Standard Oil Controlled Police, Vote to Resume Work."[86] Although *Call* editors framed the strike as a failure, historian George Dorsey argues that Bayonne marked a milestone because it forced the Rockefellers to re-examine their draconian labor practices. Standard Oil created an annuity and benefits plan for retirees and introduced death, accident, and sickness benefits. It established hiring and firing guidelines and procedures for discipline, wage adjustments, and appeals. Socialists renounced such reforms as palliatives, however, since they made workers less inclined to reject capitalism.

Conflicting Identities of Class, Gender, and Race

Eighteen-year-old Dorothy Day, future founder of the Catholic Worker movement and its newspaper, the *Catholic Worker*, joined the *Call* as a cub reporter during the middle of the Bayonne strike.[87] "MR. J. D. ROCKEFELLER, 26 BROADWAY: HERE'S A FAMILY LIVING ON DOG FOOD," read the headline above one of Day's first bylines on November 13, 1916, one of her series of exposés about hunger in the city. The subhead referenced the recent Standard Oil strike, "They're Italians, Like Yours in Bayonne, and Their Diet Is Liver and Chicken Feet Which They Once Served the Hound." Day ended her story: "There are six little children that they want to give the same chance in life that they themselves have had. 'If there only hadn't been so many,' Mrs. Salvatore said wistfully, 'And yet I love them all.'"[88]

Day's veiled reference to the poor woman's lack of access to birth control reflected the *Call*'s pioneering role in legalizing birth control, which it called "the most revolutionary doctrine yet preached by brave men and women to a headstrong world."[89] The socialist press narrative framed birth control as a class issue, arguing that the criminalization of contraception kept the lower classes impoverished because they could not limit their family size, while upper-class women could obtain the contraband through private physicians. Day chronicled the saga of birth-control pioneer Ethel Byrne, who embarked on a hunger strike at the Blackwell's Island workhouse after she was sentenced to thirty days for opening the nation's first birth control clinic in Brooklyn on October 16, 1916, with her sister, socialist nurse Margaret Sanger. Margaret became world famous for her fight to legalize birth control, but the eleven-day hunger strike that her nearly forgotten sister launched on January 22, 1917, briefly made Byrne a national cause célèbre.[90]

After 185 hours without food or water, Byrne became the first female American political prisoner to be force-fed when prison doctors jammed a feeding tube down her throat. Day scored a front-page scoop when Sanger gave her the first account of her sister's experience.[91] The *Call*'s relationship with Sanger dated back to 1911, when she first wrote about sex in veiled terms for a parenting column. She grew more daring in her column, "What Every Girl Should Know," broaching taboo topics such as menstruation and masturbation. The Post Office declared her column about syphilis (February 9, 1913) obscene and that issue of the *Call* non-mailable under federal obscenity laws.[92] The *Call* defiantly filled the empty space where Sanger's banned column would have appeared with this message:

"What Every Girl Should Know,"
NOTHING!
By Order of the Post Office Department

The *Call* supported other aspects of the feminist movement swirling across New York. A 1912 editorial, for example, urged women to wear red sashes in the upcoming Fifth Avenue suffrage parade to show socialist support for votes for women.[93] "Woman's Sphere" provided a forum for women to debate their changing role, although its conflicting messages about women's place in the home and the reality of the workingwomen whose struggles it documented reflected social confusion on gender roles.[94] Woman's editor Anita Block supported a separatist movement among women who felt discriminated against in the Socialist Party, where a "male superiority complex" reigned, according to historian Ira Kipnis.[95] In July 1908, the newspaper was instrumental in organizing the New York Socialist Women's Conference, which voted to create a separate women's educational organization that would nurture their political skills. The state party quashed the plan, however, indicative of its dismissive attitude toward female members.

African Americans received virtually no support from the *Call*, although a Socialist Party founding resolution promised equality to black members. Black Americans were nearly invisible in the white world portrayed by the socialist press, which tended to collapse racism into a mere symptom of class that would magically disappear along with capitalism. Beyond editorializing against segregated socialist locals, the *Call* had little to offer African Americans.[96] It refused to acknowledge injustice based on race. One of the *Call*'s earliest editorials boasted that it would do "NOTHING to secure the negro vote."[97] The next month Socialist leader Eugene Debs stated in an open letter in the *Call* to the Negroes National League, "There is no negro question outside of the class question."[98] Such statements made it impossible to forge a socialist identity among black citizens. Furthermore, Debs's letter displayed the era's pervasive casual racism, the main reason why socialism failed to engage the nation's most oppressed group. "The Socialist party knows that the great mass of negroes are ignorant and it is the only party that refuses to traffic in that ignorance," Debs wrote.[99] Racist cartoons in the *Call*'s early years surely offended potential converts, as did its refusal to capitalize the word "negro."[100] W. E. B. Du Bois, erudite editor of the National Association for the Advancement of Colored People magazine the *Crisis*, briefly belonged to the Socialist Party. After he quit in frustration over its unacknowledged racism, he raised his concerns in a new socialist journal, the *New Review*. "I have come to believe that the test of any great movement toward social reform is the Excluded Class," he wrote. "If you're saving dying babies, whose babies are you going to let die?"[101] The cooperative commonwealth envisioned by the socialist press remained a white man's land.[102] It would take nearly another century before white social justice journalists, at the urging of activists and scholars of color, began to consider the intertwined oppressions of race, gender, and class.

Mobilizing the Socialist Vote

The *Call's* main mission besides supporting labor was to elect Socialist Party candidates. Going into the 1912 presidential election, the Socialist Party claimed its national all-time high of 150,000 members and had elected more than a thousand local officials in 33 states and 337 towns and cities.[103] Socialist presidential candidate Debs's 901,551 votes in 1912, 6 percent of the national total, inspired gleeful front-page headlines in the *Call*, but so did every election no matter how poor the Socialist showing.[104] The newspaper once editorialized that a group of "good, active, aggressive, militant, class-conscious" socialist Congressmen could "do more in a year for Socialism and the working class than in ten years of steady agitation."[105] The *Call* stressed practical applications of socialism over theory in essays that answered such questions as, "Why Not Own the Roads?"[106] The newspaper informed readers of numerous citywide socialist meetings and rallies, sometimes filling entire columns with notices especially during campaigns.

Political cartoons appeared on the *Call's* front and editorial pages when the newspaper could afford them. *Masses* historian Leslie Fishbein claims that radical artists in the 1910s created "a new genre of politically conscious art intended as a weapon in the class struggle."[107] Historian Cohen has demonstrated how cartoons were "an active force in framing socialist ideology and goals."[108] Cartoons' powerful visual rhetoric—a mix of imagery and text meant to persuade—telegraphed injustice. A *Call* cartoon during the 1908 election, for example, symbolized the socialist vote as a big fist smashing the ugly face of capitalism.[109] Another, in which a child laborer was nailed to a cross, made instantly clear the *Call's* stance on the practice.[110] A popular strip featured "Henry Dubb," drawn by Ryan Walker, a successful commercial cartoonist converted to socialism.[111] "He can tell a story in three strokes of a pen," *Call* editors bragged of their occasional contributor. "A very great tenderness for the unhappy and the suffering and a great love for humanity fill his soul."[112] Walker portrayed Dubb as a worker too dumb to wake up to his own exploitation, a questionable choice for recruiting converts or building a socialist collective identity. Dubb proved so popular, however, that Walker toured the East sketching his character's misadventures, indicating socialist audiences identified the unenlightened Dubb as "other" and felt superior to him.

As in its strike coverage, the *Call* played an active role in political campaigns. It enlisted readers to distribute a hundred thousand copies of the Socialist Municipal Platform, for example, before the 1913 election.[113] The

Call helped elect several Socialist state legislators. The newspaper and the New York Socialist party enjoyed their biggest political success when Meyer London, a Lithuania-born labor activist, was elected the nation's second social-ist congressman in 1914 (following *Milwaukee Leader* publisher Victor Berger in 1910). An important voice for urban immigrant workers in the Lower East Side that he represented, London fought for many progressive causes ahead of their time, including federal disability, unemployment, health, and old-age insurance. London also was the only member of the House to vote against the wartime Sedition Act of 1918, which made it a crime to "utter, print, write, or publish any disloyal, profane, scurrilous, or abusive language" about the U.S. government, Constitution, or military.[114] The act expanded on the wartime Espionage Act of 1917, which granted the Post Office virtually absolute power to ban from the mails any matter that it determined hindered the U.S. war effort or encouraged its enemies.

Silencing the Socialist Press in World War I

The espionage and sedition acts are reminders of how hegemonic powers can silence social movement media. The federal government decimated the rad-ical press, and governmental suppression is among the reasons that socialism never gained traction in the United States. Socialists had been vocal critics as the United States began its "preparedness" buildup to enter Europe's sense-less "Great War." The *Call* published a "great anti-war edition" on March 31, 1917, in a desperate bid to keep the United States out. Failing that, the *Call* endorsed the Socialist party's 140–31–5 vote to oppose the war. The fed-eral government moved quickly. The Post Office charged fifteen periodicals with Espionage Act violations that summer, including the socialist *Milwaukee Leader*, and sentenced Berger to twenty years in prison.[115] Postmaster Gen-eral Albert Sidney Burleson revoked the inexpensive second-class mail rate of thirty-six radical periodicals in fifteen states, forcing most to close due to prohibitive first-class postage rates.[116]

The *Call* led the rest of the socialist press in fighting the suppression, and Hillquit represented many of the accused in court and at public rallies.[117] In contrast, mainstream newspapers like the *New York Times* supported the federal suppression.[118] The *Call* lost its second-class postage rate due to an October 3, 1918, article headlined, "Bankers Hope to Sue Soldiers Back from War to Cut Wages." Staffers struggled to publish and distribute the newspaper through newsstands and street sales throughout the war. After the November 11, 1918, armistice, Hillquit filed a half-million-dollar lawsuit against Burleson to restore the *Call's* mail privileges, but an appeals court ruled in favor of the Post Office.[119] The *Call's* mail privileges were not restored until May 25, 1921. By then circulation had plummeted, partly because the creation of the American Communist Party in 1919 had further decimated socialist ranks. The WCPA sold the *Call* for $100,000 and stock to a corporation formed by several unions, which turned the socialist daily into an official labor newspaper renamed the *Leader*. Workers seemed indifferent, and three months later the paper disappeared until January 19, 1924, when it resurfaced as the *New Leader* weekly broadsheet— "Devoted to the Interests of the Socialist and Labor movements."[120] It evolved into a provocative liberal intellectual magazine that lasted for the next eighty-two years, succeeded by an online edition that survived until summer 2010.[121]

Socialist Journalism in the Twenty-First Century: *Jacobin* Magazine

No socialist daily newspaper today reports on New York, but Brooklyn is home to hip-looking socialist *Jacobin* magazine, visited online by a million viewers monthly in fall 2018. The bigger surprise is that 30,000 subscribers pay to read *Jacobin's* glossy quarterly print edition, even though most content is free online. Ironically, the online-only version that founder Bhaskar Sunkara launched in 2010 was virtually ignored in the vast Internet universe, so the twenty-one-year-old George Washington University student produced a print version in his student dormitory room that he published in January 2011. Revenue from *Jacobin's* first hundred subscriptions financed Sunkara's next print run, which gained another hundred subscriptions, until he far exceeded his original goal of producing eight print issues.[122]

Jacobin's success indicates that room remains for print in the twenty-first-century social movement media landscape. "*Jacobin* has [in the early 2010s] become the leading intellectual voice of the American left, the most vibrant and relevant socialist publication in a very long time," a *Vox* profile enthused.[123] The magazine got a boost in its early years from the Occupy Movement, Wisconsin's union showdown, and Vermont Senator Bernie Sanders's campaign to be the Democratic presidential nominee in 2016. Even though subscriptions dropped from 36,000 after the election of President Donald

Trump, Sunkara tripled the magazine staff as part of his goal to bring socialist ideas back into the American mainstream. Like the *Call*, *Jacobin* advocates change through electoral politics, although it publishes many stripes of leftist thought. Sunkara describes his magazine as roughly the socialist equivalent of the *New Republic* or as a less doctrinaire *Monthly Review*, the Marxist political journal. He adds, "*Jacobin* is like nothing else in this space: it's explicitly Marxist, it's programmatically socialist, yet our goal is to speak to as many people as possible."[124] The son of Trinidadian immigrants of Indian descent, Sunkara at age seventeen joined the Democratic Socialists of America, the largest successor to the Socialist Party, edited the Young Democratic Socialists blog, the *Activator*, and wrote for *Dissent*. He kept his day job at the progressive magazine *In These Times* for several years after launching *Jacobin* and continued to contribute to *VICE*, the *Guardian*, the *Nation*, and other progressive media.

The magazine's striking aesthetics are designed to help popularize socialism. "*Jacobin* was meant to be bold, young, easy to read," Sunkara says. Paragraphs are short, and decks below headlines help explain articles. Sunkara told the journalism think tank Nieman Lab that he aimed for no less than "creating a visual identity for the new left."[125] Creative director Remeike Forbes, who designed its look, told *Vox*: "Readers often notice that the magazine is unusually colorful for a left-wing rag, and that reflects a particular attitude I've tried to project through the visual content, which is confident, optimistic, forward-looking, and less bogged down in the dreariness so many have come to associate with the socialist left."[126]

Jacobin's literary style likewise avoids pedantic left-wing writing. Sunkara wants to help socialism shed its Stalin-era stigma and celebrate what he calls its libertarian streak.[127] Its social justice journalism doesn't just discuss problems but offers suggestions for solving them. A print-only feature, for example, that examined the failure of cap and trade programs to lower carbon emissions also suggested how to make them work. An example of Sunkara's editorial sensibility was his handling of a scathing analysis of the U.S. Constitution by one-time contributor Seth Ackerson (now executive editor). "Seth had a title with nine words and a semicolon," Sunkara told a reporter. "I crossed it out and wrote 'Burn the Constitution.'"[128] *Jacobin*'s title is equally incendiary, inspired by the Haitian "Black Jacobins" led by Toussaint L'Ouverture. L'Ouverture's army of self-emancipated slaves defeated three great empires— Spain, England, and France—in history's only successful slave revolution.[129]

A six-person editorial board makes decisions about content, a collective strategy that echoes the *Call*'s WCPA board. Besides Sunkara and Ackerman, the masthead lists a managing editor, associate editor, three staff writers, and two assistant editors who shepherd a thousand articles annually onto the *Jacobin* website. *Jacobin* lists eighteen contributing editors but publishes a lot of new writers, mostly under thirty-five and often graduate students, professors, activists, or union organizers who often began as *Jacobin* readers, a more successful experiment in citizen journalism than the *Call*'s attempt in the 1910s. Issues are themed, like the Summer 2017 "Earth, Wind and Fire" environmental number. "Green Islands" addressed "Eco-socialism in one city or gated communities?" "Digging Free of Poverty" explored tensions in Ecuador between development needs and the environmental cost of natural resource extraction. Some articles surprise, like Canadian F. T. Green's critique of Uber as a reactionary "permissionless innovation"—the libertarian idea that just about everything should be legal, so that consumer choice instead of elected officials dictates the shape of society.[130] In the wake of revelations about Russian meddling in the 2016 U.S. election, New Zealander Branko Marcovic described how the United States interfered with Mongolia's 1996 elections.[131] "Thinking Small" likened the acceptance of urban "micro-unit" housing as a return to the Gilded Age tenements exposed by Jacob Riis in *How the Other Half Lives*.

Like the *Call*, *Jacobin* takes an activist role in its journalism. It produced *Class Action: An Activist Teacher's Handbook* in 2014 in conjunction with the Chicago Teachers Union, whose big strike *Jacobin* covered. It also published the book version of perhaps its best-known article, "Four Futures," in which author Peter Frase coined the term "exterminism"—a genocidal war of rich against poor—to describe the worst of four post-capitalist scenarios he envisions (Frase is rooting for socialism).[132] The book was reminiscent of the role of the Kerr publishing house in distributing socialist literature, but its marketing showed how the Internet has revolutionized social movement media. Jacobin streamed the *Four Futures* book launch in New York on its social media as well as readings Frase performed on a cross-country tour, which also were publicized on *Jacobin*'s Facebook page. *Jacobin* Facebook fans could hear the late actor and civil rights activist Paul Robeson sing a tribute to IWW songwriter Joe Hill on the anniversary of his 1915 execution, one of frequent historical posts that pay homage to radical culture. *Jacobin* also produces "The Dig," a podcast in which host Daniel Denvir interviews activists and academics about the politics of "class warfare."[133]

Sunkara works to foster that culture in the real world as well as online, like a debate between himself and Vivek Chibber with the editors of libertarian

Reason magazine, one of dozens of live events *Jacobin* cohosts annually, often with its neighbor Verso books. Another is a panel on "Building Unions Under Trump," part of Labor Now, a three-part monthly winter series in which trade unionists, labor journalists, and labor historians talked about worker power. Sunkara also throws parties at church halls or grassroots social movement spaces with free beer to celebrate each new issue's release. *Jacobin* also sponsors about three dozen *Jacobin* Reading Groups globally, harkening the socialist reading rooms that formed an important part of socialist print culture at the cusp of the twentieth century. They are key to building the socialist collective identity that Sunkara says, in so many words, is the magazine's main mission. The Internet takes the concept a step farther by enabling the geographically dispersed groups to discuss their readings online—a classic imagined community. "When I started the magazine, I wanted people to read it because they thought of themselves as active members of a political project," he told an interviewer. "I was very wary of *Jacobin* being seen as just a consumer product." The idea is to use the magazine to instigate action more concrete than reading. Local organizers initiate the clubs, and *Jacobin* provides free syllabi and magazines and helps groups find meeting spaces, not unlike Kerr's socialist group lesson plans. Sunkara has even talked of resurrecting *Appeal to Reason* publisher Julius Wayland's "*Appeal* Army," a network of independent salespeople who earned commissions on subscriptions and competed for prizes.

Socialist Sunkara runs the educational nonprofit on strict business principles. Sales of tax-deductible subscriptions ($29.95 in 2018) and print copies earned about a half million dollars in revenue in 2016. "I think there's certain people who will buy print as a physical object," Sunkara says, "like a beautiful physical object that they can put on their coffee table or whatever and keep for life." Limited advertising by the likes of Duke University Press and SAGE Publications slightly bumps up revenue. Sunkara invested early in custom mailing and subscription software for long-term savings. Online stories are shorter than in print, and *Jacobin* posts them at peak web traffic times. "We try to attract web traffic, and then try to turn a certain proportion of visitors to the site into subscribers," Sunkara explains.[134] Social media also are sales tools. A December tweet offering a subscription discount asked, "Are you the type of person who would give a scholarly left journal as a Christmas gift?"

Although *Jacobin* offers an intriguing look at how social movements can blend old and new media, the organizing potential of its unique combination of face-to-face engagement and digital communication remains a question mark. Sunkara wants to increase the number of print editions per year and publish more long-form journalism. Like his socialist editor forbears, Sunkara believes publishing—in print and online—is the best way to build a social democratic electoral force, although he knows it will take years. "Ultimately," he says, "what a socialist movement needs is active militants on the streets, and then eventually a mass party."[135]

Notes

1. "News from the Front of New York's Back Door—Bayonne," *Call*, October 12, 1916, 6.

2. Philip Sheldon Foner, "The Standard Oil Strikes in Bayonne, New Jersey, 1915–1916," in *The History of the Labor Movement in the United States: On the Eve of America's Entrance into World War I, 1915–1916*, vol. 6, ed. Philip Sheldon Foner (New York: International Press, 1957), 60.

3. All quoted in "Newspaper Incitement to Violence," *New Republic* 8 (October 21, 1916), 283–85.

4. "The March of the Murderers," *Call*, October 13, 1916, 1.

5. Paul Buhle, *Marxism in the USA: Remapping the History of the American Left* (London: Verso, 1987), 90–91; and Leonard J. Teel, *The Public Press, 1900–1945* (Westport, CT: Praeger, 2006), 23.

6. Matthew Schneirov, *The Dream of a New Social Order: Popular Magazines in America 1893–1914* (New York: Columbia University Press, 1997), 62.

7. Jason Martinek, "'Mental Dynamite': Radical Literacy and American Socialists' Print Culture of Dissent, 1897–1917," Ph.D. dissertation, Carnegie Mellon University, 2005, 6.

8. Michael Cohen, "'The Ku Klux Government': Vigilantism, Lynching, and the Repression of the IWW," *Journal for the Study of Radicalism* 1, no. 1 (2007): 33.

9. Nathan Fine, *Labor and Farmer Parties in the United States 1828–1928* (New York: Russell & Russell, 1961), 232; and Robert Hunter, "The Socialist Party in the Present Campaign," *American Review of Reviews* 38 (September 1908): 298.

10. Buhle, *Marxism in the USA*, 90–91.

11. "The Socialist Party: Indianapolis Convention Effects Union of All Parties Represented in Response to Call of the Social Democratic Party," *Social Democratic Herald*, August 17, 1901, 2–3; and editorial, "The Unity Conference," *Challenge* 2 (August 14, 1901): 10.

12. Cohen, "Ku Klux Klan Government," 32.

13. Daniel Bell, *Marxian Socialism in the United States*, paperback ed. (Ithaca, NY: Cornell Paperbacks, 1996), 71.

14. See Paul Heideman, "The Rise and Fall of the Socialist Party of America," *Jacobin*, February 20, 2017, https://www.jacobinmag.com/2017/02/rise-and-fall-socialist-party-of-america.

15. Elliott Shore, *Talkin' Socialism: J.A. Wayland and the Role of the Press in American Radicalism, 1890–1912* (Lawrence, KS: University Press of Kansas, 1988), 4.

16. "The Temple of the Revolution," *Appeal*, September 7, 1907, 1.

17. Paul Buhle, "Introduction to the *Appeal to Reason* and the *New Appeal*" in *The American Radical Press*, reprint ed., vol. 1, ed. Joseph Conlin (Westport, CT: Greenwood Press, 1974), 50.

18. See Upton Sinclair, "The Jungle, Chapter I," *Appeal*, February 25, 1905, 1–3. See also Shore, *Talkin' Socialism*, 167–71. The next year, millions of readers devoured the melodramatic *The Jungle* published by Doubleday, Page & Company, which ignored its radical politics in favor of its sensationalist revelations about food processing. Within months Congress passed the landmark Meat Inspection Act and Pure Food and Drug Act of 1906. Christopher Wilson, "The Making of a Best Seller, 1906," *New York Times Book Review*, December 22, 1985, BR1, 25, 27.

19. See "By a Special Correspondent: The Southern Slave Camps," *Appeal*, December 15, 1906, 2; George Shoaf, "Revolutionary Farmers: Salvation Through Violence," *Appeal*, October 8, 1910, 1; "Revolutionary Farmers: How One Family Fought the Trust," *Appeal*, October 1, 1910, 1; and John Kenneth Turner, "Conditions More Appalling than in Barbarous Mexico," *Appeal*, May 17, 1913, 1.

20. See "John Kenneth Turner Opens Fire on Government by Gunmen," *Appeal*, May 9, 1914, 1.

21. Allen Ruff, *"We Called Each Other Comrade": Charles H. Kerr & Company, Radical Publishers* (Champaign: University of Illinois Press, 1997), 103.

22. The *International Socialist Review* [hereafter *ISR*] is available at https://www.marxists.org/history/usa/pubs/isr/index.htm#contents.

23. Tom Mann, "Diamond Mining in South Africa," *ISR* 11 (July 1910): 1–6; and Mark Sutton, "Standard Oil in China," *ISR* 13 (March 1913): 681–83. See also John Kenneth Turner, "Why Mexican Workers Rebel," *ISR* 11 (April 1911): 589–92; Henry Flury, "Manila's Shame," *ISR* 12 (August 1911): 108–109; "The Coming Economic Revolution in Abyssinia," *ISR* 12 (October 1912): 229–30; "Capitalist Agriculture in Argentina," *IRS* 13 (February 1913): 607–11; Marion Wright, "The Hawaiian Pineapple," *ISR* 17 (August 1916): 414–16; and George Hardy, "Blacks and Whites in the Congo," *ISR* 17 (January 1917): 414–16.

24. Oscar Ameringer, *If You Don't Weaken: The Autobiography of Oscar Ameringer*, 2nd ed., (Norman: University of Oklahoma Press, 1983), 308.

25. Ehud Manor, *FORWARD: The Jewish Daily Forward (Forverts) Newspaper: Immigrants, Socialists, and Jewish Politics in New York, 1890–1917* (Brighton, UK: Sussex Academic Press, 2009), 123n2, 46. One of thirteen socialist periodicals published in Yiddish in 1902, *Forward*'s circulation topped 200,000 in 1915, and it continues today as a bilingual weekly, http://www.forward.com.

26. John Kennedy, "Socialistic Tendencies in American Trade Unions," *ISR* 8 (December 1907): 330–45.

27. See Leslie Fishbein, *Rebels in Bohemia: The Radicals of The Masses, 1911–1917* (Chapel Hill: University of North Carolina Press, 1982); Margaret C. Jones, *Heretics & Hellraisers: Women Contributors to The Masses, 1911–1917* (Austin: University of Texas Press, 1993); William O'Neill, *Echoes of Revolt: "The Masses," 1911–1917* (Chicago: Quadrangle Books, 1966); and Rebecca Zurier, *Art for "The Masses": A Radical Magazine and Its Graphics, 1911–1917* (Philadelphia: Temple University Press, 1988).

28. See Florence Tager, "A Radical Culture for Children of the Working Class: *The Young Socialists' Magazine*, 1908–1920," *Curriculum Inquiry* 22, no. 3 (Autumn, 1992): 271–90; and Theodore Kornweibel, *No Crystal Stair: Black Life and The Messenger, 1917–1928* (Westport, CT: Greenwood, 1975).

29. For more on the Chicago newspaper, see Jon Bekken, "Contradictions of a Socialist Daily," *American Journalist* 10 (Winter-Spring 1993): 61–83. For more on the *Leader*, see Sally M. Miller, *Victor L. Berger and the Promise of Constructive Socialism, 1910–1920* (Westport, CT: Greenwood Press, 1973).

30. Report, Publications of the WCPA New York Call, Workingmen's Co-operative Publishing Association, Archives of Tamiment Library, New York University [hereafter called WCPA].

31. "What We Are and Why We Are," *Call*, May 30, 1908, 8.

32. Editorial, "Uncovering the Enemy!," *Call*, September 28, 1916, 6. See also "The Advertiser and the Editor," *Call*, February 3, 1909, 6.

33. WCPA Constitution, Workingmen's Co-operative Publishing Association; and Progressive Labor Organizations, nd, Box 2, both in WCPA.

34. "Girl Crushed in Elevator Accident," *Call*, August 18, 1911, 4; and "Four Workmen Are Boiled Alive," *Call*, November 17, 1911, 1.

35. "This is the Biggest News in the Paper," *Call*, December 14, 1914, 1.

36. "Are You Working in a Firetrap Factory? Let the *Call* Know," *Call*, November 10, 1915, 1; and "Factory Fire Laws Ignored," *Call*, November 11, 1916, 1.

37. "Every Man to His Trade" and "The Ship that Passed in the Night," both *Call*, April 24, 1912, 6; and "Titanic Passengers in Steerage Brave," *Call*, April 25, 1912, 2. See also "Tens of Thousands of Unfortunates Starve and Suffer While They Seek Employment," *Call*, June 19, 1909, 1, 2; "Bread Lines Everywhere," *Call*, January 15, 1909, 3; and "Bread as a Public Utility," *Call*, August 19, 1913, 6.

38. See for example, "Chicago Socialist Poet Sings of World's Hog Butcher in New Book," *Call*, April 7, 1916, 5; "Isadora Duncan and a Free People," *Call Sunday Magazine*, March 28, 1915, 5; "Sculpture at Rand Exhibit," *Call*, May 21, 1909, 5; "The Democratic Theatre—Its Necessary Conditions," *Call*, August 29, 1915, 6; and poems, "A Prostitute's Soliloquy," *Call*, February 10, 1909, 6; "The Bread Line," *Call*, March 31, 1909, 6; and "Martyrdom," *Call*, December 18, 1910, 6.

39. "Reflections on the Fair," *Call*, April 13, 1909, 6.

40. See "Children Starve," *Call*, June 3, 1908, 1; "Socialists Fed School Children," *Call*, June 5, 1908, 1; and editorial, "Feed the Children and Starve the Pharisees," *Call*, June 16, 1908, 6.

41. William Morris Feigenbaum, pamphlet, "Ten Years of The Call," 18, in WCPA.

42. "Nameless Babies Given Way," *Call*, April 3, 1910, 14; and "Menacing the Lives of Babies," *Call*, April 10, 1910, 7.

43. "Jungle Beaten by New York Gilded Hostelries," *Call*, June 13, 1912, 1. See also "The Origin, Growth and Waste of Life Insurance," *Call*, March 13, 1911, 4; and F. J. Boyle, "How U.S. Treats Panama Workmen," *Call*, November 22, 1910, 4.

44. See for example, "Loan Sharks and Their Victims," *Call*, February 3, 1909, 1; "Tragedy Follows in Wake of Loan Sharks' Persecution," *Call*, February 6, 1909, 2; and "Loan Sharks Lay Traps for the Unwary," *Call*, February 6, 1909, 3. For more on yellow journalism, see W. Joseph Campbell, *Yellow Journalism: Puncturing the Myths, Defining the Legacies* (Westport, CT: Praeger, 2001).

45. *Call*, August 4, 1908, 6; and *Call*, September 28, 1908, 1. See also editorial, "We Blow Our Own Horn a Little Bit," *Call*, November 28, 1908, 6; "Pittsburg [sic] Aroused by Evening *Call* Exposé," *Call*, February 16, 1909, 1; "Forced to Act by *Call's* Exposé," *Call*, July 26, 1910, 1; ad, "We Publish a Great Story This Morning—A Story No Other Paper Will Publish," *Call*, May 8, 1916, 6; and "Department of Measures Recognizes Meat Frauds Shown in *Call* Exposé," *Call*, October 10, 1916, 3.

46. See "Effort to Break Cloak Strike Ends in Laughable Fizzle," *Call*, August 9, 1910, 1; "Ridgewood Bosses Settle with Bakers," *Call*, July 6, 1910, 1; "Police Beat Up Garment Strikers Who Defy Injunctions Forbidding Picketing of the Tied Up Shops," *Call*, January 23, 1913; 1; "The *Call*—Six Years Old," *Call*, May 30, 1914, 6; and "173,600 Answer First Strike Call; 300,000 Quit Today with Builders," *Call*, September 28, 1916, 1.

47. "Railroad Men Endorse *Call's* 8-Hour Report as Only Accurate One," *Call*, January 29, 1917, 1.

48. "Throwing Down the Waiters," *Call*, June 5, 1912, 6; cartoon, *The Bosses' Model Waiter*, *Call*, June 5, 1912, 6; Charles Edward Russell, "Why Should the Waiter Cringe?," *Call*, June 5, 1912, 6; "Big Meeting of Waiters Tonight Under Socialist Party Auspices," *Call*, June 5, 1912, 1; "3,500 Waiters Jam Carnegie Hall," *Call*, June 6, 1912, 1; "The Father of Six Calls to His Fellow Workers," *Call*, June 12, 1912, 2; and photo, *Group of Hotel Strikers at Socialist Picnic*, *Call*, June 19, 1912, 2.

49. "*Call's* Special Edition Bombshell in Ranks of the Hotel Managers," *Call*, June 13, 1912, 1.

50. "Tyrants," *Call*, September 9, 1916, 4.

51. "Instead of an Advertisement," *Call*, March 1, 1917, 3.

52. "Shirt Waist Strike Now in Full Swing," *Call*, November 24, 1909, 1. See also "7,000 Waist-Makers Win Speedy Victory," *Call*, November 25, 1909, 1.

53. The Women's Trade Union League was an organization of progressive middle-class and upper-class women founded in 1903 to help women workers organize. See Susan Amsterdam, "The National Women's Trade Union League," *Social Service Review* 56, no. 2 (June 1982): 259–272. For more on the shirtwaist strike, see Nancy Shrom Dye, *As Equals and Sisters: Feminism, the Labor Movement, and the Women's Trade Union League of New York* (Columbia: University of Missouri Press, 1981), 88–103; Nan Enstad, *Ladies of Labor, Girls of Adventure, Working Women, Popular Culture, and Labor Politics at the Turn of the Century* (New York: Columbia University Press, 1999), 84–159; and Annelise Orleck, *Common Sense and a Little Fire: Women and Working Class Politics in the United States, 1900–1915* (Chapel Hill: University of North Carolina Press, 1995), 53–86.

54. "The Strike of the Forty Thousand," *Call*, November 27, 1909, 5.

55. "Waist Strikers will March on City Hall," *Call*, December 3, 1909, 1; and "Record of Police Persecution in the Waistmakers' Strike," *Call*, December 23, 1909, 1.

56. "10,500 Shirt Waist Makers Triumph in 4 Days," *Call*, November 27, 1909, 2.

57. "Rules for Pickets," *Call*, December 7, 1909, 1.

58. "Help is Needed," *Call*, December 14, 1909, 6. See also "The Shirt-Waist Makers," *Call*, December 19, 1909, 8; and "Freedom, Chivalry and Workhouse," *Call*, December 20, 1909, 6.

59. "'Fight!' Mother Jones Urges Waist Strikers," *Call*, December 10, 1909, 1.

60. "Police, Magistrates, and Strikers," *Call*, December 27, 1909, 6; and "Incident in the Shirt-waist Strike," *Call*, December 29, 1909, 6.

61. December 26, 1909, *Sunday Call Magazine*, 15.

62. "Waist Strikers Firm in Their Fight for Union's Recognition," *Call*, December 31, 1909, 1.

63. "Hillquit Bares Waist Bosses' Nefarious Plot," *Call*, December 14, 1909, 1.

64. Information about each victim is available at the excellent website, Remembering the 1911 Triangle Factory Fire: http://trianglefire.ilr.cornell.edu/index.html. For more on the Triangle fire, see David von Drehle, *Triangle: The Fire That Changed America* (New York: Atlantic Monthly Press, 2003).

65. See David W. Dunlap, "Triangle Fire: A Frontier in Photojournalism," *New York Times*, March 23, 2011, https://cityroom.blogs.nytimes.com/2011/03/23/triangle-fire-a-frontier-in-photojournalism/?_r=0; and Elizabeth Burt, "The Triangle Fire and Working Women: Press Coverage of a Tragedy," *Journalism History* 30 (Winter 2005): 189–99.

66. See also *Call* cartoons, April 5, 1911, 1; and March 31, 1911, 6.

67. Editorial, *Call*, March 27, 1911, 6.

68. See "The Same Thing Can Happen in These Cloak Death-Traps," *Call*, March 29, 1911, 3; "Authorities in Fear of Great Demonstration on Funeral Day," *Call*, March 29, 1911, 1; "Triangle Workers Tell of Locked Doors," *Call*, March 30, 1911, 1; "Great Throng of Workers Pack Memorial Meeting, Many Faint," *Call*, March 30, 1911, 1; and "Officials Move to Kill Demonstration," *Call*, March 31, 1911, 6. The headline on a November 6, 1911, story on the dedication of a memorial to the victims read, "Harris and Blanck Cursed by Parents of 145 Victims of Asch Building Tragedy."

69. *Call*, March 28, 1911, 1; and "Triangle Shops Like Other Hell-Holes," *Call*, March 28, 1911, 1.

70. "The Indictments," *Call*, April 13, 1911, 6. See also, editorial, "Fireproof Buildings," *Call*, March 29, 1911, 6.

71. "March On!" *Call*, April 5, 1911, 6.

72. Quoted in Phillips Russell, "God Did It," *ISR* 12 (February 1912): 472–73. See also "Harris and Blanck, Triangle Bosses, Acquitted by a Jury of their Peers, for Causing 147 [sic] Deaths in Fire Trap," *Call*, December 28, 1911, 1.

73. Chester Wright, "Bayonne Explodes, and Nobody Cares About It," *Sunday Call Magazine*, October 22, 1916, SM5.

74. For more on the strike, see George Dorsey, "The Bayonne Refinery Strikes of 1915–1916," *Polish American Studies* 33, no. 2 (Autumn 1976): 19–30.

75. "Another Local Armageddon Looming Up?," *Call*, October 11, 1916, 6.

76. "Bayonne Strikers Shot Down," *Call*, October 11, 1916, 1; and "Woman Killed and Many Wounded as Bayonne Cops Charge Strikers," *Call*, October 12, 1916, 1.

77. "March of the Murderers," *Call*, October 13, 1916, 1; and Foner, "Standard Oil Strikes," 60, n65.

78. "Will You Enlist in the Fight?" *Call*, January 22, 1909, 1.

79. Quoted in Foner, "Standard Oil Strikes," 62.

80. *New York Times*, October 19, 1916, 18.

81. "Police Army in Bloody Bayonne Street Fight Kills Lawyer, Wounds Nine Strikers and Shoots Up Town," *Call*, October 13, 1916, 1.

82. "Rockefeller Will Use his Power as Long as He Has It," *Call*, October 14, 1916, 6.

83. "A State of Anarchy Exists in New Jersey—What is the Answer?," *Call*, October 16, 1916, 6. See also Chester Wright, "Bayonne Explodes!" *Call Sunday Magazine*, October 22, 1916, SM5.

84. "Strike or Face Starvation, and Bayonne Struck," *Call*, October 19, 1916, 1.

85. "Confiscation of the Press in Czar Rockefeller's Domain," *Call*, October 17, 1916, 6.

86. *New York Times*, October 20, 1916, 1; and *Call*, October 20, 1916, 1.

87. See Tom McDonough, *An Eye for Others: Dorothy Day, Journalist: 1916–1917* (Washington, D.C.: Clemency Press, 2016).

88. The 39 bylined articles Day wrote for the *Call* are available at http://www.catholicworker. org/dorothyday/browse/call.html.

89. Sam Schmalhausen, "Motherhood by Coercion," *Call*, May 2, 1915, SM112.

90. See Jill Lepore, *The Secret Life of Wonder Woman* (New York: Alfred A. Knopf, 2014), 90–96. A committee of 100 members of the National Birth Control League organized to protest the Brownsville Clinic arrests. It helped arrange a meeting between Sanger and Governor Whitman that led to Byrne's early release from prison. "Birth Control Organizations: The Brownsville Clinic and Committee of 100," Margaret Sanger Papers Project, http://www.nyu.edu/projects/sanger/aboutms/organization_brownsville_clinic.php, accessed October 26, 2018.

91. Dorothy Day, "Mrs. Byrne Tells Her First Story of Life During Hunger Strike," *Call*, February 6, 1916, 1.

92. See Nicola Beisel, *Imperiled Innocents: Anthony Comstock and Family Reproduction in Victorian America* (Princeton, NJ: Princeton University Press, 1997).

93. "Socialists and the Suffrage," *Call*, November 9, 1912, 6.

94. See for example, "Is Your Home Threatened?," *Call*, October 17, 1909, 15; "The Emancipation of Women," *Call*, September 10, 1908, 6; "For Women Who Work at Home," *Call*, November 21, 1909, 13; and "What Will Socialism Do for Women?," *Call*, August 29, 1908, 5.

95. Ira Kipnis, *The American Socialist Movement 1897–1912* (New York: Columbia University Press, 1952), 262.

96. "The Negro and Socialism," *Call*, January 24, 1911, 6.

97. "What Socialism Has to Offer the Negro," *Call*, July 2, 1908, 6.

98. Eugene Debs, "Not Racial But Class Distinction," *Call*, August 27, 1908, 1. See also "Race and Class," *Call*, June 4, 1909, 6; "A Negro Leader's Advice," *Call*, August 28, 1910, 15; and "The Editor's Desk," *Call*, June 5, 1910, 1.

99. Debs, "Not Racial but Class Distinction," 1.

100. See for example, *Call* illustrations, July 8, 1908, 4; July 23, 1908, 3; and July 27, 1908, 6.

101. W. E. B. Du Bois, "Socialism and the Negro Problem," *New Review* 1 (February 1913): 138–41.

102. For more on socialism and race, see Linda J. Lumsden, "'The Black Man's Burden': Race and the Radical Press," in *Black, White, and Red All Over: A Cultural History of the Radical Press in Its Heyday, 1900–1917* (Kent, OH: Kent State University Press, 2014), 212–39.

103. Kipnis, *American Socialist Movement*, 364, 346.

104. "Most Class-Conscious Socialist Vote in History of Nation Will Total Approximately 900,000," *Call*, November 7, 1912, 1; and "Working Class Vote Throughout Nation Climbing Resistlessly Toward the One Million Mark," *Call*, November 8, 1911, 1. See also "Roosevelt—An Unconscious Tool of Socialism," *Call*, August 8, 1912, 6.

105. "A Socialist Group in Congress," *Call*, May 20, 1914, 6.

106. *Call*, July 18, 1910, 6. See also "Socialism and the Farmer," *Call*, August 5, 1910, 6; "Socialism and the General Situation," *Call*, November 16, 1910, 6; and "Let the City Own the Whole Traction System," *Call*, September 8, 1916, 4 [strike edition].

107. Fishbein, *Rebels in Bohemia*, 191.

108. Michael Cohen, "'Cartooning Capitalism': Radical Cartooning and the Making of American Popular Radicalism in the Early Twentieth Century," *International Review of Social History* 52, supp. 15, (January 2007): 35.

109. A *Smasher*, *Call*, November 4, 1908, 6. See also untitled illustrations in the *Call*, June 16, 1908, 1; and September 19, 1908, 6.

110. *"Behold! The Child!,"* *Call*, October 27, 1908, 6.

111. See Ryan Walker, "The New Adventures of Henry Dubb: Cartoons" (Chicago: Socialist Party, 1915), accessed November 8, 2009, http://www.marxists.org/subject/art/visual_arts/satire/walker/index.htm.

112. "Ryan Walker and His Funny Pen," *Call*, December 25, 1916, 1.

113. "A Pointer for New York Socialists," *Call*, September 26, 1913, 6.

114. See Gordon J. Goldberg, *Meyer London: A Biography of the Socialist New York Congressman, 1871–1926* (Jefferson, NC: McFarland, 2013).

115. Miller, *Victor L. Berger*, 194. Berger never served the sentence but his Congressional colleagues refused to seat him. See Edward J. Muzik, "Victor L. Berger: Congress and the Red Scare," *Wisconsin Magazine of History* 47 (Summer 1964): 309–18.

116. Third Assistant Postmaster General WCW to The Solicitor, January [?] 1918, file 47606, Box 44, Entry 40, Records of the Post Office Department, Office of the Solicitor General (Records Group 28.2.5), National Archives, Washington, D.C.

117. See "Sedition," *Call*, February 6, 1917, 6; "The Shadow of Coming Repression," *Call*, February 8, 1917, 6; "Where Is Free Speech," *Call*, April 3, 1917, 6; and Morris Hillquit, *Loose Leaves from a Busy Life* (New York: Rand School Press, 1934), 169.

118. "Punishment for the Disloyal," *New York Times*, April 3, 1918, 12.

119. *Burleson v. U.S. Workingmen's Co-operative Publishing Association*, 274 Fed. 749 (1921).

120. See Norman Thomas, "Labor and the Press," *Forum* (May 1924): 587–96.

121. Charles McGrath, "A Liberal Beacon Burns Out," *New York Times*, January 23, 2006, http://www.nytimes.com/2006/01/23/arts/a-liberal-beacon-burns-out.html.

122. "No Short-Cuts: Interview with the *Jacobin*," *Idiom*, March 16, 2011, http://idiommag. com/2011/03/no-short-cuts-interview-with-the-jacobin/.

123. Dylan Matthews, "Inside *Jacobin*: How a Socialist Magazine Is Winning the Left's War of Ideas," *Vox*, March 21, 2016, https://www.vox.com/2016/3/21/11265092/jacobin-bha skar-sunkara.

124. "New Masses, New Media," *New Left Review* 90 (November–December 2014), https:// newleftreview.org/II/90/bhaskar-sunkara-project-jacobin.

125. Caroline O'Donovan, "*Jacobin*: A Marxist Rag Run on a Lot of Petty-Bourgeois Hustle," *Nieman Lab*, September 16, 2014, http://www.niemanlab.org/2014/09/jacobin-a-marxist-rag-run-on-a-lot-of-petty-bourgeois-hustle/.

126. Mathews, "Inside *Jacobin*."

127. "No Shortcuts."

128. Jennifer Schuessler, "A Young Publisher Takes Marx into the Mainstream," *New York Times*, January 20, 2013, http://www.nytimes.com/2013/01/21/books/bhaskar-sunkara-editor-of-jacobin-magazine.html.

129. Remeike Forbes, "The Black Jacobin," *Jacobin*, March 3, 2012, https://www.jacobinmag. com/2012/03/the-black-jacobin-2/.

130. F. T. Green, "Uber's Consumer Democracy," *Jacobin*, May 11, 2016, https://www. jacobinmag.com/2016/05/uber-ride-sharing-toronto-permissionless-innovation-disruption.

131. Branko Marcetic, "How Washington Hacked Mongolia's Democracy," *Jacobin*, November 29, 2017, https://www.jacobinmag.com/2017/11/mongolia-elections-mccain-interna tional-republican-institute.

132. Peter Frase, "Four Futures," *Jacobin*, December 13, 2011, https://www.jacobinmag.com /2011/12/four-futures/.

133. "The Dig," http://podbay.fm/show/1043245989/reviews.

134. O'Donovan, "*Jacobin*: A Marxist Rag."

135. "New Masses, New Media."

· 3 ·

TRAILBLAZER

The *Sierra Club Bulletin* Helps Build the Environmental Movement

Long before legendary Sierra Club Executive Director David Ross Brower was anointed "father of the modern environmental movement"—its "Archdruid," the "Knight Errant of Nature," "a latter-day Savonarole"[1]—the lanky teenager read the entire run of the *Sierra Club Bulletin* in the early 1930s.[2] He bought copies dating all the way back to its first number in January 1893. The novice mountaineer drank in its state-of-the-art panorama photographs of the Sierra Nevada and vivid descriptions of new climbing routes, but his favorite part of the *Bulletin* was club founder John Muir's essays extolling wilderness.

Decades later, Brower recalled, "I read that the way one would read the Bible."[3] As Sierra Club executive director, he published a photo-offset reproduction of the five *Bulletin* volumes published before 1906, when the San Francisco earthquake destroyed all of the plates, type, overrun, manuscripts, and photos of the first U.S. environmental action journal, known today as *Sierra* magazine.

Today, it's the rare nature lover who has not heard of Brower or his media genius for saving redwoods and wild rivers: filming a home movie that revealed the dammed Hetch Hetch Valley's desolation; loading reporters and senators aboard rafts that spun through Dinosaur National Monument; placing a full-page ad in the *New York Times* that likened damming the Grand Canyon to flooding the Sistine Chapel. Yet few people know about the vital role the venerable *Sierra Club Bulletin* played in building the modern environmental movement. Articles of Incorporation for the pioneering wilderness preservation organization created on May 28, 1892, in San Francisco by Muir and 181 fellow Sierra Nevada enthusiasts established the organization as more than a hiking club. They stated media were intrinsic to its mission: "To explore, enjoy, and render accessible the mountain regions of the Pacific Coast; to publish authentic information concerning them; to enlist the support and co-operation of the people and the Government in preserving the forests and other natural features of the Sierra Nevada Mountains."[4]

The early Sierra Club introduced many Americans to the radical idea that saving civilization meant protecting rather than conquering wilderness. While the earlier Boone and Crockett Club (1887) and National Audubon Society (1905) organized to advocate professional management of natural resources, the Sierra Club was the first organization to advocate preservation of wilderness solely for its natural beauty. Muir's view that nature possessed intrinsic value was revolutionary, as was its corollary that wilderness mattered more than development.[5] This embryonic environmental movement predates by eight decades the "new" social movements of the late twentieth century described by sociologist Alain Touraine, which focus on issues of identity, lifestyle, or culture, in contrast to "old" movements such as labor or socialism, which centered around issues of economic privation.[6] The Sierra Club today is an institution of modern environmentalism, regarded by some as "one of the greatest social movements of the twentieth century, surpassing in significance the peace, labor, women's, civil, and human rights movements of earlier decades."[7] In 2018, the Sierra Club boasted that its 3.5 million members comprise the nation's "most enduring and influential grassroots environmental organization."[8] The *Bulletin* continues as *Sierra* magazine both in print and online, offering an unusual opportunity to explore how social movement media adapt to the inevitable change that social movement organizations must undergo to stay relevant.

This chapter first traces how the *Bulletin* forged a collective identity among early Sierrans, then concentrates on its role in three milestone campaigns against dams: the loss of Hetch Hetchy Valley in Yosemite National Park, 1906–1913; saving Echo Park canyon in Dinosaur National Monument, 1952–1956; and stopping two dams proposed just outside Grand Canyon National Park, 1963–1969, set in the context of roiling internal power struggles that nearly destroyed the club.

Collective Identity in the Early *Sierra Club Bulletin*

A few other mountaineering journals existed before the *Sierra Club Bulletin* (*Alpine Journal* in London; *Mountaineer* in Seattle; *Mazama* in Portland, Oregon; *American Alpine Journal*), but they stuck to recreation. Although accounts of members' mountaineering explorations and descriptions of routes pioneered by club climbers dominated the early *Bulletin*, the journal advocated for wilderness from its first issue. The Sierra Club board sent a memorial to Congress, the *Bulletin* reported in January 1893, to "use every effort to defeat" a proposed bill to reduce the size of Yosemite National Park, founded just three years earlier.[9] Accounts of speeches—one describing a hike along Yosemite's Tuolomne River, another on the discovery of a grove of giant sequoia trees—helped members who missed the club's first general meeting on September 16, 1892, feel connected.

Early Sierrans were a well-educated bunch. J. Henry Senger, a German professor at the University of California, Berkeley, headed the Committee on Publications and Communications that produced the first four biannual *Bulletin* numbers.[10] Bolston Coit Brown, a Stanford University drawing professor, illustrated his hiking accounts with drawings he made on the spot. More than their privilege, this cadre of scholars and professionals shared a sense of wilderness as liberation from urban life. A lawyer wrote of camping with college pals and their dogs: "When we could escape the busy turmoil of life we fled to nature and gathered strength, elasticity, and moral equipoise from her sacred touch."[11] His language echoed Muir's view of nature as sublime.

Perhaps the *Bulletin's* most distinguishing feature was its high-quality glossy plates of black-and-white photographs. Appearing a decade before *National Geographic Magazine* began publishing photographs, they elevated the *Bulletin* to a higher aesthetic plane than most popular magazines of the time. The May 1895 *Bulletin* featured thirty-one such images, not only of mountains and glaciers but also of Sierrans hiking, camping, and canoeing.[12] Imagery would remain key to Sierra Club messaging. Book reviews began in 1897, and soon "Notes and Correspondence" and "Forestry Notes" tracked conservation issues. *Bulletin* pages offer a peek back at recreational camping in the 1890s. Theodore Solomon recounted how, after four feet of snow fell on him and a companion, they shivered through the night squeezed between two logs and covered by branches. But when the storm stopped and they awoke, "The great Sierra world was robed in virgin white. ... Never have I seen a sight so purely and transcendently beautiful."[13]

Among the reveries appeared calls to action. "Forestry Notes" in 1898 called for a national redwoods park along the California coast—a feat finally accomplished in 1968.[14] An 1899 essay suggested the UC Board of Regents double as an independent forestry board to stop destruction of forests by fire, sheep, and logging.[15] An 1896 Muir speech suggested transferring underfunded Yosemite Valley State Park to the surrounding national park, which became the club's first major conservation victory in 1905. The *Bulletin* quoted Muir: "[I]f people in general could be got into the woods, even for once, to hear the trees speak for themselves, all difficulties in the way of forest preservation would vanish."[16]

Muir's wish became reality with the inauguration in 1901 of the club's annual High Trips—elaborate, month-long excursions that were the antithesis of wilderness solitude: the 1903 outing included 210 people and dozens of mules and horses that packed in 30,000 pounds of baggage, food, and equipment.[17] Club leaders believed people must experience wilderness first-hand to value and protect it. The *Bulletin* amplified, preserved, and extended this exercise in building collective identity through personal essays that described the first outing's daily tramps and evening outdoor lectures on biology, songs, and stories.[18] The February 1903 *Bulletin* included a photograph of happy campers lining up at a Fourth of July buffet in King's River Canyon; a double-truck image in June 1903 featured thirty-two men and seventeen women in single file ascending the slopes of 13,886-foot Mt. Brewer.[19] *Bulletin* editor Francis Farquhar insisted throughout his twenty-year tenure (1926–1946) on engaging stories about outings, which he celebrated as "reeking with nostalgic propaganda."[20] One club president explained, "[O]ur outings have been not only for the purpose of *exploring* and *enjoying* wilderness, but for *protecting* wilderness."[21] Sierra Club leaders had stumbled upon scholars' later discovery of the profound effects that emotional commitments can work to inspire collective action.[22] Future executive director Brower deemed the outings "one of the political forces in the Sierra Club."[23] Little did Sierrans who in 1904 camped one night amid Hetch Hetchy's wildflowers, however, realize how soon they would need to summon those forces.

The Loss of Hetch Hetchy Valley

Even as the Sierra Club celebrated the addition of Yosemite Valley to the national park, San Francisco cast covetous eyes on Hetch Hetchy's roiling river in Yosemite's sister valley. In 1905, the city requested federal permission to dam the river and flood the valley for drinking water. Diametrical forces debated utilitarian versus aesthetic values of nature in the first of perpetual public policy battles over Western water. The club faced an uphill battle. "In those days the word conservation was scarcely known," former *Bulletin* editor Farquhar recalled.[24] A vocal minority of Sierrans supported the dam, splitting the club's collective identity and threatening its mission as a protector of wilderness. Club secretary William Colby forced the schism to a vote. The 589–161 tally in support of the board's August 31, 1907, resolution against the dam reaffirmed the club's commitment to advocating public policy to preserve wilderness. Leaders nonetheless deflected the threat to club collective identity by forming another group, the Society for the Preservation of National Parks, which for all practical purposes was a division of the club, even naming Muir as president.

The first of innumerable emergency *Bulletin* "specials," the "SPECIAL YOSEMITE NATIONAL PARK NUMBER" alerted members in January 1908 to the threat not only to Hetch Hetchy but also to all national parks. It framed wilderness in religious terms and challenged capitalist values. "It is impossible to overestimate the value of wild mountains and mountain temples as places for people to grow in, recreation grounds for soul and body," the issue began. "In these ravaging money-mad days monopolizing San Francisco capitalists are now doing their best to destroy the Yosemite Park, the most wonderful of all our great mountain national parks."[25] In his debut as a *Bulletin* contributor, Muir declared, "Dam Hetch-Hetchy! As well dam for water-tanks the people's cathedrals and churches, for no holier temple has even been consecrated by the heart of man."[26] The board's resolution followed, along with subtler arguments for saving the valley, including a photograph of sunrise above the luminous valley and descriptions of Hetch Hetchy's geological gems. The Outings report rated 1907 as the best High Trip yet, especially the "gem-like Hetch-Hetchy Valley."[27] Colby reported to members on the club's seminal claim that local interests had no right to a national "public treasure."[28] The *Bulletin*, however, mainly addressed its several hundred members.

The June 1908 "Notes and Correspondence" reported the Secretary of the Interior's approval of the dam.[29] The club engaged in its first campaign to sway national public opinion by enlisting influential newspapers and magazines that, save for the pro-dam *San Francisco Call*, supported keeping national parks inviolate.[30] The club also published thousands of circulars and pamphlets to mobilize collective action far beyond the Sierra Nevada. Club historian Holway Jones asserts the beautifully illustrated pamphlets accompanied by a letter from Muir motivated hundreds of letters and telegrams to Washington prior to the January 1909 hearings, prompting Congress to hold off on San Francisco's request.[31] Hetch Hetchy supporters' hope that they might win as the debate spilled into the new Wilson Administration dissolved when he appointed San Francisco's former city attorney as Secretary of the Interior. On December 19, 1913, Wilson signed the bill authorizing the dam. Muir died a year later, felled, Colby was convinced, by the "tremendous blow."[32] The valley disappeared under water.[33]

The conventional view of nature as instrumentally valuable triumphed over the view of nature as intrinsically valuable, at least in political backrooms. The public, however, had embraced the principle that national parks should be untouchable. A 1914 *Bulletin* editorial noted the national press agreed the decision created a "perilous precedent." Editor William Badé wrote, "The widespread and vigorous expressions of public sentiment and elsewhere for commercial and utilitarian projects has been of permanent value in making similar projects more difficult if not impossible for the future, and our National Parks as a whole are more secure as a result of the Hetch-Hetchy fight."[34] The *Bulletin* editorialized for a National Park Service in 1915 to provide a "consistent policy of protecting and improving these parks."[35] Ironically, the Sierra Club's first failure resulted in the 1916 founding of the NPS, which in its centennial year oversaw 417 protected areas covering more than eighty-four million acres.[36] The emotions stirred by the Hetch Hetchy campaign marked it a success in the long run.

Brower Joins the *Bulletin*

By the 1920s, "*Bulletin* Outings" sections had expanded into *Bulletin* annual editions numbering well over a hundred pages. Farquhar modeled them on the prestigious British *Alpine Journal*. He packed the annuals with lengthy features on Sierra history and science, mountain ascents around the world, Sierran hiking adventures, and dozens of lush photographs on coated paper. An accountant by trade, Farquhar also was a historian, book collector, and connoisseur of fine printing who was at the center of the circle of University of California Press editors associated with the *Bulletin*. His brother Samuel Farquhar ran the press's large printing operations. Francis Farquhar in 1941 fatefully helped David Brower get a job as an editor at the UC Press, where he worked for publishing director August Frugé, another Sierran who in the 1950s would head the club publications committee.[37]

The club fortuitously stumbled upon Ansel Adams during its 1923 High Trip to Yosemite, where he was custodian of LeConte Memorial Lodge when not experimenting in his darkroom. He became climbing pals with Brower, who recalled that Adams "taught me about everything I knew about photography."[38] Adams doubled for a decade between the wars as the High Trips' camp advance man and photographer. As an editorial board member and *Bulletin* photo editor, he strived to keep the journal's imagery "on a simple, clean-cut plane." He once complained of a caption, *Snow-Covered Tree:* "[E]very serious photographer has been trying to get away from the 'Pictorial' coyness of titles. It's a good picture, but the connotations of the title destroy the mood."[39] The early occasional circulars were replaced in 1923 with short bi-monthly *Bulletins* similar to newsletters. Farquhar expanded them into monthlies in 1940 before World War II forced the schedule to revert to bimonthly, and a shortage of coated paper forced him to replace the annual's lavish cover photograph with the club logo. The war's end launched a new era not only for the nation but also for the Sierra Club when Brower succeeded Farquhar as *Bulletin* editor and editorial board chair.

Brower's first *Bulletin* byline in summer 1933 topped his account of a knapsack trip. His second article about a ten-week trip with pack mules led the 1935 annual *Bulletin* after some heavy editing by Farquhar. The editor placed Brower on the editorial board in 1935 and assigned him to write book reviews. "From then my interest in books began and never left," Brower recalled.[40] Farquhar kicked Brower off the editorial board when he missed deadlines, but Brower continued to help work on the *Bulletin* in Farquhar's home office, first editing the short bimonthly numbers, then the annual. As an associate editor, he learned a lot from Farquhar about typography and how to work with authors and printers. "Francis imposed high standards in graphic arts on the *Bulletin* for me," Brower said.[41] The club paid him in 1938 to produce a members' handbook. His black-and-white image of a rock climber's view of roaring Upper Yosemite Falls was the April 1941 *Bulletin's* full-page cover photograph. Brower remained on the masthead as associate editor through the war, when he served in Europe as an intelligence officer for the 86th Mountain Infantry.

Brower's crusading style lit up the *Bulletin* as soon as it returned to monthly status in January 1947. The year's first three issues devoted forty-three pages to saving California's San Gorgonio Mountains from development by creating a San Gorgonio Primitive Wilderness Area. Another sixteen pages countered "misinformation" that threatened Olympic National Park. "The monthly *Bulletin* has been one of the club's best weapons in the fight to save these areas," stated the 1947 *Sierra Club Handbook* that Brower authored. "It requires a publication to bring matters of great importance to all the members of as large a club as this one has grown to be."[42] Privately, Brower wrote, "the club's publishing mission is to take sides, to try to save something, to have a point of view, to be unashamed of good propaganda."[43] Brower even embraced a charge that the *Bulletin* was didactic. "I want to see our members informed of a point of view that gets too little budget for publication—to wit, the preservation of irreplaceables." He felt no obligation to give equal space in the letters-to-the-editor column to well-financed corporate opponents. "I probably do pontificate," he acknowledged in 1963. "I am didactic. … The main thing is that our 20,000 x 2 readers should be given a minimum of excuses for not doing things."[44]

After he was hired as the club's first executive director in 1952, Brower was still expected to edit both the annual and the more prosaic monthly. Almost immediately he resigned as editor of the latter, in part a protest against overwork and low pay that marked his first disagreement with the board of directors.[45] The next year, the board appointed volunteer Fred Gunsky to produce the monthlies, while Brower continued to helm the showcase annuals. Directors rejected Brower's suggestion they increase to publishing them quarterly while replacing the monthlies with an offset newssheet that would cut expenses for just "talking to ourselves."[46] The humble monthly *Bulletin*, however, would soon play a key role in the Sierra Club's second crusade against a dam.

The Fight to Save Dinosaur National Monument

The federal government in 1952 announced its mammoth Colorado River Storage Project, which included plans to build a 524-foot-high hydroelectric dam in magnificent Echo Park canyon, just downstream of where the Yampa and Green rivers converged in Dinosaur National Monument in Utah. The Sierra Club took a lead role in the Council of Conservationists, an unprecedented coalition of ten groups united to stop the dam. While Sierra Club new-media innovations in the Dinosaur campaign have received abundant attention in numerous works—Brower's *Two Yosemites* home movie equating Echo Park with Hetch Hetchy; Charles Eggert's exciting color films of rafting the Green River; and Alfred K. Knopf's groundbreaking *This is Dinosaur*, forerunner of the phenomenal Sierra Club exhibit-format books—scholars have paid little attention to the *Bulletin's* central role in connecting them all in resuming the fight for the principle that all national park lands were inviolate.[47]

The *Bulletin's* social justice journalism in the service of saving wilderness relied on the emotional power of imagery. A May 1952 special *Bulletin* introduced "The Dinosaur Story," with Martin Litton's dramatic photographs of the river canyons. "You get a person down in that canyon looking up—your pictures give the beholder a feeling of being there," Sierran Charlotte Mauk wrote Litton. "And that is what is good for making our readers want to defend Dinosaur."[48] Litton long puzzled how to convey in two dimensions the river's cathedral-like power. The November 1953 *Bulletin* cover featured his solution: an image of rafters dwarfed by the striped cliffs towering above the Yampa River. Litton shot the photo on one of the raft trips the club had organized the previous summer to rouse the public to save Dinosaur, following the philosophy behind the High Trips to immerse potential environmentalists in wilderness.[49]

The *Bulletin* informed members of the trips' itineraries, costs, and registration address, enticing hundreds to sign up with its rollicking accounts of running rapids and camping under stars. Publicity-savvy Brower invited congressmen, Bureau of Reclamation officials, and newspaper editors.[50] When he learned the Interior Department was taking the *New York Times* environmental columnist John Oakes on a competing raft trip through Dinosaur, Brower got himself invited along.[51] At the end of the raft trip in Provo, Oakes leaned into Brower's ear to tell him he had just filed an editorial opposing Echo Park Dam.[52] The cover of "Trouble in Dinosaur," another special twelve-page *Bulletin* in February 1954, framed the fight as a civic duty in an urgent summons to collective action:

> The rainbow canyons of the Yampa and the Green, corridors through a primitive paradise unequalled anywhere, are a unique gem of the National Park System. They are now needlessly threatened. Men of vision saved this place for us. Now it's turnabout.
>
> URGENT: Please read this issue now—and lend a hand.

The versatile Litton took up his pen in this heavy-hitting number to challenge the bureau's economic claims for the dam. "It's easy to show the park-value of Dinosaur, but that won't save it," he advised club leaders before turning in his well-researched attack on the bureau's claims for the dam's economic necessity.[53] As his fact-based piece showed, the crusading *Bulletin* also produced solid journalism. The *Bulletin* was not a collection of propagandistic rants; its tone was more like that of the turn-of-the-century moralistic muckrakers. Brower believed facts were powerful persuaders. His main interest "was getting facts which were hard to get to—unearthing the facts that the government agencies, for the most part, or particularly self-serving corporations, were not willing to let out. We had to get the facts and expose them. ..." During one dramatic Congressional hearing, Brower exposed massive errors in bureau calculations for the planned reservoir's evaporation rates. He explained later how his editorial training informed his research: "As I began to look at it with just an editor's mind, not an engineer's ... we found they were doing some very haywire things in their whole program."[54]

The deluge of urgent *Bulletins* was part of club strategy to stir collective action. The February 1954 special was filled with agency frames: the inside cover named ten cities where members could obtain Eggert's new film, *Wilderness River Trail*, to screen before as many audiences as possible. The editor noted that the film's color, sound, and action conveyed the river's excitement in a way black-and-white halftones could not. "You can't see this film, and then stand idly by while they try to destroy Dinosaur," he wrote.[55] The rest of the issue used impassioned pleas, decoded statistics, inspiring photographs, a paean to Hetch Hetchy, suggestions for alternative sites (the sacrificed Glen Canyon, now under Lake Powell),[56] energy sources (coal and nuclear power), and a list of tangible ways organizations and individuals could join the fight.[57]

The June 1954 *Bulletin* annual resumed the battle in twenty-six pages that transcribed eleven pages of Brower's testimony at Congressional hearings and drew more analogies with Hetch Hetchy, an important symbol in Sierran collective memory. Both dramatically illustrated Interior's false promise that the reservoir had improved upon the valley.[58] Frugé's illustrated account of the club's third float down the Yampa offered a buoyant blend of adventure and of human and natural history that only mentioned the proposed dam once, in the words of a woman whose ranch would be flooded.[59] When the court of appeals in October 1954 reaffirmed the legal viability of "intangible recreation values," Sierra Club President Richard Leonard instructed editor Gunsky to get this "extremely important decision, into the *Bulletin* to get it to the attention of conservationists," indicative of its influence.[60] The *Bulletin* launched a new annual conservation review in January 1955 that seemed contrived to offer an opportunity to declare the Echo Park dam the previous year's top conservation issue.[61] On the eve of the House vote, the *Bulletin* used parental guilt to mobilize *Bulletin* readers: "[A]s Dinosaur goes, so goes the national park system," it wrote. "It is this generation's obligation to see that it goes up, not down."[62]

Letters flooded the Capitol. The club once more summoned the emotional power of Litton's imagery when his self-portrait on a raft on the river graced the January 1956 *Bulletin* annual cover. A full-color version also served as the color dust jacket of the newly published *This is Dinosaur*. The book held symbolic significance as "a tangible artifact and a lasting statement about conservation." "The mere weight of a book," wrote editor Wallace Stegner, the Pulitzer Prize–winning writer and historian, "does some good; anything worth making a book about should be worth saving."[63]

Environmental historian Roderick Nash deems the Interior Department's April 11, 1956, announcement that it had abandoned dam plans "the finest hour" of the American wilderness movement.[64] Dinosaur remained untamed, but more importantly the principle stood that national land protections were forever. Author John McPhee, who rafted through Echo Park with Brower, marks the Dinosaur victory as "the birth of the modern conservation movement."[65] Congress added a line to the 1956 Colorado River Storage Project bill: "No dam or reservoir constructed under the authorization of the Act shall be within any National Park or Monument."[66] It said nothing, however, about the edges of national parks.

Turbulence Rifles the Grand Canyon and the Sierra Club

The campaign in the 1960s to stop dams proposed on the edges of the Grand Canyon unfolded in an atmosphere as turbulent as the Colorado River that ribboned through it, both within the club and across American society. A sense that the *Bulletin* was inadequate to meet club needs had surfaced as membership soared to ten thousand during the Dinosaur campaign and fights to save sequoias throughout the 1950s, but tradition and financial constraints stymied change. As early as 1954, Gunsky suggested to Publications Committee Chair Frugé that they convert the splashy annual into a general magazine called *Sierra* to differentiate it from the monthly that appeared nine times a year.[67] His idea rejected, Gunsky began to place more emphasis on the monthlies in fall 1956 but asked to more than double their budget to $5,000 and increase their size to sixteen pages. An eight-page monthly could not adequately serve the club, he warned. "As the only means of general commu-nication in the club," he stated, "the *Bulletin* fulfills a vital function."[68] The board granted his request, and when Gunsky stepped down as *Bulletin* editor in 1957, Frugé stepped in to help out. He brought in yet another UC Press editor, Max Knight, as an associate editor in an unsuccessful attempt to bring order to the annual's chaotic production process.[69] Frugé reluctantly stayed on as editorial board chair in 1959 due to its "serious" staffing problems.[70] The board finally acknowledged *Bulletin* needs when it hired Bruce Kilgore, editor of NPS's *National Parks* magazine, as the Sierra Club's first paid managing editor of publications on May 1, 1960.

A "militant liberalism" infused the club by 1960, notes environmental historian Susan Schrepfer, not unlike the restlessness of disaffected American youth.[71] The *Bulletin's* January 1960 lead article reflected the mood: "A New Decade and a Last Chance—How Bold Should We Be?" In 1962 Brower told the board's executive committee to stop "being polite"; instead, he urged the club to be "insistently critical" of government and industry,[72] a view in line with the emerging 1960s counterculture's distrust of all authority. The rebel-lious atmosphere also probably contributed to what one club president called the club's "civil war."[73]

The club took full advantage of mainstream media as a tool in its third and biggest campaign against dams and for the national parks idea.[74] Adams sounded an early call for a full-throttle push to save the Grand Canyon from two proposed dams (in Bridge Canyon and Marble Canyon) just outside national park boundaries. He wrote Frugé, "[T]his is THE great job of the Club in this decade."[75] The *Bulletin* reassumed its role as campaign forum and connection to all other campaign media. The club also published a Grand Canyon newsletter that issued timely updates. More exhibit-format books provided elegant visual rhetoric in defense of wild rivers: Eliot Porter rushed to finish photography for the elegiac *The Place No One Knew: Glen Canyon on the Colorado* (1963) to summon comparisons with the new threat to the river, while Brower collected seventy-seven color photographs and quotes for *Time and the River Flowing: Grand Canyon* (1964).

Brower scored another social movement media innovation when he placed full-page advertisements against the dams in newspapers and magazines, a tactic the club first used in 1965 in its redwoods campaign. The club's June 9, 1966, ads in the *New York Times* and *Washington Post* exclaimed, "This time it's the Grand Canyon they want to flood." The ads asked, "Should we also flood the Sistine Chapel so tourists can get nearer the ceiling?" The Internal

Revenue Service revoked the club's tax-free status, a ham-handed move that backfired when donations poured in and membership soared. "Good for the Sierra Club—Down with IRS!!" wrote a California woman who enclosed a check.[76] *Bulletin* editor Hugh Nash issued a call for collective action in the August 1966 issue: "Raise a storm of protest in any way you know how," he told readers. "*It's the Grand Canyon!*" September 30, 1968, became a landmark day when President Johnson signed a dam-less Central Arizona Project bill into law.

Growing Pains at the *Bulletin*

The victory brought the Sierra Club into the national spotlight, but the sudden growth severely strained what had been mainly a regional organization. Conflict over the *Bulletin*'s future illustrates challenges to club collective identity. Kilgore's hiring failed to resolve how to help the *Bulletin* keep up with the club, as the books were his main responsibility. In 1962 Adams resurrected the ideas of expanding the annual for outreach and retooling the monthly as a members' newsletter: "I do feel the potential Annual could be the real 'showcase' and accomplish enormous good!"[77] Board member Fred Eissler wanted to combine the monthly and annual into a bimonthly magazine following the annual's format. Something like *Audubon* magazine, he suggested. Eissler's reference to "growing pains" revealed escalating tensions, a common challenge for social movements. "There is dissatisfaction with the *Annual* as it exists and with the S.C.B. in its present form," he wrote. Eissler suggested converting the club's occasional "emergency" newsletter into a bimonthly newssheet for member news to improve what he termed poor internal communication. [78]

The refusal to transform the *Bulletin* into a real magazine even may have been the impetus for the Sierra Club's acclaimed series of lavish exhibit-format nature photography books. The books paradoxically dispersed Sierrans' wilderness gospel while cleaving and nearly bankrupting the club. Brower in old age told an interviewer that he built up the books program to get around a 1959 board resolution that forbade criticism of government agencies in the *Bulletin* or other club publications.[79] He also was frustrated that the board refused to expand the monthly *Bulletin* into a full-fledged magazine. "We could be the *American Heritage* of parks and wilderness," he enthused in his 1962 proposal for a larger, more attractive format and articles more appealing to general readers. "We have a job of conservation journalism to do, conservation journalism made attractive, interesting, even beautiful."[80]

Beautiful Big Books, Mounting Debt

Brower recently had attained a new standard of beauty and eloquence in conservation media with the third of the nineteen exhibit-format books he produced for the club, the exquisite *"In Wildness Is the Preservation of the World."* It paired Henry Thoreau quotes with seventy-two color plates of Eliot Porter's photographs on brilliant chrome-coated paper. It followed the format of the club's initial 1960 exhibit-format offering, the wildly popular and provocative *This is the American Earth*, patterned after *This is Dinosaur*.[81] By 1969, book sales exceeded ten million dollars, and the stunning coffee table books brought the Sierra Club into "the national frame of reference," as McPhee observed.[82] The evocative big books nonetheless ballooned club debt to six figures and literally obsessed consummate crusading editor Brower, who was convinced only beautiful books could save wilderness.[83]

The burgeoning books program drained club resources, including the *Bulletin*. Members requested that the periodical cover more club news and fewer crusades.[84] Club chapters complained that their submissions never appeared in the *Bulletin*. Former president Leonard claimed that by the late 1960s every issue of the *Bulletin* appeared about three months late.[85] As early as 1963, the concerned board had created a new Publications Committee to oversee Brower's publishing empire.[86] It dictated that the business manager under the committee's general supervision plan and produce the *Bulletin*. Brower scribbled on his copy, "It spells ruin."[87]

President Alexander Hildebrand's suggestions were even more extreme in his 1965 attempt to steer the *Bulletin* from "fascism and communism." He wanted to ban partisan politics and even "political discussions." Hildebrand sought "objectivity" in *Bulletin* articles. "The Club shall criticize public policies and actions only in an objective and constructive manner and with strict regard for the truth," he stated, instead of "innuendo, attacks on inferred motivation, allegations of questionable integrity or insufficient social conscience, quotations made out of context, creation of villains, use of half truths, presentation as factors of unchecked and/or doubtful information, deliberate misrepresentation, etc."[88]

The debate aired a fundamental disagreement on the role of an organization's media. *Bulletin* editors welcomed editorial guidelines but championed controversy. "The publication of controversy can often be interesting," stated Brower, who worried about censorship. "The purpose of the policy is not to stifle but to instill a feeling of responsibility."[89] Hugh Nash, who edited the *Bulletin* in the late 1960s, opposed a total ban on dissent but agreed the editor should get approval from the board or president if an article appeared partisan. "Club publications are basically journals of opinion, it seems to me."[90]

Club organs also were sources of power. In 1966, incoming Sierra Club President George Marshall instigated a publishing reorganization after he accused Nash of censoring and slanting *Bulletin* coverage to favor Brower's view in a public brawl over a proposed nuclear power plant that exposed fissures in club policy and among individuals.[91] In 1967, the board established a five-person *Bulletin* Policy Committee that—not surprisingly—concluded that the periodical was emphasizing conservation at the expense of fulfilling its internal main function of informing members and the public about the Sierra Club.[92] Affirming that *Bulletin* contents be "diverse and national in scope," the 1968 recommendations indicated a hunger for more material closer to home: individual Outings stories; personal mountaineering or conservation experiences; personality profiles; historical articles about the club, Sierra Nevada, national parks, and the conservation movement; articles on club purposes, programs, proposals, and projects. A recommendation for a permanent mechanism for reviewing *Bulletin* policy maintained the overseers would wield no editorial review authority.[93] It recommended expanding editorial resources with "talent scouts" and a special fund to buy "extraordinary" manuscripts. A suggested budget increase, however, mainly would help chapter newsletters expand.

The omission of any reference to increasing the *Bulletin* budget caught editor Nash's eye. He detailed his unpaid overtime and requested an associate editor. "I feel on a treadmill," he wrote. "I feel little pride of achievement, knowing that each issue could be and should be better."[94] A recommendation to shelve the popular annual unless bookstore sales recouped its cost shocked him. He wrote, "The annual's long tradition is part of the club's long tradition. ... It is the only publication available to all members without charge that reflects the 'class' for which the club is noted and admired. To abolish it might be costly in terms of the image members have of their club."[95]

Battle Over the *Bulletin*

As the club's main communications channel, the *Bulletin* inevitably became
ensnared in the colossal clash between the board and its executive director,
which culminated in 1969 when the directors fired Brower at the same meeting at which they congratulated him for the landmark Grand Canyon victory.
The struggle over *Bulletin* editorial policy offers a rare glimpse into the role
social movement media play in internal power struggles. The club periodical
was at least perceived by leaders to hold the key to control of the club, and the
Brower–board brouhaha affected the entire environmental movement.[96] The
final straw occurred on January 14, 1969, when a $20,000, full-page Sierra
Club ad in the *New York Times* surprised directors with Brower's grandiose
vision for an Earth International Park in the Galapagos Islands, subject of
the first volume of an expansive—and expensive—new Sierra Club International Book Series.[97] The 1967 annual *Bulletin* had unveiled Brower's ambi-
tious Galapagos park plans in a lavish full-color spread. His text's manic tinge
hinted at a runaway agenda: "In this action, all the nations could unite against
the one real common enemy—Rampaging Technology."[98] Brower claimed he
bought the *Times* ad because current President Edgar Wayburn forbade Nash
from promoting the two-volume set in the *Bulletin*.[99] Wayburn had been taken
aback when a quarter of the October 1968 *Bulletin* advertised media products such as the Sierra Club calendar, notecards, films, and the "Sierra Club
Christmas Book List."

When the board moved that autumn to remove Brower as executive
director, Wayburn and *Bulletin* editor Nash fought over how to cover the
controversy. The incident illuminates the challenges a journal faces trying
to remain neutral in organizational power struggles. The percolating debate
over *Bulletin* editorial policy exploded following the appearance of a short
January 1969 item that devoted one cryptic paragraph to an October 19,
1968, board meeting. It stated the board had declined to pursue one of three
grounds for Brower's dismissal—the charge that Brower had diverted unauthorized club funds, a charge three directors considered criminal. The board
gave Brower more time to reply to the other charges of insubordination and
financial irresponsibility.[100] The item probably perplexed most readers, but the
brief infuriated Wayburn. The president had instructed Nash to print the club
president's longer version, in which he elaborated on the accusations to clarify
the dispute, which Nash deemed even more damaging. "I could not be a party

to their dissemination in the club's official publication without abandoning journalistic ethics," he stated.[101]

The battle reverberated in chapter newsletters, which tried to fill the gaps in the *Bulletin's* circumscribed coverage. Brower threatened libel suits against the volunteer editors who reported on the criminal allegations dropped at the October 19 meeting.[102] His threat offended the volunteers as an assault on a free press. "What hypocrisy!" one exclaimed.[103] The dispute grew more complicated when Brower announced in January his candidacy for a seat on the board in the April election, after which he would resign as executive director. He took leave to campaign. *Bulletin* editor Nash fired off a five-page memo defending Brower to the Sierra Club Council of volunteers and club chapters and circulated a petition among staff supporting Brower. He accused Wayburn of banning Brower from the *Bulletin* for political gain. Editorial board chair Frugé asked Wayburn to rebuke Nash for distributing a "political memorandum" through official club mail.[104] When Nash declined to go on leave, Wayburn suspended him without pay for six weeks. The editor quit. Acting executive director Mike McCloskey informed department heads that Nash's departure stemmed "from a basic disagreement over editorial policy."[105] The post-Nash *Bulletin* of March 1969 quoted Wayburn saying that Brower's ad purchase was "grossly irresponsible."[106] Brower blamed his loss in the election on his blocked access to the *Bulletin*, the main avenue for communicating with 77,000 Sierra Club members.[107]

Moving from Social Movement to Institution

The election proved a referendum on the sanctity of club collectivity. Members mattered as did lines of authority, club leaders believed, no matter how successful the messianic Brower's leadership in building the environmental movement. The national movement was less significant to club leaders than was preservation the club. "[H]e felt that the Grand Canyon was more important than the Sierra Club itself, more important than his own career," Leonard said of Brower.[108] After Brower resigned, the board of directors retained the books program while cutting capital expenditures and tightening its focus.[109] Back in the black by 1975, Sierra Club Books were hugely popular and profitable throughout the twentieth century.[110] In 2015, however, the club discontinued its Sierra Club Books and Sierra Club Books for Children imprints. Its explanation demonstrates social movements' struggle to continually define and redefine goals: "The closure stems from the organization's aim to refocus its resources on its core conservation mission."[111]

The *Bulletin* survived but evolved, as social movement media must, with a renewed focus on "the ordinary member." Its evolution further demonstrates the fluidity of social movement media. In a move to reengage membership, new editors in 1974 added a page of news about the club, its forty-five chapters, nine regional conservation committees, numerous national committees, and individual members. Despite "tremendous overall improvement," internal news editor Robert Irwin feared the *Bulletin* still lacked a "distinctive Sierra Club stamp." He added, "If the news page can foster a sense of belonging, a realization that what one individual does is important, that the Sierra Club really matters, then the Sierra Club will become more effective."[112] Theorists could not offer a better explanation of the imperative for collection identity to facilitate collective action.

The full-color glossy cover became *SIERRA: The Sierra Club Bulletin* in October 1977 as part of a major revamping to full-fledged magazine status in hopes of attracting attention among the general public. "[W]e've brought environmental thinking into the everyday consciousness of millions of people," editor Frances Gendlin told readers. "Now it's time to involve them further, showing them the process of cohesive citizen action and how it works."[113] Finances remained strained, however, and the magazine reverted to a thicker bimonthly at the end of 1978. The capitalized "*SIERRA*" stood alone on the November/December 1981 color cover of ski campers, although *Sierra Club Bulletin* remained on the masthead (or logotype) through January/February 1986. *SIERRA* and the subhead *Sierra Magazine* followed on the March/April 1986 as part of another redesign. Reader reaction was mixed.[114] Octogenarian Brower was not a fan of the changes. He said, "You don't really know from *SIERRA* quite what the Sierra Club should be about."[115]

The philosophical split that cleaved the club even as it led the successful fight to save the Grand Canyon marked its evolution from social movement into an environmental institution. The 1969 election results reaffirmed its collective identity as an orderly reformist organization that valued structure and respected hierarchical authority, in contrast to the contentious confrontational politics of the 1960s social movements. Its collective action occurred in courts and in the Capitol building that its lobbyists prowled, where they won considerable environmental victories. If not totally supportive, mainstream media's abundant coverage demonstrated that the environmental movement fell well within sociologist's Daniel Hallin's "circle of legitimate controversy."[116] President Richard Nixon's declaration of the "environmental decade" on January 1, 1970, further signaled environmentalism's emergence into the mainstream, a goal reaffirmed on the first Earth Day on April 1,1970.

A new generation of radical "eco-warriors" surfaced in the 1980s, typified by Greenpeace. The organization targeted television audiences with dramatic "image events," like videos of volunteers in tiny Zodiac watercraft placing themselves between whales and the giant ships that hunted them.[117] While Greenpeace was a nonprofit entity like the Sierra Club, the radical EarthFirst! rejected the club's comparatively staid environmentalists' corporate structures and Washington lobbyists. "We felt that if we took on the organization of the industrial state, we would soon accept their anthropocentric paradigm, much as Audubon and the Sierra Club already had," Earth First! cofounder Dave Foreman explained in 1991.[118] As editor of *Earth First! Journal* from 1982 to 1988, Foreman published lively debates on the ethics and effectiveness of "monkeywrenching," forms of industrial sabotage that Earth First! performed to protect nature. Although Foreman renounced the practice and left the militant organization after the FBI arrested him in 1990—even serving on his one-time nemesis Sierra Club's board of directors—*Earth First! Journal* continues to attack the Sierra Club as a corporate sellout.[119]

Sierra Joins the Climate Justice Movement Online

A visit to the Sierra Club website confirms it is a huge operation, but its expansive digital offerings do not appear to cozy up to corporations. The home page at the end of 2017 was filled with ads and links encouraging readers to tell Congress not to open the Arctic National Wildlife Refuge for oil drilling. Actor Edward James Olmos narrated a video explaining why natural gas is "Dirty, Dangerous, and Run Amok." "Take Action" let readers push a button to "Protect Illinois' Air from Corporate Greed!," "Stop Puget Sound Energy from Doubling Down on Fossil Fuels," or "Tell Your Representative to Vote 'NO' on Massive Tax Cuts for Corporate Polluters." Anticapitalist crusader Naomi Klein's cover story for *Sierra* magazine—just one destination among dozens on the site—appealed to Americans to reclaim the spirit that has fueled "so many transcendent social movements in the past."[120] Season 2 of its "The Land I Trust" podcast features westerners' tales of coping with the elements. Klein and Sierra Club executive director Michael Brune's Facebook Live conversation in conjunction with her article, a call to resist the Trump

Administration's assault on the past century's hard-won environmental protections, highlights how the Internet amplifies the magazine's content.

Despite the Sierra Club's emphasis on digital media, *Sierra* magazine still plays an instrumental role in its messaging. Polls show the slick print edition is members' most prized benefit and an important retention tool. The high-quality glossy also offers an "unmatched literary experience and artistic expression," according to senior editor Paul Raub, who embodies the merger between old and new media as he toils at a standing desk in front of a monitor propped up on a thick, dusty old dictionary.[121] The magazine's online audience of 150,000 monthly unique visitors in 2016 was actually smaller than its paid print circulation of 515,000, an inversion of the typical ratio. Editor-in-chief Jason Mark sees the magazine's social media as a recruiting tool. "The Holy Grail of activism is you move people from online to offline—to the streets or at a hearing, say about delisting wolves," Mark explains. The club's Facebook page had nearly a million followers in 2018. Twitter zaps *Sierra* stories around the world and also provides ideas for them. Raub, who routinely retweets possible gems to his colleagues, maintains, "Twitter is the best thing ever for journalism."[122] Virtual engagement is valuable, but Mark says participants in real-world Sierra Outings—more than three hundred destinations in 2018—continue to spark a "emotional, visceral connection" to the club that feeds its collective identity.

Sierra hired Mark in late 2015 to boost the magazine's journalistic heft. The former editor of the Earth Island Institute's award-winning quarterly, *Earth Island Journal*, increased political reporting and investigative journalism, expanded its pool of freelance writers, and doubled the number of original online stories. He also contributes stories, traveling to Tucson, Arizona, to research how the proposed border wall would affect wildlife and the local Tohono O'odham tribe, and to Puerto Rico to witness firsthand the devastating effects of Hurricane Maria. *Sierra*'s climate justice journalism emphasizes the club's commitment to eliminate fossil fuels as energy sources. Almost every issue in 2016 included a story financed by the club's "Beyond Coal" campaign donations. The club uses a blog, mapping, podcasts, video, social media, and investigative reporting in the campaign. Editor Mark says the magazine "upholds the highest principles of journalism": it is compelling, accurate, thorough, fair, and advances a clear worldview. "It's media with a purpose."[123] Stories under his watch include interviews with influential climate researchers and journalists; profiles of anticoal activists; investigations into the fossil fuels industry; and updates and analyses on legislative actions.[124] The activist magazine makes its case through evidence but makes no bones about its agenda. "I absolutely take a point of view," editor Tom Balton states. "Our mission is so critical."[125]

A Vanguard of Activist Journalists

Climate change, in fact, has spawned a raft of online social justice journalism outlets focused on the environment. The nonprofit InsideClimateNews.org won a Pulitzer Prize for its coverage of a 2010 pipeline oil spill in Michigan's Kalamazoo River. *Grist*, an independent, nonprofit newsroom started in 1999, pursues in-depth stories that incorporate solutions. It is a founding member of Climate Desk, a journalistic collaboration with influential publishers like the *Atlantic* and the Huffington Post. The climate justice movement seems especially open to innovations in activist journalism. Media scholar Adrienne Russell puts noted environmental writer Bill McKibben in the "media vanguard" she argues is reinventing journalism by combining it with activism. McKibben created a climate justice advocacy organization group thirty years after the 1989 publication of his *The End of Nature*, one of the first books to describe climate change. He started "350.org," a reference to carbon emissions, when he realized that providing information was insufficient to push government and industry to combat global warming. 350 uses online campaigns, grassroots organizing, and mass public actions to stop new coal, oil, and gas projects, and to build clean energy solutions that work for all. Rich multimedia reports explain global warming on its website, which offers a wealth of resources as of 2017—69,000 photos on Flickr, a set of 350 icons for presentations—and myriad links to get involved in 350 chapters in 188 nations. McKibben sees no conflict between his journalism and activism. For McKibben, as it is for other journalists in the climate justice movement, according to Russell, "the space of journalism is the network rather than the newsroom, and the reigning value is not neutrality but fact-based opinion."[126]

Notes

1. "Honoring the Life and Legacy of David Brower, July 1, 2010," *Berkeley Daily Planet*, June 28, 2010, http://www.berkeleydailyplanet.com/issue/2010-06-29/article/35704?head line=Honoring-the-Life-and-Legacy-of-David-Brower-July-1-2010--; John McPhee, *Encounters with the Archdruid* (New York: Farrar, Straus and Giroux, 1971); "Knight Errant to Nature's Rescue," *Life* 60 (May 27, 1966): 37–42; John Oakes, "Introduction," in "David R. Brower: Environmental activist, publicist, and prophet," interview by Susan Schrepfer,

1974–1978, Regional Oral History Office, University of California, Berkeley, 1980, xx. [hereafter cited as Brower interview]; and "Sierra Club Legend Dies," *San Francisco Chronicle*, November 7, 2000, A-ll.

2. For more on Brower, see David Brower, *For Earth's Sake: The Life and Times of David Brower* (Salt Lake City, UT: Peregrine Smith Books, 1991); Peter Dreier, "Today's Environmental Activists Stand on David Brower's Shoulders," *Huffington Post*, June 20, 2012, http://www.huffingtonpost.com/peter-dreier/todays-environmental-acti_b_1613782.html; Tom Turner, *David Brower: The Making of the Environmental Movement* (Berkeley: University of California Press, 2015); and Robert Wyss, *The Man Who Built the Sierra Club: A Life of David Brower* (New York: Columbia University Press, 2016).

3. Brower interview, 12.

4. Michael P. Cohen, *The History of the Sierra Club: 1892–1970* (San Francisco: Sierra Club Books, 1988), 9. The club removed the "render accessible" clause when cars began to clog parks after World War II. See Jason Henry Schultz, "To Render Inaccessible: The Sierra Club's Changing Attitude Toward Roadbuilding" (MA Thesis, University of Maryland, 2008).

5. See J. S. Holliday, "The Politics of John Muir," *California History* 63 (Spring 1984): 135–39. See also Gretel Ehrlich, *John Muir: Nature's Visionary* (Washington, D.C.: National Geographic, 2000); and Donald Worster, *A Passion for Nature: The Life of John Muir*, reprint ed. (New York: Oxford University Press, 2011).

6. See Alain Touraine, *The Voice and the Eye: An Analysis of Social Movements* (Cambridge: Cambridge University Press, 1978) and *The May Movement: Revolt and Reform, May 1968—the Student Rebellion and Workers' Strikes—the Birth of a Social Movement.* Trans. Leonard F. X. Mayhew (New York: Random House, 1971); and Steven M. Buechler, *Social Movements in Advanced Capitalism* (Oxford: Oxford University Press, 1999).

7. Mark Dowie, "American Environmentalism: A Movement Courting Irrelevance," *World Policy Journal* 9, no. 1 (Winter 1991/1992), 67.

8. "About the Sierra Club," *Sierra Club*, accessed October 27, 2018, https://www.sierraclub.org/about-sierra-club.

9. Untitled, *Sierra Club Bulletin* 1 (January 1893): 24. [hereafter cited as SCB]

10. Article XI, sections 1 and 3, of the Articles of Incorporation stated that the *Bulletin* editorial board was a standing committee whose chair is bulletin editor. UC English professor Cornelius Beach Bradley edited the *Bulletin* from January 1895 to 1897. Warren Gregory succeeded him through 1899. From 1900 to 1903, David Starr Jordan, the president of Stanford University, was the editor (he also chaired the Committee on Publications in 1925), while lawyer James S. Hutchinson served as assistant editor. Hutchinson became editor in 1903. Elliot McAllister succeeded him from 1905 through 1910. Dr. William Frederic Badé edited from 1911 to 1922; C. Nelson Hackett, to 1924; and Hutchinson again in 1925, followed the next year by UC Press editor Francis Farquhar, who remained in the volunteer position the next twenty-two years. "Publications," *Sierra Club: A Handbook*, SCB (November 1947), 12.

11. Hon. John R. Glascock, "A California Outing," SCB 1 (January 1895): 148.

12. See also Anne Farrar Hyde, "Temples and Playgrounds: The Sierra Club in the Wilderness 1901–1922," *California History* 66, no. 3 (September 1987): 208–19.

13. Theodore S. Solomon, "A Search for a High Mountain Route from the Yosemite to the King's River Canon," *SCB* 1 (January 1895): 223.

14. *SCB* 2 (June 1898): 245.

15. Marsden Manson, "Observations on the Denudation of Vegetation—A Suggested Remedy for California," *SCB* 2 (June 1899): 309.

16. John Muir, "The National Parks and Forest Reservations," *SCB* 1 (January 1896): 271–83. See also "Report of the Secretary," *SCB* 5 (June 1905): 311.

17. "Report of the Outing Committee," *SCB* 5 (January 1904): 74.

18. Ella M. Sexton, "Camp Muir in the Tuolumne Meadows," *SCB* 4 (January 1902): 12–18.

19. Charlotte Sanderson, "With the Sierra Club in Kings Canon," *SCB* 4 (February 1902): 185–92; and ibid., Plate LXX, npg.

20. "Report of the Editor of the *Sierra Club Bulletin*," Sierra Club Records, The Bancroft Library, University of California, Berkeley [hereafter cited as SCR], Carton 303, Folder 19.

21. Edgar Wayburn, "Why We Have Summer Outings," *SCB* 42 (March 1957): 32.

22. See Jeff Goodwin, James M. Jasper, and Francesca Polletta, "Why Emotions Matter," in *Passionate Politics: Emotions and Social Movements*, ed. Jeff Goodwin, James M. Jasper, and Francesca Polletta (Chicago: University of Chicago Press, 2001), 1–24.

23. "David Ross Brower: Reflections on the Sierra Club, Friends of the Earth, and Earth Island Institute," interviews conducted by Ann Lage, 1999, Regional Oral History Office, University of California, Berkeley, 99. [hererafter cited as "Brower: Reflections"]

24. "Francis P. Farquhar on Accounting, Mountaineering, and the National Parks," interviewed by Willa K. Baum, 1958, Regional Cultural History Project, University of California, Berkeley, 1960, 61.

25. *SCB* 6 (January 1908): 212.

26. John Muir, "The Hetch-Hetchy Valley," *SCB* 6 (January 1908): 220.

27. "Report of Outing Committee," ibid., 261.

28. "Of Secretary of Sierra Club on Same," ibid., 265–68.

29. "Decision of the Secretary of the Interior," *SCB* 6 (June 1908): 321–29.

30. See W.F. Badé, "Despoiling Hetch Hetchy," *Suburban Life* 8 (1909): 117–18; Robert Underwood Johnson, "Dismembering Your National Park," *Outlook* 91 (January 30, 1909): 252–53; John Muir, "Endangered Hetch Hetchy," *Century* 77 (1909): 464–69; and E. A. Whitman, "Argument Against the Despoiling of the Hetch Hetchy Valley," *Outlook* 91 (February 27, 1909): 507–508.

31. Holway R. Jones, *John Muir and the Sierra Club* (San Francisco: Sierra Club, 1965), 102.

32. "Reminiscences of William Edward Colby," interview by Corinne Gilb, 1954, Regional Oral History Office, University of California, Berkeley, 2001, 51.

33. For more on Hetch Hetchy, see Kendrick A. Clements, "Politics and the Park: San Francisco's Fight for Hetch Hetchy, 1908–1913," *Pacific Historical Review* 48, no. 2 (May 1979): 185–215; Jones, *John Muir and the Sierra Club*, 82–169; Roderick Nash, "Hetch Hetchy," in *Wilderness and the American Mind* (New Haven: Yale University Press, 2014), 161–81; and Christine Oravec, "Conservationism vs. Preservationism: The 'Public Interest' in the Hetch Hetchy Controversy (1984)," in *Landmark Essays on Rhetoric and the Environment: Volume 12*, ed. Craig Waddell (Mahwah, NJ: Lawrence Erlbaum Associates, 1998), 17–34.

34. "The Hetch Hetchy Situation," *SCB* 9 (January 1914): 175–76.

35. "A National Park Service," *SCB* 9 (January 1915): 288.
36. "Frequently Asked Questions," National Park Service, accessed November 7, 2018, https://www.nps.gov/aboutus/faqs.htm.
37. See "A Publisher's Career with the University of California Press, the Sierra Club, and the California Native Plant Society: August Frugé," interview by Suzanne B. Riess, 1997–1998, Regional Oral History Office, University of California, Berkeley, 2001. [hereafter cited as Frugé interview]
38. Brower interview, 218.
39. Ansel Adams to David Brower, [April] 1948, Sierra Club Office of the Executive Director Records, 1933–1994, The Bancroft Library, University of California, Berkeley [hereafter cited as SCEDR], Box 1, Folder 1.
40. *SCB* 20 (February 1935): 69–77; and Brower interview, 9. See also David R. Brower, "Beyond the Ski-Ways," *SCB* 23 (April 1938): 40–45; and ibid., "Exploring the Yosemite Point Couloir," *SCB* 24 (June 1939): 63–67.
41. Brower interview, 40.
42. "Publications," *Sierra Club: A Handbook*, *SCB* (November 1947), 11. Congress in 1964 designated the San Gorgonio Wilderness, which became part of the Sand to Snow National Monument designated by President Barack Obama in February 2016. "Presidential Proclamation—Establishment of the Sand to Snow National Monument," February 12, 2016, https://www.whitehouse.gov/the-press-office/2016/02/12/presidential-proclamation-establishment-sand-snow-national-monument.
43. David Brower to August Frugé, August 23, 1963, SCEDR, Carton 20, Folder 8.
44. David Brower to Bruce Kilgore, April 24, 1963, SCEDR, Carton 23, Folder 13.
45. Edgar Wayburn to The Board of Directors, February 6, 1952, SCR, Carton 302, Folder 41.
46. David Brower to Tom Jukes, May 1, 1953, SCR, Series 10, Carton 303, Folder 21.
47. See Finis Dunaway, "Nature on the Coffee Table," in *Natural Visions: The Power of Images in American Environmental Reform* (Chicago: University of Chicago Press, 2005), 117–47; Mark Harvey, *A Symbol of Wilderness: Echo Park and the American Conservation Movement* (Seattle: University of Washington Press, 2000); Debra E. Jenson, "Echoes of Opposition: The Media Campaign to Stop Echo Park Dam and Save Dinosaur National Monument," *Journalism History* 44, no. 1 (Spring 2018): 32–39; Nash, *Wilderness*, 212; and Turner, *David Brower*, 73–76.
48. Charlotte Mauk, assistant secretary, to Martin Litton, June 12, 1952, SCR, Carton 64, Folder 18.
49. "The 1954 Wilderness Outings," *SCB* 38 (November 1953): 5.
50. David Brower to William Voigt, May 11, 1953, SCR, Carton 64, Folder 19.
51. Oakes, "Introduction," Brower interview, viii.
52. David Brower to Phil S. Bernays, April 30, 1953, SCR, Carton 303, Folder 4. The Sierra Club board voted Oakes an honorary life member in 1958, which some journalists would consider a conflict of interest. Harold C. Bradley to John B. Oakes, December 1, 1958, SCEDR, Box 7, Folder 8.
53. Martin Litton to Richard Leonard, September 19, 1953, SCR, Carton 64, Folder 22. See also Kenneth Brower, "Appreciation: Lessons from the Man Who Stopped Grand Canyon Dams," *National Geographic*, December 2, 2014, http://news.nationalgeographic.com/news/2014/12/141202-grand-canyon-dams-colorado-river-martin-litton-conservation/.

54. Brower interview, 3, 118.

55. "New Color Film on Dinosaur, Ready February 1," SCB 39 (February 1954): 2.

56. See Russell Martin, *A Story That Stands Like a Dam: Glen Canyon and the Struggle for the Soul of the West* (New York: Henry Holt, 1989). Brower always said his biggest regret was failing to fight to save Glen Canyon.

57. "Two Wasteful Dams—Or a Great National Park?," SCB 39 (February 1954): 3–4; "For the Defense of Dinosaur—An Outline," ibid., 5; "Gist of the Claims," ibid., 6–7; "The Dry Swim," ibid., 10; "Which Shall It Be?," ibid., 7–9; and "Some Alternatives," ibid., 11.

58. David R. Brower, "Preserving Dinosaur Unimpaired," SCB 39 (June 1954): 1–10; and Robert K. Cutter, "Hetch Hetchy—Once is Too Often," ibid., 11–12; "Once is Too Often—A Picture Story," ibid.; plates following 12; and "Footnote to Hetch Hetchy," ibid., 13.

59. August Frugé, "River Journal," SCB 39 (June 1954): 15–26.

60. Richard Leonard to Frederic Gunsky, November 17, 1954, SCR Carton 301, Folder 36.

61. "Number One Issue of the Year: River Canyons or Dinosaur Dams," SCB 40 (January 1955): 11, 14–15; and untitled photo essay, plates following page 11.

62. "Dinosaur: Hour of Decision," SCB 40 (May 1955): 3.

63. Dunaway, *Natural Visions*, 130.

64. Nash, *Wilderness*, 219. See also David Perlman, "Our Winning Fight for Dinosaur," SCB 41 (January 1956): 5–8.

65. McPhee, *Encounters*, 165.

66. Chapter 203-Public Law 48, "An Act to authorize the Secretary of the Interior to construct, operate, and maintain the Colorado River storage project and participating projects, and for other purposes," U.S. Bureau of Reclamation, accessed October 27, 2018, http://www.usbr.gov/lc/region/pao/pdfiles/crspuc.pdf.

67. Fred Gunsky to August Frugé, December 14, 1954, SCR Carton 303, Folder 21.

68. Fred Gunsky to Dan L. Thrapp, September 25, 1956, SCR, Carton 302, Folder 42.

69. Fred Gunsky to David Brower, April 4, 1957, SCEDR, Carton 23, Folder 15.

70. August Frugé to Nathan Clark, June 16, 1959, SCR, Series 10, Carton 303, Folder 20.

71. Susan R. Schrepfer, *The Fight to Save the Redwoods: A History of Environmental Reform, 1917–1978* (Madison: University of Wisconsin Press, 1983), 103.

72. Sierra Club Board of Directors Executive Committee Minutes, October 14, 1962, accessed October 27, 2018, http://cdn.calisphere.org/data/28722/6s/bk00079546s/files/bk00079546s-FID222.jpg.

73. Phillip Berry, "President's Message," SCB 54 (June 1969): 2.

74. See Hillary Atkin, "Sierra Club Has Message For Media," *Television Week* 27 (October 13, 2008): 33.

75. Ansel Adams to August Frugé, October 15, 1963, SCEDR, Carton 20, Folder 9.

76. Mrs. John M. Barnes to David Brower, September 1, 1968, SCEDR, Carton 16. Two folders are filled with similar letters.

77. Ansel Adams to David Brower, September 30, 1962, SCEDR, Box 1, Folder 2.

78. Fred Eissler to Bruce Kilgore, May 12, 1962, SCEDR, Carton 20, Folder 12.

79. "No statement should be used that expressly, impliedly, or by reasonable inference criticizes the motives, integrity, or competence of an official or bureau." Sierra Club Board of Directors Resolutions, December 5, 1959, in Brower interview, 322.

80. David Brower to Weldon Heald, November 28, 1962, SCEDR, Carton 23, Folder 15.
81. See *This Is the American Earth*, 1955 exhibit and 1960 book, Sierra Club, accessed October 27, 2018, http://vault.sierraclub.org/education/leconte/history/this_is_the_american_earth.asp.
82. McPhee, *Encounters*, 15. The series won *Publishers Weekly's* 1964 Carey-Thomas Award for the best achievement in creative publishing.
83. See Brower interview, 232. See more about the exhibit-format books in Dunaway, "Nature on the Coffee Table," 117–47; "Big Books for a Cause," in *David Brower*, 93–104; and Wyss, "Books," in *The Man Who Built the Sierra Club*, 152–68.
84. Wendell Stilwell to Editors, July 10, 1965; Herbert D. Staebler to Dear Sierra Club, April 5, 1965; and Braeme Gigas to Gentlemen, February 17, 1966; all in SCEDR, Carton 23, Folder 16.
85. John and Ruth Mendenhall, "An Open Letter to the Sierra Club Board of Directors," December 8, 1968, the *Mugelnoos*, December 18, 1968, 3, in David Ross Brower Papers, The Bancroft Library, University of California, Berkeley [hereafter cited as DRB Papers], Carton 20, Folder 25. See also *Hi! Sierran*, March 1969, ibid. The folder is full of chapter newsletters commenting on the dispute.
86. Brower interview, 210. See also August Frugé, Memorandum: Re Publications Program of the Sierra Club, August 9, 1963, SCEDR, Carton 20, Folder 6.
87. "The Publications Committee," September 7, 1963, SCEDR, Carton 20, Folder 6.
88. Alex Hildebrand to William Siri, June 20, 1965, SCEDR, Carton 20, Folder 6. See also Alex Hildebrand to William Siri, March 29, 1965, ibid., Folder 12.
89. David Brower, "Supplementary Notes on the Publications Policy," SCR, Carton 302, Folder 22.
90. Hugh Nash to Will Siri, "Random Thoughts Pertinent to Publications Policy," October 16, 1965, SCEDR, Carton 20, Folder 6.
91. George Marshall to Hugh Nash, September 28, 1966, SCEDR, Carton 23, Folder 14. See Susan R. Schrepfer, "The Nuclear Crucible: Diablo Canyon and the Transformation of the Sierra Club, 1965–1985," *California History* 71, no. 2 (Summer 1992): 212–37.
92. *Bulletin* Policy Committee to Sierra Club Board of Directors, May 4, 1968, SCR, Carton 26, Folder 38. Members were George Marshall, John Mitchell, Wallace Stegner, and Peggy Wayburn.
93. Ibid.
94. "Is the Sierra Club Bulletin Adequately Staffed?," nd, SCEDR, Carton 23, Folder 14.
95. Hugh Nash to Board of Directors et al., April 26, 1968, SCR, Carton 26, Folder 38.
96. Brower immediately founded Friends of the Earth and its eponymous magazine. He later served on the Sierra Club board from 1983 to 1988 and from 1990 to 1995. Re-elected in 1998, he resigned due to differences with the board shortly before his death in 2000. "David Brower, an Aggressive Champion of U.S. Environmentalism, Is Dead at 88," *New York Times*, November 7, 2000, http://www.nytimes.com/2000/11/07/national/07BROW.html?pagewanted=all.
97. See "Photos by Eliot Porter," in *Galapagos: The Flow of Wildness. Vol. 1: Discovery*, ed. Kenneth Brower; and ibid., *Galapagos: The Flow of Wildness. Vol. 2: Prospect*, ed. Kenneth Brower, both San Francisco: Sierra Club, 1968.

98. "Toward an Earth International Park," *SCB* 52 (October 1967): 20. A dozen color plates followed, half from Porter's Galapagos portfolio. Maria Buchinger and John Milton, "Man and the Land in Ecuador," ibid., 8. By 1969, Brower envisioned a twenty-year program featuring at least twenty-five books. Minutes of Publications Committee, January 10, 1969, SCEDR, Carton 20, Folder 3.

99. David Brower to Edgar Wayburn, January 21, 1969, DRB Papers, Carton 19, Folder 35.

100. Minutes, "Special Meeting of the Board of Directors," October 19, 1968, Sierra Club Board of Directors Meeting Minutes, 1892–1995, Reel 4, BANC FLM 2945, Special Collections, Bancroft Library, University of California, Berkeley; and "Actions of Board at December Meeting," *SCB* 54 (January 1969): 5.

101. Hugh Nash, "Suspended Editor of *Bulletin* Charges It was Misused for Political Purposes," 2, nd, Brower Papers, Carton 20, Folder 22.

102. David Brower to the Editorial Staff of Chapter Newsletters and Chapter Executive Committees, *Mugelnoos*, March 19, 1969, 3, Brower Papers, Carton 20, Folder 25.

103. Bill Olmsted to David Brower, January 14, 1969, SCEDR, Box 7, Folder 11.

104. Hugh Nash to Council Representatives and Chapter Chairmen, February 1, 1969; and Resolution and Memo from Hugh Nash, February 3, 1969, both in Brower Papers, Carton 20, Folder 22.

105. Mike McCloskey to Department Heads, March 9, 1969, Brower Papers, Carton 20, Folder 22. See also Hugh Nash to Board of Directors, July 1, 1969, SCEDR, Carton 23, Folder 14.

106. "February Board of Directors Meeting," *SCB* 54 (March 1969): 5, 14.

107. "Brower: Reflections," 225.

108. Richard M. Leonard, "Mountaineer, Lawyer, Environmentalist," vol. 2, Interviews conducted by Susan R. Schrepfer, 1972–1975, Regional Oral History Office, University of California, Berkeley, 1975, 361.

109. August Frugé, "Preliminary Report on Publications Program," May 19, 1969, SCEDR, Carton 20, Folder 8. See also Publications Committee Meeting Minutes, May 5, 1969, ibid., Folder 5.

110. Robert Irwin, "Sierra Club Books—How a Small Publisher Prints a Big Book," *SIERRA* (September/October 1981): 76–77.

111. Press release, "Sierra Club Closes Book Publishing Program," *Sierra Club*, May 27, 2015, http://content.sierraclub.org/press-releases/2015/05/sierra-club-closes-book-publishing-program.

112. Memo, Robert A. Irwin, July 1, 1974, SCR, Carton 302, Folder 42.

113. Frances Gendlin, Editorial, "Some News of Sierra and the NNR," *SIERRA* 63 (October/November/December 1978): 5.

114. Letters under "*Sierra's* New Design," *SIERRA* (July/August 1986): 7.

115. "Brower: Reflections," 175, 200.

116. Daniel C. Hallin, *The Uncensored War: The Media and Vietnam* (Oakland: University of California Press, 1989), 116–18.

117. See Kevin Michael DeLuca, *Image Politics: The New Rhetoric of Environmental Activism* (New York: Routledge, 2005).

118. Dave Foreman, *Confessions of an Eco-Warrior* (New York: Crown, 1991), 21.

119. Red Emma, "Greenwashing 101: (Or How Sierra Club Learned To Stop Worrying About The 99% And Love Wall Street)," *Earth First! Newswire*, accessed October 27, 2018, http://earthfirstjournal.org/newswire/articles/big-greenwashing-101/. See also Rick Scarce, *Eco Warriors: Understanding the Radical Environmental Movement*, paperback ed. (New York: Routledge, 2007).

120. Naomi Klein, "Hope Trumps Nope: A Blueprint for Resistance," *Sierra*, December 14, 2017, https://www.sierraclub.org/sierra/2018-1-january-february/feature/hope-trumps-nope-blueprint-for-resistance. The all-caps version of the magazine title did not survive the twentieth century.

121. Paul Raub, interview with author, April 13, 2016, Sierra Club, San Francisco.

122. Ibid.

123. Jason Mark, interview with author, April 13, 2016, Sierra Club, San Francisco.

124. See Jonathan Hahn, "The Sinking Cities and Rising Seas of (Near) Future Tomorrow," *Sierra*, November 17, 2017, https://www.sierraclub.org/sierra/sinking-cities-and-rising-seas-near-future-tomorrow; Jason Mark, "Meet the Grandmother Standing Up to the Coal Mining Industry," *Sierra*, April 24, 2017, https://www.sierraclub.org/sierra/meet-grandmother-standing-coal-mining-industry; John Brinkley, "The Coal Industry Is Bankrupt," *Sierra*, April 6, 2016, https://www.sierraclub.org/sierra/2016-3-may-june/feature/coal-industry-bankrupt; and Jason Mark, "Trump Slashes Two National Monuments in Utah," *Sierra*, December 4, 2017, https://www.sierraclub.org/sierra/trump-slashes-two-national-monuments-utah?mostpopular=true.

125. Tom Balton, interview with author, April 13, 2016, Sierra Club, San Francisco.

126. Adrienne Russell, *Journalism as Activism: Recoding Media Power* (Cambridge: Polity Press, 2016), 120.

· 4 ·

SUFFRAGIST

Reframing Militant Notions of Patriotism

American Quaker Alice Paul was twenty-four when on November 9, 1909, she and a fellow suffragette disguised as charwomen sneaked into London's Guildhall and made their way to the gallery above its medieval great hall. They remained hidden until that evening, when cabinet members filed in as guests of the annual London Mayor's Banquet. Just as the politicians were about to toast the king, the women rose up from their hiding place, shouted "Votes for Women!" and hurled a shoe through a stained-glass window. The incident cost Paul thirty days in infamous Holloway Jail, where she joined other suffragettes on a hunger strike. It took five guards to hold down the ninety-five-pound social worker while a doctor force-fed her a mixture of eggs and milk through a tube plunged down her throat. "I didn't give in," she told reporters, a statement that also sums up Paul's lifelong crusade for women's rights.[1]

Paul returned to the United States at the end of the year determined to reinvigorate the moribund U.S. suffrage movement by incorporating the British Women's Social and Political Union's (WSPU) confrontational tactics and flair for spectacle. Paul rejected the National American Woman Suffrage Association's (NAWSA) slogging, state-by-state approach to winning the vote, which since 1896 had remained stuck at four victories (Colorado,

Idaho, Utah, and Wyoming). Near the top of her list for jump-starting a campaign for a federal constitutional amendment was to start a national suffrage newspaper dedicated to that single cause, following the example of the WSPU journal, *Suffragette*.[2] Selling *Suffragette* on rough-and-tumble street corners, in fact, was Paul's initiation into the militant movement. Paul's *Suffragist* is a prime example of how social movement strategies spread. Beginning in 1913, the weekly chronicled how her British-inspired civil disobedience shook up the American suffrage movement during the final, fruitful seven years of the seven decades since the first woman's rights convention resolved on July 20, 1848, that women would seek "their sacred right to the elective franchise."[3]

Woman's Rights Press

Paul's *Suffragist* may have been almost the last suffrage newspaper created during the long campaign, but its laser-trained focus on a federal suffrage amendment was new. Women had created dozens of newspapers to advocate for their civil rights since Amelia Bloomer founded the *Lily* in Seneca Falls six months after the upstate New York village hosted the woman's rights convention.[4] Feminism is barely discernible in Bloomer's calls for dress reform and temperance, however, and it would be twenty years before Susan B. Anthony and Elizabeth Cady Stanton produced their boldly titled *Revolution* (1868–1870). "Men, their rights and nothing more; women, their rights and nothing less," was its slogan. Anthony and Stanton's sweeping agenda truly was revolutionary for the times, as it called for revamping laws on marriage, property rights, child custody, women's dress, access to the professions and education, working women, and, most radical of all, votes for women. It also addressed taboo subjects such as domestic abuse and abortion.[5] The woman's rights press filled a gap left by mainstream newspapers, which were largely hostile to the woman's rights movement.[6]

The weekly *Revolution* was part of a broad nineteenth-century woman's rights press that taught isolated women empowering new ways to talk, dress, and think about themselves.[7] These newspapers were an important part of a vibrant and imaginative print culture that suffrage scholar Mary Chapman argues was largely responsible for women winning the vote.[8] Some eighty nineteenth-century suffrage publications identified, legitimized, and sustained a far-flung community of "new women" who challenged restrictive gender roles, according to historian Linda Steiner. "[S]uffrage papers persuasively illustrated alternative versions of a satisfying life style for women," she writes, "and brought suffragists into a new and exhilarating world in which their lives had special purpose and meaning."[9] *Suffragist* offered twentieth-century readers that same soaring sense of possibility and sorority.

Suffragist challenged the government, and hence American patriarchal power, with a militancy matched only by Anthony thirty years earlier and women's liberationists a half century later. Paul and other suffragists challenged no less than "the oldest, most rigid caste/class system in existence, the class system based on sex," as radical feminist Shulamith Firestone described patriarchy in 1970.[10] One project of the feminist Second Wave that Firestone helped lead in the 1960s (discussed in Chapter Seven) was the reclamation of the First Wave's forgotten history. "The history of the struggle for suffrage alone is an absolutely incredible amount of tooth and nail opposition from the most reactionary forces in America," Firestone stated in her fierce *Notes from the First Year*, the first periodical of the women's liberation movement.[11] The seemingly simple notion of women entering the ballot box required a "reconception of the female body in public space," according to scholar Shelley Stamp Lindsey.[12] Scholars have shown how patriarchal culture relegated women to the private, domestic sphere and apportioned the public, political sphere to men, creating the fundamental dichotomy on which all society rested.[13]

Women, however, had expanded the private, domestic sphere until they wielded considerable influence in public affairs through massive organizing into women's clubs and associations. The suffrage movement represented the convergence of these two parallel yet separate strands of American political life. Historian Barbara Welter claimed the transition from the homebound Victorian "true woman" to the Progressive Era's independent "New Woman" marked change "as startling in its way as the abolition of slavery or the coming of the machine age."[14] NAWSA President Carrie Chapman Catt enumerated women's decades of struggle to "get the word 'male' out of the Constitution":

> During that time they were forced to conduct 56 campaigns of referenda to male voters, 480 campaigns to get legislatures to submit suffrage amendments to voters, 47 campaigns to get state constitutional conventions to write woman suffrage into state constitutions, 277 campaigns to get state party conventions to include woman suffrage planks, 30 campaigns to get presidential party conventions to adopt woman suffrage planks in party platforms and 19 campaigns with 19 successive Congresses.[15]

Taking Suffrage to the Streets

Catt's list omits the contributions of her militant rival, Harriot Stanton Blatch. Beginning in 1908, the daughter of Elizabeth Cady Stanton had imported to New York City the British soapbox speaking campaigns and spectacular suffrage processions she had experienced while living in London. Catt and other older suffragists disliked the idea of suffragists taking to the streets, which violated social norms for proper female behavior. Paul determined to change their minds. She joined NAWSA and volunteered to chair its Congressional Committee. With committee Vice Chair Lucy Burns, who like Paul had survived jail in London for her suffrage militancy, she organized a spectacular national suffrage parade and pageant on Pennsylvania Avenue, witnessed by a half million people in Washington, D.C., on March 3, 1913, the eve of President Woodrow Wilson's inauguration.

Paul's vision of female politics wed feminism with femininity. The press lauded the sight of beautiful parade herald Inez Milholland astride a white horse at the head of the colorful procession of floats, bands, and 5,000 marchers. The San Francisco Examiner editorialized that the event was "an historical event of extraordinary beauty and dignity."[16] The suffragists scored an even greater public coup when a drunken mob swarmed the avenue, harassed the marchers, and injured some one hundred people. Milholland won front-page headlines for galloping into the mob to lead the women to their destination at the U.S. Treasury Building portico. The press's defense of the women's right to peaceably assemble was an important step toward acknowledging that women possessed other civil rights—like voting.[17] The publicity reinforced Paul's political strategy to always "keep the people watching the suffragists."[18]

The parade also revealed the racism that tinged the suffrage movement. Paul had reluctantly agreed to allow twenty-two members of historically black Howard University's Delta Sigma Theta sorority to march—but only after parade herald Milholland threatened to quit.[19] Suffragist reflected the Progressive Era's pervasive racism. Suffragist displayed racism in other ways as well. Black faces never appeared in Suffragist photographs, and its columns contained neither news of numerous black suffrage clubs nor commentary on the double burden borne by African American women seeking equal rights.[20] Several articles in Suffragist argued that woman suffrage would uphold white supremacy in the South, part of the pragmatic campaign to win Southern Congressional votes.[21] Its publishers' racism remains a stain on their record of fighting for women's civil rights.[22]

Paul next maneuvered for a journal dedicated to the federal suffrage amendment. In April 1913, she created the Congressional Union for Woman Suffrage (CU), whose policy and funding she controlled, and persuaded NAWSA's executive board to publish a periodical dedicated to publicizing the CU's campaign for a constitutional amendment. NAWSA leaders hesitated because they feared it would compete with the venerable weekly *Woman's Journal*, founded in Boston in 1870 by Lucy Stone and fellow suffragists, including William Lloyd Garrison. To lower their resistance, Paul suggested the committee publish a humble weekly bulletin. A bulletin was the pragmatic choice, Paul wrote to historian and suffrage newspaper editor Mary Beard, "because it will secure us the cooperation of the National Board, and also obviate the hostility which would come to us from the followers of the *Journal*, if we started the paper on a large scale."[23]

Only a handful of bulletins appeared, however, before the larger, graphically striking *Suffragist* debuted on November 15, 1913. As Paul stated on its front page, the *Suffragist* was a single-issue journal: "The purpose of this paper is to aid in securing an amendment to the Constitution of the United States enfranchising the women of the whole country." Its first editorial called for "A Federal Amendment Now." But it was the inaugural issue's cartoon caricature of an insolent President Wilson receiving suffrage guests that caught Catt's eye. She was furious, as was the NAWSA president's respected predecessor, Anna Howard Shaw, who wrote to Burns, "I must confess I was sick at heart."[24] The month following *Suffragist*'s debut, NAWSA cut ties with the Congressional Union.

The Only Political Newspaper Published by and for Women

Suffragist was unique as "the only political newspaper published in the United States by and for women," as its editors liked to boast.[25] It encouraged women to identify with their gender rather than other identities, although its audience was solidly middle class. The journal embodied the feminism that coalesced in the 1910s as women flooded colleges, the professions, factories, the new department stores, amusement parks, and other parts of the public previously deemed a male preserve.[26] The college-educated, professional women who published *Suffragist* typified this emerging "New Woman," whose independence was reflected in its pages. Paul envisioned the newspaper as "the backbone" of the federal amendment campaign.[27] She and Burns strategically set up shop in the nation's capitol at Cameron House just off Pennsylvania Avenue to better lobby legislators. *Suffragist* was the CU's forum for distributing news the organization created.

Editor Rheta Childe Dorr, for example, in spring 1914 arranged several CU meetings with Wilson and other officials. Dorr, formerly a muckraking New York City reporter who had also discovered the WSPU in London, had been hired in 1913 to give *Suffragist* a professional panache, but she did not return from Europe until February 1914.[28] The politicians' responses to the provocative questions the women posed elicited newsworthy quotes that spilled beyond *Suffragist's* pages into the mainstream press.[29] Dorr's dual role had her making news as well as reporting it. When some newspapers criticized CU deputations to Wilson, *Suffragist* editorials countered that as disfranchised citizens women had no alternative to make their cause heard.[30]

Dorr's short stint as *Suffragist* editor illustrates some differences between mainstream and social movement media. The professional journalist also was author of the popular feminist book, *What Eight Million Women Want* (1910), and would later cover the Russian Revolution. Despite her personal support for suffrage, Dorr followed the emerging standards for the information model of journalism that demanded neutral reportage. She was appalled when she discovered that Paul had been revising editorials without her permission, and she resented the positive spin Paul demanded on the suffrage campaign. "You want a little newspaper to advertise the Union," Dorr wrote Paul in April before resigning. "I have no idea of sacrificing my reputation as a serious journalist, which is exactly what I am doing in editing—or pretending to edit—a paper which is run in this fashion."[31] Dorr's comment reflects concerns about editorial independence in social movement media and questions about when advocacy journalism crosses over into propaganda. After Dorr left, Burns and Paul put out the newspaper themselves for the next three years. Paul recalled pulling all-nighters to meet the deadline before hiring a new editor, Vivian Pierce, a seasoned reporter who had covered politics for the Scripps newspapers in California.[32]

Mobilizing Collective Action in the *Suffragist*

The *Suffragist* encouraged all kinds of collective action. Articles suggested that groups send resolutions, letters, petitions, and telegrams to their representatives or lobby their local press to write supportive editorials. Issues provided forms and addresses for readers to write their representatives, Senate leaders, and Wilson.[33] Volunteers sold the paper on the street, and students at a CU-sponsored suffrage school were required to sell copies before they could move on to more challenging campaign techniques such as soapbox speaking in the streets.[34] *Suffragist* also kept readers apprised of legislative activity related to the federal amendment's progress through Congress and highlighted campaign events. Photographs figured prominently. Much editorial space was devoted during the first year to explaining to readers why the federal approach was superior to NAWSA's state-by-state campaign. The weekly also reported on other developments in the votes-for-women campaign at home and abroad. Regular features included a report on the current status of the suffrage amendment, "Comments of the Press," "Notes of the Week," a listing of new subscribers, and a treasurer's report. Within months of *Suffragist's* debut, the Senate reconsidered the amendment for the first time since 1887, although it was again rejected. The CU intensified its efforts.

Self-Interested Social Justice Journalism

Suffragist's greatest challenge occurred when Paul initiated picketing of the White House in 1917. Over the next two years, police arrested about half of the thousand women involved in the peaceful protests, jailing 168 of them.[35] The *Suffragist* risked suppression and its publishers prison in their fight for First Amendment rights of assembly, petition, free press, and free speech. Its self-interested coverage of the saga was also its best social justice journalism, in the service of fighting for women's civil rights. The newspaper and its publishers reframed patriotism by championing the pickets' wartime picketing.

The November 25, 1916, death of 1913 parade herald Milholland sparked the protest. Earlier that year, the CU had joined with the Woman's Party of Western Voters, another Paul creation, to campaign against Wilson's reelection. (The two groups merged in March 1917 into the National Woman's Party.) Milholland was one of a handful of "flying envoys" the Woman's Party dispatched across the Western states where women voted as part of Paul's strategy to "protest the party in power," another replication of the British suffragette campaign. The strategy misfired, however, as it was based on parliamentary politics that did not readily apply to the American republican system. Despite *Suffragist's* frequent claims to the contrary, for example, the

Woman's Party appeared to be campaigning for Republican candidate Charles Evans Hughes—not against Wilson. The policy also pitted the Woman's Party against Democratic Party candidates who supported votes for women.

Milholland collapsed onstage on October 23, 1916, while giving a speech in Los Angeles and died a month later. Paul capitalized on the tragedy in a December 23 special *Suffragist* "Inez Milholland Memorial Edition" that framed her as a martyr. On Christmas Day, Paul conducted the first memorial service for a woman ever held in the U.S. Capitol Building. The *Suffragist* lavished coverage on the solemn pageantry, which ended with calls for Wilson to make Milholland's death meaningful by coming out for the federal suffrage amendment.[36] He agreed to meet the Inez Milholland Memorial Deputation of some three hundred women in the East Room on January 9, 1917, but angrily stalked out after a stream of speakers lectured him on his responsibility to stop more women from dying for the right to vote. As chronicled by the *Suffragist*, picketing began the next day, when two sets of six women marched silently from Cameron House to the White House's east and west gates. A pair of women bearing the party's purple, gold, and white flags on each side of the gates bracketed a third woman who held a large yellow silk banner. One read, "MR. PRESIDENT, WHAT WILL YOU DO FOR WOMAN SUFFRAGE?"; the other proclaimed Milholland's final public words, slightly revised to ask, "HOW LONG MUST WOMEN WAIT FOR LIBERTY?"[37]

Wilson initially tipped his hat to the "silent sentinels" when his car rolled through the gates, but his geniality disappeared once the United States joined World War I on April 6, 1917. Pickets began hoisting signs quoting him on democracy, a subversive move to sidestep new Espionage and Sedition Acts that criminalized even the mildest antiwar expression. The NWP defied patri-archal politics by pledging allegiance to women over nationalism. *Suffragist* ignored the war and focused solely on passage of a federal suffrage amend-ment.[38] Picketing continued even though opposed by many NWP members who quit the party. Blatch was the best-known American to abandon suffrage for the war. "War!" she wrote in her book, *Mobilizing Woman-Power*. "It does make the blood course through the veins."[39]

As a Quaker, it was relatively easy for Paul to ignore the war, but she knew that picketing during wartime would brand the NWP as unpatriotic and be cited as more evidence that women were unfit for citizenship. Centuries-old cultural dictates demanded that women rally when men declared war. Even the militant WSPU had abandoned its suffrage campaign for the war effort when England entered the war in 1914. *Britannia* replaced the WSPU's

Suffragette newspaper, rededicated to patriarchal politics: "For King, for Country, for Freedom." Paul nonetheless stuck to her strategy.

NAWSA's leaders voted 63–14 on February 23, 1917, to pledge the war services of its two million members, betting that suffragists' show of civic responsibility would earn them the vote after the war's end. In June 1917 NAWSA renamed the fifty-year-old *Woman's Journal* the *Woman Citizen*, highlighting her rightful place in American society. The *Citizen* kept its 50,000 readers well apprised of women's war work. A series of comely and capable "Win the War Women" graced *Citizen* covers in 1918, including a woman doctor, tram conductor, farmer, munitions worker, nurse, and Red Cross knitter.[40] Besides working to demonstrate women's worthiness of the vote, the *Citizen* argued that granting women the vote would free their energies for the war effort.[41]

Suffragist, in contrast, argued for the vote as a natural right of American women. "Let us take the stand that American women do not need to prove their fitness for liberty," wrote elderly suffragist Mary Winsor. "It is our birth right—a debt long overdue." *Suffragist* demanded a federal amendment as a war measure almost immediately after Wilson declared war on April 6, 1917.[42] The newspaper never framed the vote as a reward, and, in fact, flaunted the NWP's militancy to attract attention to its cause. It never ran stories exhorting housewives to recycle stale bread or praising volunteers who rolled bandages. Winsor urged readers to realize "the folly of trying to win the ballot by concessions to masculine opinion, by trying to please men with 'womanly work.'"[43] Paul, in fact, was well aware that male politicians and reformers failed to reward Anthony and Stanton with the vote after the Civil War even though the pair had dropped suffrage work to lobby for the Thirteenth Amendment granting slaves their freedom. Male suffragists abandoned women and worked exclusively for suffrage for male ex-slaves.[44] *Suffragist* editorials tried to justify the NWP's controversial decision to protest during wartime.[45]

Meanwhile, the National Association Opposed to Woman's Suffrage charged that the pickets put the president at risk of assassination. Congressmen hurled gendered insults that ridiculed pickets as "militant Amazons" and "unwomanly."[46] *Woman Citizen* condemned them as "absurd, ill-timed, and susceptible of grave and demoralizing suspicion," although it did speak out against the "harshness and injustice of measures" taken against the pickets.[47] NAWSA even tried unsuccessfully to censor news about the NWP.[48] Breaching male-dominated public space also opened women to physical attack. Worse, when crowds began to attack the pickets, police charged the women with obstructing traffic. Dozens were sentenced to dismal Occoquan work-house in Virginia.

Reframing Patriotism in the *Suffragist*

Authorities secretly locked Paul into a District prison psychiatric ward near the beginning of a seven-month sentence for picketing. She launched a hunger strike that several Occoquan inmates quickly joined. Prison officials began force-feeding them a mixture of eggs and milk through tubes rammed down the women's throats, a tactic that backfired by repelling the public and press. The publicity-savvy Paul recognized the propaganda value of the hunger strikes. In a note she smuggled from the prison hospital in November 1917, Paul advised the NWP executive board that force-feeding her and other harsh acts provided "excellent ammunition" against the administration. She instructed her associates to exploit their ordeal in the *Suffragist* and press releases to mainstream newspapers. "The more harsh we can make the Administration seem … the better," Paul wrote on the flyleaf torn from her copy of the *Oxford Book of English Verse*.[49] "What splendid advertising we are getting from all of the papers," millionaire suffragist Alva Belmont wrote to Burns that July. "I never imagined the situation would be so brilliant."[50]

Suffragist raised the stakes of the suffrage debate by challenging the standard militarist definition of patriotism. Editors reframed the pickets as the epitome of patriotism in their quest for the basic democratic right to vote. "It is without the shadow of a doubt the finest service a woman can do for the country, to take her place in the women's picket line," *Suffragist* editorialized.[51] Editors stated that the anti-war vote of freshman Congresswoman Jeannette Rankin of Montana (a NWP member) "declared the possibility of a patriotism other than war patriotism, a service other than war service."[52] An editorial stated, "It is unpatriotic, we are told, to complain of injustice now. We believe that it is unpatriotic not to complain."[53] The newspaper took a jab at NAWSA when it quoted a prediction that the picketing suffragists would be remembered "to have had a truer perception of patriotism in the loftiest sense than those who believed they were serving the nation by meek self-abnegation in palliative services."[54] New editor Pauline Clarke privately worried the paper sounded "contemptuous" of women's war work.[55]

The war did provide suffragists with a new argument against disfranchisement, as they emphasized the hypocrisy of Americans fighting abroad for democracy while half its citizens lacked the franchise. The newspaper exploited that contradiction. "The United States Convicts Eleven More Women for Demanding Democracy," one headline proclaimed.[56] One editorial charged that authorities had plotted to "terrorize" the pickets.[57] When some women left Occoquan, it crowed, "Prisoners of Freedom Released."[58] Wilson's many pronouncements on the primacy of democracy provided more editorial fodder. "American Women Burn President Wilson's Meaningless Words on Democracy," *Suffragist* informed readers after a 1918 protest.[59] The *Suffragist* held Wilson personally responsible for the mob attacks upon the women.[60] A subscription ad noted *Suffragist* was the only newspaper telling the prisoners' side of the story.[61]

Besides *Suffragist*, the NWP also operated an aggressive Press Department that harnessed the weekly's media synergy to generate content for press releases it spewed out for the wire services, the Washington Press Club, and the Capitol Building press galleries. The NWP press office illustrates how social movements remain dependent on mainstream media to move their causes onto the public agenda. Paul made sure each member of Congress and the Senate and other key federal officials received free copies of the weekly number. Paul even proofread *Suffragist* pages on the picket line.[62] Generous donors such as executive board member Belmont kept the NWP afloat, and volunteers sold *Suffragist* on the street in what sociologist Marjory Nelson termed a significant rite of initiation into the organization.[63]

Reframing the Image of Suffrage Pickets

Suffragist initially resisted the label "militant," bestowed upon the NWP by the mainstream press, because members believed their pickets were legal and represented American democratic principles. The label had been tossed at them every time their campaign transgressed the bounds of acceptable female behavior. But as the suppression intensified the newspaper became more defiant: on December 15, 1917, the cover featured Nina Allender's illustration of a pretty young woman titled *The Militant*. The image reframed the image of pickets as unfeminine or insane. Allender was perhaps the most prominent of several dozen woman suffrage artists. Others included Edwina Drumm, Blanche Ames, Ida Sedgwick Proper, Rose O'Neill, and Annie "Lou" Rogers, the first woman suffrage cartoonist according to the *Woman's Journal*, which frequently published her work in the 1910s.[64]

Allender's clever covers helped transform the image of the suffragist from dour to glamorous. One typically coquettish Allender cartoon in 1916 was *The Wall-flower*, in which a woman labeled "East" sitting alone at a dance looks enviously at the men fluttering around another woman labeled "West"— who flutters a fan labeled "Voter."[65] Allender's emphasis on suffragists' youth, beauty and femininity, however, reinforced stereotypes of women as decorative rather than as powerful political players, in the view of historian Elisabeth Israels Perry.[66] Allender also could be serious, addressing, for instance, class issues. The ironic *Woman's Place is in the Home*, for example, depicted a row of five children watching their mother trudge off from their shack to a factory.[67] She also had picketed the White House in addition to organizing CU open-air meetings.[68] Once pickets were jailed, Allender's art grew more militant. She addressed the discrepancy between the suppression of disenfranchised women pickets and Democratic ideals in *Celebrating Independence Day in the National Capital* in 1917, which depicted police and a mob threatening a banner-wielding woman.[69] The satirical caption turned the illustration into powerful visual rhetoric.

The tabloid also hired photographers to make its case, publishing 173 photos during fiscal year 1917–1918, the height of its protests.[70] Paul's strategy to keep the nation "always watching the suffragists" upended a core element of western culture—the display of woman as spectacle to be looked at by men.[71] This omnipresent "male gaze" as conceived by feminist visual theorist Laura Mulvey juxtaposes male activity against female passivity.[72] "Men act and women appear. Men look at women. Women watch themselves being looked at," observes John Berger. "Thus she turns herself into an object."[73] But the female pickets in the images were the antitheses of objects. *Suffragist* treated them as not as objects but as subjects—agents of their lives. Photographs showed women bearing banners, standing in the cold, withstanding hecklers. Putting themselves on public display, however, did put women at risk. Photographs of police and hecklers harassing female pickets in respectable middle-class dress highlighted the women's vulnerability.[74]

Suffragist alternated between framing the jailed pickets as victims and as heroes. Most accounts calculatedly exploited the protesters' gender, favoring diminutives, for example, when describing its campaign: the NWP's was a "little protest" and the pickets "little" women. One news article claimed that the officers who arrested Katharine Morey were four times her size.[75] The newspaper pointed out the pickets' ladylike behavior—"demure and silent."[76] Another article referred five times to the pickets as "young."[77] Other accounts, however, emphasized the women's strength and resistance. An article describing a particularly rough Occoquan incident, for example, described sixteen prisoners' decision to hunger strike as a "revolution."[78] Both the public and press decried the force-feeding as barbarous. The embattled District freed the women after a court ruled their incarceration illegal at the end of November 1917. Wilson came out for the suffrage amendment on January 10, 1918.

While NAWSA's war work and intense lobbying definitely influenced the president, several historians agree it was no coincidence that Wilson announced his change of heart a year to the day after the picketing began. The House narrowly approved the suffrage amendment the next day. More NWP demonstrations and arrests followed, however, before the Senate approved the amendment on June 4, 1919.[79] The *Suffragist* also followed the "Prison Special," a troupe of NWP Occoquan veterans who in 1919 toured the nation by train in their prison uniforms singing their suffrage prison songs to keep the federal amendment alive in the public imagination.[80] *Suffragist* paid subscriptions in fact rose to their zenith of 5,599 subscribers on February 1, 1918.[81] After ratification by the requisite thirty-sixth state, President Wilson signed the Nineteenth Amendment granting women the vote on August 26, 1920.

Paul's greatest accomplishment is that she kept votes for women—a joke a generation earlier—on the political agenda even as world war charred the planet. *Suffragist* made sure the NWP's dramatic publicity stunts, among the earliest "media events" of the twentieth century, did not go unnoticed. Lively accounts of NWP protesters lighting "watch fires of freedom" at the White House and climbing the statue at Lafayette Park earned the NWP enmity but did prod reaction from Wilson and won some sympathetic coverage in the mainstream press, obsessed with war but not blind to such infringements upon freedom of expression as imprisoning suffrage pickets.

The Wilson administration was the most oppressive in American history, convicting more than a thousand antiwar dissidents and shuttering more than a dozen publications during World War I under the Espionage and Sedition Acts for content less provocative than some *Suffragist* contents, such as its editorial headlined "Kaiser Wilson."[82] Why did the *Suffragist* escape being banned as seditious? Gender and class in part protected the newspaper as well as the pickets. The *Suffragist* never directly criticized the war or the draft. *Suffragist*'s single-issue stance focused on winning votes for women, a message far less threatening to the federal government than the radical critiques of American democracy that filled the many banned periodicals of socialists, anarchists, and the Industrial Workers of the World. First Amendment scholar Haig Bosmajian concludes that the NWP and its newspaper escaped prosecution under the Espionage and Sedition Acts due to the government's selective enforcement of the law.[83]

After the Nineteenth Amendment

Woman suffrage is one of the few social movements that achieved its goal: women won the vote. The larger feminist movement, however, sputtered after that victory. Women are not a monolithic group and were unable to coalesce around a movement less cut-and-dry than obtaining the vote. Further, African American women in the South could not exercise their right because of institutionalized racism. NAWSA became the apolitical League of Women Voters after the Nineteenth Amendment took effect. Its *Woman Citizen* reverted to coverage of women's clubs and domestic affairs, even changing its name back to *Woman's Journal* for broader appeal in 1927, but it closed in 1932.[84] *Suffragist* suffered a similar identity crisis. The paper suspended publication in October 1919, reappeared as a monthly in February 1920, and ceased publication a year later. The newspaper mirrored the strengths and weaknesses of the NWP: it was passionate, idealistic, intelligent, articulate, and courageous, and it possessed great style.

It also was elitist, racist, and narrowly focused. Although some NWP members were working-class or socialist, most were like Paul, who held a Ph.D. in economics, or Vassar College alumna Burns, making them part of what Nancy Woloch called a female "new elite."[85] Having rejected the patriarchal call to arms in 1917, the NWP found itself largely ostracized by the male political establishment after 1920. Many reformist women also objected to the NWP's refusal to expand its platform to address racial, sexual, and labor issues that affected women. Most women rejected the NWP's one-note platform, which in the post-suffrage decades focused exclusively if vainly upon passage of an Equal Rights Amendment. *Equal Rights* succeeded *Suffragist* in 1923.

The NWP formally called for an ERA on July 23, 1923. As its inaugural editorial stated, *Equal Rights* sought to unite "free-souled women together, to hearten them by contact with others of like spirit."[86] Most American women failed to heed the call, partly because they feared the ERA would abolish hard-won protective legislation for working women and partly because they had moved on to pursue individual accomplishments after the collective victory for the vote. *Equal Rights* appeared in various forms until November

1954.[87] The ERA campaign did not succeed despite a big push in the 1970s, and it remained one state short of ratification before the 1982 deadline.[88]

Social Media Mobilize the 2017 #womensmarch

The NWP's peaceful picketing of the White House in 1917 moved back into the spotlight when some hundreds of thousands of people gathered in Washington on January 21, 2017, for the National Women's March to protest the election of President Donald Trump.[89] This time women used social media to organize via #womensmarch.[90] The swift mobilization of the mammoth march highlights social media's ability to facilitate collective action. "From its inception, it was a social-media phenomenon, not a mainstream-media one," noted *Washington Post* reporter Paul Farhi, who ventured that the march was "perhaps the largest single demonstration of the power of social media to create a mobilization."[91] Farhi observed that mainstream news media were late in catching up to the story.

Most of the estimated 3.3 to 4.6 million people who marched in rallies that spread to Los Angeles, London, and other cities around the world learned about it from Facebook.[92] The march began as a single Facebook post the day after Trump's election, when retired attorney Teresa Shook asked on her Facebook page from her home in Hawaii whether women were interested in rallying in Washington around Inauguration Day. Some virtual friends helped create an event page on which forty people had expressed interest when Shook went to bed that night; the next morning, the number had jumped to 10,000. In New York City, fashion entrepreneur Bob Bland had come up with the same idea on election night. Thanks to the viral success of the "Nasty Woman" T-shirt she had designed during the presidential campaign, Bland boasted several thousand politically active Facebook followers who signed on to her Facebook event. Bland and Shook joined forces and enlisted veteran organizers Tamika Mallory, Carmen Perez, and Linda Sarsour as national co-chairs to lend expertise and diversity to the march.[93]

Women of color and trans women, however, complained that the march ignored issues that affect them.[94] Their charges of exclusion echo critics of the 1913 suffrage parade in Washington. Unlike the suffragists, however, the 2017 organizers strived to be inclusive. The tensions within what purports to be an intersectional movement reveal the challenges of sustaining collective identity in a large social movement comprising multiple publics. Organizers struggled to maintain momentum over the next year,[95] with only 4,000 women attending the movement's first national convention in October 2017 in Detroit. Hundreds of thousands of women, however, reprised the original march in cities across the United States on January 20, 2018—galvanized, the *New York Times* reported, "by their disdain for Mr. Trump and his administration's policies."[96] One political scientist said the march's broad call untied to a specific policy goal helped draw big numbers.[97]

That breadth also could be interpreted as a vagueness that can mitigate against change. Shared identities, ideologies, and interests cohere social movements, so the larger the group the more difficult to sustain collective identity. Conversely, movements can become so inclusive they are rendered meaningless. As Bart Cammaerts observes in his study of the anti-austerity movement in the United Kingdom, "[B]uilding a very long and almost endless chain of equivalence," he writes, "leads to the constitution of a chain that is weak, ephemeral and easily breakable."[98] Women of color who stayed home in 2018 said they felt the Women's March ignored racial issues important to them. Black Lives Matter Cincinnati, for instance chose not to participate in that city's Women's March after event organizers refused to change the event's slogan from "Hear our vote!" to "Hear our voice!"[99]

Power to the Polls

The Women's March organized a massive "Power to the Polls" rally in Las Vegas on January 21, 2018, kicking off a new phase—its launch of a national tour to register a million new voters before the 2018 midterms.[100] An unprecedented 529 women filed to run for Congress in 2018, according to the Center for American Women and Politics at Rutgers University. By Election Day, 210 Democratic women and 63 Republican women remained on the ballot—and won fourteen seats in the Senate and 102 seats in the House, sending a record 126 women to the 116th Congress in 2019 and raising women's representation to 23 percent.[101]

Many candidates ran grassroots, outsider campaigns. They bucked conventional political wisdom by running campaigns that, according to political scientist Kelly Dittmar, "embraced gender and race as an asset they bring to candidacy and office-holding, instead of a hurdle they have to overcome to be successful."[102] A third of female House nominees were women of color. The first two Native American women and the first two Muslim women were elected to the House. Massachusetts and Connecticut voters elected the first African American women to represent them in the House of Representatives. Texans elected their state's first two Latinas to the House. Another Latina, Alexandria Ocasio-Cortez of New York City, at twenty-nine became the youngest woman elected to Congress.[103] Female candidates' sweeping success marked the transformation of the Women's March from a one-time protest into a social movement that relied on electoral politics. Observers noted that women still had a long way to go to achieve parity in politics, but the victories marked a milestone in the century since Alice Paul instructed *Suffragist* editors to wield her arrest as "excellent ammunition" for the campaign for votes for women.

Notes

1. "Miss Paul Describes Feeding by Force," *New York Times*, December 10, 1909, 1.
2. See John C. Zacharis, "Emmeline Pankhurst: An English Suffragette Influences America," *Communication Monographs* 38, no. 3 (1971): 198–206.
3. *Report of the Woman's Rights Convention* (Rochester, NY: John Dick, 1848), 10, https://www.nps.gov/media/photo/gallery.htm?id=C5F5A21C-155D-451F-67E9D17421B0E587.
4. For more on individual suffrage newspapers, see Elizabeth Burt, "Dissent and Control in a Woman Suffrage Periodical: 30 Years of the *Wisconsin Citizen*," *American Journalism* 16, no. 2 (Spring 1999): 39–62; Sherilyn Cox-Bennion, "Woman Suffrage Papers of the West, 1869–1914," *American Journalism* 3, no. 3 (Summer 1986): 129–41; "The *New Northwest* and *Woman's Exponent*: Early Voices for Suffrage," *Journalism Quarterly* 54, no. 2 (Summer 1977): 286–92; "The *Pioneer*: The First Voice of Women's Suffrage in the West," *Pacific Historian* 25, no. 4 (Winter 1981): 15–21; and "The *Woman's Exponent*: Forty-two Years of Speaking for Women," *Utah Historical Quarterly* 44, no. 3 (Summer 1976): 222–39; Patricia Grimshaw and Katherine Ellinghaus, "'A Higher Step for the Race': Caroline Nichols Churchill, the 'Queen Bee' and Women's Suffrage In Colorado, 1879–1893," *Australasian Journal of American Studies* 20 (December 2001): 29–46; Tiffany Lewis, "Winning Woman Suffrage in the Masculine West: Abigail Scott Duniway's Frontier Myth," *Western Journal Of Communication* 75, no. 2 (2000): 127–47; Lynne Masel-Walters, "A Burning Cloud by Day: The History and Content of the *Woman's Journal*," *Journalism History* 3, no. 4 (Winter 1976–1977): 103–10; Lynne Masel-Walters, "Their Rights and Nothing More: A History of The *Revolution*, 1868–1870," *Journalism Quarterly* 53, no. 2 (Summer 1976): 242–51; Martha Solomon, ed., A *Voice of Their Own: The Woman Suffrage Press, 1840–1910* (Tuscaloosa: University of Alabama Press, 1991); Linda Steiner, "Finding Community in Nineteenth Century Suffrage Periodicals," *American Journalism* 1, no. 1 (Summer 1983): 1–15; and Jean Ward and Elaine Maveety, *Yours for Liberty: Selections from Abigail Scott Duniway's Suffrage Newspaper* (Eugene: Oregon State University Press, 2000).

5. See Lana F. Rakow and Cheris Kramarae, eds., *The Revolution in Words: Righting Women 1868–1871* (New York: Routledge, 1990); and Ann Russo and Cheris Kramarae, eds., *The Radical Women's Press of the 1850s* (New York: Routledge, 1991).

6. See Rodger Streitmatter, "Slowing the Momentum for Women's Rights," in *Mightier than the Sword: How the News Media Have Shaped American History* (Boulder, CO: Westview Press, 1997), 30–44.

7. Linda Steiner, "The History and Structure of Women's Alternative Media," in *Women Making Meaning: New Feminist Directions in Communication*, ed. Lana F. Rakow (New York: Routledge, 1992), 131.

8. Mary Chapman, *Making Noise, Making News: Suffrage Print Culture and U.S. Modernism* (New York: Oxford University Press, 2014), 4. See also Sara Egge, "Strewn Knee Deep in Literature: A Material Analysis of Print Propaganda and Woman Suffrage," *Agricultural History* 88, no. 4 (September 2014): 591–600.

9. Steiner, "Finding Community," 2, 12. See also Mary M. Carver, "Everyday Women Find Their Voice in the Public Sphere: Consciousness Raising in Letters to the Editor of the *Woman's Journal*," *Journalism History* 34, no. 1 (Spring 2008): 15–22.

10. Shulamith Firestone, *The Dialectic of Sex: The Case for Feminist Revolution* (New York: William Morrow, 1970), 16.

11. Shulamith Firestone, "The Women's Rights Movement in the U.S.: A New View," *Notes from the First Year* (New York: New York Radical Women, 1968), 2.

12. Shelley Stamp Lindsey, "'Eight Million Women Want—?' Women's Suffrage, Female Viewers and the Body Politic," *Quarterly Review of Film and Video* 16, no. 1 (1995): 7.

13. See Elizabeth Janeway, *Man's World, Woman's Place: A Study in Social Mythology* (New York: William Morrow, 1971); Linda Kerber, *Women of the Republic: Intellect and Ideology in Revolutionary America* (Chapel Hill: University of North Carolina Press, 1980); Glenna Matthews, *The Rise of Public Woman: Woman's Power and Woman's Place in the United States, 1630–1970* (New York: Oxford University Press, 1992); and Mary Ryan, *Women in Public: Between Banners and Ballots, 1825–1880* (Baltimore: Johns Hopkins University Press, 1980).

14. Barbara Welter, "The Cult of True Womanhood: 1800–1860," in *Dimity Convictions: The American Woman in the Nineteenth Century* (Athens: Ohio University Press, 1976), 41.

15. Carrie Chapman Catt and Nettie Rogers Shuler, *Woman Suffrage and Politics* (New York: Charles Scribners Sons, 1923), 107.

16. "Discounted Chivalry of the American Man," *San Francisco Examiner*, March 13, 1913, 28. See also "Suffrage Crusaders in Thrilling Pageant Take City by Storm," *Washington Evening Star*, March 3, 1913, 1, 4; "Women's Beauty, Grace, and Art Bewilder the Capital," *Washington Post*, March 4, 1913, 1; and Teri Finneman, "'The Greatest of Its Kind Ever Witnessed in America': The Press and the 1913 Women's March on Washington," *Journalism History* 44, no. 2 (Summer 2018): 109–16.

17. See Linda J. Lumsden, "Beauty and the Beasts: The Significance of Newspaper coverage of the 1913 National Suffrage Parade," *Journalism & Mass Communication Quarterly* 77, no. 3 (Autumn 2000): 593–611; and Sarah J. Moore, "Making a Spectacle of Suffrage: The National Woman Suffrage Pageant, 1913," *Journal of American Culture* 20 (Spring 1997): 89–103.

18. Inez Haynes Irwin, *The Story of the Woman's Party* (New York: Harcourt, Brace, 1921), 31.

19. "Black Sorority Project," October 13, 2013, https://www.youtube.com/watch?v=aNWr 0kOkd74. NAWSA also told Ida B. Wells-Barnett she could not march, but friends helped her sneak into the line. See Wanda Hendricks, "Ida B. Wells-Barnett and the Alpha Suffrage Club of Chicago," in *One Woman, One Vote: Rediscovering the Woman Suffrage Movement*, ed. Marjorie Spruill Wheeler (Troutdale, Oregon: New Sage Press, 1995), 263–76.

20. At least thirty African American suffrage groups or women's clubs focused on the vote in the 1910s. Rosalyn Terborg-Penn, "Afro-Americans in the Struggle for Woman Suffrage," (PhD. diss., Howard University, 1977), 313.

21. "National Suffrage and the Race Problem," *Suffragist*, November 14, 1914, 3; and Helena Hill Weed, "The Federal Amendment and the Race Problem," *Suffragist*, February 6, 1915, 4.

22. Louise Michele Newman argues that feminism was founded upon racial politics. See Louise Michele Newman, *White Women's Rights: The Racial Origins of Feminism in the United States* (New York: Oxford University Press, 1999). For more on race and the suffrage movement, see Janet M. Cramer, "Woman as Citizen: Race, Class, and the Discourse of Women's Citizenship, 1894–1909," *Journalism and Mass Communication Monographs*, Iss. 165 (March 1998): 1–39; Ann Dexter Gordon with Bettye Collier-Thomas, eds., *African American Women and the Vote, 1837–1965* (Amherst: University of Massachusetts Press, 1997); Gail H. Landsman, "The 'Other' as Political Symbol: Images of Indians in the Woman Suffrage Movement," *Ethnohistory* 39, no. 3 (Summer 1992): 247–84; Jen McDaneld, "White Suffragist Dis/Entitlement: The *Revolution* and the Rhetoric of Racism," *Legacy: A Journal of American Women Writers* 30, no. 2 (2013): 243–64; Nell Irvin Painter, "Voices of Suffrage: Sojourner Truth, Frances Watkins Harper, and the Struggle for Woman Suffrage," in *Votes for Women*, ed. Jean H. Baker (New York: Oxford University Press, 2002), 42–55; Rosalyn Terborg-Penn, *African American Women in the Struggle for the Vote, 1850–1920* (Bloomington: Indiana University Press, 1998); Valethia Watkins, "Votes for Women: Race, Gender, and W. E. B. Du Bois's Advocacy of Woman Suffrage," *Phylon* 53, no. 2 (Winter 2016): 3–19; and Teresa Zackodnik, "'I Don't Know How You Will Feel When I Get Through': Racial Difference, Symbolic Value, and Sojourner Truth," in *Press, Platform, Pulpit: Black Feminist Publics in the Era of Reform* (Knoxville: University of Tennessee Press, 2011), 93–126.

23. Alice Paul to Mary Beard, June 28, 1913, quoted in Katherine H. Adams and Michael L. Keane, *Alice Paul and the American Suffrage Campaign* (Champaign: University of Illinois Press, 2010), 43.

24. Anna Howard Shaw to Lucy Burns, November 19, 1913, Reel 34, *National American Woman Suffrage Association Papers*, microfilm ed. (Sanford, NC: Microfilm Corp. of America, 1979). [hereafter cited as NAWSA Papers]

25. Advertisement, *Suffragist*, February 21, 1914, 7.

26. See Nancy Cott, *The Grounding of Modern Feminism* (New Haven, CT: Yale University Press, 1987); and June Sochen, *The New Woman: Feminism in Greenwich Village, 1910–1920* (New York: Quadrangle Books, 1972).

27. Alice Paul to Rheta Childe Dorr, February 21, 1914, Reel 9, *National Woman's Party Papers*, microfilm ed. (Glen Rock, NJ: Microfilm Corporation of America, 1977–1978). [hereafter referred to as NWP Papers]

28. See Zena Beth McGlashan, "Club 'Ladies' and Working 'Girls': Rheta Childe Dorr and the New York *Evening Post*," *Journalism History* 8, no. 1 (Spring 1981): 7–13.

29. See "Suffrage Delegation Interviews President Wilson," *Suffragist*, November, 22, 1913, 13; "Suffrage Deputation Interests Congressmen," *Suffragist*, January 3, 1914, 6; and "President Wilson Sees Working Women," *Suffragist*, February 7, 1914, 5.

30. "Silly, Silent and Offensive," *New York Times*, January 11, 1917, 14; "Heckling the President," *Suffragist*, June 11, 1914, 2; and "Heckling the President," *Suffragist*, May 22, 1915, 4.

31. Dorr to Paul, April 21, 1914.

32. Press release, Reel 89, Donald Haggerty, ed., *National Woman's Party Papers: The Suffrage Years 1913–1920*, microfilm ed. (Sanford, NC: Microfilm Corporation of America, 1981). [hereafter referred to as NWP Papers: The Suffrage Years]

33. "Help Win Suffrage This Session," *Suffragist*, December 29, 1917, 6; and "The Vote in the House of Representatives Telegraph Your Representative!," *Suffragist*, January 2, 1915, 6.

34. "Paper Sellers," *Suffragist*, December 6, 1913, 32; and "Learning How to Be a Successful Suffragist," *Suffragist*, December 13, 1913, 45.

35. Doris Stevens, *Jailed for Freedom* (New York: Boni & Liveright, 1920), 177.

36. "The National Memorial Service in Memory of Inez Milholland," *Suffragist*, December 30, 1916, 7; and "To the President and Congress," ibid., 6.

37. Stevens's classic contemporary account of the NWP pickets, *Jailed for Freedom*, has been followed by "Picketing Wilson," in Adams and Keane, *Alice Paul*, 157–90; Linda Ford, *Iron-Jawed Angels: The Suffrage Militancy of the National Woman's Party 1912–1920* (Lanham, MD: University Press of America, 1991); Linda J. Lumsden, "Picketing: Women's First Battle for First Amendment Rights," in *Rampant Women: Suffragists and the Right of Assembly* (Knoxville: University of Tennessee Press, 1996), 114–43; and Christine Lunardini, *From Equal Suffrage to Equal Rights: Alice Paul and the National Woman's Party, 1920–1928* (New York: New York University Press, 1986).

38. See Linda J. Lumsden, "'Excellent Ammunition': Suffrage Newspaper Strategies During World War I," *Journalism History* 25, no. 2 (Summer 1999): 53–64.

39. Harriot Stanton Blatch, *The Mobilization of Woman-Power* (New York: Woman's Press, 1918), 124.

40. See *Woman Citizen*: May 11, 1918, 1; May 18, 1918, 1; June 8, 1918, 1; April 13, 1918, 1; May 4, 1918, 1; and June 1, 1918, 1. See also Carolyn Kitch, "Alternative Visions," in *The Girl on the Magazine Cover: The Origins of Visual Stereotypes in American Mass Media* (Chapel Hill: University of North Carolina Press, 2001), 75–100; E. Michele Ramsey, "Inventing Citizens During World War I: Suffrage Cartoons in the *Woman Citizen*," *Western Journal of Communication* 64, no. 2 (Spring 2000): 113–47; and Rachel Schreiber, "She Will Spike War's Gun: Suffrage, Citizenship and War," in *Gender and Activism in a Little Magazine: The Modern Figures of The Masses*, ed. Rachel Schreiber (Farnham: Ashgate Publishing, 2011), 124–58.

41. See *Woman's Journal*, April 28, 1917, 97; and *Woman Citizen*, September 28, 1918, 345, 353.
42. *Suffragist*, April 21, 1917.
43. *Suffragist*, August 18, 1917, 8.
44. Susan B. Anthony, Matilda Gage, and Elizabeth Cady Stanton, eds., *History of Woman Suffrage*, vol. 2, Classic Reprint ed. (London: Forgotten Books, 2017), 267–70.
45. "Why We Keep on Picketing," *Suffragist*, September 1, 1917, 6.
46. Ford, *Iron-Jawed Angels*, 63.
47. "The Pickets and the Public," *Woman Citizen*, June 30, 1917, 79; "Pickets Are Behind the Times," *Woman Citizen*, November 17, 1917, 470; and *Woman Citizen*, November 24, 1917, 490.
48. Undated letter from Carrie Chapman Catt to press correspondents, Reel 33; and Carrie Chapman Catt, "An Open Letter to the Public," July 13, 1917, Reel 60, both in NAWSA Papers; and "Minutes of the Meeting of the Executive Committee of the National Woman's Party," August 10, 1917, Reel 87, NWP Papers: The Suffrage Years.
49. Alice Paul to Dora Lewis, (?) November 1917, Reel 53, NWP Papers.
50. Alva Belmont to Lucy Burns, July 19, 1917, Reel 45, NWP Papers: The Suffrage Years.
51. *Suffragist*, June 9, 1917, 6.
52. *Suffragist*, April 14, 1917, 4.
53. *Suffragist*, June 30, 1917, 4.
54. *Suffragist*, June 9, 1917, 5.
55. Pauline Clarke to Clara Wolfe, November 5, 1917, Reel 51, NWP Papers: The Suffrage Years.
56. *Suffragist*, July 14, 1917, 4.
57. "Opposition, Direct and Indirect," *Suffragist*, July 13, 1918, 4.
58. "Prisoners of Freedom Released," *Suffragist*, September 15, 1917, 4.
59. *Suffragist*, December 21, 1918, 6–7. See also "President's Words Burn at Suffrage Protest in Front of White House," *Suffragist*, September 28, 1918, 6–7.
60. "President Onlooker at Mob Attack," *Suffragist*, August 18, 1917, 7; and "Opposition, Direct and Indirect," *Suffragist*, July 13, 1918, 4.
61. "Suffragists, Attention!," *Suffragist*, October 27, 1917, 12.
62. Unidentified newspaper clipping, Reel 33, NAWSA Papers.
63. "Learning How to Be a Successful Suffragist," *Suffragist*, December 13, 1917, 45; and Marjory Nelson, "Ladies in the Street: A Sociological Analysis of the National Woman's Party," (PhD. diss., State University of New York at Buffalo, 1976), 156–57.
64. Alice Sheppard, *Cartooning for Suffrage* (Albuquerque: University of New Mexico Press, 1994), 22.
65. *Suffragist*, January 22, 1916. See also Nina Allender, *The President's Valentine*, *Suffragist*, February 19, 1916, 1.
66. Elisabeth Israels Perry, "Introduction," in Sheppard, *Cartooning for Suffrage*, 12.
67. August 29, 1914, *Suffragist*, 1.
68. "The Women Who Are 'Guarding' the White House," *Washington Post*, February 7, 1917, 1.
69. *Suffragist*, July 14, 1917, 1. See also *First to Fight (Government Recruiting Poster Slogan)*, *Suffragist*, September 8, 1917, 1.

70. Annual Report of the *Suffragist* Editorial Department, Reel 87, NWP Papers: The Suffrage Years.

71. Liesbet van Zoonen, "Spectatorship and the Gaze," in *Feminist Media Studies* (London: Sage Publications, 1994), 103.

72. See Laura Mulvey, "Visual Pleasure and Narrative Cinema," in *Visual and Other Pleasures* (Bloomington: University of Indiana Press, 1989); and Susan Rubin Suleiman, "(Re) Writing the Body: The Politics and Poetics of Female Eroticism," in *The Female Body in Western Culture: Contemporary Perspectives* (Cambridge: Harvard University Press, 1986), 7–29.

73. John Berger, *Ways of Seeing* (London: British Broadcasting Company, 1972), 47.

74. Untitled, *Suffragist*, July 7, 1917, 7; and untitled, *Suffragist*, August 10, 1918, 9.

75. "Six Suffragists Are Tried by the United States Courts," *Suffragist*, July 7, 1917, 5; and "The Fight Must Go On," *Suffragist*, July 7, 1917, 4.

76. *Suffragist*, January 17, 1917, 7.

77. "Suffragists Wait at the White House for Action," *Suffragist*, March 3, 1917, 5.

78. "A Week of the Women's Revolution," *Suffragist*, November 23, 1917, 4.

79. See for example, "Women's Protests Against Disfranchisement Broken Up by Federal Police," *Suffragist*, August 17, 1918, 5; "Woman's Party Protests Against Wilful [sic] Senators," *Suffragist*, October 19, 1918, 6–7; "American Women Burn President Wilson's Meaningless Words on Democracy," *Suffragist*, December 21, 1918, 6–7; and "The Watchfire Goes On," *Suffragist*, February 8, 1919, 8–9.

80. See "Prison Special Arouses South," *Suffragist*, March 8, 1919, 4; "The Prison Special," *Suffragist*, March 15, 1919, 8–9; and "The Prison Special through the West," *Suffragist*, March 27, 1919, 7–8.

81. Report of the *Suffragist* Circulation Department, February 1, 1918, in Reel 87, NWP Papers: The Suffrage Years.

82. "Kaiser Wilson," *Suffragist*, August 18, 1917, 6; Margaret Blanchard, *Revolutionary Sparks: Freedom of Expression in Modern America* (New York: Oxford University Press, 1992), 76; and H. C. Peterson and Gilbert C. Fite, *Opponents of War, 1917–1918* (Madison: University of Wisconsin Press, 1987), 95. See also "An Arraignment of the Police," *Suffragist*, July 14, 1917, 4.

83. See Haig Bosmajian, "The Abrogation of the Suffragists' First Amendment Rights," *Western Speech* 38, no. 4 (1974): 218–32.

84. See Sheila M. Webb. "The *Woman Citizen*: A Study of How News Narratives Adapt to a Changing Social Environment," *American Journalism* 29, no. 2 (Spring 2012): 9–36.

85. Nancy Woloch, *Women and the American Experience, A Concise History* (New York: McGraw-Hill Education, 2001), 193.

86. "The Picket Line," *Suffragist*, February 17, 1923, 8.

87. See Linda J. Lumsden, "*Equal Rights*," in *Women's Periodicals in the United States: Social and Political Issues*, ed. Kathleen L. Endres and Therese L. Lueck (Westport, CT: Greenwood Press, 1996), 72–77.

88. Bill Chappell, "One More To Go: Illinois Ratifies Equal Rights Amendment," *NPR*, May 31, 2018, https://www.npr.org/sections/thetwo-way/2018/05/31/615832255/one-more-to-go-illinois-ratifies-equal-rights-amendment.

89. Nancy Benac, "Women's March in Washington D.C. is an Echo of the Past," *Boston Globe*, January 21, 2017, https://www.boston.com/news/history/2017/01/21/womens-march-in-washington-d-c-is-an-echo-of-the-past; and Mary Bowerman, "This Isn't the First Time Thousands of Women Have Taken to the Streets in D.C.," *USA Today*, January 21, 2017, https://www.usatoday.com/story/news/nation-now/2017/01/21/isnt-first-time-thousands-women-have-taken-streets-dc/96891544/.

90. Susan Chira and Yamiche Alcindor, "Defiant Voices Flood U.S. Cities as Women Rally for Rights," *New York Times*, January 21, 2017, https://www.nytimes.com/2017/01/21/us/women-march-protest-president-trump.html; "More Than 1 Million Rally at Women's Marches in US and Around World," *ABC News*, January 22, 2017, http://abcnews.go.com/Politics/womens-march-heads-washington-day-trumps-inauguration/story?id=44936042; Elana Schor and Madeline Conway, "Millions Join Trump Protest Marches Around the Globe," *Politico*, January 21, 2017, https://www.politico.com/story/2017/01/womens-march-dc-democratic-tensions-233945; and Julie Turkewitz, "How Marches in Washington Have Shaped America," *New York Times*, January 21, 2017, A10.

91. Paul Farhi, "How Mainstream Media Missed the March That Social Media Turned into a Phenomenon," *Washington Post*, January 22, 2017, https://www.washingtonpost.com/lifestyle/style/how-mass-media-missed-the-march-that-social-media-turned-into-a-phenomenon/2017/01/21/2db4742c-e005-11e6-918c-99ede3c8cafa_story.html?utm_term=.513df0f81bf1.

92. Kaveh Waddell, "The Exhausting Work of Tallying America's Largest Protest," *Atlantic*, January 23, 2017, https://www.theatlantic.com/technology/archive/2017/01/womens-march-protest-count/514166/.

93. Charlotte Alter, "How the Women's March Has United Progressives of all Stripes," *Time*, January 20, 2017, http://time.com/4641575/womens-march-washington-coalition/.

94. See Beatrice Dupuy, "Some Women of Color Are Boycotting the Women's March, Here's Why," *Newsweek*, January 20, 2018, http://www.newsweek.com/some-women-color-siting-out-womens-march-785861; and Paula Rogo, "Why Are Some Black Women Skipping this Year's Women's March?," *Essence*, January 20, 2018, https://www.essence.com/culture/black-women-boycott-womens-march.

95. Perry Stein, "It Has Been Six Months Since the Women's March. How Can Organizers Keep the Momentum Alive?," *Washington Post*, July 20, 2017, https://www.washingtonpost.com/local/it-has-been-six-months-since-the-womens-march-how-can-organizers-keep-the-momentum-alive/2017/07/20/00cdb804-6bee-11e7-9c15-177740635e83_story.html?tid=a_inl&utm_term=.d900546af996.

96. "Women's March 2018: Protesters Take to the Streets for the Second Straight Year," *New York Times*, January 20, 2018, https://www.nytimes.com/2018/01/20/us/womens-march.html.

97. Waddell, "Exhausting Work."

98. Bart Cammaerts, *The Circulation of Anti-Austerity Protest* (London: Palgrave MacMillan, 2018), 192.

99. Dupuy, "Some Women of Color."

100. "We Are the Leaders We Have Been Waiting for," *Power to the Polls*, accessed October 2, 2018, http://www.powertothepolls.com/.

101. "2018 Election Night Tally," Center for American Women and Politics, updated November 28, 2018, http://www.cawp.rutgers.edu/2018-election-night-tally.

102. Susan Chira and Kate Zernike, "Women Lead Parade of Victories to Help Democrats Win House," *New York Times*, November 7, 2018, https://www.nytimes.com/2018/11/06/us/politics/women-midterms-historic.html?action=click&module=Spotlight&pgtype=Homepage.

103. See Elana Schor, "Voters Send Record Number of Women to Congress," *Politico*, November 7, 2018, https://www.politico.com/story/2018/11/07/women-congress-2018-midterm-election-results-970324; and Mary Jordan, "Record Number of Women Heading to Congress," *Washington Post*, November 7, 2018, https://www.washingtonpost.com/politics/record-number-of-women-appear-headed-for-congress/2018/11/06/76a9e60a-e1eb-11e8-8f5f-a55347f48762_story.html?utm_term=.8129f68b6701.

· 5 ·

AGITATOR

The *Arkansas State Press* Makes
Black Lives Matter in 1942

The West Ninth Street section of Little Rock, Arkansas, rocked when soldiers training at nearby Camp Robinson barracks gathered there to let off steam on weekends. Early Sunday evening on March 22, 1942, was typical until two white military officers arrested an African American soldier named Albert Glover on charges he was disorderly and drunk in public. Two Little Rock police officers jumped in and began clubbing Glover. Sergeant Thomas D. Foster, a member of the all-black 92nd Engineers Battalion stationed at the camp, stepped from the gathering crowd and demanded an explanation for the use of force. Instead of explaining, the two MPs arrested Foster and began to drag him down the street. He broke free and ran into a nearby church alcove, pursued by city police officer Abner Hay. The crowd watched appalled as Hay pounced on Foster and the other officers piled on, clubbing him until the battered sergeant collapsed. Standing over Foster, Hay then pulled out his revolver and shot him. As Foster lay dying in front of him, Hay lit up his pipe and casually began to puff on it. The crowd was furious. "CITY PATROL-MAN SHOOTS NEGRO SOLDIER" screamed the front-page banner head-line atop the following Friday's edition of the *Arkansas State Press*, the city's weekly black newspaper. Several subheads penned by publisher and editor L.C. Bates told the story:

Body Riddled While Lying on Ground
White Military Police Look on;
Brandishing Guns to Hold Crowd Back

Dozens of eyewitnesses interviewed by the *State Press*'s Daisy Bates for the story her husband wrote contradicted Hays's claim of self-defense. L.C. Bates framed the injustice as murder. "[T]he Policeman deliberately stood over Sgt. Foster while he lay helpless on the ground," the *State Press* reported, "and with death-dealing effect, pumped five bullets into the helpless frame, who just a few minutes before, was the highest specimen of military manhood, training to make the world safe for a Democracy, that now, he will never know."[1] As Arkansas historian Grif Stockley observes, "The paper's tone throughout the article was a militant call to action with no pretense of objectivity."[2] Bates's demand that a white man—a police officer no less—be held accountable for killing a black man in Arkansas was unprecedented.

The *State Press*'s reliance on eyewitnesses instead of authorities, in contrast, had precedents in the nineteenth century and descendants in the twenty-first century. After police in Ferguson, Missouri, killed unarmed teenager Michael Brown on August 9, 2014, data analyst Sam Sinyangwe discovered that no official statistics existed on police shootings. He connected via Twitter with two fellow activists to create the interactive website Mapping Police Violence, which documented 1,175 police killings in 2014. The digitally savvy trio were following in the footsteps of nineteenth-century journalist Ida Wells-Barnett, the African American publisher of *Memphis Free Speech* who documented terrorism against blacks across the South in her 1892 pamphlet, *Southern Horrors: Lynch Law in All Its Phases*.

Wells-Barnett went beyond white authorities to interview victims' families and neighbors to determine the truth behind lynching, what she termed "that last relic of barbarism and slavery."[3] Wells-Barnett's findings reframed lynching—a popular public spectacle in some southern communities—as terrorism.[4] An unacknowledged precursor of the muckrakers a decade later, Wells-Barnett also marshaled facts and emotion. By citing dozens of cases, she exposed the "thread-bare lie" that the black men tortured and killed by white mobs had raped white women. She claimed white men committed the crime against black females with impunity:

> In Nashville, Tenn., there is a white man, Pat Hanifan, who outraged a little Afro-American girl, and, from the physical injuries received, she has been ruined for life. He was jailed for six months, discharged, and is now a detective in that city.[5]

Wells-Barnett asserted the real motivation behind lynching was to maintain white supremacy. She blamed the white-owned press for maintaining "lynch law" through lies and false reporting. She called on African Americans to support black newspapers so they could afford to investigate the truth behind 728 reported southern lynchings over the previous eight years. "The people must know before they can act," Wells wrote, "and there is no educator to compare with the press."[6] Media historian David T. Z. Mindich has shown how Wells-Barnett's impassioned reporting revealed the truth about lynching that eluded the *New York Times*'s business-as-usual accounts that typified its emerging information model of journalism.[7]

This chapter explores the *State Press*'s two-punch combination of activism and journalism in campaigns against police brutality and white supremacy dating back to World War II. L.C. and Daisy Bates's complementary roles as activists and journalists set the stage for their famous leadership in the landmark integration of Little Rock Central High School in 1957. The *Arkansas State Press*'s experience in mid-twentieth-century America provides context for the role and function of twenty-first-century racial justice media. The newspaper's act of witnessing and condemning Foster's death in 1942 was a precursor of the citizen cell phone videos and social media that mobilized Black Lives Matter in 2014. A comparison of how the *State Press* and Black Lives Matter mobilized illuminates the continuities and disparities in the Civil Rights Movement as well as in social movement media.

Editor Lucius Christopher Bates

Born in Mississippi on April 27, 1901, Lucius Christopher Bates was tall, reed thin, and wore black-rimmed glasses. The soft-spoken minister's son "got ink in his veins" while working as a teenaged apprentice in a print shop and worked for several Midwest newspapers before he launched the *Western Ideal* in Pueblo, Colorado, at age twenty-two. His first bitter lesson in politics occurred when he agreed to boost the candidate of some shady politicians on his hunch that their win could be good for business. They lost and the paper folded. The lesson that "one does not 'sell out'" steeled Bates for his role in Little Rock.[8] His new career as a traveling insurance salesman in the South edified him about the indignities of segregation. On one trip to Little Rock in 1927, he witnessed the burning body of lynching victim John Carter in the center of the intersection at West Ninth Street and Broadway—near where

Sergeant Foster met his fate fifteen years later.[9] On another trip the married L.C. met a teenaged Daisy Gatson. Vague on the details of their first decade together, the Bateses wed in Little Rock on March 4, 1942, nearly a year after L.C. began publishing the *Arkansas State Press* on May 9, 1941.

Bates wanted to fill the void in news about the black community. "The only newspaper coverage the white man saw of blacks was about crimes black people committed," he recalled.[10] He disdained the city's three black-owned newspapers for their passive coverage of racial discrimination. L.C. believed that "newspapers should serve the public as vehicles for progressive social change, as distributors of the truth, and as defenders of social justice and equality," Daisy later told an interviewer.[11] Bates described himself as an unabashed agitator. "When you agitate something," he once said, "it comes clean."[12] Emotion infused his commentary in the *State Press*. "Segregation is the South's substitute for slavery," stated his inaugural editorial.[13]

The second issue of the paper offered an agency frame that called on the federal government to ban race discrimination in the defense industry as a war measure. "This is no time to quibble with stupid race prejudice," he wrote.[14] He criticized organized labor for relegating blacks to the most menial jobs.[15] In September 1941, a front-page story reported that a white policeman kicked a black pregnant woman standing in the whites-only line at a theater. The article suggested a boycott of the theater as the only recourse to preventing further such "brutal and uncalled for" violence.[16] L.C. edited, wrote articles, sold advertising, and served as a typesetter and photographer for the newspaper, which initially employed only one other reporter. Daisy did not work at the newspaper in its early years.[17] In 1945, Bates bought his own printing press and moved the *State Press* into its permanent home at 610 West Ninth Street. Peak circulation reached 22,000.

The Black Press in the United States

The *Arkansas State Press* was part of an extensive network of black newspapers that by the time the Japanese bombed Pearl Harbor were read by as many as six million of the nation's thirteen million African Americans.[18] The black press always had been a "protest press" and acted as a "huge sounding board" for thoughts and feelings in the Negro world, according to the *Journal of Negro Education*.[19] Its intrinsic opposition to racial injustice stretched back to March 16, 1827, when African American publishers Samuel Cornish and John Russworm argued in the inaugural issue of *Freedom's Journal* that the U.S. Constitution applied to the nation's half million free blacks.[20] More than eleven hundred black-owned papers appeared by the end of the nineteenth century, including abolitionist newspapers produced by Frederick Douglass and Mary Ann Shadd Cary. The black press really took off in the early twentieth century, when Robert Sengstacke Abbott founded the *Chicago Defender* in 1905. The *Baltimore Afro-American* appeared in 1907, and the *Pittsburgh Courier* in 1910, the same year that the National Association for the Advancement of Colored People persuaded Atlanta professor W.E.B. Du Bois to move north to New York to edit its new magazine, the *Crisis*.[21]

These newspapers changed America. As Juan Gonzalez and Joseph Torres write, historically mainstream news media not only perpetuated racist views but also fomented mob violence against nonwhite communities. People of color were virtually excluded from newsrooms until the 1970s, and efforts to diversify newsrooms remain stalled a half-century later.[22] The black press was inherently ingrained in social justice journalism as it advocated for racial equality. *Defender* publisher Abbott helped instigate the great migration of southern blacks to Chicago after World War I[23] and challenged segregation of the armed forces in World War II.[24] *Courier* sports editor Wendell Smith campaigned for the Brooklyn Dodgers to hire Negro League star Jackie Robinson in the 1940s.[25]

The 1940s proved plush for the black press in light of the wartime demand for news. Twenty-eight publishers joined together in March 1940 as the Negro Newspaper Publisher Association, which launched its own newsgathering service.[26] The *Arkansas State Press* was one of a dozen black weeklies launched in the United States in 1941 and the 118th black journal in the state since Little Rock hosted the short-lived *Arkansas Freeman* in 1869.[27] The *State Press* was among dozens of black newspapers that embraced the *Courier's* Double V campaign to symbolize African Americans' desire to defeat Nazis abroad and segregation at home.[28] L.C. Bates's first response to the declaration of war following the bombing of Pearl Harbor asserted that African Americans expected to receive equal rights in return for their service. The column framed the issue as a matter of social justice: "The Black man has contributed his share in every conflict this country has ever been involved, and he always come through with honors. … The Negro wants to enjoy some of the privileges that he fought and shedded [sic] blood for."[29]

When black editors declined the federal government's request that they cut back on coverage of racial discrimination, FBI Director J. Edgar Hoover tried to prosecute editors like Bates, who continued to report on racially charged issues, on sedition charges. The harassment echoed the black press experience in World War I, when the editor of the *San Antonio Inquirer* was sentenced to two years in prison because a jury agreed that his criticism of the dishonorable discharge of 167 black soldiers in Brownsville, Texas, violated federal Espionage and Sedition Acts.[30]

Federal officials again blamed black newspapers for instigating racial unrest during World War II. Foster's death was one of many racial incidents that flared up between 1942 and 1945, two-thirds of them in the South, site of three-quarters of all military training facilities for African American troops. Black soldiers from the North frequently ran afoul of Jim Crow laws, which southern white authorities enforced with a vengeance.[31] A few weeks after the Foster killing, the *Richmond Times-Dispatch* blamed the NAACP's *Crisis* magazine for encouraging the "bloody encounters" on Southern army bases.[32] The army's Intelligence Division urged camp commanders to "reduce and control the publication of inflammatory and vituperative articles in the colored press."[33] Black newspapers, however, were the only news media that "consistently exposed the racial insults, inferior living conditions, and physical abuse the black soldiers faced," according to Gonzales and Torres.[34] Black editors proclaimed their patriotism but refused to countenance terrorism and segregation. Bates kept readers apprised of the ill treatment accorded black soldiers training in the South, combining reportage with emotional appeals against the injustice. "The city police had a field day beating the Negro soldiers who came into town on weekend passes and who ran afoul of the law," Daisy Bates recalled in her memoir. "The *State Press* printed stories. Citizens protested. Nothing happened."[35]

Bates Battles Police Brutality

A *State Press* editorial a month before Foster's death had warned that "serious trouble could happen here with the black boys in uniform." White MPs patrolling the soldiers could stir conflict "because it is a customary rule for southern police to interfere, regardless to instruction, whenever a Negro and a white man enter in any 'discussion' above a whisper." The chief should instruct city police be more cautious when dealing with soldiers, Bates had warned, especially when they were under the MPs' supervision. Bates republished the column alongside its front-page account of Foster's death. He told readers Foster could have been saved had the chief heeded his advice.[36] Bates pressured Little Rock's black leaders to form a Negro Citizens Committee to investigate Foster's death.

Eight thousand people—one of the largest crowds ever assembled in the small city—gathered at the First Baptist Church to hear the committee's findings. They reported that white and black witnesses confirmed that Hay had stood over Foster and deliberately shot the soldier five times as he lay helpless on the ground. The committee's report also claimed the military police simply looked on as the shooting unfolded and declared as false white press claims that rioting followed the shooting. The *State Press* published the entire speeches of two ministers who wrapped their charges in patriotic rhetoric. "We love America—our blood is in her soil," began Reverend G. Wayman Blakely. "All the Negro desires is justice and fair play." Reverend E. C. Dyer was much more religious, although he departed from Scripture to add, "We will lick the Japs; We will lick the Axis. ... Why waste ammunition on each other?"[37]

"The beastial murder of Sgt. Foster shall never be forgotten," Bates editorialized. An anonymous letter writer advised the editor to keep quiet to avoid "arousing the ire of the white people." Bates responded, "If the killing of an American soldier, without any provocation, didn't arouse the ire of the white man, nothing this paper can say in relating the story, can arouse him."[38] The *State Press* also pledged in the same April 3, 1942, number to support any police efforts to clean up the area "as long as it is done in a manner to gain respect for the law, rather than resentment."[39]

The *State Press* and the NCC secured an unprecedented federal investigation into Foster's death, which concluded the shooting warranted a grand jury investigation into whether to bring murder charges against Hay. The grand jury, however, failed to indict him.[40] *State Press* editorials kept up the pressure until the Little Rock City Council hired its first black police officers in October 1942 to patrol Ninth Street, despite objections from the local police association. Little Rock's white-owned *Arkansas Democrat*, in contrast, claimed the uproar over Foster's death was merely a cover for the black press and the NAACP to "undermine white supremacy on the home front."[41] Nonetheless, the military began to prosecute white police officers that killed black soldiers on the grounds that the soldiers' civil rights had been violated.[42] The *State Press* credited military officials for arresting two Texas policemen later that year on charges of killing a black soldier accused of violating Jim Crow laws.

Bates attributed the arrest to the military's realization "that if Japan and Germany are to be conquered, the south [sic] must be conquered first."[43]

The *State Press* paid a price for its impassioned coverage of Foster's murder, a boycott that Daisy described as the newspaper's "first crippling blow in the struggle for human rights and dignity."[44] Major white advertisers dropped the paper after L.C. declined the Chamber of Commerce's offer "to keep my paper full of ads" in exchange for toning down coverage of Foster's death. He made the bold decision to rely on subscriptions instead of ads for most *State Press* revenue, he recalled in an oral history, and hired two distributors to build up subscriptions statewide. He never solicited white advertisers again.[45] The Bateses worked twelve to eighteen hours a day in their campaign against police brutality, which hit a responsive note. Some smaller white merchants remained loyal, and in months circulation doubled to 20.000. Daisy recalled, "The Negroes supposedly fighting a war in the name of freedom had through our paper found a voice to express their feelings."[46]

Social Justice Journalism: Challenging Segregation

The *State Press* continued to push for racial equality after the war ended, part of a vanguard of post-war protests against Jim Crow laws. L.C. called for desegregated housing as early as 1947, and the couple moved into an all-white neighborhood in the early 1950s. "Nothing can be more foolish, futile, and short-sighted than to begin court action against segregation with the left hand while setting up segregated housing with the right hand," a *State Press* contributor wrote in 1953.[47] The *Press*'s social justice journalism targeted all forms of racial injustice. It protested the poll tax[48] and contested the stereotype of black men as criminals.[49] As Daisy recalled, "It fought to free Negroes from muddy, filthy streets, slum housing, menial jobs, and injustice in the courtrooms."[50] Another early campaign championed paying local black teachers the same as their white counterparts, part of a nationwide NAACP crusade.[51] When *Ebony* magazine solicited black press editors for the headline they would most like to see in 1950, Bates replied: "South Abolishes All Jim Crow."[52] Bates urged *State Press* readers "to keep the pot boiling" for civil rights. He wrote, "It is a sign of weakness to make a demonstration and then allow the enthusiasm to cool off."[53]

The Bateses' challenges to white supremacy provoked legal retaliation. Both Bateses were jailed in 1946 over a front-page article that criticized a judge who sentenced three picketing black strikers to a year in prison.[54] The couple spent seven hours in a cell before their lawyer bailed them out. Convicted on April 29 of publishing articles "to influence, intimidate, impede, embarrass, and obstruct the Pulaski Circuit Court," the Bateses successfully appealed their ten-day jail sentence and $100 fine for contempt of court.[55] The judge's ruling was a significant victory for a free press that reiterated the right to free expression.

The *State Press* challenged school segregation as early as 1947, when it championed black parents in DeWitt, Arkansas, who sued the local school board to integrate schools.[56] A front-page editorial that celebrated a Kentucky court ruling for school integration concluded, "the only way to equalize good education in the South is through integration."[57] The newspaper also protested self-imposed segregation in journalism by supporting a name change from the Negro Newspaper Publishers Association to the National Newspaper Publishers Association, explaining that any division of people based on race promoted exploitation and worse.[58]

By 1952, Bates was editorially campaigning to integrate Little Rock's public institutions.[59] The *State Press* was the only Arkansas newspaper to demand an immediate end to segregated schools following the historic May 1954 ruling in *Brown v. Education*. "We feel that the proper approach would be for the leaders among the Negro race—not clabber mouths, Uncle Toms, or grinning appeasers—to get together and counsel with the school heads," wrote L.C., who was as tough on readers as he was on city officials. "Let the school officials understand that we are going to get a square deal in education."[60]

The next year, L.C. skewered the Supreme Court's vague "with all deliberate speed" order in *Brown II*, which effectively blocked integration by handing over its implementation to southern authorities. "Hi Court Decision Favors Dixie," screamed the week's lead headline.[61] "But we have news for them," a July 15, 1955, editorial announced, "desegregation is COMING and desegregation means a better educational system for America."[62] That evening Bates moved beyond the editorial page to participating in a North Little Rock school board meeting, where he voiced his displeasure with its decision to delay desegregation for two years. He got no reply from a local segregationist leader whom he asked, "How long is it going to take for democracy to start to work?"[63]

Media and the Murder of Emmett Till

Black Mississippians were asking the same question that summer after Emmett Till, a fourteen-year-old Chicago youth visiting relatives in Mississippi, was kidnapped and brutally murdered. The boy's decomposing body was retrieved from the Tallahatchie River on August 31, his head bashed in, one eyeball dangling from its socket. He had been shot behind his left ear. The *New York Times* mentioned the lynching on September 6, 1955, in a three-paragraph Associated Press wire-service item buried on page fifty-two.[64] The buried news brief's placement reflected mainstream media's disinterest in confronting white supremacy in the South. The African American press, write historians Hank Klibanoff and Eugene Roberts, "had the front-row seat during the early dramas, while the white press sat in the balcony, if it came to the performance at all."[65] The Till tragedy changed that. Historian David Halberstam called the teen's lynching the first great media event of the civil rights movement— largely because of photography.[66]

Photographs that appeared only in the black press played a crucial role in elevating the Till tragedy from a statistic to a cause célèbre that sparked the Civil Rights Movement. They were a harbinger of the emotional impact of imagery in the Civil Rights Movement. Emmett's devastated mother, Mamie Till Bradley, insisted authorities return his body to Chicago, where photographers from the *Chicago Defender* and other newspapers followed her to the train station to meet her son's coffin.[67] Mamie insisted on an open casket at the funeral "so everyone can see what they did to my boy."[68] *Jet* magazine's September 15, 1955, issue featuring the horrific close-up photograph of Emmett's bloated, mutilated face immediately sold out, forcing pioneering black magazine mogul John L. Johnson for the first time to reprint an issue to meet demand. Two days later the gruesome image resurfaced on the *Defender*'s front page, followed by eight more images of the funeral attended by thousands.[69] Charles Diggs, a former congressman from Detroit, called the photograph "probably one of the greatest media products in the last forty or fifty years, because that picture stimulated a lot of anger on the part of blacks all over the country."[70]

As Johnson Publications held the rights to the image, it never appeared in mainstream media, but it caught the attention of editors at the nation's biggest newspapers and magazines, who dispatched dozens of white reporters to the five-day trial in Mississippi in September. They joined a dozen veterans of the black press: Johnson sent Simeon Booker for *Jet* and *Ebony*, James L.

Hicks represented the *Baltimore Afro-American* and sister papers in the East, and Moses Newson and Alex Wilson reported for the *Defender*.[71] After some wangling, the black press was allowed to cover the trial from inside the court-room—but only from the spectator section.[72]

When the all-white jury quickly acquitted the two defendants,[73] the *New York Times* pushed the story up to page one, alongside a damning photograph of the grinning defendants and the woman who claimed Till sexually harassed her (falsely, she admitted decades later).[74] The malicious murder that galvanized southern blacks also awakened mainstream news media to the rising antisegregation tide. The *Times* blanketed the South with ten reporters to explore the racial climate, although they proved naively optimistic about the South's openness to integration.[75] On December 1, 1955, Alabaman Rosa Parks's refusal to sit in the "colored" section at the back of a Montgomery bus launched the first mass protest against segregation. The Montgomery bus boycott continued for 381 days until the city integrated transportation on December 20, 1956. The NAACP next set its sights on integrating southern schools.

The *State Press* and the Little Rock Nine

Daisy Bates was elected president of the Arkansas NAACP in 1952, thanks in part to support from the *State Press*, which published countless notices and accounts of NAACP meetings Daisy organized and tirelessly editorialized for integrating Little Rock schools. The newspaper served as the state NAACP's unofficial organ, apprising readers of local integration plans and meetings. The couple saw no conflict in the newspaper's dual roles. Daisy's connections to the *State Press* eventually gave her a unique ability to set the state's civil rights agenda, according to John Lewis Adams's dissertation on the couple. "L.C. displayed a genius and mastery of the written word," Adams observes of their partnership. "Daisy had a gift for speaking them."[76] More than a decade of challenging racial discrimination had prepared the couple for the draining campaign to integrate Little Rock Central High School.

An example of their synergy occurred on January 23, 1956, when Daisy accompanied eight girls and their parents to Central High and asked the principal to register them. He sent her to the school superintendent, who denied the request and then refused to set a date for integration. *State Press* photographer Earl Davy's image of the group in the superintendent's office illustrated that Friday's newspaper front-page story. On February 8, Daisy filed suit in federal district court to desegregate city schools. In August, the *State Press* exploded when a federal judge denied the request. L.C. Bates wrote, "Gradualism in allowing the Negro to exercise his rights, is what the South says, but what the south [sic] means is **NEVER**."[77] According to historian C. Calvin Smith, L.C. plotted most of the following school integration campaign's strategy and tactics but remained in the background to avoid the fate that often awaited "assertive black males who championed unpopular causes."[78]

Yet Daisy's gender failed to protect the Bates from white supremacists. When a burning cross lit up their front lawn on October 11, 1956, private guards stood watch at the Bates home and police stepped up patrols.[79] When a second burning cross appeared on their lawn, L.C. declared in an editorial: "The Negro has had the taste of freedom. ... It is the height of foolishness, for any un-American group to foster any idea that the Negro will stop now at the mere burning of crosses, burning and bombing of homes, and with an occasional slaying."[80] He rarely slept over the next two years, and carried a pistol at all times.[81] The Bateses' home was even bombed in 1959.[82] Largely due to the Bateses' agitation, the school board finally agreed to allow nine Negro teenagers to enroll at Central under a two-year plan beginning on September 3, 1957. Daisy helped choose and mentor the honor-roll students who comprised the Little Rock Nine. Two weeks before the opening day of school, she was reading in the living room when a large rock crashed through the window. She threw herself on the floor and picked up the rock, entwined in a scrawled note that read: "STONE THIS TIME. DYNAMITE NEXT."[83] Years later she explained that the couple resolved to continue because if they had fled, "the movement would have died."[84]

On September 2, Arkansas Governor Orval Faubus announced on television he was calling out the Arkansas National Guard to surround the high school, which he declared would bar the African American students, a move decried not only by the *State Press* but also by Little Rock's mayor and both white-owned daily newspapers.[85] Faubus's move, widely denounced as political grandstanding, put Little Rock on the national news agenda. The next day a federal judge ordered that desegregation proceed the next morning. White protestors from across the state converged on Little Rock.

The stars of the black press also gathered in Little Rock, including Till trial veterans Newson, Hicks, and Wilson. Ethel Payne, the popular Washington correspondent of the *Chicago Defender*, pulled no punches in her first-person dispatches. She couldn't find a decent restaurant that served African

Americans, and the white couple that served her dinner were evicted from their apartment. "Little Rock to me is about the crummiest corner on the map," she told readers.[86] The Bateses put up visiting black reporters in their home, where they joined in strategy sessions around the Bates dining table, comfortable both covering the story and being part of it. They also mingled with the students who frequented the Bates home.[87] Ted Poston, an African American reporter for the *New York Post*, profiled each of the nine throughout fall 1957. The public only heard the students' voices by reading the *State Press*, since Daisy sheltered them from the white-dominated mainstream media.[88]

National television network news crews also descended on Little Rock, the first time the broadcast technology played a role in a social movement. 1957 marked a media milestone when the number of American homes with televisions—forty-one million—surpassed that of homes receiving a daily newspaper—thirty-nine million.[89] Scenes of hundreds of angry whites that caravanned from across Arkansas shocked Americans outside the state who witnessed the ugly mob on television screens from the safety of their living rooms. Television delivered the moral shock of seeing the violence and hatred that cell phones would later deliver in citizen videos of police shootings of unarmed black men. The Little Rock standoff dominated national print and broadcast media through September.[90] Although the confrontation's ugliness was unanticipated, the moral suasion of witnessing the abuse of innocent black children by hate-spewing white people would continue at the heart of the Reverend Martin Luther King Jr.'s media strategy, as when the world saw police dogs sic peaceful teens in Birmingham or assault marchers on Selma's Bloody Sunday. Halberstam called King the "dramatist of a national morality play."[91]

Cameras were ready to roll on the morning of September 4, when parents delivered the Little Rock Nine to the Bateses' home, so they could ride together to Central, accompanied by several black and white ministers. But Daisy had overlooked informing fifteen-year-old Elizabeth Eckford of the meeting place because her family had no telephone. Soon after Elizabeth stepped off a bus she rode to school, the mob surrounded the lone teenager outside Central. "Lynch her!" someone shouted. "Send that nigger back to the jungle!" Ira Wilber "Will" Counts, a twenty-six-year-old photographer for the daily *Arkansas Democrat*, felt sorry for Eckford but kept snapping his camera shutter. Before Elizabeth escaped on a bus escorted by Grace Lorch—the same white woman who cooked Payne dinner—Counts captured the image of a clenched-teethed Hazel Bryan, also fifteen, screaming from behind at

Eckford.[92] The newspaper hit the streets that afternoon with Counts's dramatic image at the bottom of the front page. The photograph stirred emotions globally when the Associated Press flashed the image around the world. A century from now, Langston Hughes posited in a *Chicago Defender* essay, this "one lone little Negro girl" would matter more than any other player in the drama.[93] The remaining eight black teens also retreated later that morning from the mob scene outside the school. Hundreds of national reporters remained in the city as the standoff between Faubus and federal officials continued over the next two weeks. Little Rock was the *New York Times*'s lead story twenty-three of twenty-five days from September 5 through September 29.[94] The National Guard left on September 20, hours after a federal judge enjoined Faubus from misusing the troops.

Three days later the Little Rock Nine finally entered the high school, evading a mob of about a thousand people.[95] The mob remained so threatening that the students had to be escorted home before lunchtime. The riots so infuriated President Dwight Eisenhower he ordered more than a thousand National Guardsmen to Little Rock the next day—this time to protect the students. The Little Rock Nine, escorted by the troops, finished the school year despite constant harassment and threats inside Central's walls and petitions and lawsuits outside. CBS News aired an unprecedented thirty-minute report on Little Rock, which featured correspondent Howard K. Smith's on-the-scene summary, commentary by Eric Sevareid and Walter Cronkite, and a video clip of an attack on Newson and his colleagues.[96] Mainstream news media subsumed black newspapers' coverage of the race beat they had pioneered. L.C. Bates's decade-long crusade to integrate city schools seemed to have succeeded.

Aftermath

The national press moved to the next big civil rights stories—Freedom Riders, March on Washington, Selma, Watts, King's assassination in Memphis. L.C. Bates continued to play both watchdog over the government and mentor to the students. "He made us all feel that what we were about had long-range implications," remembered Ernest Green, one of the Little Rock Nine.[97] Faubus, however, closed all Little Rock schools in 1958. The entire school board resigned. That July a bomb carved a small crater in the Bateses' front lawn.[98] A federal appeals court eventually overturned Faubus's school-closing order, and city schools continued their uneven lurch toward integration.[99] The now-defunct *Arkansas Gazette* won two Pulitzer Prizes for its critical news coverage and editor Harry Ashmore's salient editorials, easing the sting of canceled advertising accounts and a dip in circulation.[100]

No Pulitzer awaited the *State Press*, which, unlike the big daily, could not withstand another advertising boycott. All city and state ads disappeared, and circulation plummeted to 5,000. The landlord cancelled the *State Press*'s lease. Bates blamed Faubus: "Arkansas' Governor entered the picture in 1957 and used his executive powers to destroy the *Press* and his police force used gestapo methods to prevent news agents from handling the paper, and when the paper was barred from the school rooms as well as most of the communities, the circulation among both white and colored dwindled considerably."[101] The newspaper rolled off the press for the last time on October 30, 1959—a "survivor of terror but victim of boycott"—as one chronicler rued.[102] Daisy Bates became a hero of the Civil Rights Movement, but the significance of fifteen years of the *State Press*'s social justice journalism in setting the stage for integrating Little Rock schools has been largely overlooked. The Civil Rights Movement that Bates spearheaded in the *State Press* helped nailed the coffin of official segregation, although much work remained.[103] L.C. Bates continued campaigning as an NAACP field representative until 1972. Feted for his contributions in 1977, the seventy-six-year-old retired editor told the audience, "The days of getting mad are over. Now is the time to get smart so that some day, we may be able to say not that we shall overcome, but that we HAVE overcome."[104]

#Black Lives Matter

Police shootings of unarmed black men in the 2010s demonstrated the distance that remained for African Americans to overcome racial injustice. Like the *State Press* a half century earlier, Black Lives Matter protested police violence and rallied resistors. Social media performed the role performed by the *State Press* and other black newspapers during the Civil Rights Movement. The hashtag germinated in July 2013 from activist Alicia Garza's distraught Facebook post after a Florida jury acquitted George Zimmerman of murdering Trayvon Martin—like Till, another unarmed black teenager. A friend condensed one of Garza's musings—"I continue to be surprised at how little Black lives matter"—into #BlackLivesMatter. Another friend created Tumblr and platforms for the hashtag. Black Lives Matter exploded into a new Civil

Rights Movement following eighteen-year-old Michael Brown's shooting death by police in Ferguson, Missouri, on August 9, 2014, fueled by activist DeRay Mckesson's live-tweeting from Ferguson.

Technology defined this new kind of social movement. The smartphone had the unintended effect of democratizing technology by bringing cheap Internet access to poor communities. The Internet became "something of a cradle for black culture and black causes," reports journalist Jeff Guo, "connecting far-flung communities and amplifying activist voices."[105] Twitter's discourse conventions, ubiquity, and social features especially appealed to black users, according to technoculture scholar André Brock, fueling astronomical growth of black online communities collectively known as Black Twitter, a new "social public" that Brock says is "Twitter's mediation of Black cultural discourse. ..."[106] Black Lives Matter did not spring out of nowhere but grew out of this phenomenon through the power of a single hashtag.

The speed and reach of that technology makes BLM very different from the original Civil Rights Movement in which L.C. Bates's weekly newspaper played a role. While a single Mckesson tweet told the world where the next Ferguson protest was assembling, in 1955 Ann Robinson of the all-black Women's Political Council in Montgomery spent hours using a hand-driven mimeograph machine to crank out more than 52,000 leaflets to announce a mass protest after Rosa Parks's arrest.[107] Journalist Bijan Stephen says there is no comparison between the speed of live tweeting in Ferguson and the complicated WATS telephone service that the Student Nonviolent Coordinating Committee used in the 1960s to alert protesters and the public of arrests, violence, or brewing actions. In the 2010s, Ferguson activists disseminated their message on numerous platforms, including Vine, Instagram, Facebook, Periscope, GroupMe, SMS, WhatsApp, and Twitter.

Social media also are powerful social movement tools because they can document, distribute, and challenge episodes of police brutality against people of color in mainstream media.[108] Just weeks before Brown died, a cell-phone video of a dying Eric Garner went viral, showing the Staten Island man whispering, "I can't breathe," eleven times while police held him in a lethal chokehold. Garner's dying words became a totemic rallying call for protestors.[109] "The tools that we have to organize and to resist are fundamentally different than anything that's existed before in black struggle," Mckesson reflects.[110] *Dissent* magazine observes that Twitter empowered Mckesson to frame events and direct the actions of hundreds of thousands of people across the nation. The intense reporting on police brutality via social media also influenced mainstream print and television coverage, multiplying attention to such incidents.

A "Hybrid, Journo-Activist Space"

New media scholar Adrienne Russell sees the #BLM hashtag not only as a tool to tag, aggregate, and mobilize but more importantly as a way to connect individual incidents of police violence in a way that illuminates larger structural problems that undergird institutionalized racism.[111] One study described #Ferguson as a "hybrid, journo-activist space" that demonstrated the ongoing shift toward more hybrid reporting practices and greater interaction between professional journalists and members of the public.[112] Smartphones also enable citizens to challenge media stereotyping and mainstream narratives of black protest. After news outlets published an intimidating photograph of Brown flashing an alleged gang sign, thousands of millennial African Americans took up the hashtag #IfTheyGunnedMeDown to tweet juxtaposing positive and "thug" images of themselves, asking which image media would choose to portray them.[113]

One of McKesson's impassioned followers was data analyst Sinyangwe. Like Ida Wells-Barnett more than a century before him, Sinyangwe possessed great faith in the power of facts to expose state-sanctioned violence against black men. With fellow #BLM activist Johnetta Elzie, the twenty-five-year-old Stanford graduate began the gargantuan task of collating all necessary statistical information on police killings nationwide. They input core data from the three largest crowd-sourced databases on police killings and augmented them by searching social media, obituaries, criminal records databases, police reports, and other sources to identify 91 percent of victims' race. The result is a high-tech combination of Wells-Barnett's research and Bates's front-page exposés.

The website's interactive map allows users to obtain information about police shootings, and graphs and charts shows national trends and compare statistics between cities or states. The site also explains its methodology, consistent with the digital activist creed of transparency. Mapping Police Violence computed that police killed at least 1,149 people in 2014, and that 304 of these—26 percent—were black. At least 101 were unarmed, and data showed black people were nearly three times as likely as white people to be killed by police. Sinyangwe also posted stories and photos of unarmed victims killed by police, augmenting the emotional power of his shocking statistics. "We have been holding a mirror up to the nation," Sinyangwe said. Other media outlets established similar police shooting databases, but in 2018 only one was still active, the *Washington Post*'s Fatal Force.[114] Mapping Police Violence uses the data journalism that Russell calls a "new public information system infrastructure."[115]

New technology also raises new concerns for activists. The same technology that makes smartphones such excellent organizing tools also makes them susceptible to government surveillance.[116] In 2017, *Foreign Policy* disclosed an FBI memo that labeled BLM activists as "black identity extremists" who posed a dangerous domestic terror threat, particularly to police officers. Color of Change and the Center for Constitutional Rights sued the FBI and Department of Homeland Security to obtain records on the surveillance of Black Lives Matters protests and its leaders. McKesson said the memo harkened the FBI's dark legacy of illegal surveillance and harassment of civil rights leaders in the 1960s.[117] Racists and misogynists also tweet, and people of color and women routinely are harassed and threatened online.[118] At least twenty-nine known Russian trolls tweeted to stoke fear about Black Lives Matter in their campaign to disrupt the 2016 election.[119] And while Black Lives Matters's outsider status allowed it to shape the dialogue surrounding race and criminal justice, *New Yorker* writer Jelani Cobb argues it also raised questions about the limits of online activism.[120]

BLM succeeded on a number of levels. The city of Ferguson replaced a slate of leaders, and body cameras became mandatory for police officers across the country. After a white supremacist murdered nine black worshippers in a Charleston church in 2015, BLM online activists helped push the state of South Carolina to remove the Confederate flag from its Capitol building. Dozens of loosely affiliated BLM chapters surfaced across North America, and BLM collective action put state-backed police violence against blacks on the political agenda. *Yes! Magazine* chose #BlackLivesMatter as one of the twelve hashtags that changed the world in 2014.

Four years later, the lasting influence of hashtag-fueled Black Lives Matter is less clear. Social media have proven tremendously effective in facilitating one-time protests or short-term campaigns, but they are so new they lack a track record for effecting lasting social change. Conventional wisdom says BLM's intentionally leaderless movement and emphasis on grassroots local action also mitigates against building a strong collective identity. Its exponential growth posed challenges for BLM, compounded by the 2016 election results. Widespread concerns about the Trump White House overshadowed BLM,[121] and it was just one of many diffuse social justice movements subsumed into a broad "Trump Resistance."[122] BLM's blueprint for change seems elusive even though its Twitter account continues to host a dynamic discourse on police violence and institutional racism as well as updates on grassroots direct actions. BLM co-founder Patrisse Cullors believes its next move will be into electoral politics.[123]

Ferguson activists Mckesson, Sinyangwe, and Brittney Packett began to move beyond direct action into public policy. They created "We the Protesters," an umbrella website dedicated to a broadly defined "movement of radical liberation" by offering tools and resources to anyone interested in fighting injustice. It is pointedly a website, not a social movement organization. It does not mention Black Lives Matter. Besides Mapping Police Violence, the site is host to Campaign Zero, which takes a public policy approach to effecting change and offers toolkits for signs and slogans. The site states, "This will never replace the pace and power of Twitter, the flow of Tumblr, or the grace of Instagram—social media has sustained the movement."[124]

Notes

1. "CITY PATROLMAN SHOOTS NEGRO SOLDIER," *State Press*, March 27, 1942, 1. [capital letters in original]
2. Grif Stockley, *Ruled by Race: Black/White Relations in Arkansas from Slavery to the Present* (Fayetteville: University of Arkansas Press, 2012), 236. See also John A. Kirk, *Redefining the Color Line: Black Activism in Little Rock, Arkansas, 1940–1970* (Gainesville: University Press of Florida, 2002), 42–46.
3. Ida B. Wells, *Southern Horrors: Lynch Law in All Its Phases* (New York: The New York Age Print, 1892), accessed October 29, 2018, https://www.gutenberg.org/files/14975/14975-h/14975-h.htm.
4. See Amy Louise Wood, *Lynching and Spectacle: Witnessing Racial Violence in America, 1890–1940* (Chapel Hill: University of North Carolina Press, 2009).
5. Wells, *Southern Horrors*.
6. Ibid. In 2015, the Equal Justice Initiative documented 4,084 "racial terror lynchings" in twelve southern states between 1877 and 1950. Another 341 African Americans were lynched in other states. See Bryan Stevenson, "Introduction," in *Lynching in America: Confronting the Legacy of Racial Terror*, 3rd ed. (Montgomery, Alabama: Equal Justice Initiative, 2015), https://lynchinginamerica.eji.org/report/.
7. David T. Z. Mindich, "Balance: A 'Slanderous and Nasty-Minded Mulatress,' Ida B. Wells, Confronts 'Objectivity' in the 1890s," in *Just the Facts: How "Objectivity" Came to Define American Journalism* (New York: New York University Press, 1998), 113–34.

8. Irene Wassell, "L.C. Bates: Editor of the *Arkansas State Press*," (MA Thesis, University of Arkansas at Little Rock, 1983), 10.

9. *Arkansas Gazette*, May 4, 1927, 1.

10. Wassell, "L. C. Bates," 11.

11. John Lewis Adams, "'Time for a Showdown': The Partnership of Daisy and L. C. Bates, and the Politics of Gender, Protest and Marriage," (PhD diss., Rutgers University, 2014), 180. The *State Press* Editorial Page Mission Statement stated: "When we live in peace and harmony with one another—irrespectively of race, color, creed, former servitude or present position in life, without mythical tolerance, but in spirit of Good Will assured in the conviction of our better judgment that we will remit to every man the indomitable rights to the admonition of his own conscience in what ever line of endeavor he pursues for his religious or material existence. When that day arrives we will be contented. Then, we all can boast of our CIVILIZATION. And not until then." "*THE DAY WE HOPE FOR*," *State Press*, May 9, 1941, 4. [capital letters, italics in original]

12. Wassell, "L.C. Bates," 1.

13. "I Give It as I Get It," *State Press*, May 9, 1941, 4.

14. "Sabotage and the Negro," *State Press*, May 16, 1941, 4.

15. "The Plight of the Worker," ibid.

16. "'Cop' Kicks Woman: Unaware of Policeman's Herding Orders—Kicked," *State Press*, September 26, 1941, 1.

17. Adams, "Showdown," 172.

18. Patrick S. Washburn, *The African American Newspaper: Voice of Freedom* (Evanston: Northwestern University Press, 2006), 177.

19. Lewis H. Fenderson, "The Negro Press as a Social Instrument," *The Journal of Negro Education* 20, no. 2 (Spring 1951): 181.

20. See Jacqueline Bacon, "The History of *Freedom's Journal*," *Journal of African American History* 88, no. 1 (Winter 2003): 2–5; and Juan Gonzalez and Joseph Torres, *News for All the People: The Epic Story of Race and the American Media* (New York: Verso Books, 2011), 111–12.

21. Roland Edgar Wolseley, *The Black Press, U.S.A.* 2nd ed. (Ames, IA: Iowa State University Press, 1990), xv.

22. See "Missed Deadline: The Delayed Promise of Newsroom Diversity," Voices, Asian American Journalism Association, accessed October 29. 2018, https://voices.aaja.org/index/2017/7/25/missed-deadlines; and "More Than Three Decades of Commitment to Diversity," American Society of Newspaper Editors, accessed February 25, 2018, http://asne.org/content.asp?pl=28&contentid=28.

23. See Ethan Michaeli, "The Great Northern Drive," in *The Defender: How the Legendary Black Newspaper Changed America* (New York: Houghton Mifflin Harcourt, 2016), 61–79.

24. "How the *Chicago Defender* Became a National Voice for Black Americans," *Daily Herald*, February 10, 2018, http://www.dailyherald.com/news/20180210/how-the-chicago-defender-became-a-national-voice-for-black-americans.

25. See Glen L. Bleske, "Agenda for Equality: Heavy-hitting Sportswriter Wendell Smith," *Media History Digest* 13 (Fall–Winter 1993): 38–42; and David K. Wiggins, "Wendell K.

Smith, the *Pittsburgh Courier-Journal* and the Campaign to Include Blacks in Organized Baseball, 1933–1945," *Journal of Sports History* 10, no. 2 (Summer 1983): 5–29.

26. See Gerald Horne, *The Rise and Fall of the Associated Negro Press: Claude Barnett's Pan-African News and the Jim Crow Paradox* (Urbana: University of Chicago Press, 2017).

27. Armistead S. Pride, "The *Arkansas State Press*: Squeezed to Death," *Grassroots Editor* 2, no. 1 (January 1962): 6. John H. Johnson's publishing empire began with the *Negro Digest* (later *Black World*) in November 1942, followed by *Ebony* (1945), *Jet* (1951), and others. See John H. Johnson, *Succeeding Against The Odds* (Chicago: Johnson Publishing, 1989).

28. Matthew Delmont, "Why African-American Soldiers Saw World War II as a Two-Front Battle," *Smithsonian*, August 24, 2017, https://www.smithsonianmag.com/history/why-african-american-soldiers-saw-world-war-ii-two-front-battle-180964616/.

29. "The Inevitable Is in Evidence," *State Press*, December 12, 1941, 1.

30. Patrick S. Washburn, *A Question of Sedition: The Federal Government's Investigation of the Black Press During World War II* (New York: New York University Press, 1986), 66–91. The *Courier* appropriated President Franklin Roosevelt's Double V campaign to win the war and the election. Regarding the Brownsville case see ibid., 15–18.

31. C. Calvin Smith, *War and Wartime Changes: The Transformation of Arkansas 1940–1945* (Fayetteville: University of Arkansas Press, 1986), 81.

32. Editorial, "The Negroes and the War," *Richmond Times-Dispatch*, April 26, 1942, 6.

33. Quoted in Daniel Kryder, *Divided Arsenal: Race and the American State During World War II* (New York: Columbia University Press, 2001), 143.

34. Gonzalez and Torres, *News for All the People*, 268.

35. Daisy Bates, *The Long Shadow of Little Rock: A Memoir* (New York: David McKay, 1962), 34–35.

36. "Note," *State Press*, March 27, 1942, 1.

37. "Eight Thousand Gather for Committee's Report," *State Press*, April 3, 1942, 1; Rev. G. Wayman Blakely, "We Want to Fight for our Country: But We Want to Fight as Free Men," *State Press*, April 3, 1942, 6; and Rev. E. C. Dyer, "Be Not Deceived; God Is Not Mocked," ibid.

38. "You Are Asking Too Much," *State Press* April 3, 1942, 4.

39. "Clean up Ninth Street," *State Press* April 3, 1942, 4.

40. "U.S. Grand Jury Failed to Turn True Bill Against Hay," *State Press*, June 12, 1942, 1.

41. Kirk, *Redefining the Color Line*, 50–51; and "Run of the News," *Arkansas Democrat*, March 23, 1942, 8.

42. Smith, *War and Wartime Changes*, 85.

43. "Remember Pearl Harbor," *State Press*, August 21, 1942, 4.

44. Bates, *The Long Shadow*, 36.

45. Wassell, "L.C. Bates," 20–22.

46. Bates, *The Long Shadow*, 37.

47. S. S. Taylor, "How to Increase and Perpetuate Segregation—," *State Press*, June 26, 1953, 4.

48. "MAY GOD HELP THEM!," *State Press*, August 7, 1942, 4. [capital letters in original] See also "Louisiana Negroes to Polls Despite Legislators' Threats" and "NAACP Starts Action on Negro Disfranchisement," both ibid., 1.

49. See "Prowlers, Negro and the Police" and "The Irony of Southern Justice," *State Press*, both November 14, 1947, 1.

50. Bates, *Long Shadow*, 38.

51. "Little Rock Teachers File Suit: Equalization in Salaries Sought," *State Press*, March 6, 1942, 1. See also "Teachers' Salary Case Filed in New Orleans," *State Press*, May 23, 1941, 1; "Chattanooga Adopts Scale for Teachers Salaries," *State Press*, October 3, 1941, 1; "N.A.A.C.P. Starts Court Action for Teachers in Eight States," *State Press*, December 5, 1941, 1; "Atlanta Threatens Teachers Who Sue for Equal Pay," *State Press*, January 2, 1942, 1; "Va. School Board Gives in on Equal Salary for Teachers," *State Press*, January 16, 1942, 1; "L.R. Teacher's Assn. Rewarded," *State Press*, April 21, 1942, 1; and "Teacher Salary Suit to Be Tried: Set for Sept. 15 in Federal Court," *State Press*, May 22, 1942, 1.

52. Quoted in Gene Roberts and Hank Klibanoff, *The Race Beat: The Press, The Civil Rights Struggle, and the Awakening of a Nation* (New York: Alfred A. Knopf, 2006), 150.

53. "Keep the Pot Boiling," *State Press*, May 16, 1941, 4.

54. "Strikers Sentenced to Pen by Hand-Picked Jury," *State Press*, March 29, 1946, 1.

55. *Bates v. State of Arkansas*, 197 S.W. 2d 45.

56. Samuel S. Taylor, "A Jump Ahead or a Jump Back?," *State Press*, July 15, 1949, 4. See also "Negroes Offered Little Hope in Dewitt School Case," ibid., 1. The parents technically won but the court tepidly suggested the state make schools equal in "a reasonable time." *Pitts v. Board of Trustees of the DeWitt Special School District*, 84 F. Supp. 975, 989 (E.D. Ark., 1949).

57. "Let's Keep Them Squirming," *State Press*, April 8, 1949, 1.

58. Robert Durr, "Don't Fight and Kiss Same Thing—," *State Press*, September 14, 1951, 4.

59. "When You Can't See for Looking … ," *State Press*, October 3, 1952, 4.

60. "After the Court's Decision—Now What?," *State Press*, May 21, 1954, 4.

61. "Hi Court Decision Favors Dixie," *State Press*, June 3, 1955, 1.

62. "And Now They Holler," *State Press*, July 15, 1955, 4.

63. "White America Meets Negro and Here's What They Said," *Arkansas Gazette*, July 16, 1955, 3.

64. "Report on Slaying Due," *New York Times*, September 6, 1955, 52.

65. Wil Haygood, "Story of Their Lives for Reporters on the Civil Rights Beat, the Trick Was to Cover the News, Not Be It," *Washington Post*, November 26, 2006, https://www.washingtonpost.com/archive/lifestyle/2006/11/26/story-of-their-lives-span-classbankheadfor-reporters-on-the-civil-rights-beat-the-trick-was-to-cover-the-news-not-be-itspan/7d408efe-ffca-40c8-a3b9-baa3746a1f33/?utm_term=.bdd566db4127.

66. Quoted in Shaila Dewan, "How Photos Became Icon of Civil Rights Movement," *New York Times*, August 28, 2005, http://www.nytimes.com/2005/08/28/us/how-photos-became-icon-of-civil-rights-movement.html.

67. "Grieving Mother Meets Body of Lynched Son," *Chicago Defender*, September 10, 1955, 5.

68. John Barrow, "Here's a Picture of Emmett Till Painted by Those who Knew Him," *Chicago Defender*, October 1, 1955, 4.

69. "Emmett Till Funeral Saddens City, Nation," *Chicago Defender*, September 17, 1955, 1, 4. See also editorial, "Blood On Their Hands … ," *Chicago Defender*, September 10, 1955, 1. For more on *Defender* coverage, see Michaeli, *The Defender*, 323–32.

70. "(Part 1) Awakenings 1954–1956," *Eyes on the Prize: America's Civil Rights Years, 1954–1965* (Washington, D.C.: PBS, 1987).

71. See Simeon Booker, "To Be a 'Negro' Newsman—Reporting on the Emmett Till Murder Trial," *Nieman Reports*, September 7, 2011, http://niemanreports.org/articles/to-be-a-negro-newsman-reporting-on-the-emmett-till-murder-trial/.

72. See *The Untold Story of Emmett Louis Till*, (New York: Velocity/ThinkFilm, 2005).

73. *Look* magazine paid the two men $4,000 to recount the murder. See Bob Ward, "William Bradford Huie Paid for Their Sins," *Writer's Digest*, September 1974, 16–22; and William Bradford Huie, "The Shocking Story of Approved Killing in Mississippi," *Look*, January 24, 1956, 46–50.

74. John Popham, "Mississippi Jury Acquits 2 Accused in Youth's Killing," *New York Times*, September 24, 1955, 1, 38. See also Timothy B. Tyson, *The Blood of Emmett Till* (New York: Simon & Schuster, 2017); and "Woman Linked to 1955 Emmett Till Murder Tells Historian Her Claims Were False," *New York Times*, January 29, 2017, A13.

75. Klibanoff and Roberts, *Race Beat*, 110–12.

76. Adams, "Time for a Showdown," 22.

77. "Gradualism, Moderation or Never—Which does the South Want?," *State Press*, September 7, 1956, 4. [boldface, capital letters in original]

78. C. Calvin Smith, "From 'Separate but Equal to Desegregation': The Changing Philosophy of L. C. Bates,"*Arkansas Historical Quarterly* 42, no. 3 (Autumn 1983): 266.

79. "Burn Cross on Publishers' Lawn: Symbol of Old KKK 'Death Warning,'" *State Press*, October 19, 1956, 1.

80. "Burning Crosses Is Not Going to Stop the Negro's Fight for His Freedom," *State Press*, November 2, 1956, 1.

81. Bates, *Long Shadow*, 94.

82. "'Arkansas-Protected' Hoodlums' Attempt to Destroy the Bateses Fails When Bomb Misses Target," *State Press*, July 17, 1995, 8.

83. Bates, *Long Shadow*, 4.

84. "Oral History Interview with Daisy Bates," interview by Elizabeth Jacoway, October 11, 1976, Southern Oral History Program Collection, electronic ed., http://docsouth.unc.edu/sohp/G-0009/G-0009.html.

85. Benjamin Fine, "Militia Sent to Little Rock; School Integration Put Off," *New York Times*, September 3, 1957, 1.

86. James McGrath Morris, *Eye on the Struggle: Ethel Payne, the First Lady of the Black Press* (New York: Armistad, 2015), 211–12.

87. "L.C. Bates: Little Rock's Forgotten Man," *Jet*, June 4, 1959, 13.

88. Roberts and Klibanoff, *Race Beat*, 174.

89. Ibid., 156.

90. Hoyt Hughes Purvis claims the national press reporters provoked and set up inflammatory crowd reactions. Hoyt Hughes Purvis, "Little Rock and the Press," (MA Thesis, University of Texas, 1963), 36–41.

91. David Halberstam, *The Fifties* (New York: Fawcett Columbine, 1994), 691.

92. David Margolick, "Through a Lens, Darkly," *Vanity Fair*, September 24, 2007, http://www.vanityfair.com/news/2007/09/littlerock200709.

93. Ibid. Counts photographed Bryan and Eckford together at the 1997 anniversary in front of the high school. See Ira Wilmer Counts, *A Life is More than a Moment, 50th Anniversary: The Desegregation of Little Rock's Central High School* (Bloomington: Indiana University Press, 2005). Eckford reportedly never forgave Daisy Bates for forgetting her that morning; see Margolick, "Through a Lens Darkly."

94. Guardsmen threatened to arrest reporters covering the controversy on incitement charges. Benjamin Fine, "Guardsmen Curb Newsmen's Work," *New York Times*, September 6, 1957, 8.

95. See Hank Klibanoff, "L. Alex Wilson: A Reporter Who Refused to Run," *Media Studies Journal* 14, no. 2 (Spring/Summer 2000): 60–68. Wilson began suffering neurological symptoms similar to those of Parkinson's disease soon after he was promoted to editor of the *Chicago Defender*. He died at fifty-one on October 11, 1960. His widow blamed blows to his head with a brick he received in Little Rock. Dylan Lovan, "Widow Believes Husband Died in Pursuit of Cause," *Jackson Sun*, accessed November 17, 2018, http://orig.jacksonsun.com/civilrights/sec6_widow_wilson.shtml.

96. Jack Gould, "TV: President Speaks," *New York Times*, September 25, 1957, 59.

97. "One of 'Little Rock Nine' Eulogizes Rights of Leader; Carter Letter Read," *Arkansas Gazette*, August 28, 1980, 6-A, 1.

98. "L.C. Bates Dies at Age 79, Pursued Equal Treatment for Races in State: Home Bombed," *Arkansas Gazette*, August 24, 1980, 15A.

99. "How They Beat Faubus," *New Republic*, June 8, 1959, 7–8. Faubus was re-elected three times.

100. For examples of *Gazette* coverage, see Purvis, "Little Rock and the Press," 46–51.

101. Pride, "Squeezed to Death," 7.

102. Ibid. Daisy tried but failed to revive the *State Press* in 1984. She sold her interest in the paper in 1988 to Darryl Lunon and Janis Kearney Lunon, who continued to publish it until 1997.

103. John A. Kirk, ed., *An Epitaph for Little Rock: A Fiftieth Anniversary Retrospective on the Central High Crisis* (Fayetteville: University of Arkansas Press, 2010), 121.

104. *Arkansas Gazette*, February 20, 1977, 3-A.

105. Jeff Guo, "What People Don't Get About Black Twitter," *Washington Post*, October 22, 2015, https://www.washingtonpost.com/news/wonk/wp/2015/10/22/why-it-can-be-offensive-to-use-the-term-black-twitter/?utm_term=.401fc2d07ab4.

106. André Brock, "From the Blackhand Side: Twitter as a Cultural Conversation," *Journal of Broadcasting & Electronic Media* 56, no. 4 (2012): 530.

107. Fredrick C. Harris, "The Next Civil Rights Movement?," *Dissent*, Summer 2015, https://www.dissentmagazine.org/article/black-lives-matter-new-civil-rights-movement-fredrick-harris.

108. Yarimar Bonilla and Jonathan Rosa, "#Ferguson: Digital Protest, Hashtag Ethnography, and the Racial Politics of Social Media in the United States," *American Ethnologist* 42, no.1 (January 2015): 4–17.

109. A grand jury declined to indict the officer who choked Garner, but the city settled a wrongful death suit with his family. See J. David Goodman, "Eric Garner Case Is Settled by New York City for $5.9 Million," *New York Times*, July 13, 2015, https://www.nytimes.

com/2015/07/14/nyregion/eric-garner-case-is-settled-by-new-york-city-for-5-9-million. html?smid=pl-share.

110. Bijan Stephen, "Get Up, STAND UP: Social Media Helps Black Lives Matter Fight the Power," *WIRED*, November 2015, https://www.wired.com/2015/10/how-black-lives-matter-uses-social-media-to-fight-the-power/.

111. Adrienne Russell, *Journalism as Activism: Recoding Media Power* (Cambridge: Polity Press, 2016), 86.

112. Stephen R. Barnard, "Tweeting #Ferguson: Mediatized Fields and the New Activist Journalist," *New Media & Society* 20, no. 7 (July 2017): 2252–71.

113. Jacqueline Schiappa, "#IfTheyGunnedMeDown: The Necessity of 'Black Twitter' and Hashtags in the Age of Ferguson," *ProudFlesh: New Afrikan Journal of Culture, Politics and Consciousness*, no. 10 (2014), http://www.africaknowledgeproject.org/index.php/proudflesh/article/view/214.

114. The British *Guardian* newspaper in 2015 launched an investigative project, The Counted, although data ends with December 2016. *VICE News* analyzed data from 2010–2016. "Police Shootings: Collect the Data," *VICE News*, December 10, 2017, https://news.vice.com/en_us/article/a3jjpa/nonfatal-police-shootings-data; *Deadspin's* research covered 2011–2013. "Police Shootings Database," *Deadspin*, latest update October 27, 2014, https://deadspin.com/tag/police-shootings-database.

115. Russell, *Journalism as Activism*, 115.

116. See Craig Timberg, "In Trump's America, Black Lives Matter Activists Grow Wary of their Smartphones," *Washington Post*, June 1, 2017, https://www.washingtonpost.com/business/technology/fearing-surveillance-in-the-age-of-trump-activists-study-up-on-digital-anonymity/2017/05/20/186e8ba0-359d-11e7-b4ee-434b6d506b37_story.html?utm_term=.3bd2359f94d5; and Brandon E. Patterson, "Police Spied on New York Black Lives Matter Group, Internal Police Documents Show," *Mother Jones*, October 19, 2017, https://www.motherjones.com/crime-justice/2017/10/police-spied-on-new-york-black-lives-matter-group-internal-police-documents-show/.

117. Jana Winter and Sharon Weinberger, "The FBI's New U.S. Terrorist Threat: 'Black Identity Extremists,'" *Foreign Policy*, October 6, 2017, http://foreignpolicy.com/2017/10/06/the-fbi-has-identified-a-new-domestic-terrorist-threat-and-its-black-identity-extremists/.

118. Maeve Duggan, "1 in 4 Black Americans Have Faced Online Harassment Because of Their Race or Ethnicity," *Pew Research Center*, July 25, 2017, http://www.pewresearch.org/fact-tank/2017/07/25/1-in-4-black-americans-have-faced-online-harassment-because-of-their-race-or-ethnicity/.

119. Kanyakrit Vongkiatkajorn, "How Russia Exploited Black Lives Matter, Sean Hannity, and Mass Shootings," *Mother Jones*, February 17, 2018, https://www.motherjones.com/politics/2018/02/how-russia-exploited-black-lives-matter-sean-hannity-and-mass-shootings/.

120. Jelani Cobb, "The Matter of Black Lives," *New Yorker*, March 14, 2016, https://www.newyorker.com/magazine/2016/03/14/where-is-black-lives-matter-headed. See also Stefania Milan, "When Algorithms Shape Collective Action: Social Media and the Dynamics of Cloud Protesting," *Social Media + Society* 1, no. 2 (July-December 2015): 6.

121. Michael Harriott, "Whatever Happened to Black Lives Matter?," *Root*, February 16, 2017, https://www.theroot.com/whatever-happened-to-black-lives-matter-1792412728.

122. Touré, "A Year Inside the Black Lives Matter Movement," *Rolling Stone*, December 7, 2017, https://www.rollingstone.com/politics/politics-news/a-year-inside-the-black-lives-matter-movement-204982/; and Mark Z. Barabak, "Trump Succeeds Where Obama Failed—Spawning a New Wave of Liberal Activism," *Los Angeles Times*, June 28, 2017, http://www.latimes.com/politics/la-na-pol-trump-spontaneous-protest-2017-story.html.

123. Ann M. Simmons and Jaweed Kaleem, "A Founder of Black Lives Matter Answers a Question on Many Minds: Where Did It Go?" *Los Angeles Times*, August 25, 2017, http://www.latimes.com/nation/la-na-patrisse-cullors-black-lives-matter-2017-htmlstory.html.

124. "Executive Summary," We The Protesters, accessed October 29, 2018, http://www.wetheprotesters.org/exe-sum-and-overview.

· 6 ·

BAD BOYS

El Malcriado and the Making of the United Farm Workers

Andy Zermeño had come a long way from his teenaged days hoeing lettuce when Cesar Chavez telephoned him one day in 1964. Zermeño had toiled alongside his father, foreman of a migrant labor camp that each spring housed some of the thousands of mostly Mexican families that streamed into California's bountiful Salinas Valley to tend the lettuce, grapes, and other crops that earned it the moniker "Salad Bowl of the World." The teen also was an artist who began drawing as a child to compensate for a severe stutter he attributes to being forced to speak English in school. His talent enabled Zermeño to exchange the backbreaking short hoe—genesis of the derisive term "stoop labor"—for a pen when he won a scholarship to art college. Twenty-eight-year-old Zermeño was lead artist of a successful animation firm in Los Angeles when Chavez called. The community organizer envisioned the National Farm Workers Association he launched in 1962 as a key step toward organizing the United States' most marginalized workers into a union powerful enough to demand decent wages, working conditions, and dignity. First, Chavez had to teach farm workers they *possessed* civil rights, then convince them that they could improve their lives.

He drove Zermeño around the valley, pointing to where people lived under bridges or in ramshackle shacks where toddlers played outside in dirt.

Chavez told the artist he needed a light-hearted way to edify the downtrodden workers. "So we came up with Don Sotaco, a farmworker who didn't know anything," Zermeño recalled. "Bumbling, ignorant, who just worked and worked and worked—did whatever the boss told him to do."[1] The hapless Sotaco cartoons could critique farm workers' passivity and explain their rights. "Instead of being offensive," Chavez once explained, "it would be funny."[2] The jug-eared, bucktoothed *campesino* debuted on the December 1, 1964, cover of *El Malcriado*, the Spanish-language farm workers newspaper Chavez had long dreamed of publishing.[3] A couple of months later, editors added the subtitle, "*La Voz del Campesino*—The Voice of the Farm Worker."

Don Sotaco was the antithesis of the scrappy *Malcriado*, whose title Chavez chose because it means a rowdy, rude child who insults elders. "The name *Malcriado* fits well because the growers are paternal and the newspaper is talking back to them like a child talking back to his father," he once explained.[4] A paper by that name had appeared during the Mexican Revolution that inspired Chavez. "El Malcriado" also had been the pseudonym of Daniel Venegas, one of a handful of Southwestern *cronistas* (pundits) in the 1920s and 1930s whose satirical text and cartoons helped preserve Mexican culture by mocking "gringoized" Hispanics.[5] *El Malcriado*'s modern version of this impudent humor accounted for much of the social justice journal's appeal. Brazen and bombastic, its unapologetic editors once boasted, "[T]here are many beautiful newspapers that do not tell the truth. And like all real *malcriados*, we are not very beautiful."[6]

It was no coincidence that farm workers began to arise across California within months after this bad boy swaggered into the valley. *El Malcriado* not only supported the strikes of summer 1965 but also offered advice on how to start them (talk to your crew; form a committee; ask NFWA's advice).[7] "We were the *malcriados*, the bad boys," founding editor Bill Esher told an interviewer later, "and we were thrilled by the strike wave."[8]

This chapter looks at the first volume of *El Malcriado* (sixty-six issues from December 1, 1964, to August 16, 1967), when it was a still a grassroots periodical designed to recruit, organize, and give voice to California's largely invisible migrant farm workers, who faced daunting obstacles: "weak bargaining position, farm worker poverty and a culture of resignation, high rates of migrancy and weak social cohesion, and a perpetual oversupply of farm labor, ensuring that growers could break any strike."[9] Complicating matters was that farm workers were excluded from the 1935 National Labor Relations Act that granted most of American labor the right to organize. Field workers were even more vulnerable and harder to organize because so many were immigrants subject to deportation. The chapter focuses on how the newspaper's visual rhetoric, especially Zermeño's cartoons, built collective identity and inspired collective action. It builds on Marshall Ganz's study that attributes the United Farm Workers' success to its leaders' superior "strategic capacity"—the timing, targeting, and tactics used to build their unprecedented social movement.[10] *El Malcriado* was a vital part of that strategy.

An Expanding Sense of Empowerment

Don Sotaco's evolution over the original bimonthly newspaper's twenty months, in fact, mirrors farm workers' expanding sense of empowerment in this dizzying period: after rose grafters unexpectedly won concessions when they walked out of giant grape-grower DiGiorgio Corporation in spring 1965, Filipino farm workers launched the landmark Delano grape strike on September 8. Chavez's NFWA joined on September 16—Mexican Independence Day. Although Chavez had been reluctant to strike so soon, from then on *El Malcriado* agency frames summoned the strike—"huelga." The newspaper ballooned to twenty-four pages by the end of its first year, as strikers bore down for a long winter. NFWA incorporated the Farm Worker Press to publish *El Malcriado* at the end of 1965 in part to protect itself from lawsuits.[11] The press run tripled to 3,000 copies, including a thousand copies of a new English edition. In January 1966, NFWA began boycotting Schenley Industries liquor brands, including Seagrams and Hiram Walker whiskey.

Chavez's widely publicized pilgrimage on foot to Sacramento that April made him famous; Schenley signed a contract within days after a jubilant crowd of thousands greeted their charismatic leader at the State Capitol. Senator Robert F. Kennedy contributed celebrity and clout when he visited. In late summer 1966, NFWA merged with Filipino workers into the United Farm Workers Organizing Committee (UFWOC; today it goes by UFW), a true union affiliated with the AFL-CIO. UFWOC won an election to represent workers at DiGiorgio in September. More growers followed throughout fall 1966. A. Perelli-Minetti & Sons winery, the final big holdout as 1967 began, however, filed a million-dollar libel suit against *El Malcriado*, in part because of a Zermeño cartoon.

Main Character in the Farm Workers Movement

El Malcriado itself was a main character in the emerging farm workers movement. Editorials that first year appeared in screaming all-capital letters under the logo, "Viva La Causa." Underlines added even more emphasis to some sections. Editors cultivated its subversive persona, as when boasting of an article, "*El Malcriado* once again exposes the lies and prints the truth."[12] (*Saturday Evening Post* writer John Gregory Dunne, however, found the NFWA newspaper as dishonest as the growers' propaganda.)[13] At its peak in the late 1960s, *El Malcriado* claimed 18,000 subscribers.[14] Initially, the paper was totally self-supporting, funded by over-the-counter sales and NFWA members, whose dues included a subscription. Besides being an apt practitioner of social justice journalism, early editor Douglass Adair also proved an adept marketer, who turned the Farm Worker Press into a surprising source of revenue by advertising in *El Malcriado* an expanding catalog of strike-related media. Strike buttons and stickers eventually were joined by UFWOC posters, calendars, records, books such as Eugene Nelson's *Huelga, the First 100 Days of the Delano Grape Strike*, and a fifty-page collection of Don Sotaco cartoons.[15] The products were visual clues to a powerful collective identity that far-flung middle-class supporters felt with the farm workers.

El Malcriado also marketed its "bad boy" image. A house ad featured a cuddling couple above a caption that read, "I will marry you but do not tell my boss that you read *El Malcriado*."[16] A reader's poem captured its popularity: "*Malcriado*'s not a daily, / Boring and repetitious, / On the day that it's released / It sells like hotcakes."[17] Brief addenda titled "*EL MALCRIADO SAYS*" tacked an editorial two cents onto articles. An account of a grower who beat a farm worker's son, for example, ended, "*EL MALCRIADO SAYS*: Justice moves slowly: without a push from the workers and their Association it doesn't move at all."[18] It called itself "the nation's leading newspaper on farm labor" and marketed months-old issues as collectors' items.[19] When a reader inquired about a proposed bill, it responded: "EL MALCRIADO SAYS: … 'This law will pass over *El Malcriado*'s dead body,'" as if the newspaper were a living creature.[20]

Although *El Malcriado* was instrumental in the farm workers movement, most scholars have focused on other factors in the movement's success.[21] An exception is Frank Bardacke's *Trampling Out the Vintage: Cesar Chavez and the Two Souls of the United Farm Workers*, which parallels *El Malcriado*'s trajectory with the community's journey "from family association to strike vehicle to independent union to big labor affiliate and movement emblem."[22] Carlos Reyes Guerrero concurs in his dissertation that El Malcriado was a cornerstone of the "cultural space" Chavez's group created in its challenge to California's $4 billion agribusiness oligarchy.[23] Other scholars credit El Malcriado as forefather of the Chicano journalism at the nexus of the 1960s Chicano/a print renaissance.[24]

Chicano Journalism, Hispanic Media

The more than fifty Chicano/a newspapers that sprang up in the U.S. Southwest by 1971 were more socially and politically activist than the nation's numerous other Spanish-language newspapers.[25] They filled a journalistic void that encompassed what Randy Ontiveros calls a "near 'brown-out' of televised news about Mexican-Americans."[26] Media historian Colin Gunckel describes El Malcriado as "highly influential in shaping Chicano movement print culture and the way it visualized emerging conceptions of identity politics."[27] El Malcriado set the template for illustration-rich Chicano newspapers, according to Chicano Studies scholar Rudy Acuna.[28] In addition to helping to forge a new genre of Mexican-American journalism, El Malcriado followed a long tradition of Spanish-language newspapers in the United States.[29]

Spaniards, in fact, in 1533 delivered the Americas' first printing press to Mexico City, the actual birthplace of journalism in the Americas, where hojas volantes (newssheets) began flying off the press in 1541.[30] At least eighty Spanish-language papers appeared before 1860 in what is now the United States.[31] By the end of the nineteenth century, the U.S. Spanish-language press played an important role in forging and preserving Hispanic identity.[32] Inherent in its mission has been defense of Hispanic civil rights. One example of its social justice journalism was a nationwide campaign by Spanish-language newspapers and Spanish-language radio, for example, which helped fund the 1954 landmark civil rights case Hernandez v. Texas, in which the Supreme Court extended to Mexican Americans constitutional rights of due process.[33]

The Farm Workers Movement

A decade later, however, civil rights remained far beyond the reach of Californian farm workers. Growers supported by the state had quashed earlier attempts at unionization, and big-city union organizers had alienated the *campesinos*. Chavez avoided the word "union" when he formed the NFWA in 1962. He figured he needed at least five years to build the collective identity and confidence a union required. Chavez's strategy fused Mahatma Gandhi's commitment to nonviolence with radical Saul Alinsky's call for theatrical, confrontational campaigns.[34] When *El Malcriado* appeared, some fifty dues-paying families comprised NFWA, which provided a modest life insurance benefit and a credit union. Local newspapers supported the growers. As Adair recalled, "There was no radio program, no mention of the union on the radio, or in the press, or on TV." Farm workers who picked up copies of *El Malcriado* for a dime in "little rinky dink stores" knew the newspaper long before they recognized the association.[35] Founding editor Esher once said that Chavez half-jokingly envisioned him as Joseph Goebbels, Hitler's propaganda minister.[36] Esher was a New York native whose parents worked with the Catholic Workers movement. The Syracuse University dropout was picking cantaloupes in the San Joaquin Valley while secretly documenting growers' abuses when a fellow activist connected him with Chavez.[37] The pair jointly developed the newspaper's defiant tone and spirit over the first half of 1965. They frequently drove to Los Angeles that spring to confer with artist Zermeño about his Don Sotaco cartoon character.

Don Sotaco, Don Coyote, and El Patron

The Don Sotaco cartoons followed a long tradition of political cartoons in American journalism, stretching back to the "Join, or Die!" severed-snake illustration Benjamin Franklin published in 1754. Thomas Nast's "Tammany Tiger" led *Harper's Weekly's* 1871 crusade against New York City's corrupt government.[38] Cartoons formed the heart of satirical magazines such as *Puck* (1877), *Judge* (1881), and *Life* (1883).[39] Radical journals were rife with satirical cartoons lampooning capitalism in the early 1900s.[40] Hundreds of political cartoonists satirized American society by 1900, although not on the *New York Times* editorial page, which deemed their visual rhetoric inherently biased.[41]

In early issues of *El Malcriado*, Don Sotaco is a hapless sad sap. Zermeño and Chavez were confident their audience would recognize this subjugated, submissive figure. The artist followed the visual rhetorical advice of rhetoricians Martin Medhurst and Michael DeSousa: "The artist must know and utilize the beliefs, values, and attitudes of his audience if he or she is to be an effective persuader."[42] Zermeño's choice of Don Sotaco made further cultural sense because comics had long been popular across Latin America because of their ability to dramatize forces of modernization.[43] The second issue's cover featured a new character, scowling Don Coyote, who also culturally resonated with the Mexican laborers. As the wily coyote has long been a cultural symbol for trickery, workers would immediately comprehend the symbolism of the stick-thin, chain-smoking caricature of the conniving Mexican contractors whom growers hired to recruit workers.

Coyote and Sotaco meet inside issue No. 3, when the contractor complains to the *campesino* about how he struggles to pay for his Cadillac and his girlfriends' fancy clothes. "Yesterday, when I was picking beets," Sotaco tells readers in an aside, "I was thinking about what a hard life my friend Don Coyote leads."[44] The cartoon demonstrates how contrast, contradiction, and commentary function as main organizing principles for cartoons, which must convey meaning in a limited space. Zermeño invites viewers to condemn Coyote as a hypocrite, as his Cadillac contradicts his claim of poverty. Sotaco drily contrasts his life in the fields with Coyote's in commentary that completes the visual rhetoric. It is notable that Sotaco dares not speak directly to Coyote but that his asides to readers draw them into a subversive alliance. This pattern of an accommodating Sotaco tolerating Coyote's complaints continued through spring 1965, although the reader increasingly realizes Sotaco is more aware of his exploitation than he lets on.

The third character in Zermeño's trio is El Patron or Patroncito, symbolizing the farm owners. The porcine boss sips lemonade as he ruminates during the grape strike, "These low-life strikers had to pick on me. Everybody knows I treat my people right and pay them the top wage. It's not my fault if they don't know how to spend their money."[45] Patron's physical bulk is a metaphor for his greed and power; one cartoon shows him tipping the scales of justice against a smaller "public."[46] Sotaco is a helpless victim in early Patroncito cartoons: in summer 1965, Sotaco is a mere pawn in Patroncito's chess game with the blind government.[47] Another depicts Don Sotaco straining to pull a rickshaw loaded with Patroncito and Coyote, who whips Sotaco—as if he is an animal.[48] Neither disempowering image seems as if it would inspire potential recruits to identify with Sotaco. Zermeño continued this theme in a parody of "The Pyramid of Capitalist System," a provocative 1911 cartoon that depicts workers at the bottom tier of capitalist society; in Zermeño's version, Patroncito is wined and dined at a table literally supported by workers' backs.[49] In fact, Don Sotaco has parallels with "Henry Dubb," the hapless worker created by socialist cartoonist Ryan Walker in the 1910s. Sotaco also harkens "Mr. Block," a similarly block-headed worker who appeared in the 1910s in *Industrial Worker*, magazine of the radical Industrial Workers of the World. "He is representative of that host of slaves who think in terms of their masters," an editor described Mr. Block.[50] Unlike his predecessors, who never comprehended they needed to organize to improve their lot, however, Don Sotaco grows smarter and more assertive.

Sotaco, Coyote, and El Patron appeared together a month after the grape strike began. Coyote lurks in the background as El Patron bemoans the lack of local workers. "Keep those *braceros* coming, man!" he tells a blindfolded man in a suit labeled "The Government," referencing the World War II *bracero* program that welcomed Mexican workers. Although the program officially ended in 1964, growers continued to import Mexicans willing to work for a pittance. The NFWA reviled them as a threat to organizing. In the cartoon, an eavesdropping Don Sotaco crouches beneath the desk, his usual exasperated expression indicating he has heard this tale a thousand times before.[51] Yet he keeps himself invisible. But hints of Sotaco's subversiveness begin to appear. Issue No. 10, which covered the rose workers strike, featured a cartoon of Patroncito and Coyote relaxing in a tree, unaware that Sotaco is chopping it down with an ax labeled "La Huelga," symbolizing the power of collective action.[52] The next issue finds Patroncito on his knees surrounded by farmers bearing "Huelga!" signs, although Sotaco is nowhere to be seen.[53] A few weeks later he gets educated along with readers about the movement and the significance of the strike in a two-page spread in which "*El Malcriado* Le Contesta Preguntas de Don Sotaco."[54]

Don Sotaco Finds His Voice

After police arrested twenty-four pickets in Arvin, however, Sotaco reveals his first signs of resistance. Coyote praises him: "You work for whatever wage I pay you, you never create any problems for me and you never forget to bring me a little present." Sotaco replies, "Coyote, if you say I'm smart it must be true." But he adds: "And there is an association that will show me the way to repay you for your generosity."[55] Sotaco's sardonic tone signals that his surface amiability belies a capacity for revenge. The cartoons condense all three of William Gamson's collective action frames into the Sotaco character as he awakens to injustice, begins to identify with the organized farm workers' resistance, and recognizes his potential to confront the growers in collective action. Sotaco grew more assertive under the influence of El Teatro Campesino, the acting troupe founded to entertain and educate pickets by Luis Valdez, a veteran of San Francisco street theater who grew up in the fields. Valdez, who also helped translate *El Malcriado*, featured Sotaco in his skits or *actos*. The timorous *campesino* became shrewder and more assertive in his onstage encounters with Coyote and El Patron at Friday night strike meetings and on the picket line throughout the cold winter of 1965–1966.

In *El Malcriado*, Sotaco first asserts himself not in a cartoon but in a narrative, No. 18's "Don Sotaco Story." In an accompanying cartoon of him hoeing, he is only three feet tall. In the story, a University of California professor shows Sotaco and his wife his lab, where scientists have solved the problem of underpaid workers by feeding them strawberry-flavored chicken feed. Sotaco says to his wife: "I can't believe my ears. This idiot ought to be locked up." He still does not address his oppressor directly. But when the professor explains that growers gave the university five million dollars to breed long-fingered babies that stop growing at three feet, Sotaco finally finds his voice. "Viva La Causa," he shouts, then turns to the professor and spits in his face.[56] Soctaco's first overt act against dominant powers marks a new stage in the movement.[57]

By January, Patroncito sweats in a small cartoon that illustrates a story headlined, "Citrus Workers Stand Up, Patroncito Trembles." At the end of the story, an *"EL MALCRIADO SAYS"* blurb adds, "We say to Patroncito, 'Wake up and join the 20th Century. Farm workers will never again lie down and let you kick them around like animals.'"[58] Zermeño's messaging was inconsistent, however, and he also continued to portray the farmer worker as subjugated by the growers. On the July 28, 1966, cover, Patroncito is about to gobble up Sotaco in a sandwich; on another cover, he is squeezed by Patroncito and Coyote.[59] The next month, however, featured a confident-looking Sotaco leading a long parade of followers in an appeal to NFWA members to vote "yes" in the upcoming election to join the AFL-CIO. In contrast to past appearances, Sotaco is the largest person in the crowd, looking upward instead of down, a hint of a smile replacing his usually furrowed brow.[60]

Sotaco finally becomes a true revolutionary in the September 9, 1966, issue marking the one-year anniversary of the grape strike. El Patroncito and Coyote drive a train with cars labeled low wages, bad housing, and bad conditions across a railroad trestle, unaware that a beaming Sotaco below is about to derail them by igniting dynamite labeled "Huelga."[61] The image is a dramatic contrast to the Sotaco who cowered beneath a desk. Two months later,

Socato stars in a full-page cartoon that contrasts "Yesterday and Today." In the top half of the drawing, Sotaco flees from El Patron and Coyote; in the bottom, he stops them in their tracks as he thrusts a "Huelga" sign in their stunned faces.[62] Zermeño's visual rhetoric telegraphs that the strike's collective action empowers farm workers. Sotaco is a new man. Gender also figures in Zermeño's cartoons, which ridicule foes by feminizing them. A corrupt government worker in another Don Sotaco scenario is a "sissy" who hides behind his mother's skirts.[63] In yet another, El Patron plays the violin as two senators tango together.[64]

Mexican Revolution Influences

While Zermeño's characters made their points with humor, almost every cover in the newspaper's first eight months featured somber works by the post–Mexican Revolution era's graphic artists, who romanticized *mestizo* peasants in simple linocuts as they strove to shape a populist Mexican identity in the 1920s and 1930s. Chavez and his followers hoped to gain moral authority and political capital by linking themselves to the celebrated Mexican revolutionaries through frame bridging.[65] January 1965 featured a woodcut of revolutionary *campsinos* singing as they sit around a fire. "The men that circled the flames of the revolution fought the revolution not only for bread, but for the dignity that man deserves," an *El Malcriado* editorial stated in a recurring theme.[66] Alfredo Zalce's woodcut of Mayan workers in the Yucatan graced the No. 6 cover, and Francisco Dosamantes's drawing of three barefoot Oaxacan girls with braids trailing to their knees appeared on the next.[67]

The ideals of the Mexican Revolution infused *El Malcriado*, stirring collective memory that helped forge the movement's collective identity. "We had members with a living memory of the Mexican Revolution, of hanging the landlord and dividing up the hacienda," Adair said.[68] A portrait of Emiliano Zapata appeared on an early cover.[69] An editorial blared, "MEN GO ON STRIKE BECAUSE THEY DARE TO FIGHT, TO RESIST UNTIL THE VERY END. THEY ARE THE SONS OF EMILIANO ZAPATA."[70] Adair even printed an unauthorized poster of Zapata shouting "*Viva La Revolucion!*" that became a best-selling piece of radical chic.[71] A series on Pancho Villa began at the end of 1966.[72] The Plan of Delano, which served as the movement's mission statement, asserted, "We are the sons of the Mexican Revolution, a revolution of the poor seeking bread and justice."[73] Once the grape strike began, *El Macriado* editorials evoked the Revolution to sustain pickets. "But what can one man do?" asked one. "Everything: The roots of this country, and the roots of the Mexican Revolution were established by a very few men. It is always a very few men who are responsible for the great social changes in the world."[74]

Frame Bridging to the Civil Rights Movement

El Malcriado also summoned the Civil Rights Movement as a role model for farm workers' collective action. "How have the African-Americans won their battles?" it asked in summer 1965. "They have united against the mad dogs and the fire hoses."[75] It argued that the voice of farm workers was the same as the voice of black people. The Plan of Delano included the pledge, "WE SHALL OVERCOME." A black Madonna and child graced a fall 1965 cover by African American artist Elizabeth Catlett, the only non-Latino so honored in volume one. When NFWA joined UFWOC's Delano grape strike in September, the newspaper likened the action to the Montgomery bus boycott a decade earlier. "The movement of the Negro began in the hot summer of Alabama ten years ago when a Negro woman refused to be pushed to the back of the bus," it editorialized. "Sometime in the future they will say that in the hot summer of California in 1965 the movement of the farm workers began."[76]

Because it framed itself as a movement and not just a labor union, NFWA won the support of the National Association for the Advancement of Colored People (NAACP) and the Student Nonviolent Coordinating Committee (SNCC), according to scholar Lauren Araiza.[77] Civil rights workers, for example, loaned the NFWA two shortwave radios so that roving bands of pickets could keep in constant touch with headquarters and each other. The newspaper framed the strike as a rainbow of unity: "For the first time in history, Filipinos, Mexican Americans, Puerto Ricans, Negroes and Anglos are all working together to win a strike," one editorial said.[78] Such lofty rhetoric also was pragmatic because success was totally dependent on these diverse groups overcoming any differences. *El Macriado* featured photographs of "Our Filipino Brothers" at the end of 1966.[79] An eight-page special bilingual section on election news supported UFWOC leader Larry Itliong's campaign for Delano City Council.[80] *El Malcriado* even published a tribute to Filipino workers in Tagalog, a Filipino language.[81]

El Malcriado injustice frames emphasized Chavez's key theme that farm workers were a part of something bigger than themselves. "What is a movement?" an editorial asked just before NFWA voted to join the grape strike in September 1965. "It is when there are enough people with one idea so that their actions are together like a huge wave of water which nothing can stop."[82] In November, an essay added, "It is a movement, because it looks toward the day when every farm worker in California: Mexican, Negro, Puerto Rican, or Anglo will have a living wage and a position of dignity."[83] At the end of the year, another editorial defined a movement: "It is a direct person-to-person response to injustice. It is an immediate, courageous reaction against lies and dishonesty. It is the idea that a man's dignity is more important than anything else."[84] And at the end of January 1966 it republished the popular "Enough People with One Idea" editorial. "Once a movement begins, it is impossible to stop," it claimed.[85] "These local tyrants become furious when they show them that the *huelga* is a huge social movement involving the respect of a whole race of people."[86] The Plan of Delano reiterated, "This is the beginning of a social movement in fact and not in pronouncements."[87]

Oppositional Framing in *El Malcriado*

A crucial complement to building unity was making enemies. *El Malcriado* crafted a strong sense of oppositional identity by demonizing growers, contractors, Teamsters, and scabs in text and imagery.[88] "[T]he resistance these thieves, these vampires, have given us only makes us stronger," it editorialized about growers during the grape strike.[89] It derided the *Delano Record* as "A Scurrilous Enemy of the Farm Worker."[90] Editors' oppositional framing took many forms. They labeled Mexican-born strikebreakers "Mexicanos Malinchistas," a reference to La Malinche, the treacherous indigenous woman who helped Hernán Cortés conquer her homeland.[91] The newspaper likened to Judas contractors who brought in strikebreakers, specifically naming and shaming individual contractors. It made it clear whom farm workers should identify with: "If you don't want to be on the side of this JUDAS, don't let yourself be seen with this stooge of the ranchers!"[92] *El Malcriado* pit Pope John XXIII against the Christian Brothers wine label, which it accused it of harassing workers attempting to unionize, in an illustration of him with a tear rolling down his cheek.[93] Editors also cast themselves as David to the growers' Goliath.[94] The Day of the Dead issue in 1966 featured lushly illustrated *calaveras*, mock obituaries in verse, that poked fun at strike "heroes" and "villains." Verse for a scab began: "A tombstone they made up / years in advance / and on the day that she died / they held a big dance."[95]

Editors also used symbolism to create an ""us versus them" mentality among farm workers. For example: "The El Malcriado Says: This monster, DiGiorgio Corporation, has grown to such gigantic size, that it acts as if it owns the state. But the eagle of the Farm Workers Association is out to tame the beast and make it give some of its fantastic wealth to the workers who make it rich."[96] Another editorial used an animal analogy to describe the difference between the two sides: "We have seen ourselves treated like cattle. They have taken the work of our hands and bodies and made themselves rich, while we are left with empty hands between the earth and the sky."[97] The camera also built oppositional identity. "The Enemy," for example, featured photographs and names of individual scabs and Teamsters, whose union was competing for farm workers.[98]

Photography as Social Justice Journalism

Photographs began to replace the historic Mexican graphic prints and Zermeño's cheeky cartoons on El Malcriado covers almost as soon as the strike began. The change signaled the movement's surge out of the past. Documentation of abuse was a form of social justice journalism. Like its illustrations, the newspaper photographs also played a key role in building collective identity. The first cover photograph featured Chavez addressing a crowd in front of the union's Aztec eagle logo, designed by Zermeño, an early step toward Chavez's emergence as the movement's public face.[99] Two weeks later, an iconic photograph of NFWA cofounder Dolores Huerta hoisting her "Huelga" sign above her head made the cover of the special strike edition. While Huerta is unidentified, photography introduced a focus on individuals that had been absent in El Malcriado's first year, when editors emphasized the movement's collective nature. The strike edition, for example, projected strength through five carefully chosen photographs that illustrated an article detailing a parade of nearly a thousand workers led by Chavez.[100] The newspaper concluded 1965 with a look back at "The Year in Pictures" that portrayed farm workers as stoic, devout, racially inclusive, and sacrificing for their families. One image showed determined-looking mothers holding babies in their arms. "Poor as we are, we have stood firm for 100 days," read accompanying text. "We are determined to win a decent life for our families."[101]

One example of photography as social justice journalism appears in a fall 1965 issue, which featured powerful images of the arrests of forty-four pickets, including a dozen ministers. The pickets had been shouting "Huelga!" from the roadside to lure strikebreakers from the fields, a popular UFWOC tactic. Charged with unlawful assembly, they spent three days in the Bakersfield jail, providing free publicity for the farm workers just as images of police maltreatment aided civil rights protesters in the Deep South.[102] The newspaper itself became part of the story when the Reverend David Havens was arrested while reading from its pages while standing in a truck bed.[103] Photographs of police harassment proved a useful tool for gaining public support.

While the newspaper could not afford to hire a photographer, several impassioned young activists eagerly wielded their cameras as tools for social justice. John Kouns, inspired by Dorothea Lange's Depression-era photography and John Steinbeck's *The Grapes of Wrath*, not only documented the farm workers movement but also organized photo exhibitions throughout California to raise money for the cause and educate people on the farm workers' plight.[104] Talented professional Jon Lewis dropped out of graduate school to become NFWA's first official photographer at five dollars a week. Photojournalism historian Richard Steven Street asserts that Lewis's strike images in *El Malcriado* "helped a movement establish its identity and chronicle its activities." He chose not to document the farm workers' poor living conditions, an important decision in how his images constructed their collective identity. "I found it hard to photograph poverty," Lewis said. "I was always photographing strength, strong men and women standing."[105]

Lewis's work came to the fore when he covered the 320-mile farm workers' pilgrimage from Delano to Sacramento that began on March 17, 1966, in a brilliant stroke of publicity conceived by Chavez.[106] He called the march *La Peregrinación*, after the Lenten *peregrinaciónes* of Mexico as well as Gandhi's Salt March to the Sea. NFWA staffers organized subscribers in each town along the route to provide food and lodging for marchers. Workers' response was a testament to the newspaper's influence. "Every house would be open to us," Adair said. "Because of the *Malcriado*."[107] As a "participant observer," Lewis shot thousands of images, often the only photographer present as he walked the entire route.[108] His constant presence granted him an intimacy with marchers, who did not mind when he stuck a camera in their faces.[109] When on Easter morning the group arrived at the Sacramento River bridge leading to the Capitol building, several thousand ebullient supporters greeted them, and Lewis found himself elbowing for position with a swarm of mainstream photojournalists and national TV news crews. Footage of the impassioned rally pressured Schenley Industries into signing the first major contract with the striking farm workers.[110]

Witnessing in *El Malcriado*

El Malcriado's social justice journalism was strongest in its eyewitness accounts. The newspaper frequently reported on police brutality[111] and violence against pickets by growers and their forces.[112] One striker's stark tale of being arrested and jailed overnight describes how police chained pickets together and drove them to a San Diego jail: "Again they took off our clothes and this time Father Salandini too. They gave us different prison clothes and put us all in one cell. But there was no room to sleep, and some were so tired that they slept on the floor."[113] A 1967 photo spread shows pickets confronting a scab foreman as they call into the vineyard, "Come out, Brothers! Come out of the field!"[114]

Occasionally *El Malcriado* actually investigated an issue. It interviewed the Delano city manager about its slow progress in fixing its contaminated water supply, and it published the findings of two UFWOC staffers who investigated arsenic contamination in the water of Allensworth. "They don't have any idea as to how long we've been drinking the poisoned water, but no one has been sick or died because of the water, yet," a local school principal said in a telling quote. "The Health Dept. of Tulare said that arsenic poisoning is a very slow process, so we'll just have to wait and see."[115] *El Malcriado*'s social justice journalism included years of stories claiming that contractor Jimmy Hronis was cheating sugar-beet workers, which finally prompted a state investigation that ended with an order for him to pay back their salaries.[116] The newspaper also followed an ultimately successful two-year rent strike by residents of the shabby Woodville and Linnell labor camps.[117] Generally, however, more complex journalistic forays lacked substance. An "investigation" into poor care at county hospitals contained no evidence backing sweeping claims such as, "Kern Hospital Staff members appear to hate all strangers, particularly their own patients."[118]

While *El Malcriado* epitomized the journalistic adage to comfort the afflicted and afflict the comfortable, its frequently erroneous claims jeopardized its role as the farm workers' champion. *El Malcriado* shared the muckrakers' moral umbrage but lacked their reverence for fact. Editors once directed a long screed at a reader who suggested improvement "in the interest of better journalism."[119] Grammar and spelling errors punctuated many articles due to Esher and Adair's poor Spanish. When a reader volunteered to proofread articles, the editors demurred: "People who want to know what is happening to farm workers around the state will take the trouble to wade through our unavoidably and regrettably poor Spanish."[120] An article ostensibly about El Teatro Campesino included the gratuitous observation, "Like a pile of mashed potatoes, Governor [Pat Brown] has proved spineless in resisting the insatiable greed of the growers for special privileges and favors."[121] It also was not above using deceit when other methods failed. Reporter Robert Dudnick posed as a reporter for a big Texas daily in 1967 to wangle an interview with the owners of union hold-out Perelli-Minnetti & Sons.[122] "We were just outrageous," Adair told an interviewer. "By then the paper had become so famous it was like a lightning rod attracting attention."[123]

Chavez began getting complaints from supporters. He and Huerta routinely reprimanded Adair and Esher for excesses that annoyed the UFWOC expanding constituencies of national union leaders, politicians, assorted social justice organizations, and the far-flung consumers it courted for the nationwide grape boycott. El Malcriado now reported on farm workers arising in Alabama, marching in Michigan, opening an office in Phoenix, and organizing in Wisconsin.[124] A large map located grape boycotts as distant as Oklahoma City, Chicago, and Boston.[125] A New Jersey donor wrote, "As I read each issue of El Malcriado, the emotions I felt years ago reading The Grapes of Wrath return."[126] Local readers resented the increasing emphasis on issues outside the valley. The Vietnam War was one bone of contention. Even though Chavez insisted UFWOC remain neutral on the subject in the 1960s,[127] the editorial malcriados opposed the war on the grounds that the Vietnamese peasants were the campesinos' comrades.[128] "It seems to me you are writing more and more about less and less and that you are not always the 'Voice of the Farm Worker' that you pretend to be," wrote "A Chavista." "And stories about negroes in Atlanta and soldiers in Vietnam have nothing to do with Mexican and Filipino farm workers here in California and down in Texas."[129]

El Malcriado Transforms with the Movement

The newspaper once taunted a Schenley executive, "EL MALCRIADO publicly calls this man a liar. If you are not lying, Mr. Woolsey, we suggest that you sue us."[130] He did not, but A. Perelli-Minetti & Sons filed a $6 million libel suit against UFWOC, Chavez, Esher, and others in response to a series of "exposés" and cartoons that were as sensational as they were false. It was one of several libel suits.[131] UFWOC had launched a boycott against the large winery after it signed a sweetheart contract with the Teamsters instead of UFWOC in September 1966.[132] The next month, *El Malcriado* slapped on its cover an illustration of a worker crucified on an agave plant's spikes to plug the story inside, "BETRAYAL IN DELANO: JUDAS IN ACTION!!!" The exposé charged Perelli-Minetti with committing a "huge swindle" against workers.[133] The zealous bad boys were wrong, however, and the next issue of *El Malcriado* published the firm's refutation of nearly every accusation. Corrections filled four pages. "No employee was fired because he refused to return to the company either his check or the money which he had received," read one.[134]

Editors kept up their campaign despite a furious Chavez; ironically, by then he also found *El Malcriado* too outrageous and uncontrollable. The newspaper mockingly called Perelli-Minetti's 85-year-old founder a member of the Mafia and Ku Klux Klan.[135] In April, *El Malcriado* likened Perelli-Minetti officials to Nazis.[136] Zermeño caricatured the firm as El Patron, a puppeteer pulling the strings of Teamsters and scabs.[137] Unamused AFL-CIO leaders charged that the newspaper had become shrill and off message and that it embarrassed key constituencies.[138] Relationships between the newspaper's real-life *malcriado* editors and its more conservative leaders frayed further.[139] Lawyers from both sides eventually negotiated a settlement in 1967, in which Perelli-Minetti agreed to hold an open election for union representation—an election that UFWOC won. The costly legal battle took a toll. Editors appealed to readers, who sent in donations ranging from five dollars to a thousand dollars.

El Malcriado still struggled, financially and editorially. The first editorial of 1967 sounded a paranoid note that foreshadowed the UFWOC split to come. "A Dangerous Enemy" warned, "Distrust, jealousy and cowardice. All these are personal failings, happening quietly amid the noise and confusion of our work."[140] Chavez dismissed a handful of associates he deemed disloyal, including the journalists' *malcriado* soulmates in El Teatro Campesino. Even Zermeño seemed untethered, penning a manic new cartoon strip with new editor Daniel de los Reyes that followed three Mexicans' misadventures in the United States; the first installment at the end of 1966 filled eight full pages, a quarter of the issue's total.[141] Union members in March stopped receiving the newspaper for free, further disconnecting *El Malcriado* from farm workers.[142] A disillusioned Adair moved to Texas in April to publish an edition to organize melon workers, and a burnt-out Esher left the movement soon after.[143] The May 10, 1967, number announced that UFWOC members would write editorials.[144] In July, Marcia Brooks, another new editor, cut the thirty-two-page tabloid to an eight-page broadsheet, with Spanish and English versions on facing pages. *El Malcriado's* trademark cover images disappeared overnight.[145] The original *El Malcriado* published its final issue on August 16, 1967.

UFWOC went without a newspaper for six months. The revamped *El Malcriado* rolled out on February 21, 1968, was a tightly disciplined and controlled periodical as the official UFWOC union organ.[146] Union lawyer Jerry Cohen read every issue in paste-up. Instead of farm workers, it addressed a distant middle-class audience of consumers, union leaders, and politicians involved with its hugely successful nationwide boycott of California produce.[147] Magazine freelancer Gloria Steinem helped Chavez plan an International Boycott Day and a Carnegie Hall fundraiser in her first foray into activism.[148] Peace Corps veteran David Fishlow, more diplomatic than his predecessors, served as the newspaper's managing editor, aided by a contrite Adair, who acquiesced to any changes Cohen ordered. "To me: no big deal," Adair told an interviewer. "It was important to have a paper, and the paper could make a tremendous contribution."[149] Along with the demise of the original *El Malcriado*, according to historian Bardacke, "The early bloom of a free-wheeling democratic Delano was gone."[150] The union, not the farm worker, now starred as the newspaper's central character—with one important exception.[151] The newspaper's reappearance seemed timed to publicize the fast Chavez had undertaken two days earlier. Chavez not only penned but also signed Volume Two's maiden editorial on nonviolence, a striking departure from the original newspaper's commitment to collectivity.[152] Now, as a supporter wrote, "Chavez is the Movement, and the Movement is Chavez."[153] On July 29, 1970, Chavez signed landmark contracts that covered 7,000 farm workers at twenty-six ranches, marking a new era of farm workers rights.[154]

Don Sotaco's Legacy

Just as the farm worker movement changed, so did Don Sotaco. The September 1, 1970, cover of *El Malcriado* that announced the contracts featured a new Zermeño character, a feisty kid whose shirt reads, *"El Campesino de Salinas."* At his back stands the robust UFWOC striker featured in Zermeño's famous "Huelga!" poster, clad in an Aztec eagle sash over his work clothes.[155] "Hands off Buster!! We Mean Business!!" the UFWOC hero bellows at a "Teamster." A tiny Patroncitio cowers behind the teamster, signaling the new order in California's fields. Even more striking is a full-page cartoon strip inside that demonstrates how *El Malcriado* symbolized the soul of the farm workers movement. In "Dear Papa…," a boy recounts the many indignities Don Sotaco suffered over the years. In the next-to-last panel, the grown son kneels before a grave marked, "RIP Don Sotaco." The caption reads, "A Dios Papa… Thank you for raising me to be your son. …" In the final panel, the boy is revealed as the powerful "Huelga!" UFWOC striker that loudly proclaims his name: *"El Malcriadooooo!!"*[156]

Farm Workers' Rights Online

El Malcriado's blunt visual rhetoric was an essential element in coalescing the embryonic and unlikely farm workers movement, a milestone for the larger Latino civil rights movement it spawned. A decade of UFWOC nonviolent strikes, boycotts, marches, and fasts culminated in California's landmark Agricultural Labor Relations Act of 1975 that secured collective bargaining for farm workers. After more reincarnations as a series of fliers and as an eight-page newsletter, *El Macriado* shuttered again in the mid-1970s, replaced by Chavez's "President's Newsletter," indicative of his starring role in the movement. It resurfaced in 1984 as a glossy bilingual magazine that appeared sporadically until its final demise in February 1989.[157] Unfortunately, UFWOC lost many of its gains in the 1980s, when California Governor Ronald Reagan's anti-union ideology ascended as Chavez descended into vindictive paranoia. Although his name is synonymous with social justice, some scholars say Chavez's saga is a cautionary tale about the benefits and drawbacks of charismatic leadership in social movements.[158] By the time Chavez died in 1993, the union, now called UFW, had lost many contracts.[159] Passage of the North American Free Trade Agreement the following year further weakened farm workers' position, and the UFW became entangled in several divisive legal proceedings.[160]

The UFW nonetheless remains the nation's largest farm workers union, with a strong digital presence that continues to fight for their hard-won rights. In 2018, the bilingual UFW website helped users tweet their senators to vote against Trump administration plans to reverse worker protections against pesticide exposure. An online pledge allowed viewers to urge the federal government to adopt a landmark California law that guarantees farm workers overtime pay. The UFW's Facebook page hosted an online petition asking the California attorney general to investigate a crash in which two Mexicans died while fleeing Immigration and Customs Enforcement (ICE) agents. A major difference from the UFW's early years is the union's connection with immigration rights and reform. In the 1970s, El Malcriado campaigned against undocumented migrant workers, whom it called "wetbacks" that the UFW viewed as threats to union jobs. In the Trump era, campaigns for immigration rights and reform dominate the UFW website.

In many ways, the web's interactivity has returned the UFW to its grass-roots level, even though the Internet now gives it a global reach. It highlights workers' voices: #WeFeedYou features photographs that workers post of themselves in the fields to remind the public and politicians where their food comes from. A garlic harvester, in one post on the union's YouTube channel, describes how pesticide poisoning affected her. The UFW also combines virtual organizing with collective action. On Labor Day weekend in 2011, 3,000 farm workers rallied at Sacramento's State Capitol building alongside twenty marchers who retraced some 200 miles of Chavez's 1966 pilgrimage to press for a law that would grant them the right to overtime pay. Social media facilitated the march, and the website encouraged supporters across the nation to march virtually by signing its online petition.[161]

Many original El Malcriado features can be found on the UFW site. Just as the newspaper identified offensive contractors and strike breakers in photographs and text, the website names and shames legislators who vote against farm workers' interests, providing users with a link to email them their displeasure. "Know Your Rights" explains dilemmas such as "What to do if immigration knocks on your door," replicating the same column that appeared in the first issues of El Malcriado. Similarly to the newspaper's back-page list of boycotted Schenley Liquors labels to avoid, the website lists brands of approved produce picked by workers under UFW contracts. The online UFW Store sells Zermeño's famous "Huelga" poster alongside #RESIST iPhone covers and t-shirts bearing the UFW Aztec eagle. In 2017, the website took another technological step when it offered a free nineteen-second ringtone to inform undocumented immigrants of their rights if confronted by ICE agents. The website also pays homage to its past by archiving videos and audio clips of Chavez that feed the organization's collective memory. An online UFW campaign succeeded in the proclamation of Cesar Chavez Day as a federal commemorative holiday every March 31, when thousands of people volunteer community service in his honor. The first face of the farm workers movement, however, is absent from the UFW website. Don Sotaco's work is done.

Notes

1. "Decade of Dissent—Andy Zermeño," in *Decade of Dissent: Democracy in Action 1965–1975*, Los Angeles: Center for the Study of Political Graphics, accessed June 10, 2017, https://www.youtube.com/watch?v=ht7HG68Vwdk. See also "The Father of Don Sotaco," *El Malcriado* [hereafter referred to as EM] 1, no. 39 (June 30, 1966), 23.
2. Yolanda Broyles-Gonzalez, *El Teatro Campesino: Theater in the Chicano Movement* (Austin: University of Texas Press, 1994), 13.
3. See "Decade of Dissent"; and Tomás Ybarra-Frausto, "The Chicano Movement/The Movement of Chicano Art," in *Beyond the Fantastic: Contemporary Art Criticism from Latin America*, ed. Gerardo Mosquera (Cambridge, MA: MIT Press; 1996), 165–82.
4. Elaine Flora Graves, "Essay," in *Remembering Cesar: The Legacy of Cesar Chavez*, ed. Cindy Wathen (Sanger, CA: Quill Driver Books, 2000), 45.
5. In the 1920s, Venegas published a one-man illustrated weekly newspaper in Los Angeles entitled *El Malcriado*, which advocated for working-class Mexicans. Nicolás Kanellos, "Cronistas and Satire in Early Twentieth Century Hispanic Newspapers," *MELUS* 23, no. 1 (Spring 1998): 3–25.
6. "Who Is Tearing Up *El Malcriado*?," EM 1, no. 65 (July 19, 1967), npg.
7. "How to Strike?," EM 1, no. 17 (nd), 5. Many numbers of the first volume are undated.
8. Frank Bardacke, *Trampling Out the Vintage: Cesar Chavez and the Two Souls of the United Farm Workers* (New York: Verso Books, 2012), 144.
9. J. Craig Jenkins and Charles Perrow, "Insurgency of the Powerless: Farmworker Movements in the U.S.," *American Sociological Review* 42, no. 2 (April 1977), 249.
10. Marshall Ganz, "Resources and Resourcefulness: Strategic Capacity in the Unionization of California Agriculture, 1959–1966," *American Journal of Sociology* 105, no. 4 (January 2000): 1003–62. Ganz worked with Chavez from 1965 to 1981. He became a lecturer in public policy at the Kennedy School of Government at Harvard University and consulted on Barack Obama's 2008 presidential campaign. See Marshall Ganz, *Why David Sometimes Wins: Leadership, Organization, and Strategy in the California Farm Worker Movement* (New York: Oxford University Press, 2009).
11. "Articles of Incorporation of Farm Worker Press Inc.," December 21, 1965, in Folder 1, Box 14, UFW Administration Department Files, Walter P. Reuther Library of Labor and

Urban Affairs, Wayne State University, Detroit, Michigan. [hereafter referred to as UFW Papers]

12. "The Growers vs. the Facts," *EM* 1, no. 28 (January 26, 1966), 10.

13. John Gregory Dunne, *Delano: The Story of the California Grape Strike* (Berkeley: University of California Press, 1971), 121.

14. Randy Ontiveros, *In the Spirit of a New People: The Cultural Politics of the Chicano Movement* (New York: New York University Press, 2013), 78. Adair placed peak circulation at 100,000 copies, most in English. Doug Adair, "*El Malcriado* 1968–1970: David Fishlow, Doug Adair, Mark Day, Editors," *El Malcriado* Archives, Farmworker Movement Documentation Project, accessed October 10, 2018, https://libraries.ucsd.edu/farmworkermovement/archives/#malcriado.

15. See also "Now You Can Own a Picture of Cesar Chavez," *EM* 1, no. 55 (March 1, 1967), 31.

16. Ad, *EM* 1, no. 7 (nd), 9.

17. Martin Lerma, "To *El Malcriado*," *EM* 1, no. 61 (May 24, 1967), 14.

18. "Rancher who Beat Worker's Child Still Walks the Streets," *EM* 1, no. 17 (nd), 6.

19. "Back Issues Now Available!," *EM* 1, no. 30 (February 28, 1966), 21.

20. "The Holland Rider," *EM* 1, no. 19 (nd), 13.

21. Jennifer Jihye Chun attributes the union's early success to its "community-based unionism." Jennifer Jihye Chun, *Organizing at the Margins: The Symbolic Politics of Labor in South Korea and the United States* (Ithaca, NY: Cornell University Press, 2009), 73. Francisco J. Lewels cites the union's savvy in manipulating mainstream media. Francisco J. Lewels, *The Uses of the Media by the Chicano Movement: A Study in Minority Access* (Westport, CT: Praeger, 1974), 22. John C. Hammerback and Richard J. Jensen credit Chavez's rhetorical genius. John C. Hammerback and Richard J. Jensen, *The Rhetorical Career of César Chávez* (College Station: Texas A&M University Press, 1998), 194. J. Craig Jenkins and Charles Perrow point to liberal elites' support. J. Craig Jenkins and Charles Perrow, "Insurgency of the Powerless: Farm Worker Movements (1946–1972)," *American Sociology Review* 42, no. 2 (April 1977): 249. While *El Malcriado* surfaces briefly in some biographies of Chavez, it mainly is relegated to the footnotes of movement histories. See Susan Ferriss and Ricardo Sandoval, *The Fight in the Fields: Cesar Chavez and the Farmworkers Movement* (Boston: Houghton Mifflin Harcourt, 1997); Ganz, *Why David Sometimes*; Matthew Garcia, *From the Jaws of Victory: The Triumph and Tragedy of Cesar Chavez and the Farm Worker Movement* (Berkeley: University of California Press, 2014); Miriam Pawell, *The Union of Their Dreams: Power, Hope, and Struggle in Cesar Chavez's Farm Worker Movement* (London: Bloomsbury Press, 2010); and Miriam Pawell, *The Crusades of Cesar Chavez: A Biography*, reprint ed. (London: Bloomsbury Press, 2015).

22. Bardacke, *Trampling Out the Vintage*, 267. Linda Baughn's Internet essay relies on *El Malcriado* to trace Chavez's ascendance from invisible staff organizer to icon, which she argues eventually doomed the farm workers movement. Linda Baughn, "César Chávez and the 1968 Fast: A Turning Point for the United Farm Workers," accessed June 26, 2017, https://www.academia.edu/25180762/CÉSAR_CHÁVEZ_AND_THE_1968_FAST_A_TURNING_POINT_FOR_THE_UNITED_FARM_WORKERS

23. Carlos Reyes Guerrero, "Silent No More: The Voice of a Farm Worker Press, 1964–1975," (PhD Diss., Claremont Graduate University, 2003), 1. See also Todd Holmes, "The Economic Roots of Reaganism: Corporate Conservatives, Political Economy, and the United Farm Workers Movement, 1965–1970," *Western Historical Quarterly* 41, no.1 (Spring 2010): 55–80.

24. Lewels, *Uses of the Media*, 64.

25. Frank Del Olmo, "Voices for the Chicano Movement," *Quill* (October 1971): 9. See also Frank Del Olmo, "Chicano Journalism: New Medium for a New Consciousness," in *Readings in Mass Communication*, 2nd ed., ed. Michael C. Emery and Ted Curtis Smythe, (Dubuque, IA: William C. Brown, 1974). Prominent Chicano newspapers included *La Raza* in Los Angeles; *El Grito del Norte*, Espanola, New Mexico; *La Verdad*, San Diego; *El Gallo*, Denver; and *Basta Ya!*, Oakland. Lewels, *Uses of the Media*, 65. See also Félix Gutiérrez and Jorge Reina Schement, "Chicanos and the Media: A Bibliography of Selected Materials," *Journalism History* 4, no. 2 (Summer 1977): 53–55.

26. Ontiveros, *In the Spirit of a New People*, 45.

27. Colin Gunckel, "Building a Movement and Constructing Community: Photography, the United Farm Workers, and *El Malcriado*," *Social Justice* 42, no. 3–4 (2015): 29.

28. Del Olmo, "Chicano Journalism," 311.

29. Félix Gutiérrez, "Reporting for *La Raza*: A History of Latino Newspapers," *Agenda* 8 (July/August 1978): 29–35.

30. A true newspaper, *Mercurio Volante*, appeared in 1693, more than a decade before the *Boston News-Letter*, the first continuously published newspaper in British colonial America. "The News Media and the Making of America," American Antiquarian Society, accessed November 1, 2018, http://americanantiquarian.org/earlyamericannewsmedia/exhibits/show/news-in-colonial-america/item/116.

31. *News for All the People*, 66.

32. Doris Meyer, *Speaking for Themselves: Neomexicano Cultural Identity and the Spanish-Language Press, 1880–1920* (Albuquerque: University of New Mexico Press, 1996). See also Rafael Chabrán, "Spaniards," in *The Immigrant Labor Press, 1840–1970: An Annotated Bibliography*, ed. Dirk Hoerder (Westport, CT: Greenwood, 1987); Carlos Cortes, "The Mexican American Press," in *The Ethnic Press in the United States: A Historical Analysis and Handbook*, ed. Sally M. Miller (Westport, CT: Greenwood Press, 1987); and Nicolás Kanellos with Helvetia Martell, *Hispanic Periodicals in the United States, Origins to 1960: A Brief History* (Houston: Arte Publico Press, 2000).

33. "A Quiet Victory for Civil Rights," *New York Times*, May 15, 2004, http://www.nytimes.com/2004/05/15/opinion/a-quiet-victory-for-civil-rights.html. *El Malcriado* also followed in the tradition of an American labor press that by the early 1830s numbered some fifty labor weeklies, although most were in the industrializing Northeast. See Rodger Streitmatter, "Origins of the American Labor Press," *Journalism History* 25, no. 3 (Autumn 1999): 99–106.

34. See Saul Alinsky, *Reveille for Radicals* (Chicago: University of Chicago Press, 1946).

35. Douglass Adair, interviewed by Greg Turex at California State University, Northridge, March 10, 1995, Farmworker Movement Oral History Project—1995, Part 1, accessed

November 1, 2018, https://libraries.ucsd.edu/farmworkermovement/media/oral_history/swf/csun/adair01.swf. [hereafter cited as Adair interview]

36. Bardacke, *Trampling Out the Vintage*, 132.

37. Pawell, *The Crusades of Cesar Chavez*, 98–99.

38. See John Adler and Draper Hill, *Doomed by Cartoon: How Cartoonist Thomas Nast and the New York Times Brought Down Boss Tweed and His Ring of Thieves* (New York: Morgan James Publishing, 2008); and Stephen Hess and Sandy Northrup, *Drawn & Quartered: The History of American Political Cartoons* (Montgomery, AL: Elliott & Clark Publishing, 1996).

39. Donald Dewey, *The Art of Ill Will: The Story of American Political Cartoons* (New York: New York University Press, 2007), 27.

40. See Linda J. Lumsden, "Striking Images: An Analysis of the Visual Rhetoric in the Radical Press," *Visual Communication Quarterly* 17, no. 4 (October–December 2010): 225–40.

41. Chris Lamb, "Drawing Power: The Limits of Editorial Cartoons in America," *Journalism Studies* 8, no. 5 (September 2007): 720.

42. Martin Medhurst and Michael Desousa, "Political Cartoons as Rhetorical Form: A Taxonomy of Graphic Discourse," *Communication Monographs* 48, no. 3 (September 1981): 204.

43. Héctor Fernández L'Hoeste and Juan Poblete, *Redrawing the Nation: National Identity in Latin/o American Comics* (New York: Palgrave Macmillan, 2009), 2.

44. *Don Sotaco y Don Coyote, EM* 1, no. 3 (nd), 9.

45. *The Boss, EM* 1, no. 17 (nd), 3.

46. *EM* 1, no. 39 (June 30, 1966,) 19.

47. "La Movide Chueca," *EM* 1, no. 18 (nd), 1.

48. *Untitled, EM* 1, no. 15 (nd), 1. Republished in *EM* 2 (June 2, 1967), 10.

49. *A Costillas de Nosotros, EM* 1, no. 14 (nd), 1. See also "Pyramid of Capitalist System," *Revolvy*, accessed October 8, 2018, https://www.revolvy.com/main/index.php?s=Pyramid+of+Capitalist+System.

50. Mike Konopacki and Gary Huck, "Labor Cartoons: Drawing on Worker Culture," in *The New Labor Press: Journalism for a Changing Union Movement*, ed. Sam Pizzigati and Fred J. Solowey (Ithaca: Cornell University Press, 1992), 129.

51. *Stewed Tomatoes, EM* 1, 19 (nd), 8.

52. *Untitled, EM* 1, no. 10 (nd [1965]), npg.

53. *Untitled, EM* 1, no. 11 (nd, [1965]), 1.

54. *EM* 1, no. 14 (nd), 8–9.

55. *Coyote Y Sotaco, EM* 1, no. 17 (nd), 11.

56. "Don Sotaco Story," *EM* 1, no. 8 (nd), 5–6.

57. *EM* 1, no. 38 (June 16, 1966), 7.

58. *EM* 1, no. 27 (January 11, 1966), 5.

59. *How Patroncito Got So Fat, EM* 1, no. 41 (July 28, 1966), 1; and *The Big Squeeze, EM* 1, no. 22 (nd), 1. See also "Historieta: Don Sotaco Como Esquirol," *EM* 1, no. 11 (nd), 8–9; and "Historieta de Don Sotaco: Chisme del Melon," *EM* 1, no. 16 (nd), 8–9.

60. *Untitled, EM* 1, no. 43A (August 26, 1966), 5.

61. *EM* 1, no. 44 (September 9, 1966), 5.

62. *Yesterday and Today, EM* 1, no. 49 (nd), 6–7.

63. "A Tale of Don Sotaco," *EM* 1, no. 38 (June 16, 1966), 12–13.

64. *EM* 1, no. 34 (April 21, 1966), 19.

65. See Robert S. Jansen, "Resurrection and Appropriation: Reputational Trajectories, Memory Work, and the Political Use of Historical Figures," *American Journal of Sociology* 112, no. 2 (January 2007): 953–1007.

66. Editorial, "Los Hombres de la Revolucion," *EM* 1 (unnumbered/nd [January 1965]), 2.

67. *Untitled, EM*, no. 77 (nd), 11. See also Leopoldo Méndez, *En el Volantin, EM* 1, no. 5 (nd), 1; David Alfaro Siqueiros, *Untitled, EM* 1, no. 7 (nd), 14; Alfredo Zalce, *Untitled, EM* 1, no. 19 (nd), 1; Jesus Escobedo, *Las Acordadas, EM* 1, no. 38 (nd), 1; and José Clemente Orozco, *The Struggle Against Injustice, EM* 1, no. 49 (nd), 22.

68. Doug Adair, "*El Malcriado* 1964–1970—Analysis," Farmworker Documentation Project, accessed July 23, 2017, https://libraries.ucsd.edu/farmworkermovement/archives/#malcriado.

69. *Zapata, EM* 1, no. 16 (nd [1965?]), cover.

70. "Editorial: Emiliano Zapata," *EM* 1, no. 16 (nd [1965?]), 2. The editorial was reprinted in *EM* 1, no. 29 (February 12, 1966), 2.

71. Adair interview.

72. "Exploits of Pancho Villa," *EM* 1, no. 52 (December 29, 1966), 20–21. See "A Friend of Villa," *EM* 1, no. 53 (January 13, 1967), 20, 10.

73. "The Plan of Delano," *EM* 1, no. 31 (March 17, 1966), 12–13.

74. "What Can One Man Do?" *EM* 1, no. 18 (nd), 15.

75. "Editorial: *Igual que los Negritos*," *EM* 1, no. 14 (nd [1965?]), 2.

76. Ibid.

77. Lauren Araiza, *To March for Others: The Black Freedom Struggle and the United Farm Workers* (Philadelphia: University of Pennsylvania Press, 2013), 28.

78. "United We Stand," *EM* 1, no. 23 (nd), 14. See also "A Union for all Farm Workers," *EM* 1, no. 39 (June 30, 1966), 18–19; and "It's Your Own Hiring Hall: How the Union Has Changed the Face of DiGiorgio," *EM* 1, no. 60 (May 10, 1967), 14–15.

79. *EM* 1, no. 52 (December 29, 1966), 31.

80. "Election News," *EM* 1, no. 32 (March 31, 1966), npg.

81. "Ang Kahuluganng Skirol," *EM* 1, no. 29 (February 12, 1966), 11; "Kasa Ysa Y Ankatapangan Ng," *EM* 1, no. 57 (March 29, 1967), 6; and "To a Bright Future," [English version] *EM* 1, no. 58 (April 12, 1967), 22. See also David Bacon, "How Filipino Migrants Gave the Grape Strike Its Radical Politics," *Dollars & Sense*, May/June 2018, http://dollarsandsense.org/archives/2018/0518bacon.html.

82. "Editorial: Enough People with One Idea," *EM* 1, no. 19 ([mid-September 1965]), 2.

83. "Why Do They Call It a Movement?," *EM* 1, no. 23 ([November 1965]), 13.

84. "Because of our Struggle Now," *EM* 1, no. 26 (December 22, 1965), 2.

85. "Enough People with One Idea," *EM* 1, no. 28 (January 26, 1966), 6.

86. "Everybody's Business," *EM* 1, no. 24 (nd), 2.

87. "The Plan of Delano," *EM* 1, no. 31 (March 17, 1966), 12–13.

88. Ana Raquel Minian, "'Indiscriminate and Shameless Sex': The Strategic Use of Sexuality by the United Farm Workers," *American Quarterly* 65, no. 1 (March 2014): 80.

89. "Editorial: Hunger ... For Justice," *EM* 1, no. 30 (February 28, 1966), 2.

90. *EM* 1, no. 56 (March 15, 1967), 3.

91. "Que Verguenza!," *EM* 1, no. 7 (nd), 14.

92. "Judas is Among Us," *EM* 1, no. 18 (nd,) 14. See also "On 'the List,'" *EM* 1, no. 19 (nd), 4.

93. "Christian Brothers—Hear Your Popes," *EM* 1, no. 56 (March 15, 1967), 8.

94. "Victory in the Grape Strike: SCHENLEY GIVES UP," *EM* 1, no. 34 (April 21, 1966), 4.

95. *EM* 1, no. 48 (November 4, 1966), 12–13. The cover featured artist Jose Guadalupe Posada's famous skeleton, "Katrina," another homage to the Mexican Revolution era.

96. "A Don Coyote Story: How the Contractors Get So Rich," *EM* 1, no. 42 (August 12, 1966), 12–13. See also "DiGiorgio: Untamed Monster," *EM* 1, no. 35 (May 5, 1966), 12–13.

97. "Dignity of the Farm Worker," *EM* 1, no. 18 (nd), 2.

98. *EM* 1, no. 46 (October 7, 1966), 19. See also *EM* 1, no. 49 (nd), 1; and "The Good … and the Bad," *EM* 1, no. 22 (nd), 3–5.

99. *Director Cesar Chavez: "Ganameros!,"* *EM* 1, no. 20 (nd), 1.

100. "The Great Parade," *EM* 1, no. 21 (nd), 4–5.

101. *EM* 1, no. 26 (nd), 10.

102. "The Day They Took Them to Jail for Shouting 'Huelga!'" *EM* 1, no. 23 (nd), 8–9.

103. "Rev. Havens Is Innocent," *EM* 1, no. 24 (nd), 5.

104. Lorenza Munoz, "An Activist's Vision," *Los Angeles Times*, April 29, 2000, http://articles.latimes.com/2000/apr/29/entertainment/ca-24552.

105. Richard Steven Street, "Delano Diary: The Visual Adventure and Social Documentary Work of Jon Lewis, Photographer of the Delano, California Grape Strike, 1966–1970," *Southern California Quarterly* 91, no. 2 (Summer 2009): 230, 234.

106. "The History of the Pilgrimage," *EM* 1, no. 33 (April 10, 1966), 5.

107. Adair interview.

108. Lewis compiled his images into a book he handcrafted, *From the Earth* (1969), and made a film version, *Nosotros Venceremos*. Street, "Delano Diary," 222, 230.

109. "Terry Scott Interviews Jon Lewis, UFW Photographer 1966/1968," Farmworker Movement Documentation Project, accessed June 25, 2017, https://libraries.ucsd.edu/farmworkermovement/media/oral_history/swf/new/JLewisAudioClip01.swf.

110. "The Schenley Contract," *EM* 1, no. 37 (June 2, 1966), 5.

111. "Police Brutality," *EM* 1, no. 27 (nd), 7; "They're Out to Get Camacho," ibid., 12; and "Farm Workers Sue DiGiorgio For $640,000," *EM* 1, no. 35 (May 5, 1966), 4.

112. "Violence by DiGiorgio," *EM* 1, no. 34 (April 21, 1966), 6; "Grower-Police Conspiracy?," *EM* 1, 41 (July 28, 1966), 14–15; and "The Ugly Face of Delano," *EM* 1, no. 47 (October 21, 1966), 1, 3–15.

113. "An Evening with DiGiorgio," *EM* 1, no. 40 (July 14, 1966), 12–13.

114. "Scabs … !" *EM* 1, no. 53 (January 13, 1967), 16–17.

115. "POISON!," *EM* 1, no. 59 (April 26, 1967), 10; and Kerry Ohta, "Allensworth," *EM* 1, no. 60 (May 10, 1967), 21.

116. Roger A. Bruns, *Encyclopedia of Cesar Chavez: The Farm Workers' Fight for Rights and Justice* (Santa Barbara, CA: ABC-CLIO, 2013), 82.

117. See "County and State Investigate Linnell and Woodville Camps," *EM* 1, no. 17 (nd), 5; "Rent Strike! The People Win!," *EM* 1, no. 23 (nd), 8; and "Tulare: Poverty Is a Crime," *EM* 1, no. 59 (April 26, 1967), 14.

118. "'Why Are the County Hospitals So Bad?,'" *EM* 1, no. 29 (February 12, 1966), 7.

119. "For Denouncing the Bad Ranchers: Is This a Bad Newspaper?" *EM* 1, no. 49 (nd), 18–19.

120. "Raul G. Hernandez to Dear Editor," and "EM Says," both *EM* 1, no. 35 (May 5, 1966), 15.

121. "Farm Workers Theatre," *EM* 1, no. 8 (January 26, 1966), 15.

122. "Perelli-Minetti Speaks: But What Did he Say?," *EM* 1, no. 57 (March 29, 1967), 21.

123. Adair interview.

124. "The Farm Workers of Alabama," *EM* 1, no. 51 ([c. mid-December 1966]) 28; "The Farm Workers' Strike Spreads to Florida," *EM* 1, no. 53 (January 13, 1967), 22; "Michigan Campesinos March," *EM*, no. 58 (April 12, 1967), 25; "Arizona: Mass Lockout," *EM* 1, no. 6 (May 10, 1967), 16; and *EM* 1, no. 62 (June 7, 1967), 15.

125. "Boycott!," *EM* 1, no. 30 (February 28, 1966), 18–19. See also *The Boycott Network*, *EM* 3, no. 57 (March 29, 1967), insert; "Friends in Washington," *EM* 1, no. 36 (May 19, 1966), 21; and "San Francisco—We've Got Friends," *EM* 1, no. 56 (March 15, 1967), npg.

126. Edwin W. Huser to Dear Editor, *EM* 1, no. 50 (December 2, 1966), 4.

127. Bardacke, *Trampling out the Vintage*, 273–74. Chavez and the UFW officially came out against the Vietnam War in October 1969. "UFWOC Joins War Protests," *EM* 1, no. 14 (October 15–31, 1969), 12.

128. "Editorial: The Fight for Humanity," *EM* 1, no. 52 (December 29, 1966), 3. See also "Farm Worker Children," *EM* 1, no. 51 ([c. mid-December 1966]), 11; "The Leprous Face of War," *EM* 1, no. 54 (January 13, 1967), 5; "A Victim of War," *EM* 1, no. 55 (March 1, 1967), 13; and "Mexicans and the Draft," *EM* 1, no. 58 (April 12, 1967), 24.

129. "'A Chavista' to Dear Editor," *EM* 1, no. 58 (April 12, 1967), 5.

130. "Schenley's Fairy Tales," *EM* 1, no. 28 (January 26, 1966), 12.

131. "Sues *El Malcriado* for One Million Dollars," *EM* 1, no. 48 (November 4, 1966), 11. See "How the Teamsters and the Growers Cheat the Workers in Salinas," *EM* 1, no. 42 (August 12, 1966), 22; *Untitled*, *EM* 1, no. 43 (August 26, 1966), 8; and "Patron Bud Antle says: 'El Malcriado is a Liar,'" *EM* 1, no. 45 (September 25, 1966,) 12–14.

132. "Libel Suit Hits Union, Chavez," *Madera Daily Tribune*, May 5, 1967, 1.

133. The illustration was by Mexican artist Fernando Castro Pacheco. "JUDAS IN ACTION Betrayal In Delano," *EM* 1, no. 45 (September 23, 1966), 4; and "Huge Swindle at Perelli-Monetti," *EM* 1, no. 47 (October 21, 1966), 12–13. [capital letters in original]

134. "Perelli-Minetti Defends Itself," *EM* 1, no. 49 (nd), 12–15. Adair blamed the libelous story on Daniel de Los Reyes, a Mexico City reporter that joined the staff in 1966. See Doug Adair, "El Malcriado, 1966–67," July 12, 2009, Farmworker Movement Documentation Project, https://libraries.ucsd.edu/farmworkermovement/ufwarchives/elmalcriado/elmalcriado4.pdf.

135. "Perelli-Minetti Never Belonged to the Mafia," *EM* 1, no. 50 (December 2, 1966), 16, 20.

136. "The P-M Firings," *EM* 1, no. 58 (April 12, 1967), 7. See also "… Something that Reminds Us of Nazi Germany," *EM* 1, no. 48 (November 1966), 10.

137. EM 1, no. 58 (April 12, 1967), 32. See also "What Is He Hiding?" EM 1, no. 55 (March 1, 1967), 15; "Tell the Truth, Mister A. Perelli-Minetti!," EM 1, no. 55 (March 1, 1967), 14; and "And the Right Answer!" EM 1, no. 55 (March 1, 1967), 15, 18, 30.

138. Adair, "El Malcriado 1968–1970."

139. Adair interview. See EM 1, no. 40 (July 14, 1966), 1.

140. EM 1, no. 54 (January 13, 1967), 3. See also Bill Esher, "The Story Behind the Crime," EM 1, no. 55 (March 1, 1967), 22, 24–25.

141. See "'La Dolce Vita' in the North," in EM 1, no. 52 (December 29, 1966), 22–29. The series continued in: ibid., no. 53 (December 29, 1967) [sic], 26–29; no. 55 (March 1, 1967), 26–29; no. 56 (March 15, 1967), 26–29; no. 57 (March 29, 1967), 26–29; no. 58 (April 12, 1967), 26–29; no. 59 (April 26, 1967), 26–29; no. 60 (May 10, 1967), 27–31; no. 62 (June 7, 1967), 20–31; and no. 63E (June 1967), 20–23.

142. "Important Notice," EM 1, no. 55 (March 1, 1967), 12.

143. See "Starr County," EM 1, 53 (January 13, 1967), 15–16; "The Hell That Is Texas," EM 1, no. 56 (March 15, 1967), 10–11, 31; "This Is the Texas Strike," EM 1, no. 57 (March 29, 1967), 9–14; "First Vote in Texas," EM 1, no. 59 (April 26, 1967), 12–13; "The Struggle to Save Texas," EM 1, no. 61 (May 24, 1967), 15–18; and "Texas Rangers Arrest 22," EM 1, no. 62 (June 7, 1967), 16.

144. "That's the Way It Should Be," EM 1, no. 60 (May 10, 1967), 3; Felix Zapata, "Editorial," EM 1, no. 62 (June 7, 1967), 2; and Editorial, "Luming Imutan," EM 1, no. 63E (June 1967), 2–3.

145. "Editorial," EM 1, no. 64 (July 5, 1967), 4–5.

146. Editorial, "We're Back," EM 2 (March 15, 1968), 2.

147. By mid-1968, grape shipments dropped by 41 percent in Chicago, 42 percent in Boston, and 98 percent in New York City. Holmes, "Economic Roots of Reaganism," 70.

148. Gloria Steinem to Manuel [Chavez], April 24, 1969 [?], Box 208, Folder 3, Gloria Steinem Papers. Sophia Smith Collection, Smith College, Northampton, MA. [hereafter cited as Steinem Papers]

149. Adair interview.

150. Bardacke, Trampling Out the Vintage, 260.

151. Guerrero, "Silent No More," 116.

152. "We Are Accused," EM 2 (February 21, 1968), 2. The twenty-five day fast followed Chavez's innocent plea to a criminal contempt of court charge of allegedly violating an injunction requiring picketers to stand fifty feet apart. "Frame Up," ibid., 1.

153. Robert A. Gutwillig to Gloria Steinem, March 3, 1969, Box 208, Folder 3, Steinem Papers.

154. "26 Ranches, 7000 Workers Covered by Latest Contracts, HUELGA ENDS," EM 4 (August 1, 1970), 4–6. [capital letters in original]

155. See "Poster of the Week," Center for the Study of Political Graphics, October 19, 2012, http://cspgblog.blogspot.com/2012/10/poster-of-week_19.html.

156. "Dear Papa … ," EM 4 (September 1, 1970), 6.

157. Bardacke, Trampling Out the Vintage, 534–35.

158. Baughn argues that Chavez's 1968 fast created "a cult of personality around Chavez" that ultimately doomed the union. Baughn, "César Chávez and the 1968 Fast," 21.

159. Nathan Heller, "Hunger Artist: How Cesar Chavez Disserved his Dream," *New Yorker*, April 14, 2014, http://www.newyorker.com/magazine/2014/04/14/hunger-artist-2.

160. See Elaine Ayala, "Marching on César Chávez's Non-birthday Is a Story of Pettiness," *San Antonio Express*, March 25, 2018, https://www.expressnews.com/news/news_columnists/elaine_ayala/article/Marching-on-Cesar-Ch-vez-s-non-birthday-is-a-12780705.php; Geoffrey Mohan, "FCC Fines Cesar Chavez Foundation Over Promotions on Its Radio Stations," *Los Angeles Times*, February 2, 2018, http://www.latimes.com/business/la-fi-ufw-fine-20180202-story.html; and Amy Wu, "UFW Ordered to Pay $1.2M in Wages, OT," *Californian*, March 29, 2107, https://www.thecalifornian.com/story/news/2017/03/29/ufw-ordered-pay-12m-unpaid-wages-overtime/99800788/.

161. Juan Lopez, "Farm Workers March for Justice," *People's World*, August 25, 2011, https://www.peoplesworld.org/article/farm-workers-march-for-justice-2/.

· 7 ·

Ms.

The First Feminist Mass Media Magazine

Forty years before actress Alyssa Milano tweeted "Me too" in fall 2017, Ms. magazine put sexual harassment on its cover. The term had barely entered the public lexicon. To avoid exploiting an actual woman, editors used puppets for the November 1977 image of a man's hand reaching into a woman's blouse. Some stores still banned it. The story cited a study in which 88 percent of women claimed they experienced sexual harassment on the job and related appalling anecdotes. The story predicted, "What we have so far seen, is only the tip of a very large and very destructive iceberg."[1]

Ms. was right, as the first feminist mass magazine usually had been since its debut six years earlier as a special forty-four-page insert tucked inside *New York* magazine; the preview issue of Ms. magazine rolled off the presses in spring 1972 and the first regular issue that July. The 1977 sexual harassment cover story reframed what had been viewed as a private problem into a political issue, in a perfect articulation of the women's liberation movement epiphany that the personal is political. Forty years later, Ms. published a cover story on the #MeToo movement, demonstrating both the snail's pace of social change and the durability of the oldest Second Wave feminist periodical still publishing.[2]

Ms. was far from the most radical women's liberation journal—one analyst described the mass magazine as an "intermediary change agent"—but it stands as the most influential and enduring product of a dynamic feminist print culture that revolutionized American women's lives.[3] In the 1970s, Ms. was the only original nationwide magazine edited for and by women, the only women's magazine regularly included in the White House press summary, the only women's magazine astronaut Sally Ride carried into space. Ms. magazine introduced millions of Americans to such concepts as feminism, pay equity, reproductive justice, LGBTQ rights, domestic abuse, date rape, and workplace sexual harassment. Feminism infiltrated mainstream America in part through Ms. magazine. Even scholar Amy Erdman Farrell, whose insightful book critiques the compromises that advertising forced upon this "fascinating hybrid," acknowledges, "Ms. played a central role in helping to create and disseminate a feminist consciousness across the nation."[4] Smaller, more radical feminist periodicals reached far fewer readers, while the mammoth "Seven Sisters" consumer magazines remained mired in outdated stereotypes.[5] Ms. was unique among social movement media because it tried to sell revolutionary ideas about women's place *and* sell the corporate advertising that fuels institutions of patriarchal capitalism.

This chapter explores the first feminist mass magazine's role as both chronicler and shaper of feminism in the latter twentieth-century, when its very name reframed female identity. "When Ms. debuted, I subscribed," a sixty-three-year-old woman wrote on the Ms. *Blog* on its forty-fifth anniversary. "For me, like so many young women of my generation, it was a lifeline to know that others felt the same as I did and were fighting the same battles. I never called myself anything but 'Ms.' from then on."[6] The chapter argues that Second Wave feminists' flawed attempt to triumph in the mass media marketplace succeeded in producing social justice journalism that instigated important social change. As one of its thousands of devoted readers wrote, "In many ways Ms. is the only major voice and hope through mass media for most people."[7] The chapter traces Ms. to 1980, when it was converted into an educational nonprofit periodical, ending the first phase of its feminist experiment in the mass-media marketplace. It concludes with a look at today's nonprofit Ms. online, where its more than 300,000 Facebook fans and nearly 150,000 Twitter followers rival the Fourth Wave's top digital influencers.[8]

Perhaps more than any other journal analyzed in this study, Ms. excelled at social justice journalism through groundbreaking investigations, interviews, editorials, and imagery. Its egalitarian management structure highlights structural differences between social movement media and corporate news media, as did its tortured relationship with advertisers. The magazine in the 1970s inspired a strong collective identity palpable in thousands of letters to the editor and nurtured by editorial innovations such as "No Comment"—a crowd-sourced smackdown of sexist advertisements; nonsexist "Stories for Free Children"; and the "Lost Women" column that retrieved to readers' historical memory heroes such as Harriet Tubman. The white-dominated, middle-class Ms. also angered and alienated some radical feminists, lesbians, women of color, transgender women, and conservative women, who charged that Ms. overlooked them, a critique that tested co-founder Gloria Steinem's sunny faith in a sisterhood that transcends all other difference. Questions of inclusion and intersectionality remain at the heart of digitally driven Fourth Wave feminism. The Internet has both widened and fractured feminism, and the Fourth Wave's online discourse is probably even more contentious than Second Wave print culture.

Second Wave Feminist Print Culture

A seminal document in Second Wave history is New York Radical Women's *Notes from the First Year*, a one-time publication founded by Shulamith Firestone that functioned as a theoretical forum and chronicler of radical feminists' theatrical bursts of collective action.[9] They tossed false eyelashes, girdles, mops, and other symbols of female oppression into a "Freedom trash can" on the Atlantic City boardwalk in their first protest at the 1968 Miss America pageant.[10] *Notes* seethed against the sexist New Left that many female activists fled. "If we have anything to say to movement men at this point it is—Fuck Male Standards!" read one essay. "We don't care what you want."[11] The twenty women who produced *Notes* rejected hierarchical systems of patriarchy by sharing equal credit. *Notes* introduced the revolutionary feminist concept that "the personal is political," refuted what it labeled "the myth of the vaginal orgasm," and advocated consciousness-raising as the key to liberation. It published founder Firestone's speech for legalizing abortion: "We are tired of being pawns in a male power game. Tired of being bought and sold and traded and used to sell your deodorants and hair sprays."[12] Firestone organized the nation's first abortion speak-out in March 1969, which Steinem covered for *New York* magazine in her first article on the women's movement. Steinem walked away a feminist.[13]

New York Radical Women rejected Betty Friedan's *The Feminine Mystique*, which in 1963 galvanized a generation of white housewives who embraced her diagnosis of their "problem with no name" as basically their lack of careers. NYRW's Marxist-influenced re-envisioning of public and private life was much more revolutionary than that of the National Organization for Women that Friedan co-founded in 1966, which sought "to bring women into full participation in the mainstream of American society." Jo Freeman (aka Joreen) gave the radical branch its name with *Voice of the Women's Liberation Movement*, the first nationwide women's liberation newsletter that she published in Chicago for seven issues, beginning in March 1968.[14] Freeman's essay "What in the Hell Is Women's Liberation, Anyway?" distinguished the movement from Friedan's liberal feminism by aligning women's lib with struggles against all oppression.[15] Freeman, who studied at the University of California, Berkeley, and registered black voters in Mississippi, knew from working in the South that a newsletter "created a sense that something important was happening."[16] She described the early women's liberation movement as "linked only by the numerous journals, newsletters and cross country travelers."[17]

Newsletters were the chief mechanism for diffusion of Second Wave ideology and strategies since women's liberation groups were small and far apart and mainly in cities.[18] Scholar Anne Mather counted more than 500 feminist periodicals created between 1968 and 1973.[19] Feminist pamphlets, newsletters, newspapers, magazines, and books were available only at feminist conferences and women's centers, sites for women's lib culture that spawned feminist publishing houses. "When male printers refused to print our articles about self-help vaginal exams, the real lives of women in prostitution, or lesbian self-esteem, we established our own printing presses so that no man could ever again tell women what we could read," recalled Carol Seajay, founder of the Feminist Bookstore Network. Feminists also established their own typesetting shops, binderies, wholesale distributors, and bookstores.[20] Historian Kristen Hogan counted more than 100 feminist bookstores that opened their doors across the United States from the 1970s through the 1990s.[21]

The title of the first women's liberation newspaper, *off our backs*, proclaimed its rejection of male supremacy. The fierce twelve-page tabloid that debuted in Washington, D.C., on February 27, 1970, defined its mission as providing "news and information about women's lives and feminist activism; to educate the public about the status of women around the world; to serve as a forum for feminist ideas and theory; to be an information resource on feminist, women's, and lesbian culture; and to seek social justice and equality for women worldwide." Besides making all decisions by consensus, the *off our backs* collective was so adamantly egalitarian it cast out co-founder Marilyn Webb because she was the only member with journalism experience.[22] Partly because of this anti-elitist ethic, early feminist papers featured "not-quite-aligned layouts, sometimes poorly written pieces, and amateur poetry and drawings. Many articles were signed simply 'Susan' or 'Randy,' or not signed at all, because the movement was hostile to the idea of intellectual property," according to Rosalyn Baxandall and Linda Gordon. "Nevertheless, it was in these homespun rags that you could find the most creative and cutting-edge theory and commentary."[23] The imagined community the periodicals forged among distant women nurtured a collective identity reminiscent of how nineteenth-century suffrage newspapers sustained far-flung readers—but with a lot more four-letter words.

Off our backs's call for women to cut all ties with mass media reflected the feminist belief that they "exploited, distorted, belittled, or patronized women and the women's movement," in the words of Linda Steiner.[24] One of Firestone's most militant acts occurred during the 1970 takeover of the *Ladies' Home Journal* office by a hundred radical feminists, when she jumped on the desk of editor-in-chief John Mack Carter and tore up copies of the magazine in his face. 1970 proved a milestone for feminist media. In January, future *Ms.* editor (and former Miss America protester) Robin Morgan led female staffers' takeover of the New Left's *Rat* and converted it into a feminist newspaper. Morgan memorably broke with the "toxic sexism of the left" in *Rat*'s first women's issue in her iconic essay, "Goodbye to All That":

> Let it seem bitchy, catty, dykey, Solaniseque, frustrated, crazy, nutty, frigid, ridiculous, bitter, embarrassing, man-hating, libelous, pure, unfair, envious, intuitive, low-down, stupid, petty, liberating. **We are the women that men have warned us about.**[25]

She and her young son received death threats.[26] Besides *Notes from the Second Year*, 1970 saw publication of Firestone's *The Dialectic of Sex: The Case for Feminist Revolution*, Kate Millett's *Sexual Politics*, and an anthology edited by Morgan, *Sisterhood Is Powerful*, named by the New York Public Library as one of the most influential books of the twentieth century.[27]

The First Feminist Mass Media Magazine

All of this literature informed *Ms.*, which was conceived in 1971 by a handful of women journalists who met in Steinem's New York apartment to discuss the idea of a national woman's periodical edited entirely by women. Steinem envisioned another newsletter, but Patricia Carbine, then editor of *McCall's*, and others protested that to be taken seriously and effect change, the publication had to look and feel like a glossy women's magazine. The cover of the forty-four-page insert inside *New York*'s December 1971 issue featured a blue Hindu-like goddess with many hands, juggling women's many roles. The issue sold out in eight days.

Inside, Steinem wrote earnestly about "Sisterhood," Jane O'Reilly immortalized the "Click!" of consciousness-raising, and Vivian Gornick addressed why women fear success. Readers found a "how to" on writing a marriage contract and ratings of political candidates on women's issues. Other feminist articles that spilled into the regular *New York* offered suggestions on getting rid of sexist pronouns and an exposé of sex roles in early childhood education. *Washington Post* publisher Katharine Graham donated $20,000 and Warner Communications invested a million dollars, elevating *Ms.* to a capitalist enterprise that dwarfed the crude pioneering women's lib newsletters by financing a print run of 300,000 copies of a 128-page, ad-packed Spring 1972 Preview Issue.

The issue offered a bold experiment in building collective identity with "We Have Had Abortions," a statement signed by fifty-three women, including Steinem, Billie Jean King, Barbara Tuchman, and Judy Collins a year before *Roe v. Wade* legalized abortion. The "American Women's Petition" for safe and legal abortion grew to more than 1,200 names of women who returned a mail-in form. *Ms.* published all their names in October, amplifying their collective action by inviting readers to add their own names and send the entire list to their legislators as the Supreme Court prepared to rule on whether abortion was a constitutional right.[28] Other articles addressed race, class, and sexuality. Eleanor Holmes Norton discussed the black family, and the head of the National Welfare Rights Organization explained why welfare is a woman's issue. Anne Koedt wrote about lesbian sex, and Pentagon Papers' leaker Daniel Ellsberg discussed women and war. "A Story for Free Children" debuted, launching the magazine's runaway commercial and critical success, a series of nonsexist tales for children. Literature included fiction by Cynthia Ozick and a play by Sylvia Plath. "Child Care Center: Who, How and Where" established the magazine's template of agency frames that offered solutions to problems it addressed.

Ms. content was nearly as significant for what was missing from its pages—the "supportive copy" about cooking, fashion, and beauty that filled other women's magazines to lure advertisers. Liquor and cigarette ads, however, abounded. Some 26,000 readers subscribed, boosting the all-female Ms. sales department's ability to land big accounts for cars, electronics, and other products that shunned traditional women's magazines.[29] Four years after its debut, Ms. boasted a half-million paid circulation and a total readership of more than two million people, higher than the *New Yorker* or the *Atlantic*. The feminist mass magazine appeared a success.

A Collective Spirit Inside *Ms.*

Women's response to Ms. revealed a hunger for the magazine's flashy feminist journalism. Tens of thousands of women in spring 1972 mailed 20,000 letters to the editors, a number ten times higher than typically received by popular magazines.[30] Historian Ruth Rosen describes the letters' revelations as a "national consciousness-raising group."[31] Steinem correctly called them "advance messengers of every major social, political, and demographic change for women. They made Ms. the forum, communicator, and pioneer of change."[32] Decades before social media made feedback instantaneous, letters to Ms. connected readers in an extraordinarily powerful and personal network. They also reveal an unusually strong bond between the magazine and its readers. In the introduction to her collection of Ms. letters, one-time executive editor Mary Thom stated, "Ms. was founded to give voice to the concerns of a movement, and the letters help us fulfill that purpose."[33]

Letter writers' sense of relief that they were not alone is almost palpable. Correspondents dealt with highly contentious social issues such as the Equal Rights Amendment, pay equity, racism, childcare, rape, body image, abortion, sexuality, and language. Some were confessional, like the reader who as a child had been raped by her sister's boyfriend. Others told tales of rebirth, like a mother of three who returned to college. A female bartender in Bronson, Kansas, sent in her sassy comebacks to rowdy bartenders; a nurse revealed how she covertly placed a Ms. article on alternatives to mastectomy in the surgeons' mailboxes at her hospital; a closeted lesbian reached out for support from Michigan's Upper Peninsula. Thom explained, "Ms. readers look to the

Letters column as a caring community to share their reactions to national events that affected them...."[34]

The staff practiced the feminism it preached. "Its agenda did make Ms. seem more like a social movement than a national magazine," recalled Thom, who began as a researcher.[35] The magazine organized itself horizontally in accord with the feminist rejection of hierarchy. All editors' names appeared alphabetically on the masthead without titles. They communally decided to set salaries according to need and experience. Only publisher and editor-in-chief Carbine had her own office; everyone else worked in a large but crowded space on Lexington Avenue. The staff conducted its own conscious-raising meetings to address issues that arose from the nontraditional setup, such as confusion about work responsibilities.

Ms. followed several conventions of mass-media periodicals. To engage readers, it favored and emphasized personal stories over feminist theory. Second Wave historian Alice Echols described Ms.'s emphasis on self-help as a "pull-yourself-up-by-your-bootstraps" feminism that appealed to many women.[36] Like traditional women's magazines, it featured reader "how-tos" rooted in individual solutions. The magazine's emphasis on individual success also contradicted collective action. "It is significant that in Ms. all women are exceptional women," a 1979 reviewer observed.[37] Another complained of the superwomen profiles: "They make you tired just to read them."[38] Thom acknowledged the "editorial bias toward an individual woman's experience" but rejected charges the magazine ignored a collective approach to ending oppression. "Over and over again, articles and news coverage argued the necessity of institutional and systemic change," she wrote.[39] The emphasis on dramatic personal narratives may have been more effective than critics realize, however, since emotion is acknowledged as a great mobilizer of collection action.

An unpublished paper from 1974 analyzing Ms. as a "change agent" claims the magazine's collective action frames emphasized injustice and identity frames over agency frames. Ms. staffers viewed themselves as members of an "insulated organization in a sexist culture," Faith Dickerson and Janet Weinglass wrote. Identity frames hostile toward "purveyors of sexism" strengthened the magazine's "us versus them" dynamic. The magazine frequently made "explicit statements of injustice experienced by women because they are women" in "relatively extreme and emotional terms." Examples cited from the November 1974 issue included: women blamed for male violence; female rock groups not taken seriously; female writers valued less than men. These frames prioritized identity over agency in the sense they offered resources for individuals to address sexism but suggested few avenues for collective action for redress. The authors applied Robert K. Merton's notion of obligation to the magazine's collective action frames: "By taking the onus off the woman reader and putting it on the society-at-large, the magazine seems to be saying, 'It's not your fault; you're O.K.; but it's up to us, women, to right these societal ills.'"[40]

Ms.'s Social Justice Journalism

Ms.'s social justice journalism, however, contradicts that assessment. The magazine invariably provided resources to solve problems it unearthed. Its groundbreaking investigations revealed complications of breast implant surgery,[41] dangerous ingredients in cosmetics,[42] and health threats to mascara factory workers.[43] When Ms. became the first national magazine to report on workplace sexual harassment, for example, it also offered suggestions on what to do about it.[44] The magazine even sponsored a speak-out in New York City where women shared stories and tactics in an effort to make state legislators take sexual harassment seriously. A trailblazing investigation into domestic abuse was accompanied by extensive information on how and where to get help.[45] The only magazine to regularly cover the long, doomed Equal Rights Amendment campaign, Ms. in 1976 was among magazines led by *Redbook* and *Glamour* that coordinated publication of pro-ERA articles in thirty-eight national women's magazines. A story on alternatives to radical mastectomy to treat breast cancer was accompanied by a list of physicians that offered the alternatives.[46] The March 1974 issue included a pullout chart on sex discrimination laws and instructions on how and where to complain. Ms. not only broke stories on the dangers facing daughters whose mothers took DES but also facilitated a DES task force that issued a national alert in October 1978.[47]

The magazine was arguably the best source of diverse news on women in the 1970s. It uncovered and published in-depth stories about Karen Silkwood and Crystal Lee Jordan, the factory worker whose story inspired the film, "Norma Rae."[48] It meticulously calculated the economic value of housework ($13,391.56 annually in 1972);[49] Sheila Tobias exposed the toll of math anxiety among girls,[50] Susan Brownmiller identified rape as a tool of war,[51] and Simone de Beauvoir pondered how she came to feminism.[52] Barbara Ehrenreich debunked the myth that female executives were prone to heart attacks.[53]

Golda Meir told Oriana Fallaci that feminists are crazy man-haters, and Bernadette Devlin explained Northern Ireland's independence movement.[54] All of these articles are evidence for editor Thom's assertion, "Ms. was a powerful catalyst for public discourse on feminist issues."[55]

Although white, heterosexual, affluent women predominated, the magazine did publish works about marginalized women. *Furies* publisher Charlotte Bunch's "Learning from Lesbian Separatism" appeared in November 1976, and in February 1977, Steinem penned "Transexualism: If the Shoe Doesn't Fit, Change the Foot," years before the transgender community had even a newsletter. Kate Millett profiled Angela Davis,[56] who in turn wrote about imprisoned rape survivor Joanne Little,[57] and Michelle Wallace deconstructed "The Myth of Black Macho."[58] The anonymous "The Birthplace of Machismo" in October 1972 was the first of several articles on Latino women's issues.[59]

Professional Journalists and "Rabble Rousers"

Unlike most social movement periodicals, Ms. staff included highly skilled professional reporters that elevated the quality of its journalism. Lisa Wohl, who exposed a fake physician experimenting with a dangerous abortion procedure, had been an Associated Press reporter; B.J. Phillips had reported for *Time* magazine; and Lindsy Van Gelder was a former *New York Post* reporter.[60] Carbine edited *McCall's* and *Look* before Ms., and for a decade before she edged into activism, Steinem herself was a successful magazine journalist, best known for her 1963 undercover exposé of exploitative working conditions in Playboy Bunny Clubs.[61]

Steinem disliked neutral reporting that lacked opinion or a point of view. "That makes for a blandness that I find it hard to relate to," she once said. The false balance generated by the "he said, she said" style of newspaper journalism annoyed her.[62] She questioned the elusive journalistic quest for objectivity in 1974 in *Folio*, the magazine trade journal. "Perhaps we need to think, all of us in this industry, less about what is supposed to be objectivity and more about accuracy."[63] Frequent Ms. contributor and one-time editor Robin Morgan also described her writing as "unabashedly nonobjective 'participatory journalism.'"[64] Editor Letty Cottin Pogrebin once described the editorial staff as "rabble-rousers." In her view, journalism was inextricable from their social justice agenda: "We publicized grass-roots organizations and local feminist leaders. We reported on street demonstrations, consciousness-raising groups, cutting-edge lawsuits, and legislative initiatives. We advocated for the beleaguered and the silenced. We helped make a revolution."[65] Pogrebin also was a successful book author and magazine columnist steeped in the power of fact. She once dug up 1,377 pages of documents that exposed FBI spying on the women's movement as part of its illegal COINTELPRO program in the 1960s.[66]

Collaborating with Readers and Writers

Ms. also encouraged readers to get involved with its content. Thom called the Ms. audience "an essential collaborator in the process of producing feminist journalism." She described its pages as "a journalism that made a text out of the lives of the participants, editor, writer, and reader alike."[67] Van Gelder, for example, not only produced tough investigative pieces but also came out as a lesbian in a February 1984 piece, "Marriage As a Restricted Club." It detailed her decision to stop attending weddings of straight friends and family members (although editors dallied two years before publishing it). Ms. editors were exceptionally receptive to the thousands of women who mailed Ms. unsolicited stories and poems every year. They read everything that came in, which on average included annually 9,000 unsolicited poems; 4,800 general story queries; 2,400 Gazette queries; 20,800 submissions to "No Comment"; and 3,300 letters to the editor.[68] If editors agreed to publish a piece, they did not change copy without the author's permission. "And if the writer really disagrees, then the writer wins," Steinem once said.[69] At least three editors read each piece, and many manuscripts were circulated among even more editors, who scribbled notes in the margins.

Steinem worked hard with new authors to get marginalized voices into the magazine. Her editorial notes on an interview with former Black Panther Ericka Huggins submitted by unknown writer Michele Russell show how editors nurtured the aspiring journalist. Alice Walker, a part-time editor and future author of The Color Purple, waxed enthusiastic: "She's radical, black, feminist and cares." Joanne Edgar found the piece moving but with many "loose ends." Steinem offered to edit the submission, recommending Russell omit her interview questions and slash the text by at least a third. She also came up with the title for the piece published that April: "What's a Nice Girl Like You Doing in the Black Panther Party?"[70] Editors were tougher on established authors. Morgan began her memo on Fear of Flying author Erica Jong's stab at an essay on feminism: "Stunningly naïve, factually inaccurate, pretentious, preachy, historically wrong, and a severe case of the terminal acute Dumbs."[71] The collective approach was time consuming, however, and one former staffer complained the practice rewarded the "lowest common denominator."[72]

Besides promoting new authors, the editors retrieved historical figures in feminist history that helped rebuild a feminist collective memory. One of Walker's first articles for Ms. recounted her hunt for the Florida grave of a forgotten black writer. "In Search of Zora Neale Hurston" in March 1975 was accompanied by a list of Hurston's books and a box filled with quotes from her work, launching the rediscovery of the Harlem Renaissance author. Editors were very conscious of Ms.'s place in feminist history and prided themselves that it served as magazine-of-record for the national women's movement. Its bibliographies, lists of publications, and local feminist organizations not only linked contemporary activists but also remain part of the Second Wave's historical record. Ms. published full texts of the La Raza Unida feminist platform (December 1972); the Bill of Rights for Household Workers (February 1973); Statement of Purpose of the National Black Feminist Organization (May 1974); and all twenty-six resolutions of the 1977 National Woman's Conference in Houston, Texas, in which many staffers actively participated. It once presciently stated, "Just as we now turn to Susan B. Anthony's magazine, Revolution, as a source on the first wave of feminism, it's probable that scholars of the next century will turn to Ms. when studying this wave."[73]

Shaping Feminist Culture

In addition to chronicling a feminist past, Ms. shaped an evolving Second Wave feminist culture by introducing women writers and highlighting women in other arts. Besides Walker, the long list of writers it introduced to a national audience included Jong, Ntozake Shange, Mary Gordon, and Barbara Ehrenreich. In addition to showcasing women in "Ms. on the Arts," it created feminist events that fostered collective identity. Ms. sponsored the Ms. Metric Mile in the 1974 U.S. Olympic trials, an important step toward women finally competing in the Olympic marathon a decade later. The following year it organized the first major concert of orchestral compositions by women, featuring Sarah Caldwell conducting the New York Philharmonic at Lincoln Center. The discography listed ninety-five pieces of orchestral music composed by forty-five women.[74] The magazine amplified the feminist message when mainstream media repurposed its contents: Maria de Dargo's essay on growing up Latina inspired a PBS TV special; an essay on Harriet Tubman became a book; and Judith Thurman's profile of Isak Dinesen led to her biography of the writer and the film "Out of Africa."[75] Ms. also was a role model for the global feminist journals F in France, Emma in Germany, and Effe in Italy.

One of Ms.'s biggest cultural influences elevated a World War II comic book character into a feminist icon. The first regular Ms. cover in July 1972 featured a giant "Wonder Woman" bounding across a toy-sized city and beneath a banner that read, "Wonder Woman for President." Historian Jill Lepore says the cover choice staked out Ms.'s turf as a serious political magazine.[76] "In a sea of women's magazines featuring models, actresses, and delicate hors d'oeuvres, the Ms. cover suggested female readers had more on their minds than beauty hacks and dinner," Katie Kilkenny averred.[77] Steinem, who relished Wonder Woman comics as a girl, republished an old strip in Ms. and collected a dozen more in a book.[78] She selected only the most empowering storylines to construct the strongest possible Wonder Woman, rejecting postwar versions that diminished the superhero's powers (or that portrayed acts of bondage, a staple of the original strip).[79] Largely thanks to the attention generated by Ms., DC Comics launched a revamped Wonder Woman in 1973 that restored the heroine's magic lasso, bulletproof bracelets, and invisible airplane. Wonder Woman became a popular television show in 1975, and in 2017, director Patty Jenkins's blockbuster film continued "to frame the classic Wonder Woman as an icon for sisterhood and equality."[80]

Constructing and Covering Feminism

The Wonder Woman cover is one among many that remain striking artifacts that make the magazine a repository of Second Wave collective memory. Like the Ms. editors, Brazilian-born art director Bea Feitler was a seasoned professional who had spent the previous decade as co-director of art at Harper's Bazaar.[81] Her lush covers often were the battleground for the magazine's clashing imperatives to succeed commercially and vanquish sexism. Covers had to be eye-catching to stand out on crowded newsstands but also stay true to Ms.'s serious agenda. The magazine struggled between aesthetics and substance in cover choices while trying to avoid stereotypes. Despite objections from the appalled sales department, for example, the August 1976 cover proved popular on newsstands even though it featured a photograph of a battered women's swollen, bruised face for a groundbreaking story on domestic abuse. Perhaps its most shocking image appeared just after the *Roe v. Wade* ruling in 1973 established women's constitutional right to abortion. The grisly black-and-white photograph showed an unnamed woman's naked corpse sprawled stomach-down, knees bent over a blood-soaked towel, the aftermath of an illegal abortion in a Connecticut motel room.[82] Editors argued over how to handle the graphic image. "We didn't want to seem to be using it for sensationalism, and we thought about it for a long time," Steinem said.[83] They ran the photograph small on an inside page, and the image became an icon of the reproductive rights movement. The most agonizing cover debate illustrated the compromises the marketplace demanded of the magazine. It pitted a story about Andy Warhol superstar Viva breast-feeding her five-year-old daughter against an exclusive exposé on the suspicious death of union activist Silkwood. "But it came down to the art: a crumpled car versus gorgeous Viva with hair flowing to the heavens," editor Harriet Lyons acknowledged. Viva won. "Of course, we all regretted it."[84]

Tensions Between Collectivity and Commercialism

The Viva cover illustrates the constraints on a social movement journal attempting to succeed in a commercial environment. The flip side of the empowering "Wonder Woman" cover, for example, featured a blond in a bikini sprawled on a beach in an ad for Coppertone. Even though "No Comment's" shaming of sexist ads bit the hand that fed it, Ms. needed advertising. Management justified ads as a necessary evil to deliver the feminist message to a mass audience even though many readers despised them. Selling ads meant that unlike other social movement media, the magazine had to view its audience as consumers. Historian Farrell argues Ms.'s reliance on advertising doomed it as a feminist platform because of what she terms the "censorship of the commercial."[85] Enmeshed in the free market system, Ms. never challenged capitalism, limiting its ability to prescribe real change in poor women's lives. Whirlpool sent the staff issues of Ms. with every sexual word underlined in a yellow marker to illustrate why it would not advertise in its pages. Yet Ms. did push back against advertiser pressure. It once put Walker on a cover much to the displeasure of its southern distributor, and it published lesbian stories even though they scared away advertisers. It refused sexist ads, like Philip Morris ads for Virginia Slims with the tagline, "You've Come a Long Way, Baby" (the only cigarette ad it declined).[86] Ms. in the 1970s contained no cover stories about women and alcoholism or about nicotine's lethal addiction. Other ads for perfume and other personal products reified conservative notions of womanhood.[87] Only after Ms. became ad-free in 1990 did Steinem somewhat hypocritically critique the corporate hold on women's magazines that rendered their contents "far below the journalistic and ethical standards of news and general interest publications."[88]

Radical Women's Critiques of *Ms.*

Advertising in Ms. was just one among many criticisms that radical feminists leveled against the magazine in the mid-1970s. "[M]any radical feminists maintain Ms. is a 'house organ of liberalism,' a false shadow of feminism," the *Los Angeles Free Press* reported.[89] Ellen Willis quit as a part-time contributing editor in June 1975,[90] writing in her resignation letter, "Ms.'s politics [include] a mushy, sentimental idea of sisterhood designed to obscure political conflicts between women."[91] The divide grew uglier. In 1975 Redstockings' Kathie Sarachild unleashed a campaign against Steinem that included false claims that Steinem spied on the women's movement for the CIA.[92] The charges split the women's movement.[93] Charges that Ms. was elitist, racist, and heterosexist further challenged Ms.'s claims of universal sisterhood. A feminist collective identity seemed illusory. Finances also frayed. Ms. circulation peaked in 1978 at a half million as paper and postage costs skyrocketed. By midyear, Ms. had a cumulative loss of $1.6 million and was losing about a half million dollars a year.[94]

In 1980, a desperate Steinem and Carbine won tax-exempt status for a new nonprofit Ms. Foundation for Education and Communication. The status converted Ms. magazine into an educational and charitable nonprofit entity, although it continued to accept advertising. The innovative approach slashed postage costs and enabled fundraising. Other magazines such as *Smithsonian* and *Mother Jones* held the same status but none had moved from profit to nonprofit status. The foundation gave Ms. a fundraising structure for sustaining its tradition of social justice journalism. Fundraisers financed some of Ehrenreich's investigations and paid for Morgan to fly to Vienna to interview four feminist dissidents who fled Russia. Ms. published the first American article on female genital mutilation in 1980, an expose of overseas sweatshops in 1981, and the first major magazine article on date rape in 1983.[95] Ms.'s reinvention of itself as a not-for-profit educational entity also marked the end of the social movement journal's unlikely experiment as a commercial media enterprise.

But its tax-exempt status prevented Ms. from endorsing candidates, weakening its political influence. The magazine also faced the decade's backlash against feminism. Money woes continued. As described by Susan Faludi, Ms. succumbed to the emerging celebrity culture under the ownership of an Australian media company that bought it in 1988, the first of six ownership changes between 1988 and 2001.[96] The Aussies suspended Ms. for seven months at the end of 1989. The company agreed to reboot Ms. in summer 1990 as an international, advertising-free, activism-oriented, hundred-page bimonthly "magabook" that was sustained by a hefty $4.50 single-issue price tag and subscriptions. Under editor-in-chief Morgan, Ms. produced some globally focused social justice journalism as the millennium approached, even as it struggled financially and editorially to remain relevant to a new generation of feminists as the Internet revolutionized mass media.

Social Media Stimulate Intersectional Feminism

In 2018, Ms. counted more than 300,000 Facebook fans. Only the digital-only feminist magazine *Everyday Feminism* at a half million claims more. Another 147,000 follow Ms. on Twitter, and its Instagram account shared photographs of women around the world participating in the 2018 Women's March. Millions view the Ms. *Blog* every year, more than a quarter of them young men. "Ms. is thriving," digital editor Carmen Rios said in June 2018 interview. "The feminist movement is growing."[97] Since the end of 2001, Ms. has been published quarterly by the nonprofit Feminist Majority Foundation cofounded by former NOW president Eleanor Smeal, which bought the magazine that year to save it from bankruptcy.[98] The quarterly print edition is available only to foundation members, but access to the Ms. *Blog* and other digital platforms is free. Ironically, nearly a half-century after its debut as the first feminist mass magazine, Ms. stands out as a pioneer of the nonprofit journalism business model that ascended in the new millennium. It failed in the commercial sector but created a sustainable model for magazines to go advertising-free. Unlike Ms., however, virtually all nonprofit journalism outlets are digital natives such as ProPublica. Ms. operates more like *Sierra* magazine, another print survivor that members of the Sierra Club receive as a benefit of membership. Like *Sierra*, Ms.'s digital platforms amplify the print magazine's message.

"We've long connected readers to events and actions in physical spaces," Rios said. "Now we can do that online." Rios, a cofounder of *Argot Magazine* with extensive feminist and journalistic credentials, joined Ms. in 2016 to build up Ms. *Blog* content and boost the online audience. The much timelier blog, she explained, can amplify stories in the quarterly magazine visible only to foundation members. When the magazine covered #MeToo in January 2018, for example, the Ms. *Blog* invited viewers to post their own #MeToo moments. Ms. social media circulated a list of tactics for staying safe while confronting harassers and solicited and shared resources for #MeTooWhatNext. Rios said Ms. remains a grassroots feminist magazine focused on the women's movement. She tries to connect activists and promote collective action. In the weeks leading up to the 2018 Women's March, for example, the Ms. *Blog* featured personal essays by women on what drew them to the march.

Ms. still follows the magazine's feminist "how to" formula, as in "We Kicked A Fake Women's Healthcare Center Off Our Campus, Here's How," linked from FMF's Feminist Campus website.[99] "No Comment" continues but actually does comment in its blog format, like in a post that condemned retail-store Target's "Trophy" t-shirt for women. It links to FMF's Feminist Daily Newswire for breaking news and depends on a global network of freelance journalists, scholars, activists, and aspiring writers for most of its content. Contributors range from a professional freelancer based in Chile who covers abortion rights across Latin America to teenagers that Ms. nurtures in its "The Future is Ms." youth reporting project. Rios champions the use of storytelling as a tool for advancing social change. She sees herself as a bridge between journalism and activism, asserting, "Everything we do is rooted in the truth and facts in a real data-driven, solutions-driven way." Like the Ms. founders, Rios seeks out young writers and new voices. "I'm making sure I do all I can to recruit and retain writers and put forth perspectives that are diverse and intersectional." The Spring 2018 issue included a profile of an activist working to provide sanitary pads and end "period poverty" among poor women in developing nations, a Mongolian woman's account of playing her country's national instrument, and an update on the fight for reproductive justice for incarcerated women.

Ms. stands like a giant redwood surrounded by saplings in a virtual forest of digital native feminist websites.[100] Feminism online is diverse and dynamic and seriously committed to intersectionality. An example is Marina Watanabe's Feminist Fridays series of brief videos on YouTube, which uses humor to tackle topics like "What the F*ck is a Tumblr Feminist?" and "Do 'White Passing' PoC Have Privilege?" Digitally driven Fourth Wave feminism began with a renewed focus on sexual harassment and sexual assault in the 2010s. Antonia Zerbisias, co-creator of #BeenRapedNeverReported, called the flood of hashtags—beginning with #gamergate and #yesallwomen—twenty-first-century versions of "Take Back The Night" marches that get a lot more attention than the protests that originated in the 1980s.[101] #MeToo and #TimesUp were like earthquakes that reshaped the workplace environment. Those movements, however, were instigated by major investigations by legacy media, the *New York Times* and the *New Yorker*. They shared a 2018 Pulitzer Prize for documenting long-simmering whispers that Hollywood mogul Harvey Weinstein was a rapist, demonstrating improvements in mainstream media coverage of women's issues. The millions of women who responded to the revelations by revealing their own experiences via #MeToo showed the power of a feminist community similar to that stirred by Ms. in so many women in the 1970s. The yellowing letters to Ms. archived at Harvard University's Schlesinger Library also continue to move readers. For her 2018 film *Yours in Sisterhood*, filmmaker Irene Lusztig traversed the nation to invite diverse women to read one of the letters from a teleprompter, then to reflect on camera what its content meant to them. The simple but staggering result, observed reviewer Megan Moodie, was "a new kind of contemporary public feminism."[102]

On February 2, 2008, one-time Ms. editor Morgan posted an online sequel to her iconic 1968 essay in the liberated *Rat* newspaper, titled "Goodbye To All That #2." Morgan excoriated the misogyny directed at Hillary Clinton in her failed presidential bid. The screed went viral, generating 800 emails a day to Morgan. "With the first one, it took about six months for it to leach out across the country. With the Internet, it's six minutes," she told a reporter. "So far, no death threats this time. ... But a lot of blogging."[103]

Notes

1. Karen Lindsey, "Sexual Harassment on the Job: and How to Stop it," *Ms.*, November 1977, 47. See also Jessica Bennett, "The 'Click' Moment: How the Weinstein Scandal Unleashed a Tsunami," *New York Times*, November 5, 2017, https://www.nytimes.com/2017/11/05/us/sexual-harrasment-weinstein-trump.html.

2. The U.S. Supreme Court recognized workplace sexual harassment as a form of unlawful sex discrimination in *Meritor Savings Bank v. Vinson*, 477 U.S. 57 (1986).

3. Ms.'s role in the women's movement has been much studied. See "Ms.," in Carolyn G. Heilbrun, *The Education of a Woman: The Life of Gloria Steinem* (New York: Dial Press, 1995), (New York: Ballantine, 1996), 189–231; Ruth Rosen, "Click! Ms. Publicizes the Personal," in *The World Split Open: How the Modern Women's Movement Changed America* (New York: Viking, 2000), 208–17; Amy Erdman Farrell, *Yours in Sisterhood: Ms. Magazine and the Promise of Popular Feminism* (Chapel Hill: University of North Carolina Press, 1998); E. Barbara Phillips, "Magazine Heroines: Is Ms. Just Another Member of the *Family Circle?*" in *Hearth and Home: Images of Women in the Mass Media*, ed. Gaye Tuchman, Arlene Kaplan Daniels, and James Benet (New York: Oxford University Press, 1978); and Mary Thom, *Inside Ms.: 25 Years of the Magazine and the Feminist Movement* (New York: Henry Holt, 1997).

4. Farrell, *Yours in Sisterhood*, 6, 3. See also Sara M. Evans, *Tidal Wave: How Women Changed America at Century's End* (New York: Free Press, 2003), 92–94.

5. The Seven Sisters were *Better Homes and Gardens*, *Family Circle*, *Good Housekeeping*, *Ladies' Home Journal*, *McCall's*, *Redbook*, and *Woman's Day*.

6. "What's Your Ms. Story?" *Ms.* Magazine Blog, September 26, 2017, http://msmagazine.com/blog/2017/09/26/whats-ms-story/.

7. Donna Whalen to Ms. Magazine, nd, Box W23, Folder 1970s: Reactions of Morgan's Writings 1, Robin Morgan Papers. Sallie Bingham Center for Women and History, Special Collections, Duke University, Durham, NC. [hereafter cited as Morgan Papers]

8. Definitions and time periods for the four waves of feminism vary, but generally: First Wave feminism centered around women's fight for the right to vote from the mid-nineteenth century until 1920. The Second Wave in the late 1960s and 1970s sought legal and cultural changes that would give women equal rights in practice. The "sex-positive" Third Wave in the mid-1990s began to incorporate legal scholar Kimberlé Crenshaw's concept of intersectionality, which critiques how class, race, age, ability, sexuality, gender, and other issues combine to affect women's experience of discrimination. Fourth Wave feminists are digital natives who embrace intersectionality and use social media to confront sexual harassment and sexual assault in the 2010s. See Kira Cochrane, *All the Rebel Women: The Rise of the Fourth Wave of Feminism* (London: Guardian Books, 2013).

9. For more on Firestone, see Susan Faludi, "Death of a Revolutionary," *New Yorker*, April 15, 2013, https://www.newyorker.com/magazine/2013/04/15/death-of-a-revolutionary.

10. See Robin Morgan, "On Freedom," *Liberation*, October 1968, 34–35; and "The Miss America Protest: 1968," *Redstockings*, accessed November 8, 2018, http://www.redstockings.org/index.php/themissamericaprotest.

11. Judith Gabree, "On Staughton Lynd's 'Good Society,'" in *Notes from the First Year* (New York: New York Radical Women, 1968), 29, https://library.duke.edu/digitalcollections/wlmpc_wlmms01037/. NYRW also published *Notes from the Second Year* (1970) and *Notes from the Third Year* (1971).

12. Firestone, "Abortion Rally Speech," *First Year*, 25.

13. Gloria Steinem, *Outrageous Acts and Everyday Rebellions* (New York: Henry Holt, 1987), 21–22; and Gloria Steinem, "The City Politic: 'After Black Power, Women's Liberation,'"

New York, April 7, 1969, 8–9. See also "At 81, Feminist Gloria Steinem Finds Herself Free of the 'Demands of Gender,'" *Fresh Air*, NPR, December 30, 2015, http://www.npr.org/2015/12/30/461441508/at-81-feminist-gloria-steinem-finds-herself-free-of-the-demands-of-gender.

14. Rosalyn Baxandall, "Re-Visioning the Women's Liberation Movement's Narrative: Early Second Wave African American Feminists," *Feminist Studies* 27, no. 1 (Spring 2001): 229.

15. *Voice of the Women's Liberation Movement* 1, no. 1 (March 1968): 1, 4, 61.

16. "Jo Freeman (1945–)," in *Significant Contemporary American Feminists: A Biographical Sourcebook*, ed. Jennifer Scanlon (Westport, CT: Greenwood Press, 1999), 104–10.

17. Jo Freeman, "The Women's Liberation Movement: Its Origins, Structures and Ideals," 3, in "Women's Liberation Movement Print Culture Collection," Duke University Libraries Digital Collections, accessed November 2, 2018, https://library.duke.edu/digitalcollections/wlmpc_wlmms01013/.

18. Rebecca Kolins Givan, Kenneth M. Roberts, and Sarah A. Soule, "Introduction: The Dimensions of Diffusion," in *The Diffusion of Social Movements: Actors, Mechanisms, and Political Effects*, eds. Rebecca Kolins Givan, Kenneth M. Roberts, and Sarah A. Soule (Cambridge: Cambridge University Press, 2010), 3.

19. Anne Mather, "A History of Feminist Periodicals, Part I," *Journalism History* 1, no. 1 (Autumn 1974): 82–85.

20. Carol Seajay, "Books: 20 Years of Feminist Bookstores," *Ms.*, July 1992, 60.

21. Kristen Hogan, *The Feminist Bookstore Movement: Lesbian Antiracism and Feminist Accountability* (Durham, NC: Duke University Press Books, 2016), xiv.

22. Marilyn Webb, Heidi Steffens, Marlene Wicks, Colette Reid, and Norma Lesser founded *off our backs*. The bimonthly moved to the Internet before its demise in 2008. See https://www.jstor.org/journal/offourbacks.

23. Rosalyn Baxandall and Linda Gordon, *Dear Sisters: Dispatches from the Women's Liberation Movement* (New York: Basic Books, 2000), 15, 16.

24. Linda Steiner, "The History and Structure of Women's Alternative Media," in *Women Making Meaning: New Feminist Directions in Communication*, ed. Lana F. Rakow (New York: Routledge, 1992), 132.

25. Robin Morgan, "Goodbye to All That," *Fair Use Blog*, accessed November 2, 2018, http://blog.fair-use.org/2007/09/29/goodbye-to-all-that-by-robin-morgan-1970/. [boldface in original]

26. Robin Morgan to "Dear Shulie," March 14, 1971, Box C5, Folder 1970s-1980s, Morgan Papers.

27. Morgan used proceeds to create a nonprofit that funded numerous women's ventures, including the Feminist Print Cooperative in Northampton, Massachusetts, the *Lesbian Tide* newsletter of Los Angeles, the *Feminist Newsletter* of Nashville, a feminist art journal in New York, and a women's bookstore in San Diego. Nancy Dyer to Robin Morgan, April 18, 1973; Jeanne Cordova to Sisterhood Foundation, December 20, 1972; Eleanor Timm to Robin Morgan, November 30 [1972?]; Robin Morgan to "Dear Mesdames," January 14, 1972; and Jean Fishbeck to Robin Morgan, November 9, 1972; all in Box W19, Folder General, 1971–1974 1, Morgan Papers.

28. "Abortion Law Repeal," *Ms*, October 1972, 116–20.

29. Thom, *Inside Ms.*, 36–37.

30. Quoted in Gloria Steinem, manuscript for "The Importance of Ms. Magazine," np, Box 112, Folder 45, Gloria Steinem Papers, Box 3, Folder 15, Sophia Smith Collection, Smith College, Northampton, MA. [hereafter referred to as Steinem Papers]

31. Rosen, World, 211. Suffrage journals also served a consciousness-raising function. See Mary M. Carver, "Everyday Women Find Their Voice in the Public Sphere: Consciousness Raising in Letters to the Editor in Woman's Journal," Journalism History 34, no. 1 (Spring 2008): 15–22.

32. Steinem, "The Importance of Ms. Magazine."

33. Letters to Ms., 1972–1987, ed. Mary Thom (New York: Henry Holt, 1987), xvii. See also Richard Beck, "Letters to Ms. Magazine," New Yorker, September 4, 2013, https://www.newyorker.com/books/page-turner/letters-to-ms-magazine.

34. Thom, Letters, xviii.

35. Ibid., 44.

36. Alice Echols, Daring to Be Bad: Radical Feminism in America, 1967–1975 (Minneapolis: University of Minnesota Press, 1989), 199.

37. Esther Stineman, "Women's Magazines: Serving Up the 'New Woman' in the Same Old Ways," Serials Review, October/December 1979, 28.

38. Laura Berman, "Portable Friend? A New Look at Ms.," Detroit Free Press, January 16, 1980, 5C.

39. Thom, Inside Ms., 80.

40. Faith Dickerson and Janet Weinglass, "Ms. Magazine as a Promoter of Change," unpublished paper, December 16, 1974, 13, 14, in Box 3, Folder 15, Steinem Papers. See Robert K. Merton & Contemporary Sociology, ed. Carlo Mongardini and Simonetta Tabboni (New Brunswick, NJ: Transaction, 1998), 253.

41. Marjorie Nashner and Mimi White, "Beauty and the Breast—a 60-Percent Complication Rate for an Operation You Don't Need," Ms., September 1977, 53–54, 84–85.

42. Linda Stewart, "Alice in Cosmeticsland," Ms., January 1973, 68–71, 106–10.

43. Barbara Garson, "The Heartbeat of an Assembly Line," Ms., March 1974, 72–83.

44. Lindsey, "Sexual Harassment," 47–48; 50–51, 74–76; and "Help for the Sexually Harassed," ibid., 49.

45. Judith Gingold, "'One of These Days'—POW Right in the Kisser," Ms., August 1976, 51–54, 94.

46. Maureen R. Michelson, "There Are Alternatives to Mastectomy," Ms., January 1979, 29–31. [underline in original]

47. Jan Worthington, "The Cancer Time Bomb: Did Your Mother Take DES?" Ms., March 1977, 16–18.

48. B. J. Phillips, "Exclusive! The Case of Karen Silkwood: Dead Because She Knew Too Much?," Ms., April 1975, 59–66.

49. Woman's Work [chart], Ms., July 1972, 59.

50. Sheila Tobias, "Math Anxiety: Why Is a Smart Girl Like You Counting on Your Fingers?," Ms., September 1976, 56–59, 92.

51. Susan Brownmiller, "The Real Spoils of War," Ms., December 1975, 82–85.

52. "The Radicalization of Simone de Beauvoir," Ms., July 1972, 60–63, 134.

53. Barbara Ehrenreich, "Is Success Dangerous to Your Health?" Ms., May 1979, 51–54.

54. "Golda Talks to Oriana Fallaci," *Ms.*, April 1973, 77, 100–104; and "Bernadette Devlin: An Interview by J. Fitzgerald," *Ms.*, January 1975, 69–71, 102–105, 108.

55. Thom, *Inside* Ms., 199.

56. Kate Millett, "On Angela Davis," *Ms.*, August 1972, 54, 56, 58–60, 105–10, 114–16; and ibid., (Part II), *Ms.*, September 1972, 58–60, 104–108, 112–14.

57. Angela Davis, "Forum: Joanne Little—The Dialectics of Rape," *Ms.*, June 1975, 74–78, 103–108.

58. Michelle Wallace, "Black Macho and the Myth of the Superwoman," *Ms.*, January 1979, 45–48, 87–91.

59. "The Birthplace of Machismo," *Ms.*, October 1972, 12–17. See also Anna Mayo, "Mexico: Mucho Macho," *Ms.*, December 1972, 116–20; Judith Thurman, "Sister Juana: The Price of Genius," *Ms.*, April 1973, 14–21; Nan Blitman and Robin Green, "Inez Garcia on Trial," *Ms.*, March 1975, 49–54, 84–88; and Maria Del Drago, "The Pride of Inez Garcia," *Ms.*, May 1975, 54, 84.

60. Lisa Cronin Wohl, "Would You Buy an Abortion from this Man? The Harvey Karman Controversy," *Ms.*, September 1975, 60–63, 113–20.

61. See Elizabeth Varnell, "Gloria Steinem Knows Firsthand How the Original Playboy Bunnies Got Their Hourglass Shape," *Vogue*, September 28, 2017, https://www.vogue.com/article/playboy-bunnies-hourglass-body-gloria-steinem-hugh-hefner-death-playboy-club-new-york.

62. John Brady, "Freelancer with No Time to Write," *Writer's Digest* 54 (February 1974): 20.

63. Gloria Steinem, "The Politics of Journalism," *Folio*, January/February 1974, 20.

64. Manuscript, *Saturday's Child 1999*, Box W4 Writings, Folder 3, Morgan Papers.

65. "Letty Cottin Pogrebin," Jewish Women's Archive, accessed November 2, 2018, https://jwa.org/feminism/pogrebin-letty-cottin-1.

66. Letty Cottin Pogrebin, "Have You Ever Supported Equal Pay, Child Care, or Women's Groups? The FBI Was Watching You," *Ms.*, June 1977, 37–44; and "Gazette—Extra," ibid., 76. See also Rosen, *World Split Open*, 237–52. Morgan's FBI files for 1969 alone contained thirty-six pages of handwritten notes that listed all meetings and protests she attended, including the number of male and female participants. Box PER2, Folders 1976–1978: FBI and CIA Files 1–2, Morgan Papers.

67. Thom, *Inside* Ms., 205.

68. "Reader Response," *Ms.*, Box 162, Folder 8, Steinem Papers.

69. Brady, "Freelancer," 21.

70. "Notes on April 26, 1977, Michele Russell interview with Ericka Huggins," Box 157, Folder 6, Steinem Papers.

71. Memo from Robin [Morgan], June 9 [?] Box W23, Folder 1970s–1980s and undated: Comments on Others, Morgan Papers.

72. Janie T. Gaynor, "I Was Humor Editor of Ms. Magazine but the Joke Was on Me," *Harper's Weekly*, June 14, 1976, 10.

73. "A Magazine of Record," Box 162, Folder 8, Steinem Papers.

74. "Here They Are—on a Plastic Platter: A Complete Discography of Women Composers," *Ms.*, November 1975, 111–14.

75. Judith Thurman, "Isak Dinesen/Karen Blixen: A Very Personal Memoir," *Ms.*, September 1973, 72–77, 90–93; and Judith Thurman, *Isak Dinesen: The Life of a Storyteller* (New York: St. Martin's Press, 1982).

76. Jill Lepore, *The Secret History of Wonder Woman* (New York: Knopf-Doubleday, 2014), 284–87. See also Joanne Edgar, "Wonder Woman Revisited," *Ms.*, July 1972, 52–55. "Wonder Woman" returned to the *Ms.* cover on its thirty-fifth and fortieth anniversary issues.

77. Katie Kilkenny, "How a Magazine Cover from the 1970s Helped Wonder Woman Win Over Feminists," *Pacific Standard*, June 21, 2017, https://psmag.com/social-justice/ms-magazine-helped-make-wonder-woman-a-feminist-icon.

78. *Wonder Woman: A "Ms." Book*, ed. Gloria Steinem (New York: Holt, Rinehart and Winston and Warner Books, 1972).

79. For an interesting critique, see Ann Matsuuchi, "Wonder Woman Wears Pants: *Wonder Woman*, Feminism, and the 1972 Women's Lib Issue," *Colloquy: Text Theory Critique*, 24 (2012): 118–42.

80. Kilkenny, "How a Magazine Cover…."

81. "Bea Feitler, Magazine and Book Designer, 44," *New York Times*, April 11, 1982, https://timesmachine.nytimes.com/timesmachine/1982/04/11/055529.html?action=click&contentCollection=Archives&module=LedeAsset&region=ArchiveBody&pgtype=article&pageNumber=34.

82. Roberta Brandes Gratz, "Never Again," *Ms.*, April 1973, 44. A 1995 documentary told the story of the woman, Gerri Santoro. See "Leona's Sister Gerri," (Newburgh, NY: New Day Films, 1995), accessed November 2, 2018, https://www.newday.com/film/leonas-sister-gerri.

83. Brady, "Freelancer," 21.

84. Abigail Pogrebin, "How Do You Spell Ms.?," *New York*, October 30, 2011, http://nymag.com/news/features/ms-magazine-2011-11/.

85. Farrell, *Yours in Sisterhood*, 196.

86. "A Personal Report from Ms.: Everything You Wanted to Know About Advertising—and Haven't Been Afraid to Ask," *Ms.*, November 1974, 56.

87. Phillips, "Magazine Heroines," 116–129.

88. Gloria Steinem, "Sex, Lies and Advertising," *Ms.*, July/August 1990, 19.

89. Jeanne Cordova, "Gloria Steinem: Can Ms. Survive?," *Los Angeles Free Press*, July 4, 1974, np, in Steinem Papers. See also Kathleen Hendrix, "Ms. Grows Up with the Movement," *Los Angeles Times*, Part V, June 18, 1982, 16–19.

90. Rosen, *The World Split Open*, 238.

91. Pogrebin, "How Do You Spell Ms.?"

92. Heilbrun, *Education of a Woman*, 286.

93. Joreen, "Trashing: The Dark Side of Sisterhood," *Ms.*, April 1976, 49–51, 92–98. See also Echols, *Daring to Be Bad*, 265–69.

94. Thom, *Inside Ms.*, 158.

95. Robin Morgan and Gloria Steinem, "Genital Mutilation: 30 Million Women are Victims," *Ms.*, March 1980, 65–67, 98–100; Barbara Ehrenreich and Annette Fuentes, "Life

on the Global Assembly Line," *Ms.*, January 1981, 53–59, 71; and Karen Barrett, "Date Rape: A Campus Epidemic?" *Ms.*, September 1982, 48–51, 130.

96. Susan Faludi, *Backlash: The Undeclared War Against Women* (New York: Crown, 1991), 121–24.

97. Carmen Rios, telephone interview with author, June 4, 2018.

98. The foundation purchased Liberty Media LLC, a corporation Steinem and others formed to publish *Ms.* in 1998.

99. Maggie Goldberger, Emma Bessire, and Natalie Jacobson, "We Kicked A Fake Women's Healthcare Center Off Our Campus, Here's How," *Feminist Campus*, April 30, 2018, http://feministcampus.org/authora/maggie-goldberger/.

100. "Top 20 Feminist Blogs and Websites for Women to Follow in 2018," *Feedspot*, last updated September 30, 2018, https://blog.feedspot.com/feminist_blogs/.

101. Antonia Zerbisias, "Feminism's Fourth Wave Is the Shitlist," *NOW*, September 16, 2015, https://nowtoronto.com/news/feminisms-fourth-wave-is-the-shitlist/.

102. Megan Moodie, "Handmade Feminism: Irene Lusztig's 'Yours in Sisterhood,'" *Los Angeles Review of Books*, May 11, 2018, https://lareviewofbooks.org/article/handmade-feminism-irene-lusztigs-yours-in-sisterhood/#!

103. Ariel Levy, "Goodbye Again," *New Yorker*, April 21, 2008, https://www.newyorker.com/magazine/2008/04/21/goodbye-again.

· 8 ·

"CRIPS" AND "GIMPS"

Creating a Disability Culture in the *Disability Rag*

Mike Ervin remembers discovering the *Disability Rag* just after he graduated from college in the early 1980s. "It was a fiery magazine written by other gimps like me," recalled the gray-bearded Chicago-based writer and blogger. "Like others, it turned me into an activist." The one-time Muscular Dystrophy Association official poster child founded "Jerry's Orphans" to protest the MDA's annual Labor Day telethon fundraisers for "Jerry's Kids," in which comedian Jerry Lewis mawkishly portrayed the children as helpless objects of pity.[1] Among the *Rag*'s countless diatribes against the telethon appeared a tongue-in-cheek report that Lewis was hospitalized; it claimed a group of MS survivors calling themselves "Jerry's Parents" were organizing a telethon for him.[2] Lewis was dismissed as host in 2010, partly because of Ervin's campaign, and the last telethon aired in 2014.[3]

Ervin was just one among thousands of readers roused to action by the combative *Rag*, a unique mix of intimate revelations by contributors about dealing with disability and exhortations to protest discrimination against disabled people. The *Rag* framed disability issues through the lens of American values of independence and participation. After rising from humble beginnings in January 1980 as a four-page newsletter in Louisville, Kentucky, its influence mushroomed far beyond its peak national circulation of 6,000 in

1986. Steven E. Brown, cofounder of the Institute on Disability Culture, cites the *Rag* for mobilizing him. "As an avid reader of the (then) newsprint *Rolling Stone* I was hooked," he recalled. "I wanted to write for it one day."[4] Brown's byline did indeed eventually appear in what historian Richard K. Scotch called "the unofficial newspaper of the disability rights movement" that came of age in the 1980s.[5] It was "one of the most important publications to come out of the movement," according to Mary Lou Breslin, former deputy director of the Disability Rights Education and Defense Fund.[6] The *Atlantic* magazine quoted the *Rag*, and the *Wall Street Journal* profiled it on its front page. Another admirer was Bob Ruffner, public affairs director for President Ronald Reagan's Committee on Employment of the Handicapped. "[U]topian ideas—ideas that can be translated into social action—start in places like the *Rag*," he told a reporter. "How else can you build a movement among people who have been left out? Its purpose is to build a fire."[7]

This chapter focuses on how the caustic Kentucky-based newspaper strived to create an empowering collective identity among a diverse population of Americans who had thoroughly internalized society's negative stereotypes about being disabled. The journal played a leading role in creating an assertive disability culture, a work-in-progress that evolves as this diverse community encounters new threats. [8] More than most social movements, the early disability rights movement relied on journals as a forum of communication and source of community because, unlike members of a labor union, for example, its constituents literally could not gather together. Buses without lifts, streets with curbs, or meeting places with even a single stair made physically organizing practically impossible. The chapter also analyzes the monthly's successful reframing of disability as a civil rights issue, an example of frame bridging that emphasized collective action frames of injustice and agency. It highlights *Disability Rag*'s social justice journalism, which paired education with calls for action in articles, exposés, first-person essays, media columns, cartoons, editorials, and special issues. A 1986 *Rag* reader's survey found that the journal had inspired nearly two-thirds of respondents to take action.[9] The chapter concludes with a look at digital disability movement media.

Roots of a Disability Culture

Some 53 million Americans—22 percent of the U.S. population—had a disability in 2015, according to the Centers for Disease Control. They may comprise the nation's most discriminated-against demographic group, and the disabled are more likely to live in poverty and less likely to be employed than the able-bodied.[10] Disabled people also are unique as the only minority group most Americans can expect to join as they age. One challenge to cohering the disabled into a social movement is the diversity clumped under that broad term's umbrella: people who are blind, deaf, have limited mobility, difficulty breathing, brain damage, AIDS, suffer some degree of intellectual disability, as well as some people diagnosed with autism spectrum disorder. The *Rag* and other groundbreaking disability rights periodicals that followed, such as *Mainstream*, *New Mobility*, and *Mouth*, rejected the medical approach that viewed a disability as an affliction to be cured before its label-bearer could become wholly human.

The new journals challenged the stock pair of media stereotypes of the disabled that dominated the twentieth-century—"Supercrip," the courageous overachiever who defies all odds to succeed, or "Tiny Tim," an impotent object of pity.[11] Several scholars have deemed typical news coverage of the disabled as negative or inaccurate and devoid of disabled voices.[12] Virtually all publications targeting the disabled audience before the 1970s were service-oriented magazines published by the nondisabled, stretching back to 1848 with the North Carolina School for the Deaf's school newspaper, the *Deaf Mute*.[13] In 1907, the mother of a sightless boy founded *Matilda Ziegler Magazine for the Blind* to give the sight-impaired access to selected periodical articles printed in Braille, tactile New York Point, and embossed Moon type.[14] The significant population of World War II veterans who used wheelchairs in 1946 resulted in *Paraplegia News* (now *PN Magazine: For Better Wheelchair Living*). An unexpected demographic became disabled over the next decade when the post-war poliomyelitis epidemic struck tens of thousands of American children before Jonas Salk discovered a vaccine in 1955. Many endured months or years in iron lungs and hospitals that they exited in wheelchairs. In 1958, a volunteer in a Cleveland hospital's polio ward launched the *Toomey Jr. Gazette* for former patients to keep in touch and share stories of self-reliance; in 1970, it became the *Rehabilitation Gazette: International Journal of Independent Living by and for Persons with a Disability*.[15] Many of the 56 newsletters, magazines, and newspapers for the disabled listed in a 1996 study were affiliated with service organizations for the disabled, and half were edited by nondisabled people.[16] Studies show that disability nonprofits' advocacy and fundraising campaigns, like mainstream media, often rely on tragedy tropes,[17] which helps explain the origins of the identity-politics slogan, "Nothing about us without us!" in the 1990s disability movement.[18]

Frame Bridging with Sixties' Social Movements

Unlike the service-oriented periodicals, new magazines like *Disability Rag* and *Mainstream* that rode the crest of the 1960s petri dish of social justice activism reframed disability discourse from a fixation on coping or curing to a demand for civil rights. They put the onus on institutions to provide access for the disabled, whom they emphasized were wholly human. Before the 1970s, virtually no one viewed the disabled population's main handicap as its members' literal lack of access to transportation, education, and employment. A curb cut on a three-inch sidewalk, a ramp alongside stairs—these were civil rights, the *Rag* asserted. It practiced frame extension when it drew analogies between slaves and the disabled.[19] The *Rag* reprinted excerpts from a 1969 *American Scholar* article that discussed how the Black Power movement could guide the disabled community's struggle to rise from invisibility.[20] The *Rag* displayed frame bridging when it editorialized that the disabled remained unconstitutionally segregated by inaccessibility that it likened to Jim Crow laws[21] and it opposed "paratransit" programs as separate but equal.[22] A call to campaign for automatic doors urged:

> It's time for us to quit playing Uncle Tiny Tim and saying, "Well, we can't expect them to put in automatic doors. It's not in the codes." Ask yourself: why didn't Rosa Parks go to the back of the bus? That was the law, after all. Answer: She was tired, that was all. When are we going to get tired of trying to make heavy doors move by themselves?[23]

Rag founder Cass Irvin, deeply influenced by *The Feminine Mystique*, also looked to the women's liberation press as a model. Irvin likened the mindset of most disabled people to that of the housewives whom Betty Friedan described as oppressed by restrictive gender roles. "The disability press is beginning to help us see ourselves as we really are—not as society tells us we are," Irvin wrote in 1982. "We today, like women ten years ago, must realize that society imposes the obstacles we are encouraged to overcome, not our disability."[24]

The first person to declare access as a civil right was Ed Roberts, a quadriplegic polio survivor known as the "father" of the independent living movement, who in 1964 entered the University of California, Berkeley at the height of the free speech and antiwar movements.[25] He successfully fought for the California Department of Rehabilitation to pay for his housing and attendants on the second floor of the campus hospital. More disabled students moved in, and in 1972 it became the first Center for Independent Living, with Roberts as executive director. Three years later Governor Jerry Brown appointed Roberts director of the state's rehabilitation department. On the other side of the country, Judy Heumann filed a widely publicized lawsuit in New York in 1970 when she was denied teaching certification because she was paraplegic. She helped found Disabled in Action, a loose conglomeration of grassroots groups of disabled people that had popped up in several cities to protest inaccessible bus systems and public buildings.[26]

Congress took heed and passed the historic Rehabilitation Act of 1973, hailed at the time as the civil rights act for the disabled. Tacked onto the bill was a little-noticed provision titled Section 504. Once the White House realized that Section 504 would cost billions to remake public spaces accessible, neither President Richard Nixon nor his successor Gerald Ford would sign it. When President Jimmy Carter's Secretary of Health, Education, and Welfare Joseph Califano tried to soften Section 504, hundreds of disabled protesters held unprecedented sit-ins in federal offices across the country. In spring 1977, protesters in wheelchairs took over Califano's Washington offices for 28 hours, and another 128 disabled activists occupied HEW's San Francisco office for twenty-five days. The sit-in organized by the American Coalition of Citizens with Disabilities marked the disability rights movement's "political coming of age," according to historian Joseph P. Shapiro. "Disabled people had risked arrest and their health by turning to civil disobedience tactics and had surprised a nation—and themselves—with their own power."[27]

After Califano signed the historic regulations on April 28, 1977, the number of independent living centers jumped almost fivefold to nearly 250 over the next decade. They included the Center for Accessible Living in Louisville, where two board members tried to raise community consciousness about the city's lack of accessible transportation by publishing a small newsletter. Disability Rag began as a single eleven-by-seventeen-inch sheet of paper folded to form four pages. "We kept feeling frustrated because there was much that needed to be said that wasn't," Irvin once recalled. "How are you going to get the disabled to work together if they can't even get together? There needed to be some way for people to connect."[28]

After polio left Irvin a quadriplegic at age nine in 1954, the Louisville schools' policy prevented her from attending classes with other children until junior high school. She grit her teeth when teachers condescendingly praised her courage but discouraged her career plans. Nonetheless, she earned a master's degree in English literature and became a college English instructor. She remained frustrated by barriers to living independently, including expensive personal attendants and an electric wheelchair. "That's when I realized there must be something wrong with the system," she told the *Wall Street Journal*, "if I couldn't be as successful as other people can."[29] She and board member Mary Johnson, a former journalist and publicist who was not disabled, initially published the *Rag* anonymously, fearing their audience would mistrust a missive published by an able-bodied person.[30] They acknowledged the ruse three years later. "Do non-disabled people have the right, ultimately, to participate in the disability rights movement?" an editor's note asked. "After much thought, we have decided that they do."[31]

The activist *Rag* emphasized agency frames. Louisville City Hall's new TTY phone number appeared in large print on page one of its second number alongside information on how to order the American Civil Liberties Union's new, unprecedented guide to disabled people's legal rights. "We wanted disabled people to realize that getting about is not totally up to them," Irvin said. "Society needs to take the responsibility for people getting around easier."[32] The *Rag* called for "a little grassroots activism, for example," against cars illegally parked in handicapped spaces. It offered windshield stickers to stick on offending vehicles that read: "I had no respect for the handicapped. I parked in the reserved zone."[33]

Shaping a Disability Culture

The *Rag*'s greatest contribution, however, was helping to shape an empowered disabled identity. Because of the *Rag*, Brown observed, "A traditional antipathy to identification as an individual with a disability turned into pride in both individual and group strength."[34] The *Rag* and its peers launched a lively discourse on disabled identity, a concept so new members struggled to find a suitable name.[35] Articles sought to reappropriate pejoratives into badges of honor. Typically irreverent, the *Rag* suggested "gimp."[36] The journal objected to the vague term "physically challenged": "The reason we can't do lots of things is not because we're lazy or because we won't accept a challenge ... but because many things are simply beyond our control. Like barriers. Like discrimination."[37] The *Rag* occasionally tried the term "survivor" instead of disabled but also solicited readers' opinions, an example of its highly collaborative relationship with readers. "Printed words are strong tools for change," an editors' note stated. "And the language that we use defines and shapes our perceptions of ourselves."[38]

Debates on whether to refer to themselves as "disabled" versus the more common "handicapped" were not merely semantics but the process of a group defining itself. As psychologist Carol Gill explained in a special double issue devoted entirely to the topic: "A disability culture movement can foster disability pride. We renew each other and our strength through shared experiences and rituals. Through our culture we can recruit people. When we present a strong image, it motivates people to want to belong."[39]

The "Disability Cool" column it launched toward the end of 1981 is a perfect example of how the *Rag* reframed disability with empowering agency frames.[40] In one column, a woman describes how she used a trendy mini-purse worn across the shoulders designed for credit cards to hold her catheter; another described a necklace designed to hide tracheotomy scars.[41] A 1987 column wondered if the trendy TV cartoon character Max Headroom would make stuttering acceptable.[42] A "Cool" column heralding the first home robot praised the fact that "Hero 1" was not a special medical device but a mass-market item. It concluded, "This is Disability Cool."[43]

The feisty cartoon "Disability Rat" in a wheelchair symbolized the *Rag's* subversive nature. Disability Rat was featured on stickers for illegally parked cars, and Irvin's Avocado Press began marketing "Disability Rat" posters and disability rights stickers and t-shirts in April 1982. The Rat is the opposite of the farm workers' timid Don Sotaco. In one cartoon, he blows up a van parked in a handicapped parking space. Disability Rat's antithesis, the passive "Uncle Tiny Tim," appeared in a June 1980 cartoon. Literature and art in the *Rag* also contributed to disability culture. It reviewed books and films dealing with disability from a disabled person's viewpoint.[44] One reviewer observed of a presidential biography, "Seldom has a gimp ever been less 'confined to a wheelchair' than President Franklin D. Roosevelt."[45] A physician who reviewed *The Unexpected Minority* supported its argument against the medical approach toward the disabled.[46] Occasional poems exposed the pain, isolation, and terror of disability.[47]

Modernist philosopher Michel Foucault's three "Stoic Technologies of the Self" are useful for analyzing the periodical's attempts to rehabilitate the meaning of disability: (1) disclosure, an expression of self, especially confession by which people reveal themselves; (2) examination, which Foucault describes as conducting "a review of what was done, of what should have been done, and comparison of the two"; and (3) remembrance, or the "memorization of deeds."[48] For example, in 1989 the *Rag* surveyed readers about their sexual experiences after a readers poll revealed an overwhelming number of readers desired articles on the topic. The painfully candid responses match the disclosure component of Foucault's system. "There is a lot of avoidance, 'shutting me out,' seeing me and quickly looking the other way (too quickly), thus never giving me the chance to smile or speak," one respondent wrote.[49] An emotional open letter from a disabled woman to her lover was intimate: "Thank you for the pleasure of new sexual experiences when so many pleasures are no longer possible."[50]

Foucault's examination function frequently flowed from contributors' disclosures. Paralyzed in a car crash, S. L. Rosen reframed the responsibility for "overcoming a handicap" from individuals to society in a thoughtful series on surviving traumatic injury.[51] He railed about "how we're supposed to overcome the handicap of houses we can't get into or out of or buses we can't ride."[52] Rosen was blunt. "The problem of having to hold your urine 12 hours or more was something that you had accept and overcome," he wrote. "We weren't taught to rage and force society to build bathrooms we could use like everybody else had a right to expect."[53] Such disclosures offered a lifeline to isolated, far-flung readers. One disabled college student in Covington, Kentucky, scribbled a note to the editors in pencil. "Thank God you're here!" he wrote. "Now I know that I'm not alone in my efforts to change things."[54] Another reader wrote, "It's nice to know that someone with the same radical attitude that I have has the guts and 'know-how' to start a 'rag' like this."[55]

Sharing stories performed an important function for the disabled rights community. Alice Wong, founder and project coordinator of the Disability Visibility Project, asserts that storytelling "is incredibly important for people with disabilities. Too often, we [disabled people] are not in control of our own narratives, and historians and the media often tell our stories through a nondisabled lens."[56] More graphic disclosure appeared *Disability Rag* in accounts of other taboo subjects. Heumann wrote about what it was like to need to have others clean her bottom in the bathroom.[57] Edward L. Hooper delivered a moral shock when he addressed attendant abuse with a harrowing tale about the solitary confinement forced on a five-year-old polio survivor in a home for "crippled children" in the 1950s; his point was that thirty years later the culture of silence surrounding such abuse endured. "I know a 22-year-old man who, for over a week, had not been bathed," Hooper wrote. "His bowels became so impacted that the contents of his small intestine had started to back up into his stomach."[58] In "Public Stripping," Lisa Blumberg recounted her humiliation and anger when as an adolescent with spina bifida she was forced to strip naked at periodic medical examinations for the edification of a gallery of medical professionals. "By and large, we want to be provided a medical service, not render one," she wrote, moving into Foucault's evaluation phase, which seeks remedies to problems.[59]

Blumberg's essay itself is an artifact that falls into the remembrance component of Foucault's framework. The *Rag* performed the important role of creating and preserving this evolving disability identity. An editor's note told readers, "The role of the disability press is to record and preserve our present and our past. ...Unlike most minority groups, we do not have our own culture and traditions. But we do have a past and we should learn about it and feel pride in the accomplishments of our forebears and we should feel anguish about how badly our people have been treated."[60]

Rejecting Handicapped Heroes

The *Rag's* unvarnished realism in accounts of dealing with disability contrasted with rosy mainstream media stories about handicapped heroes. The journal and its readers despised the portrayal of ordinary disabled people as special.[61] As an exasperated teacher with cerebral palsy wrote to the *Rag*, "I can't tell you how many times a week I hear that '*#!% What! You drive a car?!!?' You *work?*'"[62] Bob Muskie wrote that feature stories on disabled athletes demeaned the group because it reinforced the belief that physical ability is valued.[63] "Myth & Media" even tore apart paragraph by paragraph a Pulitzer Prize–winning feature story on a blind boy functioning in a seeing world.[64] Ironically, *Ladies' Home Journal* honored Irvin as one of fifty "American Heroines" in 1984. The *Rag's* antipathy toward handicapped heroes inspired a popular new feature in 1982 called "We wish we wouldn't see," modeled on *Ms.* magazine's "No Comment" department that called out sexist texts. Both relied on reader submissions of offensive media portrayals. The July 1983 "We wish we wouldn't see," for example, featured an ad for a TV special on amputee skiers titled "The Bravest Athletes in the World." A March/April 1988 submission featured an ad "For Executives Who Are Tired of Being 'Computer Cripples.'..." April 1983 offered a twist—an ad for a Holly Near concert that also listed "Susan Freundlich, Sign Language Artist," winning a rare thumbs up from the editors.

Editors also empowered readers by encouraging participation that encouraged collective identity. The *Rag's* second number sought information on consciousness-raising groups in Louisville for a future story—an early example of crowdsourcing that the short-staffed *Rag* frequently called upon. The *Rag* surveyed readers for a story on attendant care, wheelchair repairs, and their thoughts about new cochlear implants that enabled some deaf people to hear. One example of how it supported agency among readers was a feature titled "You Decide." One installment let readers weigh in on whether a bakery's panel of colored lights to direct deaf employees was exploiting or supporting them. Others asked readers to consider whether a paraplegic woman giving birth was news or if special shopping days for the disabled (and elderly) were desirable.[65] When *Playboy* published nude photos of a 23-year-old paraplegic woman, the *Rag* asked readers to weigh in on whether the images were liberating or exploitative.[66] A robust discussion on disabled female sexuality ensued.[67]

Barrett Shaw, a *Rag* editor in the early 1990s, once said its "biggest single influence" was improving media representation of the disabled.[68] Media watchdog *Rag* skewered clichés and offensive stereotypes.[69] In her "Myth & Media" column, Anne Peters scored an Associated Press story on the suicide of a Nobel Prize–winning scientist with Lou Gehrig's disease, for example, for perpetuating the myth that "being a quadriplegic is a fate worse than death."[70] "Phys Diz Showbiz," which monitored TV shows,[71] accused fitness guru Richard Simmons of apartheid when he published an exercise book for the "physically challenged." Lauri Klobas asked, "Why aren't your everyday fitness spas wheelchair accessible?"[72] A themed December 1983 issue on "Images" explored improving representations of the disabled in entertainment media, an example of the *Rag*'s activist bent. Another was a feature on a reader whose letter-writing campaign instigated change in references to the disabled in the *Toledo Blade*. An accompanying box offered tips on how to write letters to editors.[73] The package exemplifies William Gamson's definition of collective action frames as showing that "we" can do something to fix "it."[74] That sensibility imbued the collective action frames that dominated the *Rag*'s social justice journalism.

Social Justice Journalism in *Disability Rag*

The *Rag* followed the social justice journalism formula of including ways to remedy the injustices it documented and discussed. Articles almost always supplied contact information on where to complain about discrimination or request removal of architectural barriers.[75] Johnson's name first appeared in the February 1982 issue atop a story about a high school girl who had recently returned to high school after her legs were amputated following a car crash. Johnson's story shows how the *Rag* contested mainstream news stereotypes, as Malinda Lamb had been featured as a hero in several *Louisville Journal* articles. "It is a personal story and nothing more," Johnson observed of the *Journal's* angle. "It is the story of one person, coping." Johnson reported what the *Journal* reporter omitted: Malinda is forced to ride the "handicapped" bus; the school has no elevator to the library; the bathrooms lack the pull-up bar she needs to lift herself off the toilet. Johnson quoted Lamb as saying she would prefer an electric wheelchair but has been bullied by a rehab counselor to use artificial legs. Johnson reframed Lamb's story as one of institutional failure rather than individual courage. She skewered the perceived institutional neglect by drily noting, "A person must learn to adjust as Malinda has."[76]

Years later, Johnson discussed how she negotiated the terrain between activism and journalism. "Looking back from my distance today," she said in 2009, "I am aware that there was an ongoing tension between activists who wanted us to be more activist and my instincts to be [the voice of] 'journalism'—reporting but not participating actively."[77] Johnson's reportage often followed the information model of journalism. She reported neutrally, for example, on a Rhode Island ironworker's successful series of suits to enforce Section 504 to win battles for access to polling places, housing, and universities.[78] In 1983, Johnson interviewed violinist Itzhak Perlman, who uses crutches, not about music but about accessibility on the eve of his performance in Louisville.[79] The interview was the centerpiece of a themed issue that critiqued access to city arts, a topic close to Irvin's heart as an usher once made a scene about her wheelchair during a play.[80] The *Rag* argued wheelchair users had the right to sit where they want in theaters.[81] It also criticized the local theater company's refusal to allow American Sign Language interpreters at performances and the Speed Museum's refusal to let blind visitors touch sculptures. It also published an Arts Access Guide.

The guide was one of many practical ways in which the *Rag* provided a public service. The *Rag* told readers unable to access polling places where to write to report the infraction. A page-one article urged readers to comment on the state's new Architectural Barriers Act, either in person or in writing.[82] It suggested readers try out its minimum specifications, like the five-foot diameter recommended for turning around in a wheelchair, and recommend better specifications if necessary.[83] It accompanied a 1981 roundup of proposed Kentucky bills with instructions on how to obtain a ballot if a polling site was inaccessible.[84] An October 1983 themed issue on accessible transportation included a "how-to" on organizing to force a community to provide accessible buses. A law column explained discrimination and how to address it.[85] In 1990, it published petition sheets for video companies to caption all releases.

The *Rag* generally organized issues by themes. "Anger" in August 1982 explored how the disabled should reclaim that taboo emotion. "Voting" the next month focused on defining and getting out the disability vote. "Cure" in January 1983 examined why the disabled rights community disliked that focus. The November/December 1984 issue explored wheelchairs from occupants' angle: the indignities of trying to hail a cab or board a plane. The September 1985 special "Independent Living" issue ran 64 pages. The June 1984 number examined the newly released 1980 U.S. Census findings on the disabled, noting it counted only people who did not work, and launched a campaign to change counting methods of the disabled in the 1990 census. The "Technology and the Disability Dream" special issue in June 1985 considered costs as well as benefits of computers and robots. Another issue considered the ethics of animal experiments, which ostensibly offered cures for the disabled. One of the very few *Rag* issues that contained photographs, it featured graphic images of cats, dogs, and chimpanzees in labs.[86]

The *Rag* offered in-depth, well-researched reports on employment, injury lawsuits, the Little League's campaign to shut down a team of disabled children, and personal care attendants.[87] A 1984 election package included articles on disability issues, the candidates' stands, the power of the disabled vote, and access issues for voting. One article described "How to Test a Candidate's D.Q." In 1988, the *Rag* also reported when all presidential candidates broke a pledge to use sign language interpreters in all debates and TV appearances.[88] A "Do-It-Yourself Political Action" column parsed bills and budgets as they affected the disabled and concluded with contact info for relevant politicians.[89] A special report considered attendant care from various angles.[90] The *Rag* also invited readers to statewide meetings to pressure Kentucky to start an attendant care program for severely disabled people.[91] "Ragout" was a roundup of briefs on disability in the news as well as testament to the editors' flair for creative license of the journal's title. The magazine also reported on a successful lawsuit in which the judge agreed that Michigan statutes against sodomy violated the constitutional rights to privacy of the dozen plaintiffs, whose disabilities prevented them from having sex in the missionary position.[92]

The January 1984 issue featured a California group that provided wheelchairs for Nicaragua, impossible to obtain in that war-torn nation because of

a U.S. trade embargo. What impressed the editors was the Nicaraguans' inge-
nuity in designing and building their own lightweight, durable wheelchairs.
Using the Nicaraguans' input, American volunteer Ralf Hotchkiss created
a sturdy chair anyone could put together in less than a week for $60 to $80.
The Nicaraguans' focus on the chair as a form of transportation instead of as a
medical device fueled the innovation, which Hotchkiss believed could make
wheelchairs affordable to people in other developing countries.[93] The *Rag*
approached the international story in its usual thorough way, packaging the
wheelchair story with another on Nicaragua's burgeoning independent living
movement and sidebars that updated readers on the lightest new wheelchairs
in the United States.[94]

Reporting on disability bills was standard.[95] The *Rag* followed the militant American Disabled for Accessible Public Transit (ADAPT) organization from its first protest at the 1983 meeting of the American Public Transit
Association in Denver. The confrontational activists used direct action and
mass arrests to make their case for fully accessible buses. The *Rag* reported on
the group's protests across the nation.[96] It slammed mainstream media coverage that focused more on the protest details than on the issue (letters to the
editor, however, showed many readers believed the *Rag* was too critical).[97]
"No editorial from a major daily supported ADAPT's position," Johnson
noted.[98] Her lively "fly on the wall" descriptions of ADAPT's door-blocking
of a federal building in Chicago offered an insider's view of the protests for
implementation of the ADA.[99]

Agency Frames in Disability Rag

Agency frames filled the *Rag*. A 1989 "Protest" issue quoted ADAPT leader
Wade Blank, who was not disabled. "We try to use the wheelchair as a source
of power and intimation," he said. "You put a wheelchair in front of bus and
you get a totally different image than a wheelchair on a corner with a tin
cup."[100] The newspaper asserted the disabled can hold down jobs and discussed
the responsibilities of successful disabled people.[101] The paper cited occasional victories, like an intentionally impossible Great Wheelchair Race and
Obstacle Derby staged to demand curb cuts in downtown Louisville.[102] That
story found its way to a reader in Asheville, North Carolina, who requested
more information to organize a similar event there.[103] Another example of
how the *Rag* amplified the disabled movement message was when a Wisconsin

independent living center asked permission to reprint one of Rosen's pieces on survival.[104]

"Groups Demand Housing" in June 1980 chronicled a disabled-rights coalition news conference announcing their demand that Louisville fund programs to provide accessible housing for disabled people.[105] In-depth articles looked at the state of curb cuts in Louisville and threats to implementation of Section 504 regulations to transportation (including addresses for every Kentucky representative).[106] An election package in September 1980 asked if the presidential debate in Louisville would be accessible and discussed a new national League of Disabled Voters. The August 1981 lead story announced, "Disabled People Plan Cross Country Rally." Readers could contact the *Rag* for information on how to participate in the caravans that planned to convene for protests in Washington on September 7. The *Rag* rallied its readers to participate in a 1982 protest against Reagan administration threats to Section 504.[107]

The *Rag* also critiqued charitable institutions for the disabled. It found "deeply troubling" the National Barrier Awareness Day publicity gimmick of following able-bodied officials using wheelchairs or blindfolds for a day.[108] It especially reviled telethons, target of a May 1982 special issue. Anne Peters explained in it why Jerry Lewis's televised event offended: it treated wheelchairs as a gift instead of a right; the MDA focused on finding a cure, implying the disabled were lesser people; it stereotyped the disabled as helpless.[109] Johnson's detailed 1992 chronicle of the decade-long campaign to remove Lewis from the annual MDA Telethon—and the MDA's campaign against their critics—contrasted to frequent first-person diatribes against its offensive "Jerry's Kids" theme.[110]

Challenging the Right to Die

The *Rag* also raised uncomfortable ethical questions about disability and challenged mainstream views on controversial issues. For example, it parsed the case of Elizabeth Bouvia, a young woman with cerebral palsy who in 1983 sued a hospital to stop force-feeding her so she could die.[111] Bouvia's desire to die contradicted the *Rag*'s empowering disability identity. "She proves that bravery, courage, overcoming are fallacies—and she fulfills society's deepest feeling about disability, that it's a fate worse than death," Irvin wrote in an editorial.[112] The *Rag* argued that Bouvia's real problem was a lack of support

that would enable her to lead a fulfilling life. A special double issue examined the Bouvia case from many angles as well as the case of Baby Jane Doe,
an infant with severe brain damage whose parents declined life-saving surgery. The double issue demonstrated the newspaper's in-depth approach to
covering issues important to its constituency. It published Bouvia's statement
requesting the disabled community respect her right to end her life[113] as well
as a mother's anguished essay about the disabled infant she lost because doctors refused to treat him.[114] Johnson's in-depth historical piece likened the
Baby Jane Doe case to Nazi genocide, when she claimed the first person they
killed was a baby born blind and missing a leg.[115]

Technology held horrors for the disabled that were invisible to others: new
amniocentesis tests that identified fetal birth defects made the disabled community collectively shudder as it saw its reflection in the imperfect fetuses.[116]
The editors' pro-life stances placed them in an uncomfortable alliance with
conservative opponents of abortion. The *Rag* strained to distance the disability rights view from them: right-to-lifers want to be heroes, Johnson argued,
but fail to recognize abortion as a disability issue—the case for the right to a
decent life. An editorial stated, "Although they talk about the rights of these
children to exist, they seem to us more concerned about winning a moral
point than about the quality of life for the disabled children they are so piously
encouraging parents to raise."[117]

The *Rag's* militant stance on other disability issues alienated some potential recruits. In contrast to enthusiastic mainstream news media, it framed
cochlear implants as a threat to deaf culture and framed as oppressive the
push for the surgery that restored hearing.[118] A *Rag* editorial charged that the
Special Olympics were a form of segregation.[119] Easter Seals telethon director John Kemp appreciated the *Rag's* perspective but disliked the newspaper's
"strident, shoot-from-the-hip approach." A reader wrote, "While I enjoy reading the *Disability Rag*, I am often left with the feeling that the attacks on
the non-disabled are unfair and the writers are their own worst enemies."[120]
Disabled actor Alan Toy once complained that the *Rag* ignored positive role
models on TV and trotted out old, outdated reruns as examples of negative
stereotyping.[121] A 1996 study found that some disabled respondents refused to
subscribe because they found the *Rag* too militant.[122] These objections illustrate that the disabled community never was monolithic and indicate the
limits of the militant *Rag's* appeal for a collective disability identity. A constant refrain in its pages criticized divisiveness among the disabled.[123] Irvin
once told an interviewer that the disabled lacked a sense of brotherhood

because they lacked a collective memory and their disabilities were so varied. She said, "Disabled people need more spirit. They need more inspiration. They need some passion."[124] Irvin's use of "they" versus "we" may offer one clue to the *Rag*'s shortcomings in cohering a collective identity.

The 1990 ADA: A New Era for Disability Rights

The *Rag*'s coverage of the landmark 1990 Americans with Disabilities Act—an "earthshaking event for disabled people," in the words of historian Shapiro—demonstrated its contrarian viewpoint.[125] The newspaper was enthusiastic in its early coverage of the proposed ADA that would grant the disabled equal rights, beginning with Johnson's July/August 1988 cover story, "A New Day for Disability Rights?"[126] Two pages of tips followed on how to keep a Discrimination Diary to send to Congressional representatives to provide evidence to persuade them to vote for the bill. The *Rag* continued to update readers on the bill's progress as it wended its way through Congress, mainly in the "Ragout" news briefs. Few believed the act would pass because of its expensive price tag for the private businesses and organizations it would force to meet the 1973 Rehabilitation Act Section 504's accessibility provisions. Both mainstream media and the public practically ignored the bill.[127] The Senate, however, passed the ADA in late 1989. When the House dallied, a thousand ADAPT protesters from thirty states descended on the U.S. Capitol on March 11, 1990. More than 60 people left their wheelchairs and crawled the 83 stone steps up to the U.S. Capitol Building. Disinterested mainstream media that missed the dramatic "Capitol Crawl" made sure to show up the next day, when protesters chained their wheelchairs together in the Capitol Rotunda. Police arrested more than a hundred people, and the House approved the bill. The Americans with Disabilities Act of 1990 became law on July 26, 1990, moving the disabled into mainstream America.

Just as the ADA marked a new era for the disabled, ADAPT's theatrical protests marked mainstream news media's discovery of ADA as a story worth covering, according to disabilities scholar Beth Haller.[128] The radical *Rag*, however, seemed displeased. It criticized the "crawl-in," which editors found demeaning.[129] It relegated to page nine a story on the historic signing of the act.[130] Johnson, in fact, believed the ADA was deeply flawed by big loopholes and by its reliance on consumers to enforce compliance through civil suits. Johnson detailed her objections in 2003's *Make Them Go Away:*

Clint Eastwood, Christopher Reeve & the Case Against Disability Rights. In 1990, however, the so-called civil rights bill for the disabled perhaps made the *Rag's* rants seem less relevant to the community, who like suffragists after the 1920 ratification of the Nineteenth Amendment focused on pursuing individual accomplishments instead of collective action in the belief all institutional barriers to their success had been removed. Although the ADA proved not to be a cure-all, its passage did mark a new era for the disability rights movement that the *Rag* helped create. The newspaper continued to publish but changed its name to *Ragged Edge* magazine in 1995, when it launched a website of the same name. The print edition continued until 2003, while the *Ragged Edge* website remained active until 2006.[131]

Mainstream and Other Early Disability Rights Magazines

While *Disability Rag* was the most militant of the early disability rights periodicals, Cynthia Jones and William Stothers's more moderate approach was embedded in their magazine's name—*Mainstream.* "The magazine was never crazy, crazy radical out-front leadership," Jones recalled. "I like the *Rag,* but if you gave the *Rag* to most of the people who are disabled in America they would think you're crazy."[132] *Mainstream,* probably the first journal produced by disabled people, originated in San Diego in 1975. It literally was the voice of founder Jim Hammitt, who had a speech impediment caused by cerebral palsy. A federal jobs-training grant enabled Hammitt to hire disabled people, including his childhood friend Jones, a polio survivor. Jones eventually bought *Mainstream,* serving as editor and publisher while developing it into a four-color glossy magazine with her husband, Stothers, a fellow polio survivor who used a wheelchair and was an editor at the *San Diego Tribune.* The couple wrote for the moderate masses they felt might follow the vanguard. It was less confrontational than the *Rag.* "There's a place to go into the street and get arrested, but not everybody has to do that," Stothers said. "But everybody can vote and should vote."[133]

The couple's philosophy of empowerment infused *Mainstream.* Unlike the *Rag,* it included an employment column. Stothers once said he was proudest of the magazine's consistency in portraying "the disability experience, not entirely in a strident advocacy way but in a broader way of trying to live one's life in a positive way, that people can be successful."[134] The couple chose to make *Mainstream* a commercial enterprise to help break the charity model of disability, selling advertising for products like wheelchairs.

A third influential disability rights periodical appeared in 1989 when brain-injury survivor Lucy Gwin began publishing her very personal *This Brain Has a Mouth*, which grew into *Mouth* magazine in 1990. It served as an uncompromising voice for social inclusion for the next twenty years, when Gwin became too ill to continue. When the former advertising copywriter and civil rights activist emerged from a three-week coma after a car accident, she was transferred to a rehabilitation facility that refused to release her until her insurance ran out. A friend helped her "escape." Gwin's exposé of its abuses helped shutter the facility. The acerbic *Mouth*'s social justice journalism tackled such tough topics as exploitative labor practices of sheltered workshops and corruption in disabled-services systems, and offered a how-to on joining the underground economy.[135] "Lucy was an extreme black-and-white thinker, with very little room for gray," recalled Josie Byzek, managing editor of *New Mobility* magazine and long-time writer and editor at *Mouth*. "For her, right was right, and wrong was unacceptable. Period."[136] The disability rights movement that these three periodicals helped create had entered a new era after passage of the ADA, even though Johnson's skepticism about the act proved prescient.

Disability Rights Activism in the Digital Age

On June 22, 2017, more than fifty ADAPT activists staged a "die-in" in the U.S. Capitol to protest massive proposed cuts to Medicaid, which they feared will force them back into institutions. Organized in less than a week through social media,[137] the protest culminated in the spectacle of police hauling protesters out of their wheelchairs. The shocking images worked, and Congress declined to make the cuts. ADAPT's website is now the nucleus of its nonviolent direct actions "to assure the civil and human rights of people with disabilities to live in freedom."[138] ADAPT's heritage of civil disobedience is important to its collective identity, which an online history museum nurtures as a repository of artifacts, articles, videos, music, ephemera, and accounts by participants in fifty ADAPT actions over twenty-five years. Facebook Moments pages feature photographs of recent actions like the 2017 protests.

Just as in the 1980s, the dramatic "wheel-ins" won a lot of media attention, demonstrating that social movement organizations still need legacy media to make an impact. Marilee Adamski-Smith, ADAPT's national media chair, alerts the media when and where an action occurs, then answers reporters' questions. ADAPT assigns some members to create and post multimedia on social media, but Adamski-Smith says it is important to have mainstream journalists witness the protests and publicize their cause. She was arrested in 2017 for the first time in twenty-one years with ADAPT during a disruption of a Congressional hearing. "People saw us, saw how it would affect our lives," said Adamski-Smith, who is a graphic designer. "I have no arms and legs. I need that home care and health services to be a productive member of society."[139]

While ADAPT continues to focus on direct action on the ground, disability rights voices have proliferated online. The Internet arguably has been more of a boon for the disability rights movement than for any other social movement because it eliminates access issues. Wheelchair user Vilissa Thompson, for example, founded Ramp Your Voice! in 2013 to fill the gap in the lack of voices of disabled people of color. Ramp Your Voice! emphasizes intersectionality in disability topics related to sex, religion, politics, racism, and education. Thompson, a social worker and blogger, argues that the erasure of black disabled women from the disability movement's history robs them of powerful role models that can help them resist discrimination. She created #DisabilityTooWhite to push the media into telling stories of people of color with disabilities. Thompson, who started kindergarten in a public school classroom in 1991, says the 1990 ADA was indispensable to her. She mixes the personal and the political in her blog to humanize the disabled experience. She once said, "Sharing my anger, pains, and joys in embracing being a woman who is Black, physically disabled, a wheelchair user, a little woman, and hard of hearing and finding space and community in the process were unexpected occurrences that strengthened my presence and advocacy."[140]

Social media are especially effective sites for connecting members of very specific and small segments of the diverse disability community. #GetYourBellyOut encourages users to post on social media images of their colostomy or ileostomy bags, often worn by people with Crohn's disease or ulcerative colitis, to help destigmatize them. The weekly Twitter chat #ChronicSex is a forum where users share tips and tricks to make sex more pleasurable for people with chronic disease or disability. Such sites emphasize collective identity, but others call for collective action. #CripTheVote is a nonpartisan online movement that engages disabled people on policies and practices regarding disability. It hosts a series of Twitter chats to educate the disabled community on a broad range of topics: the House farm bill and its effect on food stamps, media coverage of the disabled, how to make activism more accessible. The Autistic Self-Advocacy Network, organized in 2006, uses the slogan, "Nothing about us without us."[141] Rooted in Rights is a nonprofit Seattle-based project of Disability Rights Washington that produces videos and social media campaigns exclusively on disability rights issues. Its global network of digital storytellers produces videos around the world. The program is active offline, too, hosting a Rooted in Rights Storytelling Festival and hosting films and workshops. A 2018 essay by #CripTheVote founder Andrew Pulrang voiced his frustration with a divide between disability activists that mainly work online and those that physically participate in actions. Pulrang argued that the division reflects the larger debate on whether disability is an adaptable social condition or if it includes an irreducible medical component. He suggested twenty ways anyone can participate in the movement, ranging from attending town council meetings as a monitor and voice for disability issues to managing online disability discussions and forums to writing an old-fashioned letter to the editor. "Any of these activities can be useful and productive," he concluded, continuing the emphasis on agency that originated in the *Disability Rag*.[142]

Notes

1. Mike Ervin, "The Founder of the *Disability Rag* Tells Its Story," *Media dis&dat*, April 20, 2009, http://media-dis-n-dat.blogspot.com/2009/04/founder-of-disability-rag-tells-its.html. Ervin is the subject of a 2005 documentary film, "The Kids Are All Right," available at http://www.thekidsareallright.org.

2. "Lewis Sick?," *Disability Rag*, December 1982, 3. [hereafter cited as *Rag*]

3. See Mike Ervin, "My Turn: Mike Ervin: Jerry Lewis Angered Many Disabled People," *Providence Journal*, August 30, 2017, http://www.providencejournal.com/opinion/20170830/my-turn-mike-ervin-jerry-lewis-angered-many-disabled-people.

4. Steven E. Brown, "Disability Culture: Beginnings, A Fact Sheet," *Institute on Disability Culture*, accessed November 2, 2018, http://www.instituteondisabilityculture.org/disability-culture-beginnings-a-fact-sheet.html.

5. Richard K. Scotch, "Politics and Policy in the History of the Disability Rights Movement," *The Milbank Quarterly* 67, Supp. 2 (October 1989): 394.

6. Frank E. James, "Why a Magazine for Disabled Ignores Handicapped Heroes—Controversial 'Disability Rag' Says Lionizing 'Supercrips' Is No Help for Majority," *Wall Street Journal*, January 11, 1985, 1.

7. David Streitfeld, "Puncturing the Pathos for the Disabled," *Washington Post*, November 6, 1986, D5.

8. Paul Longmore and Lauri Umansky, "Introduction," in *The New Disability History: American Perspectives*, ed. Paul Longmore and Lauri Umansky (New York: New York University Press, 2001), 4–5; and Steven E. Brown, "What Is Disability Culture?," *Disability Studies Quarterly* 22, no. 2 (Spring 2002): 34–50.

9. "The Results Are In!," *Rag*, March/April 1986, 33.

10. "CDC: 53 Million Adults in the US Live with a Disability," *Centers for Disease Control*, July 30, 2015, https://www.cdc.gov/media/releases/2015/p0730-us-disability.html.

11. Ten recurring disabling stereotypes in the mass media are: the disabled person as pitiable and pathetic, as an object of curiosity or violence, as sinister or evil, as the super cripple, as atmosphere, as laughable, as her/his own worst enemy, as a burden, as non-sexual, and as being unable to participate in daily life. Colin Barnes, "Discrimination: Disabled People and the Media," *Contact*, no. 70 (Winter 1991): 45–48.

12. See Genevieve Belmaker, "Reporting on Disability with Sensitivity, not Sensationalism," *Nieman Reports*, March 30, 2016, http://niemanreports.org/articles/reporting-on-disability-with-sensitivity-not-sensationalism/; Douglas Biklen, "Framed: Print Journalism's Treatment of Disability Issues," in *Images of the Disabled: Disabling Images*, ed. Alan Gartner and Tom Joe (New York: Praeger, 1986), 79–96; Elizabeth Ride, "Media Portrayals of People with Handicaps: Does Accuracy Matter?," *Studies in Popular Culture* 16, no. 2 (April 1994): 85; and Roland Yoshida, Lynn Wasilewski, and Douglas Friedman, "Recent Newspaper Coverage About Persons with Disabilities," *Exceptional Children* 56 (1990): 418–23.

13. Beth Haller, "The Little Papers Newspapers at 19th-Century Schools for Deaf Persons," *Journalism History* 19 (Summer 1993): 46–47.

14. An online version continues at http://www.matildaziegler.com. For more on early advocacy magazines for the blind, see Catherine J. Kudlick, "The Outlook of *The Problem* and the Problem with the *Outlook*," in Longmore and Umansky, *New Disability History*, 187–213.

15. The original gazette is available at http://www.polioplace.org/GINI.

16. Lillie Sharon Ransom, "Disability Magazine and Newsletter Editors: Perceptions of the Disability Press, Community, Advocacy, Mainstreaming and Diversity" (PhD. diss., University of Maryland, 1996), 41, 120. Ransom identified 131 publications for people with disabilities. Ibid., 252.

17. See Jessica M. F. Hughes, "Changing Conversations Around Autism: A Critical, Action Implicative Discourse Analysis of US Neurodiversity Advocacy Online" (PhD. diss., University of Colorado Boulder, 2015).

18. Eli A. Wolff and Dr. Mary Hums, "'Nothing About Us Without Us'—Mantra for a Movement," *HuffPost*, September 5, 2017, https://www.huffingtonpost.com/entry/nothing-about-us-without-us-mantra-for-a-movement_us_59aea450e4b0c50640cd61cf.

19. Robert Muskie, "Slaves' Rights," *Rag*, January 1981, 3–4; reprinted in October 1982, 1–2.

20. Leonard Kriegel, "Uncle Tom and Tiny Tim," *Rag*, October 1980, 3–4.

21. "Shades of Jim Crow," *Rag*, February 1983, 15.

22. "What's Wrong with Paratransit?," *Rag*, September 1983, 7.

23. "Proposed by *Rag*: Doors an Issue," *Rag*, April 1980, 1.

24. "Why We Do What We Do," *Rag*, January 1982, 14.

25. See Victoria Dawson, "Ed Roberts' Wheelchair Records a Story of Obstacles Overcome," *Smithsonian.com*, March 13, 2015, https://www.smithsonianmag.com/smithsonian-insti tution/ed-roberts-wheelchair-records-story-obstacles-overcome-180954531/.

26. See Emily Pate, "Spotlight on Disability Rights Advocate Judy Heumann," *Rooted in Rights*, May 11, 2015, https://www.rootedinrights.org/spotlight-on-disability-rights-advoca te-judy-heumann/.

27. Joseph Shapiro, *No Pity: People with Disabilities Forging a New Civil Rights Movement* (New York: Three Rivers Press, 1993), 68.

28. Streitfeld, "Puncturing," D5.

29. Frank E. James, "Why a Magazine for Disabled Ignores Handicapped Heroes—Controver- sial '*Disability Rag*' Says Lionizing 'Supercrips' Is No Help for Majority," *Wall Street Journal*, January 11, 1985, 1.

30. "To Our Readers," *Rag*, February 1980, 2.

31. "Ragtime," *Rag*, July 1983, 2. See also Rebecca Rouillard, "A 'Non-disabled' Person Speaks Out," ibid., 3; Cass Irvin, "Is There a Place for Nondisabled People?," ibid., 5; and Mary Johnson, "The Passiveness of the Deceitful Wheelchair User," ibid., 7–10.

32. Streitfeld, "Puncturing," D5.

33. "Remember April 7," *Rag*, April 1980, 1.

34. Brown, "Disability Culture." See also Tom Shakespeare, "Cultural Representation of Dis- abled People," *Disability & Society* 9, no. 3 (1994): 283–99; and Lingling Zhang and Beth Haller, "Consuming Image: How Mass Media Impact the Identity of People with Disabil- ities," *Communication Quarterly* 61, no. 3 (June 2013): 319–14.

35. See for example, "Are You Disabled or Handicapped—or Neither?," *Rag*, April 1982, 6; and "'But Words Will Never Hurt Me,'" *Rag*, June 1982, 14.

36. Anne Peters, "Developing a Language: What About 'Gimp?,'" *Rag*, May/June 1986, 20, 22; and ibid., "Developing a Language: Do We Have to Be Named?" and "'…cripple?,'" both *Rag*, November/December 1986, 31.

37. "Ragtime: The Problem with Challenge," *Rag*, July 1985, 22.

38. "Editor's Note," *Rag*, April 1982, 2.

39. Mary Johnson, "Emotion and Pride: The Search for a Disability Culture," *Rag*, January/ February 1987, 4. See also Ed Hooper, "Seeking the Disabled Community," *Rag*, August 1985, 4; K. Hirsch, "Studying Culture," *Rag*, May/June 1987, 8, 38–39; and Peters, "Devel- oping a Language."

40. Ellen Cristopf, "Disability Cool: Signs of the Times," *Rag*, January 1982, 13; and "Disabil- ity Cool," *Rag*, June 1982, 15.

41. Mary E. McKnew, "Disability Cool," *Rag*, September 1982, 15; and "Disability Cool," *Rag*, November/December 1982, 14.

42. Anne Peters, "Disability Cool: Max H-H-Headroom?," *Rag*, September/October 1987, 8.

43. "Disability Cool: Our Heroes," *Rag*, May 1983, 1.

44. Mary Johnson, "Ending the Aloneness," *Rag*, March/April 1986, 28; and Mary Johnson, "Anthologies, Good and Bad," *Rag*, July/August 1986, 18.

45. Rob Muskie, "Reading: Looking for the Real FDR," *Rag*, August 1985, 12.

46. Dr. John Gliedman, "Minority Report," *Rag*, July 1980, 3–4.

47. "Poems," *Rag*, July 1981, 6. See also untitled, *Rag*, November/December 1982, 12; and Ed Hooper, "The Way Downtown," *Rag*, August 1983, 13.

48. Michel Foucault, "Technologies of the Self," in *Technologies of the Self: A Seminar with Michel Foucault*, ed. Luther H. Martin, Huck Gutman and Patrick H. Hutton (London: Tavistock Publications, 1988), 33, 35, 45.

49. "The Sex Survey: A First Look At Your Responses," *Rag*, November/December 1989, 15–17.

50. Patricia Smith Ranzoni, "Dancing Out the Dream," *Rag*, Fall 1985, 15.

51. "I Call Myself 'Survivor,'" *Rag*, May 1983, 8–10.

52. S. L. Rosen, "A Survivor's Manual," *Rag*, November 1980, 3.

53. S. L. Rosen, "Learning to Be Handicapped," *Rag*, December 1980, 3. See also Rosen, "Becoming a Survivor," *Rag*, March 1981, 3–4; and "Are You a Survivor?," *Rag*, May 1981, 7.

54. "Thank you, thank you, thank you," *Rag*, September 1983, 13.

55. Scott Hutchinson to "Dear *Disability Rag*," *Rag*, September 1980, 2.

56. Alice Wong, "Storytelling and the Disability Visibility Project," July 11, 2015, https://www. youtube.com/watch?v=8bgBOX42WyE.

57. Judy Heumann, "The Great Unspoken Issue of Our Movement," *Rag*, July/August 1991.

58. Edward L. Hooper, "The Room of Pain and Loneliness," *Rag*, March/April 1988, 5. See also Hooper, "Aphasia," *Rag*, August 1985, 1, 3–5.

59. Lisa Blumberg, "Public Stripping," *Rag*, January/February 1990, 18–19.

60. "Editor's Note," *Rag*, April 1982, 2.

61. "Models, Not Heroes," *Rag*, January 1982, 3.

62. Jane Zirinsky to the Editor, *Rag*, November/December 1984, 24.

63. Bob Muskie, "Some Thoughts at the End," *Rag*, January 1982, 5–6. See also "The Jock Image is Risky," *Rag*, July/August 1986, 5.

64. Anne Peters, "Heart-wrencher Wins Journalism's Top Prize," *Rag*, August 1985, 18–19.

65. "You Decide," *Rag*, July 1985, 26; and "You Decide," *Rag*, November/December 1988, 30. See also "You Decide About Elizabeth Bouvia," *Rag*, July/August 1986, 24.

66. *Rag*, July/August 1987, 14.

67. Caroline Kaufman, "One Woman's Efforts at Being Sexual," *Rag*, September/October 1987, 17–18.

68. Ransom, "Disability Magazine and Newsletter Editors," 230.

69. "Reporters' Favorite Clichés," *Rag*, January/February 1986, 7; "Hype, Hope and Hearts," *Rag*, March/April 1986, 27; "Crip-bashing in the Press," *Rag*, September/October 1989, 25.

70. Anne Peters, "A Fate Worse Than Death," *Rag*, August 1983, 14. See also Peters, "Images of Ourselves," *Rag*, November 1981, 1, 4.

71. "TV Treats Worth Waiting For," *Rag*, May/June 1986, 22; and "The Romance of Blindness," *Rag*, July/August, 34.

72. Lauri Klobas, "A New Form of Apartheid," *Rag*, September/October 1986, 30.

73. Laura Younkin, "To Stem the Tide," *Rag*, September/October 1989, 19–21. See also Mary Johnson, "Changing the Words in News," *Rag*, March/April 1987, 14–19.

74. William A. Gamson, "Constructing Social Protest," in *Social Movements and Culture*, ed. Hank Johnston and Bert Klandermans (Minneapolis: University of Minnesota Press, 1995), 90. [emphasis in original]

75. "How to Complain" and "How to Get Funds," both *Rag*, January 1981, 1.

76. Mary Johnson, "Malinda: the Untold Story," *Rag*, February 1982, 11–12; and "News Reporter Tells Why She Did What She Did," *Rag*, January 1982, 13.

77. Ervin, "The Founder."

78. Mary Johnson, "The Power of One Person," *Rag*, January/February 1992, reprinted in *The Ragged Edge: The Disability Experience from the Pages of the First Fifteen Years of the Disability Rag*, ed. Barrett Shaw (Louisville, KY: Avocado Press, 1994), 156–64.

79. Mary Johnson, "An Interview with Itzhak Perlman," *Rag*, February 1983, 1, 8. See also "Itzhak Perlman on Heroes, Leaders and the Disability Rights Movement," *Rag*, March 1983, 4–5.

80. Cass Irvin, *Home Bound: Growing Up with a Disability in America* (Philadelphia: Temple University Press, 2004), 160.

81. "If You Don't Mind the Backs of the Theater," *Rag*, February 1983, 4; and "Joining the Battle," ibid., 6.

82. "New Design Rules Issued: It's Your Turn," *Rag*, May 1981, 1.

83. "Check These Measurements," *Rag*, May 1981, 3.

84. "Making Laws" and "Get a Ballot," both *Rag*, October 1981, 1.

85. See for example, "It's the Law: Housing Rights," *Rag*, April 1980, 3.

86. "Leslie Pardue, "Should Animals Suffer So That We Might Be Cured," *Rag*, September/ October 1986, 1, 4–8.

87. "About This Matter of Work," *Rag*, March 1982, 3–4; "Insult to Injury," *Rag*, May/June 1986, 1, 4–6; Thomas R. Riley, "Playing Hardball," *Rag*, July/August 1988, 16–18; Laura Younkin, "Personal Care," *Rag*, January/February 1989, 1, 4–8; and "Housing for All?" *Rag*, May/June 1989, 16–20.

88. "Sign Language Pledge Already Broken by All Candidates," *Rag*, March/April 1988, 18.

89. See Sylvia Wyman, "The Uncontrollables," *Rag*, March 1983, 14.

90. "An Attendant Can Make a Difference," *Rag*, March 1983, 3.

91. "Attendant Care in Other States," *Rag*, March 1983, 12; and "A Call to Action," ibid., 9. See also Ellen Cristoph, "Why Not Take it to the Streets?" *Rag*, May/June 1986, 32.

92. Anne Finger and Barbara Fay Waxman, "We Could Be Next," *Rag*, September/October 1986, 27; and Barbara Fay Waxman, "It's Time to Politicize Our Sexual Oppression," *Rag*, March/April 1991, reprinted in Shaw, *Ragged Edge*, 82–87.

93. "Trickle Up," *Rag*, January 1984, 3–7.

94. Hotchkiss went on to win a 1989 Macarthur Foundation "genius" award of $260,000, which he used to help establish Whirlwind Wheelchair International. Hotchkiss has worked in 42 countries teaching people who need wheelchairs how to build and maintain them. "Mr. Mobility/Wheelchair Pioneer Assembles Global Network of Designers," *SFGATE*, April 19, 1999, http://www.sfgate.com/news/article/Mr-Mobility-Wheelchair-pioneer-assembles-2935591.php; and Whirlwind Wheelchair, accessed November 2, 2018, https://whirlwindwheelchair.org/staff/.

95. "Disability Rights: What Is in the Legislature?," *Rag*, February 1982, 1.

96. "ADAPT Rolls on—in Chicago," *Rag*, January/February 1987, 9; and "ADAPT Meets Phoenix" and "ADAPT Marches in Detroit," both in *Rag*, July/August 1987, 8.

97. Mary Johnson, "Improving Issue Coverage of ADAPT?," *Rag*, November/December 1987, 25.

98. Mary Johnson, "ADAPT Coverage: A Reappraisal," *Rag*, January/February 1988, 28.

99. Mary Johnson, "On the Barricades with ADAPT," *Rag*, July/August 1992, reprinted in Shaw, *Ragged Edge*, 137–48.

100. Laura Younkin, "Protest: What's the Most Effective Way to Change Things?," *Rag*, May/June 1989, 7.

101. "The 'I Can't Work,' Syndrome," *Rag*, March 1982, 5–6; and "The Best of Both Worlds," ibid., November/December 1982, 1, 3; and Deanne and Lew Wallace, "Passing," ibid., 3.

102. "Four Real Victories," *Rag*, December 1980, 1, 4.

103. Richard Clark to "Dear *Rag*," *Rag*, January 1981, 2.

104. Barbara Hummel to "Dear Editor," *Rag*, July 1981, 2.

105. *Rag*, June 1980, 1.

106. "Curb Cuts," *Rag*, July 1980, 1, 4; and Rebecca Rouillard, "Transit Amendment Threats," *Rag*, August 1980, 1, 4. See also "HUD Lags on 504; Gets Sued," *Rag*, March 1981, 1.

107. "Take Action June 3 to Protest Changes in 504," *Rag*, June 1982, 1.

108. Geeta Dardick, "Disability Puff," *Rag*, July/August 1987, 1, 4–6.

109. Anne Peters, "Telethons," *Rag*, May 1982, 2–3, 12.

110. Mary Johnson, "A Test of Wills: Jerry Lewis, Jerry's Orphans, and the Telethon," *Rag*, September/October 1992, reprinted in *Ragged Edge*, 120–30.

111. Anne Peters, "What Is It, Elizabeth?," *Rag*, January 1984, 14. [italics in original]

112. "A Mixed-up Woman," *Rag*, March/April 1986, 23. See also Mary Johnson, "Drab Curtains—or How the Press Didn't Cover the Issues that Led to David Rivlin's Suicide," *Rag*, September/October 1989, 25–26; and "Bouvia in Hospital Again—'Issue's different,' attorney says," *Rag*, March/April 1986, 1.

113. "I Am Fully Aware … ," *Rag*, February/March 1984, 5.

114. Julie Shaw Cole, "Silence Surrounding the Fear," *Rag*, February/March 1984, 14–17. See also "Secret Aversions: Mothers Talk About Disabled Babies," *Rag*, February/March 1984, 18.

115. Mary Johnson, "A Life Worth Living," *Rag*, January/February 1987, 24–26. See also "Ragtime: Stealing History for Ourselves," ibid., 30.

116. "'The Right Not to Be Born," *Rag*, November/December 1989, 21–22.

117. "Ragtime: Raising Vegetables," *Rag*, February/March 1984, 12. See also Mary Johnson, "Killing Babies: Left and Right," *Rag*, May 1983, 2, 6.

118. "Cochlear Implants: The Final Put-down?," *Rag*, March/April 1986, 1, 4–6; and "The Hope of 'Cure,'" ibid., 6.

119. "Ragtime: Troubling Questions about the Special Olympics," *Rag*, September/October 1987, 32.

120. Stephanie E. Phillips to the Editor, *Rag*, May 1985, 2.

121. Alan Toy, "'Pejorative Inaccuracies,'" *Rag*, March/April 1990, 37.

122. Ransom, "Disability Magazine and Newsletter Editors,"109.

123. Mary Jane Owen, "Like Squabbling Cubs," *Rag*, March/April 1985; and David T. Williams and Frances Dwyer McCaffery, "A Divided Lot," *Rag*, May/June 1986, 28.

124. "Local Woman Wins National Post," *Rag*, July 1981, 6.

125. Shapiro, *No Pity*, 140. See also "Introduction," *New Disability History*, 1.

126. *Rag*, July/August 1988, 1.

127. Shapiro, *No Pity*, 117.

128. Beth Haller, "Crawling Toward Civil Rights: News Media Coverage of Disability Activism," in *Cultural Diversity and the U.S. Media*, ed. Yahya Kamalipour and Theresa Carilli (Albany: State University of New York Press, 1998), 89–98.

129. "The Crawl In," *Rag*, May/June 1990, 21. See also "Opportunity Lost," ibid., 31.

130. "Movement Celebrates Signing of Disabilities Act," *Rag*, September/October 1990, 11–12. See also Robin Garr, "ADA: Too Early to Celebrate?," *Rag*, July/August 1990, 10.

131. See *Ragged Edge Online*, accessed November 2, 2018, http://www.raggededgemagazine.com/.

132. "Cynthia Jones, *Mainstream Magazine* Editor and Publisher," an oral history conducted in 1999 by Mary Lou Breslin in *Mainstream* Magazine: Chronicling National Disability Politics, Regional Oral History Office, The Bancroft Library, University of California, Berkeley, 2000, 90.

133. "William Stothers, Journalist and Managing Editor for *Mainstream Magazine*," an oral history conducted in 1999 by Susan O'Hara in *Mainstream Magazine*: Chronicling National Disability Politics, Regional Oral History Office, The Bancroft Library, University of California, Berkeley, 2000, 212.

134. Ibid.

135. See Douglas Lathrop, "Challenging Perceptions," *Quill* 83 (July/August 1995), 36–38.

136. Janine Bertram Kemp, "Lucy Gwin: The Brain with a Mouth," *Independence Today*, accessed November 2, 2018, http://www.itodaynews.com/2014-issues/12-2014-issue50/Cover.htm. Gwin died in 2014. Ibid.

137. "Why Disability Rights Activists Stormed Mitch McConnell's Office," *Rolling Stone*, June 2, 2017, https://www.rollingstone.com/politics/news/why-disability-rights-activists-stormed-mitch-mcconnells-office-w489441.

138. "Welcome to ADAPT!," *ADAPT*, accessed November 2, 2018, http://adapt.org/.

139. Marilee Adamski-Smith, telephone interview with the author, May 8, 2018.

140. Trimiko Melancon, "Ramp Your Voice: An Interview with Vilissa Thompson," *Black Perspectives*, March 18, 2017, https://www.aaihs.org/ramp-your-voice-an-interview-with-vilissa-thompson/.

141. "About," *Autistic Self-Advocacy Network*, accessed November 2, 2018, http://autisticadvocacy.org/about-asan/.

142. Andrew Pulrang, "Can We Stop Arguing About the 'Right Way' to Be a Disability Activist?," Rooted in Rights, May 4, 2018, https://www.rootedinrights.org/can-we-stop-arguing-about-the-right-way-to-be-a-disability-activist/.

· 9 ·

FTM NEWSLETTER

Louis Sullivan Finds Himself and Fosters a Movement

When a thin young woman wearing black Levis and a leather jacket approached the founder of the Gay People's Union in Milwaukee in the early 1970s and asked if they could talk, Eldon E. Murray figured she wanted to discuss her lesbian feelings. He was surprised but not shocked when Sheila Sullivan confided over coffee that she felt like a man trapped in a woman's body. More surprising was the future Louis Graydon Sullivan's disclosure that he felt not just like a man, but a gay man. Experts agreed there was no such thing as a gay transgender man.

Sullivan proved them wrong. Before dying from AIDS complications at thirty-nine on March 2, 1991, Sullivan founded the first support and educational group for FTMs—female-to-male trans people. He forced the medical establishment to acknowledge the existence of gay FTM transsexuals, as transgender people were called back then, and to recognize the distinction between sexual orientation and gender identity, a finding that rocked age-old assumptions about human identity. He literally wrote the book on FTM sex reassignment (or gender reassignment). Sullivan created a grassroots support network for FTM transsexuals and cross-dressers, and he educated physicians and psychiatrists about the process and dynamics of FTM transition. He offered his own body as a case study of FTM transition in photographic and video archives that unsparingly document his experience. One of Sullivan's many contributions was *FTM Newsletter*, the first periodical devoted to issues affecting trans men. It became a lifeline for people around the world, fostering a unique community of journalism as fervent as the abolitionist readership of William Lloyd Garrison's *Liberator*. Colleague Kevin Horwitz wrote of Sullivan: "He was somebody who forced others to validate the condition of female-to-male transsexualism, and finally, he had the very good sense to write books on this subject, to establish a newsletter, and to form a support group. All of this was done even during the times when he could barely drag himself out of bed."[1]

This chapter examines the role of *FTM Newsletter* in the transgender social justice movement, the last major American social movement to originate in print culture. Transgender journals developed in parallel with the evolving lesbian and gay press as each group confronted essential questions about identity that delved deeper than the gay/straight dichotomy—a concept already beyond the ken of many heterosexual, cisgender Americans. Gay men and lesbians frequently competed with—and often were less than welcoming—to trans people like Sullivan, who did not conform to their binary model. Trans folk revolutionized conceptions of the basic marker of human identity by arguing that gender identity is not the same as sexual orientation and can be fluid and temporary. Their views pushed various segments of the community into a more expansive LGBT movement—although language remains contentious as this diverse community continues to define itself. Calls for inclusivity by some groups have stretched the acronym's latest iteration to the tongue-in-cheek LGBTQQIAAP, while a few have reverted to LBG, a pointed exclusion of trans people.[2]

FTM Newsletter made visible one segment of this diverse movement, shaped an empowering collective identity among them, and helped move its focus beyond individual FTM issues to a collective fight for civil rights. Before analyzing the newsletter's role and contents, the chapter will trace the history of the first transgender journal as well as the gay and lesbian press from postwar America through the 1970s, when the transsexual movement was still struggling for recognition. As historian John D'Emilio observes, the gay and lesbian press played a decisive role in building and mobilizing the Gay Liberation Movement. "The community press was, really, the only resource other than word of mouth for letting people know that a new world, a new outlook, and a new community were in formation," he wrote.[3] Historian and

Windy City Times editor Tracy Baim concurs that gay and lesbian newspapers were the community's voice. She adds, "They were activists and historians."[4]

Demonized by Mainstream Media

The postwar preoccupation with communism and conformity made homosexuals an easy target in Cold War America. The FBI established a "Sex Deviates Program" in 1951, and twice as many people were fired from the State Department for suspected homosexuality than for suspected loyalty to communism between 1947 and 1953, according to Craig M. Loftin.[5] The press fanned a moral panic about "sexual deviation" by highlighting sex crimes—which included acts of homosexuality in public parks or entering a gay bar.[6] News media demonized gay men and lesbians as misfits, degenerates, or depraved.[7] "Mainstream journalism had been one of the bastions of homophobia," D'Emilio stated.[8] Typical was a 1963 front-page story in the *New York Times* that called gays and lesbians "deviates" [sic] who were "condemned to a life of promiscuity."[9] The first American documentary to address homosexuality originally was titled "The Gay Ones," but by the time it aired on KQED on September 11, 1961, it had become "The Rejected." Despite the depressing name, the documentary's featured experts advanced the enlightened view of the 1948 Kinsey Report that homosexuality was a normal variation of human sexuality.

"Homophile" Magazines in the 1950s

Alfred Kinsey was a hero to activists in the "homophile" movement that originated on the West Coast in the 1950s, beginning with Los Angeles's Mattachine Society in 1950. Chief organizer Harry Hay, an actor whom the Communist Party expelled in the 1930s when his homosexuality was revealed, envisioned a national civil rights organization along the lines of the National Association for the Advancement of Colored People. The political climate was such that Mattachine members drew the shades and posted a lookout whenever they met, even though all they did was talk.[10] Frustrated by the society's snail-like pace, several members launched an independent, pamphlet-sized magazine called *ONE*. Unlike the secretive Mattachine Society, *ONE* editors boldly placed their names on the masthead when it appeared in January 1953, making *ONE* the nation's first openly gay magazine.[11] The society finally published its own *Mattachine Review* in January 1955, which provided access to information and positive, affirming frames of homosexuality in keeping with its publishers' assimilationist perspective.

ONE was more combative than the *Mattachine Review*. "While many in the movement sought the right to be like everyone else, we asserted the right to be different," editor Jim Kepner once explained, "with the rights and privileges attendant on that difference."[12] The crisply designed journal offered fiction, poetry, editorials, and scientific and scholarly articles on the gay experience. Like *Ms.* magazine in the 1970s, *ONE* provided a forum where for the first time closeted readers could share stories and ideas about what it meant to be a gay man. *ONE* hit a nerve among gay Americans who poured their souls into letters to the editor, sharing coming-out stories and describing what it was like to meet other homosexuals for the first time. Historian Loftin described how letters to the editor foretold coming-out strategies during the Gay Liberation Movement in the late 1960s. "*ONE* circulated the idea of gay visibility as a political strategy for thousands of other gay men and lesbians to ponder," he noted.[13] A common theme of letters was police harassment and antihomosexual witch-hunts in industry and the military, persecution that would soon reach *ONE*. Circulation had peaked at 16,000 copies by October 1954 (many mailed to subscribers), when the city postmaster declared *ONE* un-mailable on the grounds it was obscene. This was the second issue the postal office had held up; the first was the August 1953 number that asked on its cover, "Homosexual Marriage?" Postal officials in Washington, D.C., however, had ruled that number suitable for mailing. The editors set a defiant tone in a cover editorial titled "*ONE* is Not Grateful":

> *ONE* thanks no one for this reluctant acceptance. ... As we sit around quietly like nice little ladies and gentlemen gradually educating the public and the courts at our leisure, thousands of homosexuals are being unjustly arrested, blackmailed, fined, jailed, intimidated, beaten, ruined and murdered. *ONE*'s victory might seem big and historic as you read of it in the comfort of your home (locked in the bathroom? hidden under a stack of other magazines? sealed first class?). But the deviate hearing of our late August issue through jail bars will not be overly impressed.[14]

When the Washington postal officials deemed the 1954 issue obscene, *ONE* editors chose to fight. Ironically, the anonymous author of that issue's cover story—"You Can't Print That!"—was a young lawyer whose ensuing four-year First Amendment fight culminated in a seminal U.S. Supreme Court ruling that discussion of homosexuality in itself is not obscene.[15] *ONE Inc. v.*

Olesen eliminated the final barrier to a gay and lesbian press. "By protecting *ONE*," said law professor David Cruz, "the Supreme Court facilitated the flourishing of a gay and lesbian culture and a sense of community at a time when the federal government was purging its ranks."[16]

The *Ladder* Lifts the Lesbian Community

Several lesbians were involved with producing *ONE*, which publicized the formation of the Daughters of Bilitis (DOB) by Del Martin and Phyllis Lyon, a couple who wanted to socialize with other lesbians elsewhere than a bar. "Women needed privacy…not only from the watchful eye of the police, but from gaping tourists in the bars and from inquisitive parents and families," they later explained.[17] As the *ONE* lawsuit slowly wound its way through the federal courts, San Francisco women in 1955 formed the nation's first lesbian civil rights organization. Martin and Lyon quickly realized that the Daughters of Bilitis needed their own journal to reach more women. The *Ladder* that appeared in October 1956 included news, DOB meeting updates, book reviews, poetry, short stories, a running bibliography of lesbian literature, and letters from readers. Future editor Barbara Gittings recalled, "We wanted people to know they had lots of company, they weren't alone, they were all right…."[18] The *Ladder* took a more political stance after Gittings took over in 1963 and added the subtitle, "A Lesbian Review." She later said, "Adding those words to the cover helped our readers gain a new sense of identity and strength. That subtitle said, very eloquently I thought, that the word *lesbian* was no longer unspeakable."[19] Generous donations from an anonymous donor enabled the magazine to publish lush covers on slick paper.

Historian Martin Meeker argued that periodicals such as *ONE* and the *Ladder* were part of a "vast variety of established networks of communication" critical to the formation of gay and lesbian communities. They were initial points of contact and sources of information for gays and lesbians who dared not be seen at an openly homosexual gathering. Meeker argued that these communications networks form perhaps the central thread through LGBT history, making it "a recognizable and unified phenomenon." He described how the DOB initiated a candid new "sexual communications network" that expanded the social role of the gay bar or house party by supplying "sturdy lines of communication over which would travel regular and reliable information about many facets of lesbian life."[20] The *Ladder* drew women to DOB discussion groups where they birthed a form of discourse that continued in the 1960s as women's liberation consciousness-raising groups. Subscriptions and newsstand sales grew to about 750 by 1960.

The homophile movement that the *Ladder* represented began to seem increasingly quaint in the revolutionary 1960s' rush of sex, drugs, and rock'n'roll. Then, on June 28, 1969, six plainclothes police officers raided the popular Stonewall Inn gay bar in Greenwich Village—and its fed-up occupants fought back. The landmark uprising launched a militant new Gay Liberation Movement. The glib *New York Daily News* headline—"Homo Nest Raided, Queen Bees Are Stinging Mad"—indicated mass media had yet to catch up.[21] In Stonewall's wake, a colorful and contentious gay and lesbian press proliferated in the 1970s; one guide lists about 150 gay and lesbian periodicals that appeared during the decade.[22] Stonewall marked the transition of the grassroots *Los Angeles Advocate* newspaper, which originated in January 1967 as a local newsletter in response to a police raid on a local gay bar, into the nationally distributed *Advocate*, which became an influential glossy magazine in the 1980s and today is the world's oldest continuously published LGBTQ periodical.

Lesbians who intersected with the radical wing of the Women's Liberation Movement shared the feminist penchant for newspapers. A Chicago collective published the radical lesbian *Lavender Woman* from 1971 to 1976. The *Furies* newspaper in 1972 was the voice of the lesbian separatist The Furies Collective in Washington, D.C. Even conservative Texas was home in 1975 to *Goodbye to All That*, a lesbian radical feminist newsletter in Austin. By 1970, the comparatively tame Daughters of Bilitis dissolved acrimoniously and members dispersed into the radical lesbian and feminist movements. The *Ladder* continued until August 1972. An article in the April/May 1970 *Ladder* was a harbinger of the coming push to make gay liberation more inclusive and to complicate dichotomized notions of gender as gay or straight: "The Transsexual Experience" was a first-person account of a female-to-male transsexual.[23] The first American trans periodical, however, predated even the pioneering *ONE*.

Transvestia and the Origins of the Transgender Rights Movement

In 1952, a cross-dressing heterosexual man in southern California who went by the name Virginia Prince (born Arnold Loman) launched *Transvestia: The Journal of the American Society for Equality in Dress*, which noted trans historian Susan Stryker described as arguably "the first overtly political transgender publication in U.S. history."[24] Although it lasted only two issues, the publication for transvestites marked the beginning of the transgender rights movement. In 1960, Prince revived the journal as *Transvestia*, which became a long-lasting and influential venue for disseminating information about trans concerns. Prince believed the binary gender system kept both men and women from realizing their full human potential. Like the homophile magazines, *Transvestia* featured essays, scientific studies, and educational outreach. *Transvestia* was a safe space for individuals to tell their stories without fear of being judged. "Virgin Views by Virginia" offered information and support to readers new to cross-dressing. "Our Cover Girl" told the story behind the trans woman featured in the cover photograph. Prince also faced federal persecution, pleading guilty to a lesser offense when charged with distributing obscenity through the mail. A requirement of her five-year probation, however, instructed Prince to educate the public about transvestites, in effect giving her a green light to publish.[25]

While Prince was writing about cross-dressing, mainstream media in the 1950s were becoming obsessed with stories of people actually changing their sex with drugs and surgery. Media accounts of what is now called sex reassignment surgery or gender confirmation surgery date back to a Viennese physiologist's "transplantation" experiments on rats and guinea pigs in the early 1910s. A handful of European doctors began to perform transformative surgery on humans several years later. The American press reported widely in 1933 on the sex reassignment of Danish artist Einar Wegener, who became Lili Elbe (subject of the 2015 film, *The Danish Girl*). David Cauldwell of the academic journal *Sexology* began in the 1950s to use the term "transsexual," which became a household word after ex-GI Christine Jorgensen returned home from sex reassignment surgery in Denmark. Media could not get enough of the glamorous and charismatic Jorgensen, although crowning her "the Cinderella of the transsexual movement" marginalized trans people who were not white or middle class in the view of scholar Edward Sagarin.[26] While the press sensationalized its coverage of Jorgensen, historian Joanne Meyerowitz argues that Jorgensen's sex reassignment saga offered a "highly informative how-to story" for frustrated transsexuals eager for a blueprint on how literally to transform their lives. Media coverage significantly boosted interest in sex reassignment surgery in the United States, and hesitant American health professionals began to endorse the procedure in the 1960s.[27]

Symbolic Annihilation of Transsexuals

A medical-psychological complex controlled who got hormones or surgery. To get treatment, trans people had to renounce any similarity to or affiliation with lesbians and gay men. Further, many gay, lesbian, feminist, and other progressive activists distanced themselves from transgender issues. Although the idea of changing sex is inherently radical, some factions of Second Wave feminism reviled trans women as dangerous reactionaries whose quest for 1950s-style femininity perpetuated oppressive gender roles even as they retained the male privilege of their birth.[28] Jorgensen, for example, once told the *Washington Post* that feminism threatened "the art of being a woman."[29] *Ms.* contributor Robin Morgan compared transsexuality to blackface in an essay published elsewhere.[30] Trans people were equally unwelcome in the gay lib camp, which emphasized its masculinity as it campaigned to join the mainstream. Media historian Rodger Streitmatter claimed the *Advocate* actively tried to separate trans women from the gay and lesbian movement.[31] Emylia N. Terry charged that the gay press practiced the same symbolic annihilation of trans people that media scholar Gaye Tuchman claimed mainstream media commit when they ignore minority groups. A particular sticking point was the gay press's erasure of drag queens' leading role in the Stonewall riots.[32]

Soon after Stonewall, trans woman Angela K. Douglas attempted to bridge the gap between gay and lesbian and trans communities. In 1970, the disillusioned member of the Gay Liberation Front of Los Angeles founded the Transsexual/Transvestite Action Organization, the first international grassroots transgender association. TAO published the *Moonshadow* and *Mirage* newsletters, described by Stryker as "always interesting hodgepodges of eccentric political screeds, psychedelic arts, photographs, activist news, and occult beliefs."[33] The newsletters also denounced gay and lesbian groups that Douglas charged oppressed transsexuals.[34] But even Douglas was guilty of the symbolic annihilation of FTM trans men. It would be nearly another decade before Sullivan would provide a voice for the invisible FTM community.

Building an FTM Culture in San Francisco

Back in Milwaukee in the early 1970s, Sullivan volunteered to help Murray with typesetting and layout for the Gay People's Union's monthly magazine, *GPU News*, skills that would stand him in good stead as a newsletter editor. A self-described "heterosexual female transvestite," he began penning political essays under the byline Sheila Sullivan while passing as a man in the city's gay bar scene.[35] One Sullivan essay, "Looking Toward Transvestite Liberation," appeared in *Transvestia* in 1978. Sullivan's political activism dated back to the 1969 Moratorium March in Washington, D.C., where the teenager joined a half million people protesting the Vietnam War.[36] In 1975, Sullivan and a boyfriend left for San Francisco. Even in the diverse Bay Area, the closest affinity group Sullivan could find was the Golden Gate Girls club for "cross dressers and cross genderists." Sullivan spent several years with the club, sitting through wig shows and electrolysis demonstrations but also transforming the group into the Golden Gate Girls/Guys. He effected major change by addressing trans men after he became editor of its fledgling newsletter, *Gateway*, in July 1979. *Gateway* under Sullivan revolutionized FTM mentoring by giving trans individuals information they needed on how to dress, speak, and pass in society without outing themselves by physically attending group gatherings. This change in the newsletter, according to OutHistory.org, transformed *Gateway* from a chatty "small town newspaper" to a global mentoring tool for trans individuals.[37]

Further, *Gateway* was the first publication in which women who wanted to transition into men could find information. Sullivan added gender parity to *Gateway*'s pages: if an issue focused on passing tips for trans women, the next issue would focus on tips for trans men. The newsletter offered intimate advice to individuals and reports on global developments in the increasingly visible transsexual community. It made calls for modest collective action. In October, *Gateway* reported on a successful petition to turn back antigay laws in Santa Clara County. It also urged readers to "act now in opposition to all blatantly discriminatory legislations—we are the targets this time."[38] The September issue included proposed medical "standards of care" for persons seeking to transition. These standards were vital to trans people at the mercy of physicians and psychiatrists who decided whether they were suitable candidates for sex reassignment. Sullivan commented that the standards "must be humane and applied with flexibility," which reflected how he felt after

Stanford University rejected his application to its "gender dysphoria" program because he was sexually attracted to men.[39]

Sullivan voiced his frustration in an unsigned *Gateway* article, "Are There Really Female-to-Male Transvestites?" The article in effect validated his existence. FTMs "often dress to share in men's roles, i.e., to be strong, business-like, aggressive, protective, dominant, manly," Sullivan wrote. Cross-dressing could also be a sexual turn-on, he added, and dismissed claims that dressing as a man was simply a fashion statement: "She must learn to walk with her hips; she must bind her breasts so they won't show or move (just by that, you can hardly say they're dressing for comfort!); she must avoid all relaxed female mannerisms and she must lower her voice tone. This all takes a lot of work."[40] Sullivan offered "Voice Tips for the F-T-M" in the September 1979 *Gateway*. He advised practicing downward inflection at the end of statements: "When in a restaurant, a woman will order 'the New York steak?' etc. Instead of asking for what you want, tell them what you want."[41] The landmark December 1979 issue featured contributor Joe Dillon's detailed account of his experience taking male hormone therapy, including frank insights about dosages, shots, and side effects.[42]

By then Sullivan had begun taking male hormones. He had finally found a psychotherapist willing to accept the idea that a woman could identify as a gay man. At the time, professionals viewed Sullivan as the ultimate contradiction: why would a woman go through stressful hormone therapy and surgeries just to have sex with a man? Wasn't female sexual desire for men the definition of heterosexuality? If the transsexual movement turned conceptions of sexuality upside down, Sullivan's description of himself as a gay man turned them inside out. Lou grew a full beard and muscles and in 1980 underwent a double mastectomy. He also became the first FTM peer counselor. Doctors refused to perform his genital reconstruction, however, because of his sexual orientation as a gay man. They told Sullivan that his kind did not exist. Frustrated by the lack of information about female-to-male surgical reconstruction, Sullivan produced the world's first handbook on the process, *Information for the FTM Cross Dresser and Transsexual*, which remains a leading guide. Its nut-and-bolts approach offered advice available nowhere else. Chapters addressed everything from shoe sizes to "How to Leave Your Lesbian Life." "What impressed me most about it was here was someone writing about the real things of the transsexual experience," a reader wrote. "How to use the bathroom, what to expect from and how to act around other men, and other tips and information."[43]

Sullivan became the center of a small but growing FTM community in San Francisco that boasted global ties. He corresponded with FTMs around the world and helped start a support group at home, fittingly called FTM. In 1986, Sullivan finally underwent what his surgeon called "genitalplasty," reconfiguring his female genitals into male anatomy. He described his journey in an essay in the *Advocate*, explaining how sex changed after his surgery: "I no long feel disassociated from my sexual fantasies or turned off by having to 'make my partner straight' when he's with me."[44] One of Sullivan's new testicles did not heal well, however, and Sullivan got even worse news at the end of the year, when he was diagnosed with AIDS.[45]

Mentoring through *FTM Newsletter*

Sullivan decided to devote whatever time he had left to educating and mentoring FTM individuals. He founded the quarterly *FTM Newsletter*. The slight September 1987 debut number was a single piece of paper printed on both sides with briefs, notice of an FTM get-together, and a pledge to make the newsletter an "open forum." By 1988, the newsletter was offering significant content like "Nicholas C.'s" account of his phalloplasty and an essay addressing issues about names as a person changes gender. "You are such a lifeline," wrote Janet from Hawaii.[46] One frustrated, future trans man recalled when he first spotted a small advertisement for the newsletter in a gay newspaper in the early 1990s. "This was pre-Internet, when it was really hard to get information," he said. When the first issue arrived, his reaction was "like kind of wow, wow!"[47] By December, the expanded eight-page *FTM*'s mailing list numbered one hundred people as far away as New Zealand. Guests came to San Francisco from Seattle and Los Angeles when FTM hosted one of its frequent gatherings.

FTM became a forum for people seeking answers to the most personal questions, like a man in rural Vermont who sought advice on how to stop "leaking" after phalloplasty.[48] A correspondent advised readers: "The most awkward stage for you will be mid-transition when you are not clearly one thing or another."[49] Other articles listed where to buy generic testosterone. Ads featured products its FTM audience could find nowhere else, like latex penile molds to wear in swimsuits.[50] The *FTM Newsletter* was virtually the only place where trans men could share experiences and medical advice and find information about hormones because doctors remained almost wilfully ignorant of trans issues. As trans activists advocated for better treatment, newsletters provided a way to share frustration as well as information.[51]

Readers seemed hungry for connection with other FTMs. A new FTM group in Georgia wanted to correspond with the San Francisco FTM, and the Seattle FTM discussed plans to start a "gentlemen's club." Gatherings were important for bonding and sharing vital information. San Francisco get-togethers attracted guests from up and down the Pacific Coast. The newsletter extended the events' impact by publishing articles about the forums and speakers that people unable to attend could read. Besides transmitting information, the articles extended community by giving readers a sense of participating in the event.[52] Isolated, closeted individuals connected. Correspondence revealed their vulnerability. A college student in Iowa sought advice on how to research insurance options for sex reassignment surgery "without blowing your cover."[53] Letters often had a confessional tone, like an author's recounting of how while traveling he tried to obtain a prescription for testosterone, which for insurance purposes required him to hide that he was trans. The author was mortified when a doctor ordered him to drop his pants to prove his sex.[54] Sharing stories of such indignities created a sense of shared injustice that fostered collective identity. While Sullivan was editor, the movement was so new FTM focused on the struggles of individual FTMs rather than advocating collective action. It reframed FTMs, however, as human instead of aberrant. The newsletter became more political in the 1990s after Sullivan was gone, fueled by AIDS activists who demanded the government fund research to find a cure and provide medical care.

The newsletter also transmitted what little history existed about transgender people. Sullivan himself became a pioneer of transgender history. He wrote a biography of Jack Bee Garland, an author and adventurer assigned female at birth who lived as a man in San Francisco in the early twentieth century.[55] His research got Sullivan involved with the city's Gay and Lesbian History Project, and he helped establish the Gay and Lesbian History Society of California. FTM Newsletter contributed to that sense of history in the making: the March 1989 cover of FTM featured Billie Tipton, a famous jazz musician posthumously discovered to be a woman. Publishing these unknown stories showed that rather than far from being an exception, transgender people had been part of the human experience for centuries. FTM helped correct the record on trans people's role in Stonewall in a September 1989 headline that shouted, "An FTM Started the Stonewall Riot!" That sense of pride helped forge an FTM culture.

Sullivan contributed to the FTM community in more personal ways in his final years, when medical professionals in the Netherlands and elsewhere began to acknowledge the existence of gay FTMs. He offered himself as a case study to two researchers, whose article is considered a landmark in gender dysphoria research.[56] His social justice journalism introduced coverage of the AIDS epidemic into *FTM*, which communicated the important message that AIDS threatened everyone.[57] Its social justice journalism was one small salvo in the gay community's collective campaign to push federal authorities into action. "Organizations like ACT UP, the Gay Men's Health Crisis, the AIDS Memorial Quilt and others gave rise to LGBT activists who were fighting for their lives and had nothing to gain by being polite, and everything to lose," asserted activist Joseph Kapp.[58] Trans people of color involved with prostitution and drugs, in fact, were among the hardest hit when AIDS broke out. The *FTM Newsletter* quoted Sullivan on his own experience with the disease in 1990. He noted that transsexuals were at greater risk of the disease because their negative body image disinclined them from taking care of their bodies. The newsletter recounted that year's spring get-together, which was devoted to AIDS prevention, including Sullivan's frank descriptions of such safe-sex innovations as dental dams and finger condoms.[59] As usual, the ailing Sullivan was even able to muster a joke about the gadgets.

FTM Newsletter after Sullivan

As Sullivan grew sicker, an assistant helped him publish the newsletter. No one was more aware than Sullivan of the irony of his AIDS diagnosis. He revealed, "I kind of took a perverse pleasure in contacting the gender clinics that rejected me and said that they've told me for so many years that it was impossible for me to live as a gay man, but it looks like I'm gonna die like one."[60] Sullivan taught tolerance even from his grave. The April 1991 memorial issue included a letter from a reader furious that lesbian cross-dressers were dominating FTM meetings. The new editors followed it with a response that a "bewildered" Sullivan had penned just before he died. "I think he forgets that we all began our transitions as 'women,'" Sullivan wrote of the author, recalling his own life from ages twenty-two to twenty-eight as a "female-to-male transvestite" not quite ready to make the transition:

> This was the most tormenting stage of my life, one during which I needed desperately to connect with others in all the varying phases of female-to-male expression. This

is the most important function of the *FTM Get-Togethers* and our *Newsletter*—presenting all the options to the searching female-to-males so that she might make an informed choice concerning her future.[61]

Sullivan was tremendously relieved when on his deathbed two friends offered to continue *FTM*. "Please keep the flame burning," his sister wrote to *FTM*, "the newsletter reaching all who want it and 'the cause' an important tool in your own transition to acceptance."[62] Friends donated $400 to keep the newsletter alive. Under editor James (later Jamison) Green, its booming contents on its five-year anniversary in July 1992 demonstrated that the FTM community no longer was invisible.[63] Leslie Feinberg's influential pamphlet that year, *Transgender Liberation: A Movement Whose Time Has Come*, heralded a new era in transgender politics. Feinberg, a lesbian who lived as a man, wrote, "We are talking here about people who defy the 'man'-made boundaries of gender. Gender: self-expression, not anatomy."[64] That same year the direct-action-oriented Transgender Nation organized in San Francisco as an offshoot of Queer Nation, marking a more militant and spectacular protest phase in the trans movement. The group forged a powerful coalition by integrating transgender concerns with the political agendas of lesbian, gay, and bisexual activists. *FTM* in the 1990s posted more and more news of academic and popular books about women transitioning to men, trans advocacy groups, service organizations, global groups, and new products. Editor Green noted a larger FTM presence at gay conferences and film festivals. Artists like playwright and performance artist Kate Bornstein put trans men on the cultural map. Yet the landmark March on Washington for Lesbian, Gay, and Bi Equal Rights and Liberation on April 25, 1993, failed to acknowledge the trans community, displeasing many. A story in *FTM* the next year illustrated trans people's vulnerability when it reported on the murder of twenty-one-year-old trans man Brandon Teena in Nebraska. "Brandon's brand of transgenderism placed him, paradoxically, both in and out of the closet," the newsletter observed.[65] The 1999 film based on Teena's murder, *Boys Don't Cry*, would greatly raise Americans' awareness of transgender people.

In 1993, the newsletter began to showcase photographs and interviews in an updated design with new typefaces in a twelve-page, stapled and bound publication. A designer mistakenly identified the group on business cards as FTM International, but the name stuck [it's now FTM*International*]. The newsletter's phenomenal growth, however, threatened its existence. It cost a thousand dollars to produce and distribute the free newsletter to some five hundred subscribers in North America and eight nations overseas.[66] The July 1994 issue portended even greater growth for the FTM movement, even though the newsletter disappeared for the next five months, when editor Green rolled out a new term for transsexuals—transgender. He explained the name lent the community political weight because it signaled a move from the personal into the political arena. "The term transgender can be applied to all persons who cross traditional gender boundaries in one way or another," Green explained.[67] The newsletter resurfaced in January 1995 with huge news: FTM was seeking nonprofit status,[68] which it achieved following year.

Chronicling the Transgender Rights Movement

The increasingly political newsletter chronicled the growth of the transgender rights movement in the twilight of the twentieth century. "Conference Shines! Movement Grows by Leaps and Bounds," blared the front page of the October 1995 special issue on the first FTM conference. FTM's social justice journalism included an August 1996 special edition that featured a four-page insert describing a wide swathe of political activism against gender discrimination. Editor Marcus de Maria Arana asked readers to fill in a survey for the first national study of violence against trans people, an invisible epidemic until trans activists raised their voices. The title of Arana's cover story, "Silence=Death" appropriated ACT UP!'s memorable anti-AIDS campaign slogan. Arana called for collective action to stop the murders because of their heavy toll on FTMs. The newsletter played a role in creation of the Transgender Day of Remembrance on November 20, which since 1999 has annually honored murdered trans people around the world.

The newsletter also documented debates on language in the 1990s. The edgy "queer" movement that grew out of AIDS activism reclaimed the pejorative term as a badge of honor for all people who rejected the confines of heterosexuality and endorsed a broad struggle against institutional forces that it charged enabled racism, sexism, and classism. By 1995, many gay and lesbian groups were adding a "T" to their names in solidarity with trans people. The National Gay Task Force formed in 1973 became the National Gay and Lesbian Task Force (NGLTF) in 1985, and rebranded in 2014 as the National LGBTQ Task Force. Its "Creating Change" conferences began in 1988, one year after the massive 1987 National March on Washington for Lesbian and Gay Rights. In 1997, NGLTF changed its mission statement to include bisexual and transgendered people and launched the Federation of Lesbian, Gay, Bisexual and Transgendered Statewide Political Organizations. A groundbreaking "Youth Issue" of *FTM* appeared in Fall/Winter 2000. Incoming co-editor Ben Singer tingled at the "constant sense of history being made."[69] By then, the Internet had revolutionized almost everything about the LGBTQ experience.

Trans Media Today

It was no coincidence that the LGBT rights movement exploded along with the rise of new technologies like the Internet. Tyler Oakley, who campaigns to stop suicide among LGBT teens, remembered the moment in 2008 that he discovered the power of YouTube. "It really was awesome," he recalled. "The commenters and subscribers began talking about their experiences and different perspectives; not holding back." Oakley's YouTube videos have since been viewed more than a half billion times, and he has raised millions of dollars for the suicide prevention nonprofit, the Trevor Foundation.[70]

The Internet has created a new public space for trans people where they can explore their options without fear of public exposure. Because of the Internet, scholars say LGBT youth come out earlier and "in increasingly varied and fluid ways," partly because of the support and role models they can find online.[71] Another advantage of the Internet is its greatly expanded opportunities for finding information about transgenderism without risking public exposure. Studies show cyberspace has also facilitated explorations of gender identity because of its anonymity,[72] and the easier access to information appears to shorten the period of time in which young trans men experience identity confusion.[73]

Blogs and social media have raised the visibility of trans people, especially people of color. When black trans actress Laverne Cox started #TransIsBeautiful on Instagram, she fostered a positive collective identity by encouraging viewers to post images of themselves.[74] As this book was going to press, an image of a proposed new Pride flag design went viral, stirring robust debate on the way it proposed to add queer people of color, the transgender community, and the stigma surrounding HIV/AIDS to the original rainbow flag by adding five arrow-shaped stripes in new colors.[75] The Internet also is a site for the expanding collective memory of the relatively young trans community. The website Remembering Our Dead that honors transgender murder victims is an example of "queer worldmaking" that K. J. Rawson describes as a broad range of online media, including blogs, videos, and online forums, whose purpose is to create a historical record of the transgender experience.[76]

While much of the online trans community is focused on shaping a collective identity, the Internet also has facilitated collective action. Kapp recalled relying on "telephone trees" and nailing fliers to telephone poles to rally protesters for AIDS protests. Now all organizing is done online. "The Internet has been a key player in the development and growth of the trans community into a social movement," asserts Eve Shapiro. She concluded after interviewing ten trans activists that the Internet enabled the trans community to move beyond support groups and emerge as a "politicized trans-gender community that challenges society's gender paradigms."[77] Trans activists write, sign, and collect petitions online, circulate templates for letters to legislators, and send out calls for action. Online organizing also has made it possible for LGBTQ activists to organize in countries where it is dangerous to do so in public.[78]

The Internet also prompted a proliferation of new LGTBQ news outlets. In 2018 the *Advocate* competed with *LGBTQ Nation*, an online news magazine founded in 2009 in San Francisco, which claims its 1.6 million followers make it the world's most followed LGBTQ news source. But the trans community does not need to seek out LGBTQ media to find coverage of its issues. Trans issues were standard fare in legacy news in the 2010s as the movement edged toward the mainstream: Vice President Joe Biden declared transgender rights the civil rights movement of the decade in 2012; the trial of transgender whistleblower Chelsea Manning raised pronoun questions for the Associated Press (2013); the HBO TV series *Transparent* proved a hit (2014); and a famous Olympic decathlete transitioned very publicly to Caitlyn Jenner in 2015, the same year that the Supreme Court ruled same-sex marriage is a constitutional right.[79]

These advances were accompanied by more disturbing reports that twenty-eight killings of trans people made 2017 the deadliest year on record. Although unsettling, that number reflects the trans community's greater visibility: someone cares enough to report and track trans murders. Virtually every news and information outlet now has an LGBTQ section, from digital natives *BuzzFeed* and *Huffington Post* to legacy media like the *U.S. World & News Report* and *USA Today*.[80] The *New York Times* launched an editorial series in support of transgender equality in 2015.[81] To celebrate Pride 2018, Google partnered with the GLAAD media advocacy group on its #ThisIsFamily campaign on Google's Pride hub, inviting users to post a picture or video of their nontraditional family. Legacy news outlets have followed LGBTQ media in providing detailed coverage and in critiquing the Trump Administration's threats to the community's civil rights gains. After a *New York Times* scoop in October 2018 divulged an administration proposal to define "sex" as a set of immutable biological traits at birth—which would again render people such as Sullivan nonexistent—the newspaper condemned the proposal. An editorial asserted that the news "understandably sent a ripple of fear and anguish through the community of 1.4 million transgender Americans, their loved ones and anyone who cares about civil rights."[82]

The trans community may be united against the Trump Administration's anti-trans policies, but online discourse reveals fissures. "The transgender movement is not monolithic," as trans activist Pauline Park stated. "It's complex, sometimes fractionalized, and often vociferous."[83] A 2017 article in the *Economist* parsed what it called the "culture war" over trans identity that stems back to the 1960s.[84] Google kicks out twenty-one million sources in 0.32 seconds when asked, "Who can use the word queer?" Social media have amplified a nasty battle between militant transgender activists and women they call TERFs (trans-exclusionary radical feminists), who believe an individual's gender identity does not change their biological sex. The escalating rhetoric—"Punch a TERF" is one slogan—spilled over into real world violence in 2017.[85] Conversely, social media is full of "gender-critical" trans women who challenge the belief that gender is an irreducible essence, distinct from biological sex or socialization. "Gender-critical trans women are a uniquely despised group," observed *Slate* columnist Michelle Goldberg. "They experience the discrimination all trans people are subject to as well as the loathing of the trans rights movement and its allies."[86]

In this raucous media landscape, the former *FTM Newsletter* seems as tame as the homophile periodicals of the 1950s. FTM*International* remains a global support group that adheres to an assimilationist approach to trans rights. More than 100,000 people daily visit its website, which hosts a half-dozen online resources including FTM*International* Law Resources, FTM*International* HealthCare, and Trans-Medicine. It also offers tips and forms for changing names and gender on legal documents, applying for asylum based on gender identity persecution, and a guide to transgender family law.[87] In 2002, *FTM* became *FTMi Newsletter*, belatedly recognizing its publishers' global name, the same year in which the organization helped fund a Transgender Law Center. Unlike the wide-ranging media offerings available online, *FTMi Newsletter* is only available by subscription to members of the organization.

The leading social justice advocacy organization to combat discrimination and violence against transgender people is the National Center for Transgender Equality. It too has a strong digital presence. Founded in 2003, the center operates out of donated office space in Washington, D.C. Its lobbyists helped organize the first Congressional hearing on transgender issues in 2008 and convinced the U.S. State Department to allow transgender people to update their passports in 2010. One of its web features is based on the idea that stories can effect change. "Share Your Story" explains: "The stories you share here help us encourage policymakers to change laws and policies, allow media to tell authentic stories of transgender struggles and triumphs, and help us introduce transgender people to potential allies who may not know any out trans people in their lives."[88]

Louis Sullivan's life is a testament to the power of telling stories. Although he did not live to see it, the medical/psychological establishment removed sexual orientation from the formal criteria used to diagnose gender identity disorders—for which Sullivan campaigned so hard. Stryker calls this a "rather remarkable accomplishment" that not only enabled trans people to chart their own destiny but also significantly shaped the queer movement of the 1990s.[89] Sullivan's story has had an extraordinary impact on individuals and institutions. Brice Smith, who earned a doctoral degree to prepare himself to write Sullivan's biography, was so inspired that he began his own trans process while researching Sullivan's life. Transgender choreographer Sean Dorsey created a suite of dances based on Sullivan's journals.[90] Artist Rhys Ernst explored Sullivan's life in a multimedia piece in 2014.[91] Louis Sullivan lives on in the collective memory of the transgender movement he helped start.

Notes

1. Kevin Horwitz, "Louis Graydon Sullivan," *FTM* (December 1990), 1. Runs of *FTM* and its successor *FTM Newsletter* are held at the GLBT Historical Society Archives in San Francisco.
2. See "LGBTQQIAAP," *Urban Dictionary*, accessed November 2, 2018, https://www.urbandictionary.com/define.php?term=LGBTQQIAAP; Chris Bodenner, "Why Is the T in LGBT?," *Atlantic*, July 8, 2016, https://www.theatlantic.com/notes/2016/07/l-g-b-t/490547/; Sunnivie Brydum, "LGBT Groups Respond to Petition Asking to 'Drop the T,'" *Advocate*, November 6, 2015, https://www.advocate.com/transgender/2015/11/06/lgbt-groups-respond-petition-asking-drop-t; and Tyler Curry, "Why Gay Rights and Trans Rights Should Be Separated," *Huffington Post*, December 6, 2017, https://www.huffingtonpost.com/tyler-curry/gay-rights-and-trans-rights_b_4763380.html.

3. John D'Emilio, "Foreword: The Leading Edge of Change: The LGBT Press in the 1970s," in *Gay Press, Gay Power: The Growth of LGBT Community Newspapers in America*, ed. William B. Kelley, Jorjet Harper, and Tracy Baim (Chicago: Prairie Avenue Productions, 2012), 10.

4. Tracy Baim, "Introduction," in *Gay Power, Gay Press*, 6. For more on the history of the gay and lesbian press, see Larry Gross, *Up from Invisibility: Lesbians, Gay Men & the Media in America* (New York: Columbia University Press, 2002); Rodger R. Streitmatter, "Creating A Venue for the 'Love That Dare Not Speak Its Name': Origins of the Gay and Lesbian Press," *Journalism & Mass Communication Quarterly* 72, no. 2 (1995): 436–47; Rodger R. Streitmatter, "Lesbian and Gay Press: Raising a Militant Voice in the 1960s," *American Journalism* 12 (Spring 1995): 142–61; and Rodger R. Streitmatter, *Unspeakable: The Rise of the Gay and Lesbian Press in America* (London: Faber & Faber, 1995).

5. Craig M. Loftin, *Masked Voices: Gay Men and Lesbians in Cold War America* (Albany, NY: State University of New York Press, 2012), 6.

6. David K. Johnson, *The Lavender Scare: The Cold War Persecution of Gays and Lesbians in the Federal Government* (Chicago: University of Chicago Press, 2004), 56.

7. Edward Alwood, *Straight News: Gays, Lesbians, and the News Media* (New York: Columbia University Press, 1996), 328.

8. D'Emilio, *Gay Power, Gay Press*, 9. See also Willow Arune, "Transgender Images in the Media," in *News and Sexuality: Media Portraits of Diversity*, ed. Laura Castañeda and Shannon B. Campbell (Thousand Oaks, CA: Sage Publications, 2006), 111–33.

9. "Growth of Overt Homosexuality in City Provokes Wide Concern," *New York Times*, December 17, 1963, 1.

10. The first lesbian magazine in 1947–1948 was a typewritten monthly with no subscribers that is notable for its positive portrayal of lesbians. Rodger R. Streitmatter asserts *Vice Versa* "made a powerful political statement two decades before gay activists organized this country's first public demonstration." Rodger R. Streitmatter, "*Vice Versa*: America's First Lesbian Magazine," *American Periodicals* 8 (1998), 84.

11. See Alwood, *Straight News*, 29–34.

12. "ONE is not Obscene," in Jim Kepner, *Rough News, Daring Views: 1950s' Pioneer Gay Press Journalism* (Binghamton, NY: Haworth Press, 1998), 393.

13. Craig M. Loftin, ed., *Letters to ONE: Gay and Lesbian Voices from the 1950s and 1960s* (Albany, NY: State University of New York Press, 2012), 5.

14. *ONE*, October 1953, 1.

15. *ONE Inc. v. Olesen*, 355 U.S. 371(1958).

16. David Savage, "Supreme Court Faced Gay Rights Decision in 1958 over 'Obscene' Magazine," *Los Angeles Times*, January 11, 2015, http://www.latimes.com/nation/la-na-court-gay-magazine-20150111-story.html. See also Jim Burroway, "Today in History: ONE Magazine versus the U.S. Post Office," *Box Turtle Bulletin*, January 13, 2008, http://www.boxturtlebulletin.com/2008/01/13/1273.

17. Martin Meeker, *Contacts Desired: Gay and Lesbian Communications and Community, 1940s–1970s* (Chicago: University of Chicago Press, 2006), 77.

18. Alwood, *Straight News*, 34.

19. Quoted in Meeker, *Contact Desired*, 98.

20. Ibid., 2, 88, 89.
21. See Dawn Evans, "Covering Stonewall: Journalism Before the Rainbow," *Advocate*, June 26, 2015, https://www.advocate.com/stonewall/2015/06/26/covering-stonewall-journalism-rainbow.
22. Quoted in Baim, *Gay Power*, 438.
23. Marcia Gallo, "Introduction," The *Ladder*: An Interpretation and Document Archive, September 2010, http://womhist.alexanderstreet.com/mgallo/intro.htm.
24. Susan Stryker, *Transgender History: The Roots of Today's Revolution*, 2nd ed. (New York: Hachette, 2017), 46–47.
25. See Richard Ekins and Dave King, "Virginia Prince: Transgender Pioneer," *International Journal of Transgenderism* 8, no. 4 (October 2005): 5–15.
26. Edward Sagarin, "Transsexualism: Legitimation, Amplification, and Exploitation of Deviance by Scientists and Mass Media," in *Deviance and Mass Media*, ed. Charles Winick (Beverly Hills, CA: Sage Publications, 1978), 249. See also Emily Skidmore, "Constructing the 'Good Transsexual': Christine Jorgensen, Whiteness, and Heteronormativity in the Mid-Twentieth-Century Press," *Feminist Studies* 37, no. 2 (Summer 2011): 270–75.
27. Joanne Meyerowitz, "Introduction," in *How Sex Changed: A History of Transsexuality in the United States* (Cambridge, MA: Harvard University Press, 2004), 1–13.
28. See Michelle Goldberg, "What Is a Woman?" *New Yorker*, August 4, 2014, https://www.newyorker.com/magazine/2014/08/04/woman-2.
29. Sally Quinn, "Christine: Explaining Transsexualism," *Washington Post*, July 8, 1970, B3.
30. Robin Morgan, *Going Too Far: The Personal Chronicle of a Feminist* (New York: Random House, 1977), 180–81.
31. Streitmatter, *Unspeakable*, 142, 214.
32. Quoted in Emylia N. Terry, "An Exclusionary Revolution: Marginalization and Representation of Trans Women in Print Media (1969–1979)" (Honors Thesis, University of Nevada, Las Vegas, 2014), 13, https://digitalscholarship.unlv.edu/honors_theses/14. Alwood's 1996 *Straight News* makes no reference to trans activism.
33. Stryker, *Transgender History*, 8.
34. Terry, "Exclusionary Revolution," 32.
35. Susan Stryker, "Portrait of a Transfag Drag Hag as a Young Man," in *Reclaiming Genders: Transsexual Grammars at the Fin de Siecle*, ed. Kate More and Stephen Whittle (New York: Bloomsbury Academic, 1989), 63.
36. Brice Smith, *Lou Sullivan: Daring To Be a Man Among Men* (San Francisco: Transgress Press, 2017), 13. See also Lani M. Rodemeyer, *Lou Sullivan Diaries (1970–1980) and Theories of Sexual Embodiment: Making Sense of Sensing* (Cham, Switzerland: Springer, 2018).
37. "*Gateway*: FTM Mentoring Through Newsletters," "Man-i-fest: FTM Mentorship in San Francisco from 1976–2009," OutHistory.org, accessed November 3, 2018, http://www.outhistory.org/exhibits/show/man-i-fest/exhibit/gateway.
38. "Your Human Rights Shot Down by Fundamental Christians," *Gateway*, October 1979, 5. A run of *Gateway* newsletter is held in the GLBT Historical Society Archives in San Francisco.

39. "Standards of Care on Drawing Board," *Gateway*, September 1979, 5. See also "Part One, HBIGDA Standards of Care," *Gateway*, May 1980, 20–23; and "Part Two, HBIGDA Standards of Care," *Gateway*, June 1980, 5–7.

40. *Gateway*, November 1979, 9. [underline in original]

41. *Gateway*, September 1979, 3.

42. Joe Dillon, "The Male Hormone Therapy Experience," *Gateway*, December 1979, 8–9.

43. Jill Enquist, "Tribute to Lou Sullivan," *FTM*, July 1991, 3.

44. L. Sullivan, "Sullivan's Travels," *Advocate*, June 6, 1989, 70.

45. Jamison Green, "I remember Lou … ," 2–3. *FTM Newsletter* Special Issue, Summer 1997, 2–3.

46. Untitled, *FTM*, September 1988, 2.

47. Quoted in Kristen Schilt, *Just One of the Guys? Transgender Men and the Persistence of Gender Inequality* (Chicago: University of Chicago Press, 2010), 33.

48. *FTM*, December 1988, 3, 4.

49. Kevin R., "An Open Letter of Encouragement and Support for the Pre-transition Female-to-Male," *FTM*, September 1989, 4.

50. Ad, *FTM*, March 1989, 4.

51. "Hormones: Transition Begins," "Man-i-fest: FTM Mentorship in San Francisco from 1976–2009," *OutHistory.org*, accessed November 3, 2018, http://www.outhistory.org/exhibits/show/man-i-fest/exhibit/hormones.

52. See for example, "Endocrinolgist Talks Testosterone at Summer 1990 Get-Together," *FTM*, Spring 1990, 1.

53. "Male Box," *FTM*, December 1989, 2–3.

54. Joseph Ellman, "A Trip to the Doctor as a Genetic Male," *FTM*, December 1990, 5.

55. Louis Sullivan, *From Female to Male: The Life of Jack Bee Garland* (Boston: Alyson Publications, 1990).

56. Stryker, "Portrait," 77. See also Eli Coleman and Walter Bockting, "'Heterosexual' Prior to Sex Reassignment—'Homosexual' Afterward: A Case Study of a Female-To-Male Transsexual," *Journal of Psychology and Human Sexuality* 1, no. 2, (1989): 69–82.

57. On May 18, 1981, *New York Native*, then America's most influential gay newspaper, published the first newspaper report on what became known as AIDS. The *Native* led early coverage of the mysterious epidemic but devolved into reporting conspiracy theories about the cause of AIDS. It closed on January 13, 1997. Robin Pogrebin, "Controversial Gay Magazine Shuts Down," *New York Times*, January 9, 1997, https://www.nytimes.com/1997/01/09/nyregion/controversial-gay-magazine-shuts-down.html.

58. Joseph Kapp, "Technology: The LGBT Community's Unsung Hero," *Huffington Post*, February 2, 2016, https://www.huffingtonpost.com/joe-kapp/technology-the-lgbt-communitys-unsung-hero_b_3179844.html.

59. "Spring Get-Together Focuses on FTMs and AIDS," *FTM*, June 1990, 1.

60. Rhys Ernst, "Dear Lou Sullivan, 2014," Vimeo video, 6:34, posted by Visual AIDS, accessed November 3, 2018, https://vimeo.com/112424796.

61. Anonymous letter to the editor, *FTM*, April 1991, 2.

62. "Dear FTM from Lou's Sister," *FTM*, July 1991, 2.

63. See Jamison Green, *Becoming a Visible Man* (Nashville, TN: Vanderbilt University Press, 2004).

64. Leslie Feinberg, *Transgender Liberation: A Movement Whose Time Has Come* (New York: World View Forum, 1992), 5.

65. "FTM Crossdresser Murdered," *FTM*, February 1994, 3.

66. "FTM International Growth Strains Funds," *FTM*, July 1994, 11.

67. James Green, "What Is Transgender?," *FTM*, July 1994, 9.

68. "Big Changes at FTM," *FTM*, January 1995, 1.

69. "Newsletter Gains New Editorial Talent," *FTM*, August 2000, 1.

70. Jonathan Wells, "Tyler Oakley: How the Internet Revolutionized LGBT Life," *Telegraph*, November 12, 2015, https://www.telegraph.co.uk/men/thinking-man/tyler-oakley-how-the-internet-revolutionised-lgbt-life/.

71. Brian Jacobson and Brooke Donatone, "Homoflexibles, Omnisexuals, and Genderqueers: Group Work with Queer Youth in Cyberspace and Face-to-Face," *Group* 33, no. 3 (2009): 223–34.

72. Katherine Angel Cross, "The New Laboratory of Dreams: Role-playing Games as Resistance," *Women's Studies Quarterly* 40, no. 3–4 (2012): 70–88.

73. Colin J. Williams, Martin S. Weinberg, and Joshua G. Rosenberger, "Trans Men: Embodiments, Identities, and Sexualities," *Sociological Forum* 28, no. 4 (2013): 719–41.

74. Julie Gerstein, "Laverne Cox's #TransIsBeautiful Hashtag Will Give You New Life," *BuzzFeed*, June 2, 2015, https://www.buzzfeed.com/juliegerstein/laverne-cox-reminds-us-that-transisbeautiful-in-a-lovely-tum?utm_term=.yao4o9b9P#.ujlwYm5mp.

75. Jeff Taylor, "Trans, QPOC Inclusive Pride Flag Campaign Going Viral," *NewNowNext*, June 8, 2018, http://www.newnownext.com/trans-qpoc-inclusive-pride-flag-campaign-going-viral/06/2018/.

76. K. J. Rawson, "Transgender Worldmaking in Cyberspace: Historical Activism on the Internet," *QED: A Journal in GLBTQ Worldmaking* 1, no. 2 (Summer 2014): 38–60.

77. Eve Shapiro, "'Trans' cending Barriers: Transgender Organizing on the Internet," *Journal of Gay & Lesbian Social Services* 16, no. 3–4 (September 2004): 166.

78. Elisabeth Jay Friedman, "The Reality of Virtual Reality: The Internet and Gender Equality Advocacy in Latin America," *Latin American Politics and Society* 47, no. 3 (2005): 1–34.

79. *Obergefell v. Hodges*, 135 S. Ct. 2584 (2015).

80. Benjamin Mullin, "Despite Its Blind Spots, the Media Is Getting Better at Telling LGBT Stories," *Poynter.org*, March 24, 2016, https://www.poynter.org/news/despite-its-blind-spots-media-getting-better-telling-lgbt-stories.

81. Editorial, "The Quest for Transgender Equality," *New York Times*, May 4, 2015, https://www.nytimes.com/2015/05/04/opinion/the-quest-for-transgender-equality.html.

82. Editorial, "Donald Trump Is Lyin' Up a Storm," *New York Times*, October 22, 2018, https://www.nytimes.com/2018/10/22/opinion/editorials/transgender-trump-lies-midterm-election.html?rref=collection%2Ftimestopic%2FTransgender%20issues&action=click&contentCollection=timestopics&region=stream&module=stream_unit&version=latest&contentPlacement=28&pgtype=collection.

83. Shapiro, "'Trans' cending," 167.

84. "Making Sense of the Culture War over Transgender Identity," *Economist*, November 16, 2017, https://www.economist.com/international/2017/11/16/making-sense-of-the-culture-war-over-transgender-identity.

85. Harvey Geni, "The Rise and Rise of Political Violence Against Women," *Medium*, September 25, 2017, https://medium.com/@GappyTales/the-rise-and-rise-of-political-vio lence-against-women-6a07390db3a9.

86. Michelle Goldberg, "The Trans Women Who Say That Trans Women Aren't Women," *Slate*, December 9, 2015, http://www.slate.com/articles/double_x/doublex/2015/12/gender_ critical_trans_women_the_apostates_of_the_trans_rights_movement.html.

87. "FTM*International* FACTS," FTM*International*, accessed January 26, 2019, http://www. ftmi.org.

88. "Share Your Story," National Center for Transgender Equality, accessed November 3 2018, https://transequality.org/share-your-story.

89. Stryker, "Portrait," 77.

90. "Sean Dorsey Dance: 'Lou' (from *Uncovered: The Diary Project*)," YouTube video, 4:06, posted by FreshMeatSF, May 7, 2010, accessed November 10, 2018, https://www.youtube. com/watch?v=zW8__oZ9E1o&list=PL986A71A2937F6259&feature=share&index=9.

91. Ernst, "Dear Lou Sullivan."

CONCLUSION

Social Media and Social Justice Journalism

"It's a strange moment for American journalism," *Washington Monthly*'s editor mused near the end of 2018.[1] The year's events were equally jarring for social justice advocates as the Trump Administration shrank national parkland boundaries[2]; authorized sweeping deportations of undocumented immigrants[3]; embraced white nationalists amid a surge in hate crimes and domestic terrorism[4]; advanced new Labor Department policies that jeopardized low-wage workers' right to organize[5]; encouraged voter suppression [6]; pushed Medicaid cuts that threatened disabled people's ability to live independently[7]; moved to limit women's access to birth control and abortion[8]; and proposed to define gender at birth as a biological, immutable condition determined by genitalia.[9] These developments were reminders of the fragility of such social justice movements. Journalism also came under attack by President Donald Trump, whose torrential tweeting rivalled that of the teenaged March for Our Lives organizers in frequency if not in tone.[10] Furthermore, the Federal Communication Commission's vote to end net neutrality was a huge loss for the independent news media responsible for much social justice journalism.[11] Media scholar Emily Bell is among critics who worry that the end of the rules, which stopped Internet service providers from discriminating against certain types of content, at best signals "an ideology that plurality of voices in the media landscape is less important than efficient business competition."[12] Media conglomerate Sinclair Broadcast Group heightened fears about the danger of media oligarchy in 2018, when it required anchors at its two hundred news stations across the nation to read an identical script encouraging viewers, in an echo of the president, to mistrust "fake news."[13] The need for social justice journalism never seemed greater.

Paradoxically, the genre kept growing like a Ponderosa pine seedling after a wildfire. So did the so-called "Trump Resistance Movement," which is the likely model for future social justice movement media. Before concluding with a look at the Resistance's virtual network and what it may bode for the future of social movement media, it is worthwhile to review the print culture functions of twentieth-century social movements. One surprising observation is that half of the periodicals profiled in this book continued online—including a PDF version of Anti-Slavery's International's *Reporter*, which originated as the first transnational social movement periodical in 1825. Such continuities harken the view of Roger Silverstone, creator of the concept of the networked "mediasphere" as successor to Jürgen Habermas's pre-Internet public sphere. Silverstone states that media change is both gradual and radical. He suggests, "Evolutions and revolutions will always shade one into the other."[14]

Collective Identity

The social justice journals studied here shared a quest to build a collective movement identity. Journal reports of social movement organization meetings and direct actions enabled distant readers to feel connected. Perhaps the biggest contribution of the world's oldest social justice journal, the *Anti-Slavery Monthly Reporter*, was its detailed accounts of the abolition meetings that encouraged readers to think themselves part of a movement greater than themselves. Similarly, *Sierra Club Bulletin* articles and photographs of the Outings Club nourished its wilderness-centered culture. In *Disability Rag*, the "Disability Cool" column offered its audience an empowering identity. Letters to *Ms.* and to the *Gateway* demonstrate how these periodicals provided a lifeline for isolated individuals. Intimate first-person essays on taboo topics in *Disability Rag* and *FTM Newsletter* shared a confessional tone that encouraged community. New York's daily *Call* showcased a lively socialist culture of books, poetry, plays, songs, and art that fostered a collective identity.

Visual rhetoric played another key role in creating collective identity. *Suffragist* cartoons confronted the stereotype of suffragists as unwomanly grumps by portraying them as youthful, attractive exemplars of the independent New Woman. *Disability Rag* readers shared in Disability Rat's acts of subversion. *El Malcriado's* Andy Zermeño used his Don Sotaco character to offer farm workers a role model for their journey from passive victims to powerful members of a union. The unflinching images that Louis Sullivan offered of his own transition from female to male emboldened others like him to dare to change their lives.

The social justice journals also shared a desire to build collective memory, like Sullivan's retrieval of the history of trans men, *El Malcriado's* summoning of Mexican Revolution heroes, Alice Walker's rediscovery of Zora Neale Hurston in Ms., or the *Sierra Club Bulletin's* essays on the natural and cultural history of the Sierra Nevada. Today, websites are important repositories of collective memory, such as ADAPT's online museum on the history of ADA protests. The website Remembering Our Dead honors transgender victims of violence. The Internet also serves as a bridge to social movement print culture. The Sierra Club website links to the Internet Archives' collection of the *Sierra Club Bulletin*, for example, and almost every issue of the first three years of *El Malcriado* can be read online.

Information Functions

The journals also performed less dramatic functions, such as providing followers and recruits with basic information about the times and locations of meetings, lectures, marches, or picketing. Readers registered for Sierra Club raft trips through Echo Park via the *Bulletin*, and *Call* listings of New York City socialists' myriad activities filled columns. Social justice journals published now-historic seminal documents like the United Farm Workers Plan of Delano, the Statement of Purpose of the National Black Feminist Organization, and the first proposed Standards of Care for the Health of Transsexual, Transgender, and Gender-Nonconforming People. The periodicals offered advice published nowhere else, such as a *Gateway's* contributor's detailed account of his experience with male hormone therapy, the *Rag's* sex advice for the disabled, and *El Malcriado's* "Know Your Rights" column on how to deal with immigration officers. Even *Sierra Club Bulletin's* descriptions of new climbing routes provided news found nowhere else. Social justice media also countered hostile mainstream media accounts or filled in their information gaps. The socialist *Call*'s coverage of state violence during the strikes in Bay-onne is one example, as is gay press coverage of the AIDS epidemic beginning in the 1980s. The *Arkansas State Press* and other members of the black press challenged institutionalized racism, prodding an end to legal segregation.

Mobilizing Collective Action

The social justice journals' main purpose was to mobilize collective action to advance their various causes. The *Call* saw itself as part of the shirtwaist work-ers' strike, so it was natural to publish a special fund-raising issue for strikers. L.C. Bates prided himself in the *State Press*'s pioneering postwar campaigns against segregation and police violence. The *Bulletin* stood squarely at the center of the fight to save Dinosaur National Monument. The single-issue *Suffragist* urged readers to send resolutions, letters, petitions, and telegrams to their congressional representatives or lobby their local press to editorialize in support of the suffrage amendment. Editor Gloria Steinem was among women who declared in *Ms.* that they had had abortions, in order to urge readers to join their petition to make access to safe abortion a constitutional right. Collective action frames dominated the social justice journalism of these peri-odicals, such as the 1989 "Protest" issue of *Disability Rag* that explored ways to effect social change.

Storytelling and Emotion

The social justice journalists often used storytelling and emotion in their nar-ratives to compel readers to action. *Ms.* favored profiles of "super women" to humanize the feminist fight. Rollicking first-person accounts in the *Bulletin* brought readers along on thrilling rides down the priceless Green River. *Dis-ability Rag* delivered moral shocks, such as the indignities revealed by con-tributors in essays about their encounters with the medical establishment, as did the *Suffragist*'s descriptions of brutality faced by jailed pickets in Occo-quan workhouse, details Alice Paul knew provided "excellent ammunition" in their campaign to win the vote. Photographs in *El Malcriado* constructed an image of lettuce pickers as brave and noble. *Ms.* published a photograph of the naked, bleeding body of a victim of an illegal abortion. The *State Press* topped its straightforward account of how during World War II police shot down an unarmed soldier on a Little Rock city street with headlines that aimed to shock.

Social Justice Journalism

To varying degrees, all of these journals—as far back as the *Anti-Slavery Monthly Reporter* in 1825—practiced social justice journalism, which uses facts and emotion to expose and remedy injustice. The *Call* reported on child hunger and poor foster care in New York. Martin Litton demonstrated in the *Bulletin* the falsity of federal claims for the economic necessity of the Echo Park dam. The *State Press* reported on racial discrimination across the South, urging readers "to keep the pot boiling" for civil rights. *Ms.* investigations brought sexual harassment, date rape, and domestic abuse to national attention. Editor Mary Johnson offered *Disability Rag* readers an insider's perspective on ADAPT's takeover of a federal building in Chicago. Photographs that documented injustice could galvanize action. Examples include the *Suffragist's* documentation of attacks upon peaceful White House pickets, *Sierra Club Bulletin's* heart-stopping images of roaring rivers, and *El Malcriado's* images of field workers' mistreatment and Cesar Chavez's *Peregrinación*.

Many of these techniques were precursors of social justice journalism tools that are products of the digital revolution. The *State Press's* use of eyewitnesses to report and decry Foster's death presaged the citizen cell phone videos and social media postings that mobilized Black Lives Matter in 2014. Storytelling is increasingly important to human rights campaigns, according to Sam Gregory of WITNESS, which trains people how to document abuses with video, because the Internet has facilitated global discourse on human rights. Video campaigns emphasize agency and voice of local human rights activists.[15] Hashtags such as #MeToo and #TransIsBeautiful proved powerful mobilizers. Tumblr communities can offer lifelines similar to those provided by the letters departments of *FTM* and *Disability Rag*.

Threats to Social Justice Journalists

The experience of the *Arkansas State Press* also demonstrates how dominant powers can strike back at periodicals that challenge their institutions. Bates's coverage of Foster's shooting death sparked an advertising boycott that the aggressive newspaper managed to survive in 1942, but the crusading newspaper was felled by a second boycott imposed by Little Rock politicians and business leaders after the *Press* forced the integration of city schools in the 1950s. Bates personified the courage demanded of many social justice journalists. Neither burning crosses nor a bomb could deter the Bates from publishing the *State Press* as a vehicle for racial integration. Bates is also a reminder that individuals can play an outsized role in social justice journalism. The stern Zachary Macaulay's meticulous eye for detail made the *Reporter* effective, just as the swashbuckling David Brower's flair for publicity animated the *Sierra Club Bulletin*, and FTM's Sullivan's almost single-handed campaign forced the medical establishment to acknowledge that gay female-to-male transsexuals exist.

The *State Press* offers an example of how social justice journalists have been on the front lines of fights for First Amendment rights. The Bateses spent a day in jail for criticizing an Arkansas court's dispensation of criminal justice. California produce growers incensed by *El Malcriado*'s outrageous portrayals sued the newspaper several times. The *Call* not only was banned in Bayonne but also was one of many radical periodicals suppressed by the federal government during World War I. In 1958, a four-year legal battle culminated in *ONE Inc. v. Olesen*, which opened the door for public discussion of homosexuality.

One common trait among many of the print social movement journals was their media criticism. *El Malcriado* mocked a Delano newspaper by giving it a best-fiction award for its coverage of farm workers. "No Comment" in *Ms.* spoke volumes about sexism embedded in mass media, the *Rag*'s "Myth & Media" deconstructed media representations of disabled people, and the *Call*'s Marxist critique charged that advertising corrupted the "news trust." The *Call*'s view of news media as a monopoly has special relevance today, as the United States enters a new era of massive media conglomeration and ownership deregulation that has serious ramifications for online social justice journalism.

Alternative Business Models

Practicing social justice journalism in a capitalist system is also financially perilous, whether a journal's publishers are disabled individuals or a multimillion-dollar foundation. Early social justice journal founders innovated alternatives. The Workingmen's Cooperative Publishing Association that collectively managed the *Call* is one example; another is *Ms.* magazine's metamorphosis from the marketplace to the world of nonprofit journalism with creation of the Ms. Foundation. Foundations, in fact, seem to be the most sustainable way to support social justice journalism. The Catch-22, however, is that publishers must already be well-established organizations with a certain cachet among mainstream Americans, such as the Sierra Club. Along with member subscriptions, the nonprofit Sierra Club Foundation funds *Sierra* magazine.

A Sustainable Model for Social Justice Journalism?

Independent investigative journalists began to turn to the nonprofit model in the 1990s, as the Internet cut into legacy journalism revenue and reporting budgets were slashed. The award-winning ProPublica was among many independent nonprofit investigative journalism centers that sprang up in the 2000s, facilitated by Internet networking and new digital media tools enabled by the Internet. The trend's most spectacular result is the Panama Papers, the global financial scandal unearthed in 2015 by the International Consortium of Investigative Reporters and more than a hundred other media partners. The Panama Papers is a dynamic exemplar of the "unprecedented legacy and digital media activism" that radical media scholar John D. H. Downing believes is the model for future social movement media.[16] On a smaller scale, Barbara Ehrenreich, who got her big break as a freelancer for Ms., cofounded the nonprofit Economic Hardship Reporting Project to fund journalism about the undercovered issue of poverty. The nonprofit won three Emmys in four years, including one for "Jackson," a documentary it executive produced about the battle to keep open Mississippi's last abortion clinic. Environmentalism is another area of social justice in which activist, nonprofit journalism entities have proliferated. The Gecko Project is an initiative by the London-based investigative research nonprofit Earthsight in collaboration with environmental news site Mongabay. Its "Indonesia for Sale" multimedia series in 2017 was released in Indonesian and English and promoted on Facebook, Instagram, and WhatsApp. Another hard-hitting environmental nonprofit outlet is Climate Progress, whose founder Joe Romm has been described as "America's fiercest climate-change activist-blogger."[17]

Netroots Nation

Climate Progress is part of ThinkProgress, a pointedly progressive news site produced by the nonprofit Center for American Progress Action Fund. ThinkProgress is in turn part of the "netroots," the universe that is home to a raft of online successors to twentieth-century social movement print culture. A contraction of "Internet" and "grassroots," the netroots comprise a network of progressive bloggers who in the early 200s created a new form of online political activism. Since 2006, several thousand have physically congregated each year at Netroots Nation to strategize and socialize. Communication workshops in 2018 highlighted the central role of digital media in social justice movements: "Live Tweet Your Way to Success"; "Using SEO for Social Change"; "Handbills and Hashtags: Cross-Generational Organizing"; and "Getting Started with Facebook Live: How to Amplify Your Action and Get More People into the Movement."

Other Netroots Nation sessions underscore how threads of social justice journalism that spool back to the *Anti-Slavery Monthly Reporter*——shocking facts, narrative, and emotion—remain fundamental to mobilizing collective action. An example is a panel headlined by the director of the Sierra Club's Beyond Coal Campaign entitled, "Telling Winning Stories When the Opponents Are Really Loud." Others include: "From 'Saying Abortion Aloud' to Undocuqueer: A Discussion of Storytelling Genres"; "Race and Justice: Telling the Stories of Black and Latino Youth in the Adult Criminal Justice System"; and "Eyes on ICE: Using Video to Expose Immigration Abuses and Advocate for Immigrant Rights." UFW co-founder Dolores Huerta addressed the crowd in 2017, and Khalid Kamau, the first #BlackLivesMatter organizer elected to public office, was a panelist in 2018, when the keynote speaker was Alexandria Ocasio-Cortez, the card-carrying member of the Democratic Socialists of America who went on to win New York's 14th Congressional district seat.[18] These progressive organizers, activists, and independent media makers also formed the heart of the Trump Resistance Movement.[19]

Trump Resistance Movement Media

President Trump's election "sparked a truly unprecedented grassroots response, different in both scale and character from anything we've seen before," in the view of L. A. Kauffman, author of *Direct Action: Protest and the Reinvention of American Radicalism.*[20] The sprawling network of progressive movements was built almost entirely online, giving it unprecedented scale and geographic reach. The Resistance embraced electoral politics but differed from the political parties because it was a grassroots movement dedicated to a progressive agenda instead of a party platform. Kauffman argues that the Resistance marks a significant new stage in social movements. There is no dominant Resistance journal, for example. Despite their significant differences, however, commonalities can be seen between the Resistance's reliance on social media and the social justice newspapers and magazines that preceded them.

Take Indivisible, an exemplar of the new movement. In December 2016, the thirty-something husband-and-wife team of Ezra Levin and Leah Greenberg, used their work experience on Capitol Hill to put together a handbook for frustrated friends and family: "Indivisible: A Practical Guide for Resisting the Trump Agenda." Just like the early pamphlets of the British abolitionist movement in the late 1700s, the Google Doc went viral, only faster. Within months, Indivisible grew into a national network of more than 6,000 local multi-issue groups. Some groups grew out of "huddles" after the Women's March, others responded to calls for action from established national advocacy organizations such as the American Civil Liberties Union. Levin and Greenberg launched the national nonprofit Indivisible organization to support the matrix of local groups, providing them with online canvassing and phone-banking tools. Local organizers, however, made their own decisions about how to run their campaigns.

Electoral politics and legislative reform are typical next steps for social movements seeking social change in a working democracy. The *Suffragist* campaigned against Woodrow Wilson; the *Sierra Club Bulletin* lobbied for the 1964 Wilderness Act; the black press championed the 1964 Civil Rights Act; and the *Call* was the voice of the Socialist Party of New York. Like the print social justice periodicals that preceded them, the social media platforms of Indivisible—its very name symbolizes collective identity—aim to mobilize collective action: voting out Trump and his congressional supporters, ready-made targets for "us" versus "him" collective action frames. Indivisible's online presence, however, is very nuts and bolts, as are those of other anti-Trump political organizations Swing Left, Our Revolution, and Run for Something.

These organizations, along with a wide swathe of other grassroots Resistance groups such as Color of Change, the Latino-focused Jolt, and Moms Demand Action for Gun Sense in America, mobilized a large midterm voter turnout that returned Democrats to control of the House of Representatives. Among the record-setting number of women they sent to Congress was Lucy

McBath (D–GA), who joined Moms Demand Action after her 17-year-old son was gunned down in 2012 for playing loud music in his car. The morning after the election, Jaclyn Corin, a teenaged co-organizer of the 2018 March for Our Lives, tweeted, "More NRA-backed politicians lost their seats last night than ever before." Gun control results actually were mixed, but Corin's medium was the real message. The Twitter-savvy March for Our Lives organizers and school-shooting survivors, who embarked on a Road for Change voter recruiting tour in summer 2018, had helped boost youth turnout (ages 18–29) to its highest rate in at least twenty-five years, and virtually half of 18- to 24-year-olds heard about the elections from at least one of the four most popular social media platforms: Facebook, Instagram, Snapchat, and Twitter.[21] The Resistance political campaign, however, also relied on such old-fashioned recruiting techniques as house-to-house canvassing. The rise of postcard-writing clubs epitomized the blend of print culture and social media in mobilizing collective action. Postcards to Voters began when Tony McMullin shared five addresses apiece with five volunteers on Facebook so that they could mail postcards to voters in a special 2017 election for Georgia's Sixth Congressional District seat, urging them to vote for the Democratic candidate. Their candidate lost but the "craftivists" handwrote and mailed nearly four million more postcards to voters in some 130 key, close races nationwide, helping flip more than half from Republican to Democrat.[22]

Social justice remains a goal rather than reality, of course, and social media have their own shortcomings. Resistance media were more diffuse than previous social movement media, and lacked a single, unifying media voice that offered a continuous, consistent message over time. One question about the long-term efficacy of a social movement built almost entirely online is the ephemeral nature of social media. Another concern is the Internet's dominance by media megaliths. British new media scholar Bart Cammaerts observes that social media are "corporate online spaces" that are "inherently mainstream" and inherently capable of stifling dissent.[23] Google search engines and other platforms that organize public debate privilege established actors and institutions, while making it more difficult for smaller actors and their arguments to appear in a relevant manner.[24] These realities follow some media scholars' skepticism about the emancipatory powers of digital media. Paolo Gerbaudo warns against "fetishizing social media as a tool of collective action."[25] Nick Couldry and Malcolm Gladwell question social media's ability to sustain collective identity.[26] Legal scholar Cass Sunstein goes even further, arguing that social media's self-reinforcing algorithms are inherently antithetical to democracy.[27]

The millennial media savants who organized the March for Our Lives, however, remained resolute. Eighteen-year-old David Hogg, one of the group's most vocal gun control activists, also turned to Twitter after the midterm elections. Almost to the day nine months earlier, the *Sun Sentinel* news intern had turned on his cell phone's video recorder as he hid in a school closet in the aftermath of the Valentine's Day shooting in Parkland, Florida, and calmly described the mayhem that had just occurred.[28] On November 7, the aspiring journalist turned activist tweeted to his nearly one million followers about the growing social movement, "This is just the beginning."

Notes

1. Gilal Edelman, "Is Journalism Thriving, or Is It on Life Support? Yes," *Washington Monthly*, November 27, 2018, https://washingtonmonthly.com/2018/11/27/is-journalism-thriving-or-is-it-on-life-support-yes/.

2. Taylor Stevens, "More Than 20 Utah Local Leaders File Court Briefs Opposing Shrinkage of Bears Ears, Grand Staircase Monuments," *Salt Lake Tribune*, November 20, 2018, https://www.sltrib.com/news/politics/2018/11/19/more-than-utah-mayors/

3. Melissa Block and Marisa Penaloza, "'They're Scared': Immigration Fears Exacerbate Migrant Farmworker Shortage," NPR, September 27, 2017, https://www.npr.org/sections/thesalt/2017/09/27/552636014/theyre-scared-immigration-fears-exacerbate-migrant-farmworker-shortage.

4. Vann R. Newkirk II, "Trump's White-Nationalist Pipeline," *Atlantic*, August 23, 2018, https://www.theatlantic.com/politics/archive/2018/08/trump-white-nationalism/568393/.

5. "On the U.S. Labor Department's Fall Regulatory Agenda," *National Employment Law Project*, October 17, 2018, https://www.nelp.org/news-releases/u-s-labor-departments-fall-regulatory-agenda/.

6. Tim Rostan, "Critics Charge True Intent of Trump Threat to Would-Be Fraudulent Voters Is Vote Suppression," *MarketWatch*, October 21, 2018, https://www.marketwatch.com/story/critics-charge-true-intent-of-trump-threat-to-would-be-fraudulent-voters-is-vote-suppression-2018-10-21.

7. Robyn Powell, "For People With Disabilities, Trump's First Year Has Threatened Nearly Every Facet of Life," *Rewire.News*, January 19, 2018, https://rewire.news/article/2018/01/19/people-disabilities-trumps-first-year-threatened-nearly-every-facet-life/

8. "How the Trump Administration Is Remaking Federal Policy on Women's Reproductive Health," *PBS*, May 30, 2018, https://www.pbs.org/newshour/politics/how-the-trump-administration-is-remaking-federal-policy-on-womens-reproductive-health.

9. "Anti-Transgender and Anti-LGBT Actions," National Center for Transgender Equality, accessed November 23, 2018, https://transequality.org/the-discrimination-administration.

10. Pete Vernon, "Trump's Press Bashing Reaches a Critical Mass," *Columbia Journalism Review*, August 6, 2018, https://www.cjr.org/the_media_today/trump-press-violence.php.

11. Tom Henderson, "The Loss of Net Neutrality: Say Goodbye to a Free and Open Internet," *Network World*, May 17, 2018, https://www.networkworld.com/article/3154091/internet/the-loss-of-net-neutrality-say-goodbye-to-a-free-and-open-internet.html. See also Eric Klinenberg, *Fighting for Air: The Battle to Control America's Media* (New York: Metropolitan Books, 2013).

12. Emily Bell, "Why We Should Be Wary of Ending Net Neutrality," *Guardian*, November 26, 2017, https://www.theguardian.com/technology/media-blog/2017/nov/26/net-neutrality-law-trump-deregulation-media.

13. Brian Stelter, "Sinclair's New Media Bashing Promos Rankle Local Anchors," *CNN Business*, March 7, 2018, https://money.cnn.com/2018/03/07/media/sinclair-broadcasting-promos-media-bashing/index.html.

14. Roger Silverstone, "The Sociology of Mediation and Communication," in *The SAGE Handbook of Sociology*, ed. Craig Calhoun, Chris Rojek, and Bryan Turner (London: Sage, 2005), 201.

15. Sam Gregory, "Transnational Storytelling: Human Rights, Witness, and Video Advocacy," *American Anthropologist* 108, no. 1 (March 2006), 202.

16. John D. H. Downing, "Looking Back, Looking Ahead: What Has Changed in Social Movement Media Since the Internet and Social Media?," in *The Routledge Companion to Media and Activism*, ed. Graham Meikle (London: Routledge, 2018), 18.

17. Joseph J. Romm, *Straight Up: America's Fiercest Climate Blogger Takes on the Status Quo Media, Politicians, and Clean Energy Solutions* (Washington, D.C.: Island Press, 2010), 2.

18. See Matthew Yglesias, "Netroots Nation, Explained," *Vox*, August 2, 2018, https://www.vox.com/policy-and-politics/2018/8/2/17635034/netroots-nation-explained; and "About," *Netroots Nation*, https://www.netrootsnation.org/about/.

19. Tim Dickinson, "How a New Generation of Progressive Activists Is Leading the Trump Resistance," *Rolling Stone*, August 24, 2017, https://www.rollingstone.com/politics/features/how-progressive-activists-are-leading-the-trump-resistance-w499221.

20. L. A. Kauffman, "The Resistance to Trump Is Blossoming—and Building a Movement to Last," *Guardian*, November 9, 2017, https://www.theguardian.com/commentisfree/2017/nov/09/resistance-trump-blossoming-movement-la-kaufmann. See also Charlotte Alter, "How the Anti-Trump Resistance Is Organizing Its Outrage," *Time*, October 18, 2018, http://time.com/longform/democrat-midterm-strategy/; Sara Fischer and Becca Rotenberg, "Rise of the Trump Resistance Movement," *Axios*, April 23, 2017, https://www.axios.com/rise-of-the-trump-resistance-movement-1513301616-003dcd62-0833-4987-bdf6-1bfd1d0f1fc9.html; Joshua Holland, "Your Guide to the Sprawling New Anti-Trump Resistance Movement," *Nation*, February 6, 2017, https://www.thenation.com/article/your-guide-to-the-sprawling-new-anti-trump-resistance-movement/; Eric Levitz, "Trump Has Turned Millions of Americans into Activists," *New York*, April 6, 2018, Intelligencer, http://nymag.com/intelligencer/2018/04/trump-has-turned-millions-of-americans-into-activists.html; and John Weiner, "This Is the Resistance: More Than 5,000 Grassroots Groups Have Sprung Up Since Trump Was Elected," *Nation*, March 9, 2017, https://www.

thenation.com/article/at-least-75-new-grassroots-groups-have-been-created-since-trump-was-elected/.

21. "'Road to Change': This Is How Parkland Students Went from Teens to Activists," *VICE News*, November 13, 2018, https://twitter.com/vicenews/status/1062570824140537856; and "Five Takeaways on Social Media and the Youth Vote in 2018," *CIRCLE* (*The Center for Information & Research on Civic Learning and Engagement*), November 15, 2018, https://civicyouth.org/five-takeaways-on-social-media-and-the-youth-vote-in-2018/.

22. William Wan, "Postcards from the Left: Resistance Groups Take Aim at Trump, One Letter at a Time," *Washington Post*, November 2, 2018, https://www.washingtonpost.com/national/postcards-from-the-left-resistance-groups-take-aim-at-trump-one-letter-at-a-time/2018/11/02/699df7e0-c1ba-11e8-a1f0-a4051b6ad114_story.html?utm_term=.8ddd0f086e6b.

23. Bart Cammaerts, *The Circulation of Anti-Austerity Protest* (London: Palgrave Macmillan, 2018), 221.

24. Jürgen Gerhards and Mike S. Schäfer, "Is the Internet a Better Public Sphere? Comparing Old and New Media in the US and Germany," *New Media & Society* 20, no. 10 (2009): 1–18.

25. Paolo Gerbaudo, *Tweets and the Streets: Social Media and Contemporary Activism* (London: Pluto Press, 2012), 8.

26. Nick Couldry, "The Myth of 'Us': Digital Networks, Political Change and the Production of Collectivity," *Information, Communication & Society* 18, no. 6 (2015): 608–26; and Malcolm Gladwell, "Small Change: Why the Revolution Will Not Be Tweeted," *New Yorker*, October 4, 2010, https://www.newyorker.com/magazine/2010/10/04/small-change-malcolm-gladwell. See also Zeynep Tufekci, "Online Social Change: Easy to Organize, Hard to Win," *TEDGlobal* 2014, accessed November 3, 2108, https://www.ted.com/talks/zeynep_tufekci_how_the_internet_has_made_social_change_easy_to_organize_hard_to_win/discussion?la.

27. See Cass R. Sunstein, *#Republic: Divided Democracy in the Age of Social Media* (Princeton, NJ: Princeton University Press, 2017). See also Siva Vaidhyanathan, *Antisocial Media: How Facebook Disconnects Us and Undermines Democracy* (New York: Oxford University Press, 2018).

28. Lisa Miller, "David Hogg, After Parkland," *New York*, August 19, 2018, Intelligencer, http://nymag.com/intelligencer/2018/08/david-hogg-is-taking-his-gap-year-at-the-barricades.html?gtm=bottom&gtm=bottom.

BIBLIOGRAPHY

Archives

David Ross Brower Papers. Special Collections, Bancroft Library, University of California, Berkeley.

Robin Morgan Papers. Sallie Bingham Center for Women's History and Culture, Special Collections, Duke University, Durham, NC.

National American Woman Suffrage Association Records, microfilm ed. Manuscript Division. Washington, D.C.: Library of Congress Photoduplication Service, 1982.

National Woman's Party Papers, 1913–1974. Glen Rock, NJ: Microfilm Corporation of America, 1977–1978.

National Woman's Party Papers: The Suffrage Years, 1913–1920, ed. Donald Haggerty. Sanford, NC: Microfilm Corporation of America, 1981.

Records of the Post Office Department (POD). Office of the Solicitor General (Records Group 28.2.5). Washington, D.C.: National Archives.

Sierra Club Office of the Executive Director Records, 1933–1994. Special Collections, Bancroft Library, University of California, Berkeley.

Sierra Club Records. Special Collections, Bancroft Library, University of California, Berkeley.

Gloria Steinem Papers. Sophia Smith Collection, Smith College, Northampton, MA.

United Farm Workers Administration Department Files. Walter P. Reuther Library of Labor and Urban Affairs, Wayne State University, Detroit.

Workingmen's Co-operative Publishing Association, Archives of the Tamiment Library, New York University.

Periodicals

Anti-Slavery Monthly Reporter [the *Reporter*] (London)
Arkansas State Press (Little Rock, AR)
Call (New York City)
Disability Rag (Louisville, KY)
El Malcriado (Delano, CA)
FTM Newsletter (San Francisco)
Gateway Newsletter (San Francisco)

Ms. (New York and Los Angeles)
Sierra Club Bulletin [*Sierra*] (San Francisco)
Suffragist (Washington, D.C.)

Primary Sources

Alger, George W. "The Literature of Exposure." *Atlantic Monthly* 96, August 1905: 210–13.

Ameringer, Oscar. *If You Don't Weaken: The Autobiography of Oscar Ameringer*. 2nd ed. Norman: University of Oklahoma Press, 1983.

Anthony, Susan B., Matilda Gage, and Elizabeth Cady Stanton, eds. *History of Woman Suffrage*, vol. 2. Rochester, NY: Susan B. Anthony, 1882. http://www.gutenberg.org/files/28039/28039-h/28039-h.htm.

Barrow, John. "Here's a Picture of Emmett Till Painted by Those Who Knew Him." *Chicago Defender*, October 1, 1955, 4.

Bates, Daisy. *The Long Shadow of Little Rock: A Memoir*. New York: David McKay, 1962.

Berman, Laura. "Portable Friend? A New Look at *Ms.*" *Detroit Free Press*, January 16, 1980, 5C.

Blatch, Harriot Stanton. *The Mobilization of Woman-Power*. New York: Woman's Press, 1918.

"Blood On Their Hands. … " *Chicago Defender*, September 10, 1955, 1.

Booker, Simeon. "To Be a 'Negro' Newsman—Reporting on the Emmett Till Murder Trial." *Nieman Reports*, Fall 2011 [originally published as Simeon Booker, "A Negro Reporter at the Till Trial," *Nieman Reports*, January 1956]. Accessed July 27, 2017. http://niemanreports. org/articles/to-be-a-negro-newsman-reporting-on-the-emmett-till-murder-trial/.

Brady, John. "Freelancer with No Time to Write." *Writer's Digest* 54, February 1974: 12–21.

Carmody, Deirdre. "Feminists Rebut Friedan Charge." *New York Times*, July 20, 1972, 29.

Carper, Jean. "*Ms.*: The Mystique Is Waning." *Washington Post*, September 21, 1975, C2.

Catt, Carrie Chapman, and Nettie Rogers Shuler. *Woman Suffrage and Politics*. New York: Charles Scribner's Sons, 1923.

Cobb, Jelani. "The Matter of Black Lives." *New Yorker*, March 14, 2016. https://www.newyorker. com/magazine/2016/03/14/where-is-black-lives-matter-headed.

Dotythe, Robert C. "Growth of Overt Homosexuality in City Provokes Wide Concern." *New York Times*, December 17, 1963, 1. https://www.nytimes.com/1963/12/17/archives/growth-of-overt-homosexuality-in-city-provokes-wide-concern-growth.html

Du Bois, W. E. B. "Socialism and the Negro Problem." *New Review* 1, February 1913: 138–41.

"Emmett Till Funeral Saddens City, Nation." *Chicago Defender*. September 17, 1955, 1, 4.

Ervin, Mike. "My Turn: Mike Ervin: Jerry Lewis Angered Many Disabled People." *Providence Journal*, August 30, 2017. http://www.providencejournal.com/opinion/20170830/my-turn-mike-ervin-jerry-lewis-angered-many-disabled-people.

Feinberg, Leslie. *Transgender Liberation: A Movement Whose Time Has Come*. New York: World View Forum, 1992.

Firestone, Shulamith. *The Dialectic of Sex: The Case for Feminist Revolution*. New York: Morrow, 1970.

Foreman, Dave. *Confessions of an Eco-Warrior*. New York: Crown, 1991.

Freeman, Jo. "The Women's Liberation Movement: Its Origins, Structures and Ideals." In Women's Liberation Movement Print Culture Collection, Duke University Libraries Digital Collections. Accessed November 2, 2018. https://library.duke.edu/digitalcollections/wlmpc_wlmms01013/.

Gaynor, Janie T. "I Was Humor Editor of Ms. Magazine but the Joke Was on Me." Harper's Weekly, June 14, 1976, 10–11.

Gendlin, Frances. Editorial, "Some News of Sierra and the NNR." Sierra 63 (October/November/December 1978): 5.

"Grieving Mother Meets Body of Lynched Son." Chicago Defender, September 10, 1955, 1.

Hendrix, Kathleen. "Ms. Grows Up with the Movement." Los Angeles Times, June 18, 1982, Part V, 16–19.

Holland, Joshua. "Your Guide to the Sprawling New Anti-Trump Resistance Movement." Nation, February 6, 2017. https://www.thenation.com/article/your-guide-to-the-sprawling-new-anti-trump-resistance-movement/.

Hunter, Robert. "The Socialist Party in the Present Campaign." American Review of Reviews 38, (September 1908): 298.

Irvin, Cass. Home Bound: Growing Up with a Disability in America. Philadelphia: Temple University Press, 2004.

Irwin, Inez Haynes. The Story of the Woman's Party. New York: Harcourt, Brace, 1921.

Irwin, Robert. "Sierra Club Books—How a Small Publisher Prints a Big Book." Sierra, September/October 1981: 76–77.

"L.C. Bates: Little Rock's Forgotten Man." Jet, June 4, 1959, 13.

Mark, Jason. "The Talking Cure." Sierra, December 18, 2017. https://www.sierraclub.org/sierra/2018-1-january-february/editor/talking-cure.

"Miss Paul Describes Feeding by Force." New York Times, December 10, 1909, 1.

Morgan, Robin. "Goodbye to All That." Fair Use Blog. 1970. Accessed November 2, 2018. http://blog.fair-use.org/2007/09/29/goodbye-to-all-that-by-robin-morgan-1970/.

———. "The Miss America Protest: 1968." Redstockings. Accessed November 8, 2018. http://www.redstockings.org/index.php/themissamericaprotest.

———. "On Freedom." Liberation, October 1968, 34–35.

"The Negroes and the War." Richmond Times-Dispatch, April 26, 1942.

"Newspaper Incitement to Violence." New Republic 8, October 21, 1916: 283–85.

Notes from the First Year. New York: New York Radical Women, 1968.

"One of 'Little Rock Nine' Eulogizes Rights of Leader; Carter Letter Read." Arkansas Gazette, August 28, 1980, 6A.

"The Perjury of July 4th." Liberator, July 5, 1836. http://theliberatorfiles.com/garrison-the-perjury-of-july-4th/.

"The Pickets and the Public." Woman Citizen, June 30, 1917, 79.

"Pickets Are Behind the Times." Woman Citizen, November 17, 1917, 470.

Popham, John. "Mississippi Jury Acquits 2 Accused in Youth's Killing." New York Times, September 24, 1955, 1, 38.

Pride, Armistead S. "The Arkansas State Press: Squeezed to Death." Grassroots Editor 2, no. 1 (January 1962): 7.

Report of the Woman's Rights Convention. Rochester, NY: John Dick, 1848, 10. https://www.nps. gov/media/photo/gallery.htm?id=C5F5A21C-155D-451F-67E9D17421B0E587.

Ross Janell, and Wesley Lowery. "Black Lives Matter Shifts from Protests to Policy under Trump." *Chicago Tribune,* May 4, 2017. http://www.chicagotribune.com/news/nationworld/ ct-black-lives-matter-trump-20170504-story.html.

"*Sierra's* New Design." *Sierra,* July/August 1986: 7.

Sierra Club Board of Directors Executive Committee Minutes. October 14, 1962. http://cdn. calisphere.org/data/28722/6s/bk00079546s/files/bk00079546s-FID222.jpg.

Steinem, Gloria. "The City Politic: 'After Black Power, Women's Liberation.'" *New York,* April 7, 1969, 8–9.

———. *Outrageous Acts and Everyday Rebellions.* New York: Henry Holt, 1987.

———. "The Politics of Journalism." *Folio,* January/February 1974, 20.

Stephen, Sir George. *Anti-slavery Recollections: In a Series of Letters Addressed to Mrs. Beecher.* London: Thomas Hatchard, 1854.

Stevens, Doris. *Jailed for Freedom.* New York: Boni & Liveright, 1920.

Sullivan, L. "Sullivan's Travels." *Advocate,* June 6, 1989, 70.

Thom, Mary. *Inside Ms.: 25 Years of the Magazine and the Feminist Movement.* New York: Henry Holt, 1997.

"To the Public." *Liberator,* January 1, 1831, 1. http://fair-use.org/the-liberator.

U.S. Census Bureau. "1830 Census: Abstract of the Returns of the Fifth Census." Washington, D.C.: Duff Green, 1832, 51. Accessed November 10, 2018. https://www.census.gov/ library/publications/1832/dec/1830b.html

Walker, David. *Walker's Appeal, in Four Articles; Together with a Preamble, to the Coloured Citizens of the World, but in Particular, and Very Expressly, to Those of the United States of America. Documenting the American South.* Accessed October 26, 2018. http://docsouth.unc.edu/ nc/walker/walker.html.

Walsh, Walter. "The White Man with the Straight Eye." *Unity: A Journal of the Religion of Democracy* 94 (January 12, 1925): 261–65.

Wells-Barnett, Ida B. *Southern Horrors: Lynch Law in All Its Phases.* New York: The New York Age, 1892. Accessed October 29, 2018. https://www.gutenberg.org/files/14975/14975- h/14975-h.htm.

"The Women Who Are 'Guarding' the White House." *Washington Post,* February 7, 1917, 1.

Secondary Sources

"2018 Election Night Tally." *Center for American Women and Politics.* Updated November 28, 2018. http://www.cawp.rutgers.edu/2018-election-night-tally.

Adams, Katherine H., and Michael L. Keene. *Alice Paul and the American Suffrage Campaign.* Champaign: University of Illinois Press, 2010.

Ahern, Stephen. "Introduction: The Bonds of Sentiment." In *Affect and Abolition in the Anglo–Atlantic, 1770–1830,* edited by Stephen Ahern, 1-21. London: Ashgate, 2013.

Alwood, Edward. *Straight News: Gays, Lesbians, and the Press.* New York: Columbia University Press, 1996.

Anderson, Benedict. *Imagined Communities: Reflections on the Origin and Spread of Nationalism.* London: Verso, 2006.

Aptheker, Herbert, ed. *One Continual Cry: David Walker's Appeal to the Colored Citizens of the World, 1829–1839: Its Setting and Its Meaning.* 1st paperback ed. New York: Humanities Press, 1965.

Araiza, Lauren. *To March for Others: The Black Freedom Struggle and the United Farm Workers.* Philadelphia: University of Pennsylvania Press, 2013.

Ardizzoni, Michela. *Matrix Activism: Global Practices of Resistance.* New York: Routledge, 2016.

Atkinson, Joshua D. *Alternative Media and Politics of Resistance: A Communication Perspective.* New York: Peter Lang, 2009.

Atton, Chris, and James Hamilton. *Alternative Journalism.* London: Sage, 2008.

Bardacke, Frank. *Trampling Out the Vintage: Cesar Chavez and the Two Souls of the United Farm Workers.* New York: Verso Books, 2012.

Barnard, Stephen R. "Tweeting #Ferguson: Mediatized Fields and the New Activist Journalist." *New Media & Society* 20, no. 7 (July 2017): 2252–71.

Barnes, Colin. "Discrimination: Disabled People and the Media." *Contact*, no. 70, Winter 1991: 45–48.

Baughn, Linda. "César Chávez and the 1968 Fast: A Turning Point for the United Farm Workers." *Independent Academia.* Accessed June 26, 2017. https://www.academia.edu/25180762/CÉSAR_CHÁVEZ_AND_THE_1968_FAST_A_TURNING_POINT_FOR_THE_UNITED_FARM_WORKERS.

Baxandall, Rosalyn. "Revisioning the Women's Liberation Movement's Narrative: Early Second Wave African American Feminists." *Feminist Studies* 27, no. 1 (Spring 2001): 225–45.

———, and Linda Gordon. *Dear Sisters: Dispatches from the Women's Liberation Movement.* New York: Basic Books, 2000.

Beckett, Charlie, and Robin Mansell. "Crossing Boundaries: New Media and Networked Journalism." *Communication, Culture and Critique* 1, no. 1 (March 2008): 92–104.

Bell, Emily. "Why We Should Be Wary of Ending Net Neutrality." *Guardian*, November 26, 2017. https://www.theguardian.com/technology/media-blog/2017/nov/26/net-neutrality-law-trump-deregulation-media.

Benford, Robert, and David A. Snow. "Framing Processes and Social Movements: An Overview and Assessment." *Annual Review of Sociology* 26, no. 1 (2000): 611–39.

Bennett, Lance W., and Alexandra Segerberg. *The Logic of Connective Action: Digital Media and the Personalization of Contentious Politics.* Cambridge: Cambridge University Press, 2013.

Berger, John. *Ways of Seeing.* London: British Broadcasting Company, 1972.

Bond, Kanisha, Erica Chenoweth, and Jeremy Pressman. "Did You Attend the March for Our Lives? Here's What It Looked Like Nationwide." *Washington Post*, April 13, 2018. https://www.washingtonpost.com/news/monkey-cage/wp/2018/04/13/did-you-attend-the-march-for-our-lives-heres-what-it-looked-like-nationwide/?utm_term=.d39faa7df6cf.

Booth, Charles. *Zachary Macaulay, His Part in the Movement for the Abolition of the Slave Trade and of Slavery: An Appreciation.* London: Longmans, Green, 1934.

Boykoff, Jules. "Framing Dissent: Mass-Media Coverage of the Global Justice Movement." *New Political Science* 28, no. 2 (June 2006): 201–28.

Brock, André. "From the Blackhand Side: Twitter as a Cultural Conversation." *Journal of Broadcasting & Electronic Media* 56, no. 4 (2012): 529–49.

Broyles-Gonzalez, Yolanda. *El Teatro Campesino: Theater in the Chicano Movement.* Austin: University of Texas Press, 1994.

Bruns, Roger A. *Encyclopedia of Cesar Chavez: The Farm Workers' Fight for Rights and Justice.* Santa Barbara, CA: ABC-CLIO, 2013.

Buhle, Paul. *Marxism in the USA: Remapping the History of the American Left.* London: Verso, 1987.

Burke, Peter. "Introduction." In *What Is Cultural History?* 2nd ed., edited by Peter Burke, 1-5. Cambridge: Polity Press, 2008.

Cammaerts, Bart. *The Circulation of Anti-Austerity Protest.* London: Palgrave MacMillan, 2018.

Carey, Brycchan. "'Read This and Blush': The Pamphlet Wars of the 1780s." In *British Abolitionism and the Rhetoric of Sensibility: Writing, Sentiment and Slavery, 1760–1807,* 107–143. New York: Palgrave Macmillan, 2005.

———. "William Wilberforce's Sentimental Rhetoric: Parliamentary Reportage and the Abolition Speech of 1789." *The Age of Johnson: A Scholarly Annual* 14 (2003): 281–305.

"CDC: 53 million Adults in the US Live with a Disability." *Centers for Disease Control and Prevention,* July 30, 2015. https://www.cdc.gov/media/releases/2015/p0730-us-disability.html.

Chapman, Mary. *Making Noise, Making News: Suffrage Print Culture and U.S. Modernism.* New York: Oxford University Press, 2014.

Chira, Susan, and Kate Zernike. "Women Lead Parade of Victories to Help Democrats Win House." *New York Times,* November 7, 2018. https://www.nytimes.com/2018/11/06/us/politics/women-midterms-historic.html?action=click&module=Spotlight&pgtype=Homepage.

Chomsky, Noam, and Edward Herman. *Manufacturing Consent: The Political Economy of the Mass Media.* New York: Pantheon, 1988.

Cohen, Jodi S. "The $3 Million Research Breakdown." *ProPublica,* April 26, 2018. https://www.propublica.org/article/university-of-illinois-chicago-mani-pavuluri-3-million-research-breakdown.

Cohen, Michael. "'Cartooning Capitalism': Radical Cartooning and the Making of American Popular Radicalism in the Early Twentieth Century." *International Review of Social History* 52, supp. 15, (January 2007): 35–58.

———. "'The Ku Klux Government': Vigilantism, Lynching, and the Repression of the IWW." *Journal for the Study of Radicalism* 1, no. 1 (2007): 31–56.

Cohen, Michael P. *The History of the Sierra Club: 1892–1970.* San Francisco: Sierra Club Books, 1988.

Couldry, Nick. "The Myth of 'Us': Digital Networks, Political Change and the Production of Collectivity." *Information, Communication & Society* 18, no. 6 (2015): 608–26.

Chun, Jennifer Jihye. *Organizing at the Margins: The Symbolic Politics of Labor in South Korea and the United States.* Ithaca, NY: Cornell University Press, 2009.

Culhane, John. "The Cartoon Killers Thrive Again." *New York Times Magazine*, November 9, 1975, 38–39, 42, 46 50, 54.

Darsey, James. "Prophecy as Krisis: Wendell Phillips and the Sin of Slavery." In *The Prophetic Tradition and Radical Rhetoric in America*, 61–84. New York: New York University Press, 1999.

Davis, David Brion. *The Problem of Slavery in the Age of Emancipation*. New York: Alfred A. Knopf, 2014.

Davis, Joseph E., ed. *Stories of Change: Narrative and Social Movements*. Albany, NY: SUNY Press, 2002.

Del Olmo, Frank. "Voices for the Chicano Movement." *Quill*, October 1971, 9–11.

Dewan, Shaila. "How Photos Became Icon of Civil Rights Movement." *New York Times*, August 28, 2005. http://www.nytimes.com/2005/08/28/us/how-photos-became-icon-of-civil-rights-movement.html.

Dewey, Donald. *The Art of Ill Will: The Story of American Political Cartoons*. New York: New York University Press, 2007.

Dowie, Mark. "American Environmentalism: A Movement Courting Irrelevance." *World Policy Journal* 9, no. 1 (Winter 1991/1992): 67–92.

Downing, John D. H. "Introduction." In *Encyclopedia of Social Movement Media*, edited by John D. H. Downing, xxv–xxvii. Los Angeles: Sage, 2011.

———. "Looking Back, Looking Ahead: What Has Changed in Social Movement Media Since the Internet and Social Media?" In *The Routledge Companion to Media and Activism*, edited by Graham Meikle, 19–28. London: Routledge, 2018.

Drescher, Seymour. *Capitalism and Antislavery: British Mobilization in Comparative Perspective*. Oxford: Oxford University Press, 1987.

Duggan, Maeve. "1 in 4 black Americans Have Faced Online Harassment Because of Their Race or Ethnicity." *Pew Research Center*, July 25, 2017. http://www.pewresearch.org/fact-tank/2017/07/25/1-in-4-black-americans-have-faced-online-harassment-because-of-their-race-or-ethnicity/.

Dunaway, Finis. "Nature on the Coffee Table." In *Natural Visions: The Power of Images in American Environmental Reform*, 117–47. Chicago: University of Chicago Press, 2005.

Dunne, John Gregory. *Delano: The Story of the California Grape Strike*. Berkeley: University of California Press, 1971.

Dupuy, Beatrice. "Some Women of Color Are Boycotting the Women's March, Here's Why." *Newsweek*, January 20, 2018. http://www.newsweek.com/some-women-color-siting-out-womens-march-785861.

Echols, Alice. *Daring to Be Bad: Radical Feminism in America, 1967–1975*. Minneapolis: University of Minnesota Press, 1989.

Edelman, Gilad. "Is Journalism Thriving, or Is It on Life Support? Yes." *Washington Monthly*, November 27, 2018. https://washingtonmonthly.com/2018/11/27/is-journalism-thriving-or-is-it-on-life-support-yes/.

"Editorial: Pussy Hats as Social Movement Symbols." *Journal of Popular Culture* 50, no. 2 (April 2017): 215–17.

Editorial, "Donald Trump Is Lyin' Up a Storm." *New York Times*, October 22, 2018. https://www. nytimes.com/2018/10/22/opinion/editorials/transgender-trump-lies-midterm-election. html?rref=collection%2Ftimestopic%2FTransgender%20issues&action=click&contentC ollection=timestopics&region=stream&module=stream_unit&version=latest&contentP lacement=28&pgtype=collection.

Editorial, "The Quest for Transgender Equality." *New York Times*, May 4, 2015. https://www. nytimes.com/2015/05/04/opinion/the-quest-for-transgender-equality.html.

Emma, Red. "Greenwashing 101: (Or How Sierra Club Learned to Stop Worrying About the 99% and Love Wall Street)." *Earth First! Newswire*. Accessed October 27, 2018. http:// earthfirstjournal.org/newswire/articles/big-greenwashing-101/.

Ervin, Mike. "The Founder of the *Disability Rag* Tells Its History." *Media dis&dat*, April 20, 2009. http://media-dis-n-dat.blogspot.com/2009/04/founder-of-disability-rag-tells-its.html.

Ewick, Patricia, and Susan S. Sibley. "Subversive Stories and Hegemonic Tales: Toward a Sociology of Narrative." *Law & Society Review* 29, no. 2 (January 1995): 197–226.

"(Part 1) Awakenings 1954–1956." *Eyes on the Prize: America's Civil Rights Years, 1954–1965*. Washington, D.C.: PBS, 1987.

"Facebooking from the Fields: Farmworkers Launch a Historic Social Media Campaign." *Daily Kos*, June 25, 2013. http://ufw.org/Daily-Kos-Facebooking-from-the-Fields-Farmworkers-Launch-a-Historic-Social-Media-Campaign/.

Faludi, Susan. *Backlash: The Undeclared War Against American Women*. New York: Crown, 1991.

———. "Death of a Revolutionary." *New Yorker*, April 15, 2013. https://www.newyorker.com/ magazine/2013/04/15/death-of-a-revolutionary.

Farhi, Paul. "How Mainstream Media Missed the March That Social Media Turned into a Phenomenon." *Washington Post*, January 22, 2017. https://www.washingtonpost.com/ lifestyle/style/how-mass-media-missed-the-march-that-social-media-turned-into-a-phenomenon/2017/01/21/2db4742c-e005-11e6-918c-99ede3c8cafa_story.html?utm_term=.513df0f81bf1.

Fay, Roger. "The Clapham Sect and the Abolition of the Slave Trade." *Evangelical Times*, July 2012. Accessed March 19, 2017. http://www.evangelical-times.org/archive/item/5605/ Historical/The-Clapham-Sect- and-the-abolition-of-the-slave-trade--3-/.

Fenderson, Lewis H. "The Negro Press as a Social Instrument." *Journal of Negro Education* 20, no. 2 (Spring 1951): 181–88.

Fine, Nathan. *Labor and Farmer Parties in the United States 1828–1928*. New York: Russell & Russell, 1961.

"Five Takeaways on Social Media and the Youth Vote in 2018." *CIRCLE (The Center for Information & Research on Civic Learning and Engagement)*, November 15, 2018. https:// civicyouth.org/five-takeaways-on-social-media-and-the-youth-vote-in-2018/.

Foner, Philip Sheldon. "The Standard Oil Strikes in Bayonne, New Jersey, 1915–1916." In *The History of the Labor Movement in the United States: On the Eve of America's Entrance into World War I, 1915–1916*, vol. 6, edited by Philip Sheldon Foner, 41–62. New York: International Press, 1957.

Ford, Linda. *Iron-Jawed Angels: The Suffrage Militancy of the National Woman's Party 1912–1920*. Lanham, MD: University Press of America, 1991.

Foucault, Michel. "Technologies of the Self." In *Technologies of the Self: A Seminar with Michel Foucault*, edited by Luther H. Martin, Huck Gutman, and Patrick H. Hutton, 16–49. London: Tavistock Publications, 1988.

Gamson, William A. "Constructing Social Protest." In *Social Movements and Culture*, edited by Hank Johnston and Bert Klandermans, 85–106. Minneapolis: University of Minnesota Press, 1995.

———. *The Strategy of Social Protest*. 2nd ed. Belmont, CA: Wadsworth, 1990.

———. *Talking Politics*. Cambridge: Cambridge University Press, 1992.

———, and Andre Modigliani. "Media Discourse and Public Opinion on Nuclear Power: A Constructivist Approach." *American Journal of Sociology* 95, no. 1 (July 1989): 1–37.

———, and Gadi Wolfsfeld. "Movements and Media as Interacting Systems." *Annals of the American Academy of Political and Social Science* 28, no. 1 (July 1993): 114–25.

Gans, Herbert. *Deciding What's News*. New York: Pantheon, 1979.

Ganz, Marshall. "Resources and Resourcefulness: Strategic Capacity in the Unionization of California Agriculture, 1959–1966." *American Journal of Sociology* 105, no. 4 (January 2000): 1003–62.

Gerbaudo, Paolo. *Tweets and the Streets: Social Media and Contemporary Activism*. London: Pluto Press, 2012.

Gitlin, Todd. *The Whole World Is Watching: Mass Media in the Making and Unmaking of the New Left*. Berkeley: University of California Press, 1980.

Goldberg, Michelle. "The Trans Women Who Say that Trans Women Aren't Women." *Slate*, December 9, 2015. http://www.slate.com/articles/double_x/doublex/2015/12/gender_critical_trans_women_the_apostates_of_the_trans_rights_movement.html.

Gonzalez, Juan, and Joseph Torres. *News for All the People: The Epic Story of Race and the American Media*. New York: Verso Books, 2011.

Goodman, J. David. "Eric Garner Case Is Settled by New York City for $5.9 Million." *New York Times*, July 13, 2015. https://www.nytimes.com/2015/07/14/nyregion/eric-garner-case-is-settled-by-new-york-city-for-5-9-million.html?smid=pl-share.

Goodwin, Jeff, James M. Jasper, and Francesca Polletta, eds. *Passionate Politics: Emotions and Social Movements*. Chicago: University of Chicago Press, 2001.

———. "The Return of The Repressed: The Fall and Rise of Emotions in Social Movement Theory." *Mobilization: An International Quarterly* 5, no. 1 (March 2000): 65–83.

Graves, Elaine Flora. "Essay." In *Remembering Cesar: The Legacy of Cesar Chavez*, edited by Cindy Wathen, 45–48. Clovis, NM: Quill Driver Books, 2000.

Gregory, Sam. "Transnational Storytelling: Human Rights, Witness, and Video Advocacy." *American Anthropologist* 108, no. 1 (March 2006): 195–204.

Gunckel, Colin. "Building a Movement and Constructing Community: Photography, the United Farm Workers, and *El Malcriado*." *Social Justice* 42, no. 3–4 (2015): 29–45.

Guo, Jeff. "What People Don't Get About Black Twitter." *Washington Post*, October 22, 2015. https://www.washingtonpost.com/news/wonk/wp/2015/10/22/why-it-can-be-offensive-to-use-the-term-black-twitter/?utm_term=.401fc2d07ab4.

Gutierrez, Felix. "Reporting for *La Raza*: A History of Latino Newspapers." *Agenda* 8 (July/August 1978): 29–35.

Habermas, Jürgen. *The Structural Transformation of the Public Sphere: An Inquiry into a Category of Bourgeois Society.* Cambridge, MA: MIT Press, 1989.

Halberstam, David. *The Fifties.* New York: Fawcett Columbine, 1994.

Hall, Stuart. "Encoding/Decoding." In *Culture, Media and Language: Working Papers in Cultural Studies, 1972–79,* edited by Stuart Hall, Dorothy Hobson, Andrew Lowe, and Paul Wills, 107–16. New York: Routledge, 1991.

Haller, Beth. "Crawling Toward Civil Rights: News Media Coverage of Disability Activism." In *Cultural Diversity and the U.S. Media,* edited by Yahya Kamalipour and Theresa Carilli, 89–98. Albany, NY: SUNY Press, 1998.

———. "The Little Papers Newspapers at 19th Century Schools for Deaf Persons." *Journalism History* 19 (Summer 1993): 46–47.

Hallin, Daniel C. *The Uncensored War: The Media and Vietnam.* Berkeley: University of California Press, 1989.

Harriot, Michael. "Whatever Happened to Black Lives Matter?" *Root,* February 16, 2017. https://www.theroot.com/whatever-happened-to-black-lives-matter-1792412728.

Haygood, Wil. "Story of Their Lives for Reporters on the Civil Rights Beat, the Trick Was to Cover the News, Not Be It." *Washington Post,* November 26, 2006. https://www.washingtonpost.com/archive/lifestyle/2006/11/26/story-of-their-lives-span-classbankheadfor-reporters-on-the-civil-rights-beat-the-trick-was-to-cover-the-news-not-be-itspan/7d408efe-ffca-40c8-a3b9-baa3746a1f33/?utm_term=.bdd566db4127.

Heilbrun, Carolyn G. *The Education of a Woman: The Life of Gloria Steinem.* New York: Dial Press, 1995.

Heller, Nathan. "Hunger Artist: How Cesar Chavez Disserved his Dream." *New Yorker,* April 14, 2014. http://www.newyorker.com/magazine/2014/04/14/hunger-artist-2.

Hogan, Kristen. *The Feminist Bookstore Movement: Lesbian Antiracism and Feminist Accountability.* Durham, NC: Duke University Press Books, 2016.

Horne, Gerald. *The Rise and Fall of the Associated Negro Press: Claude Barnett's Pan-African News and the Jim Crow Paradox.* Urbana: University of Chicago Press, 2017.

Hutton, Frankie, and Barbara Straus Reed. *Outsiders in 19th-Century Press History: Multicultural Perspectives.* Bowling Green, OH: Popular Press, 2002.

Hyde, Anne Farrar. "Temples and Playgrounds: The Sierra Club in the Wilderness 1901–1922." *California History* 66, no. 3 (September, 1987): 208–19.

Jacobson, Brian, and Brooke Donatone. "Homoflexibles, Omnisexuals, and Genderqueers: Group Work with Queer Youth in Cyberspace and Face-to-Face." *Group* 33, no. 3 (2009): 223–34.

James, Frank E. "Why a Magazine for Disabled Ignores Handicapped Heroes—Controversial 'Disability Rag' Says Lionizing 'Supercrips' Is No Help for Majority." *Wall Street Journal,* January 11, 1985, 1.

Jarvis, Jeff. "Networked Journalism." *BuzzMachine,* July 5, 2006. https://buzzmachine.com/2006/07/05/networked-journalism/.

Jasper, James M. "Emotions and Social Movements: Twenty Years of Theory and Research." *Annual Review of Sociology* 37 (2011): 285–303.

————, and Jane D. Poulsen. "Recruiting Strangers and Friends: Moral Shocks and Social Networks in Animal Rights and Anti-Nuclear Protests." *Social Problems* 42, no. 4 (November 1995): 493–512.

Jenkins, J. Craig, and Charles Perrow. "Insurgency of the Powerless: Farm Worker Movements (1946–1972)." *American Sociology Review* 42, no. 2 (1977): 249–68.

Jeske, Jeff. "Why Social Justice Journalism?" *College Media Review*, June 3, 2013, 17.

Johnson, David K. *The Lavender Scare: The Cold War Persecution of Gays and Lesbians in the Federal Government.* Chicago: University of Chicago Press, 2004.

Jones, Angela. *African American Civil Rights: Early Activism and the Niagara Movement.* Santa Barbara, CA: ABC–CLIO, LLC, 2011.

Jones, Holway R. *John Muir and the Sierra Club.* San Francisco: Sierra Club, 1965.

Kanellos, Nicolás. "Cronistas and Satire in Early Twentieth Century Hispanic Newspapers." *MELUS* 23 (Spring 1998), 3–25.

Kapp, Joseph. "Technology: The LGBT Community's Unsung Hero." *Huffington Post*, February 2, 2016. https://www.huffingtonpost.com/joe-kapp/technology-the-lgbt-communitys-unsung-hero_b_3179844.html.

Kauffman, L. A. "The Resistance to Trump Is Blossoming—and Building a Movement to Last." *Guardian*, November 9, 2017. https://www.theguardian.com/commentisfree/2017/nov/09/resistance-trump-blossoming-movement-la-kaufmann.

Kelley, William B., Jorjet Harper, and Tracy Baim, eds. *Gay Press, Gay Power: The Growth of LGBT Community Newspapers in America.* Chicago: Prairie Avenue Productions, 2012.

Kemp, Janine Bertram. "Lucy Gwin: The Brain with a Mouth." *Independence Today.* Accessed November 2, 2018. http://www.itodaynews.com/2014-issues/12-2014-issue50/Cover.htm.

Kepner, Jim. *Rough News, Daring Views: 1950s' Pioneer Gay Press Journalism.* Binghamton, NY: Haworth Press, 1998.

Kerr-Ritchie, Jeffrey. *Rites of August First: Emancipation Day in the Black Atlantic World.* Baton Rouge: Louisiana State University Press, 2007.

Kessler, Lauren. *The Dissident Press: Alternative Journalism in American History.* Beverly Hills, CA: Sage, 1984.

Kilkenny, Katie. "How a Magazine Cover from the 1970s Helped Wonder Woman Win Over Feminists." *Pacific Standard*, June 21, 2017. https://psmag.com/social-justice/ms-magazine-helped-make-wonder-woman-a-feminist-icon.

King, Gilbert. "The Woman Who Took on the Tycoon." *Smithsonian*, July 5, 2012. https://www.smithsonianmag.com/history/the-woman-who-took-on-the-tycoon-651396/.

Kipnis, Ira. *The American Socialist Movement 1897–1912.* New York: Columbia University Press, 1952.

Kirk, John A. *Redefining the Color Line: Black Activism in Little Rock, Arkansas, 1940–1970.* Gainesville: University Press of Florida, 2002.

Klibanoff, Hank. "L. Alex Wilson: A Reporter Who Refused to Run." *Media Studies Journal* 14, no. 2 (Spring/Summer 2000): 60–68.

"Knight Errant to Nature's Rescue." *Life* 60 (May 27, 1966): 37–42.

Knutsford, Viscountess [Margaret Jean Treveylan]. *Life and Letters of Zachary Macaulay.* London: Arnold, 1900.

Konopacki, Mike, and Gary Huck. "Labor Cartoons: Drawing on Worker Culture." In *The New Labor Press: Journalism for a Changing Union Movement*, edited by Sam Pizzigati and Fred J. Solowey, 126–40. Ithaca, NY: Cornell University Press, 1992.

Kovach, Bill, and Tom Rosenstiel. *The Elements of Journalism: What Newspeople Should Know and the Public Should Expect, Updated and Revised*. New York: Three Rivers Press, 2007.

Kryder, Daniel. *Divided Arsenal: Race and the American State During World War II*. New York: Columbia University Press, 2001.

Lamb, Chris. "Drawing Power: The Limits of Editorial Cartoons in America." *Journalism Studies* 8, no. 5 (September 2007): 715–29.

Lathrop, Douglas. "Challenging Perceptions." *Quill* 83 (July–August 1995): 36–38.

Lepore, Jill. *The Secret Life of Wonder Woman*. New York: Alfred A. Knopf, 2014.

Levy, Ariel. "Goodbye Again." *New Yorker*, April 21, 2008. https://www.newyorker.com/magazine/2008/04/21/goodbye-again.

Lewels, Francisco J. *The Uses of the Media by the Chicano Movement: A Study in Minority Access*. Westport, CT: Praeger, 1974.

L'Hoeste, Héctor Fernández, and Juan Poblete, eds. *Redrawing the Nation: National Identity in Latin/o American Comics*. New York: Palgrave Macmillan, 2009.

Lindsey, Shelley Stamp. "'Eight Million Women Want—?' Women's Suffrage, Female Viewers and the Body Politic." *Quarterly Review of Film and Video* 16, no. 1 (1997): 1–22.

Loftin, Craig M., ed. *Letters to ONE: Gay and Lesbian Voices from the 1950s and 1960s*. Albany, NY: SUNY Press, 2012.

Lofton, John. *The Press as Guardian of the First Amendment*. Columbia, SC: University of South Carolina Press, 1980.

Longmore, Paul, and Lauri Umansky, eds. *The New Disability History: American Perspectives*. New York: New York University Press, 2001.

Lovan, Dylan. "Widow Believes Husband Died in Pursuit of Cause." *Jackson Sun*. Accessed November 17, 2018. http://orig.jacksonsun.com/civilrights/sec6_widow_wilson.shtml.

Lumsden, Linda J. "Beauty and the Beasts: The Significance of Press Coverage of the 1913 National Suffrage Parade." *Journalism and Mass Communication Quarterly* 77, no. 3 (Autumn 2000): 593–611.

———. *Black, White, and Red All Over: A Cultural History of the Radical Press in Its Heyday, 1900–1917*. Kent, OH: Kent State University Press, 2014.

———. "'Excellent Ammunition': Suffrage Newspaper Strategies During World War I." *Journalism History* 25, no. 3 (Autumn 1999): 53–64.

———. "*The New York Daily Call*: Challenges of Sustaining a Socialist Identity in the Daily Newspaper Market, 1908–1923." *Journalism History* 39, no. 4 (Winter 2014): 219–30.

———. "Striking Images: An Analysis of the Visual Rhetoric in the Radical Press." *Visual Communication Quarterly* 17, no. 4 (October–December 2010): 225–40.

———. "*Suffragist*: The Making of a Militant." *Journalism & Mass Communication Quarterly* 72, no. 3 (1995): 525–38.

"Making Sense of the Culture War over Transgender Identity." *Economist*, November 16, 2017. https://www.economist.com/international/2017/11/16/making-sense-of-the-culture-war-over-transgender-identity.

Manor, Ehud. *FORWARD: The Jewish Daily Forward (Forverts) Newspaper: Immigrants, Socialism and Jewish Politics in New York, 1890–1917.* Brighton, UK: Sussex Academic Press, 2009.

Margolick, David. "Through a Lens, Darkly." *Vanity Fair*, September 24, 2007. http://www.vanityfair.com/news/2007/09/littlerock200709.

Mather, Anne. "A History of Feminist Periodicals, Part I." *Journalism History* 1, no. 3 (Autumn 1974): 82–85.

Matthews, Dylan. "Inside *Jacobin:* How a Socialist Magazine Is Winning the Left's War of Ideas." *Vox*, March 21, 2016. https://www.vox.com/2016/3/21/11265092/jacobin-bhaskar-sunkara.

Mayer, Frederick W. *Narrative Politics: Stories and Collective Action.* New York: Oxford University Press, 2014.

Mayer, Henry. *All on Fire: William Lloyd Garrison and the Abolition of Slavery.* New York: St. Martin's Press, 1998.

McAdam, Doug. "Culture and Social Movements." In *New Social Movements: From Ideology to Identity*, edited by Enrique Larana, Hank Johnston, and Joseph R. Gusfield, 36–57. Philadelphia: Temple University Press, 1994.

———. "Social Movement Theory and the Prospects for Climate Change Activism in the United States." *Annual Review of Political Science* 20 (May 2017): 189–208.

McCarthy, John, and Mayer Zald. *The Trend of Social Movements in America: Professionalization and Resource Mobilization.* Morristown, NJ: General Learning Press, 1973.

McDonough, Tom. *An Eye for Others: Dorothy Day, Journalist: 1916–1917.* Washington, D.C.: Clemency Press, 2016.

McPhee, John. *Encounters with the Archdruid.* paperback ed. New York: Macmillan, 1977.

Medhurst, Martin, and Michael Desousa. "Political Cartoons as Rhetorical Form: A Taxonomy of Graphic Discourse." *Communication Monographs* 48, no. 3 (September 1981): 204, 232, 226–27.

Melancon, Trimiko. "Ramp Your Voice: An Interview with Vilissa Thompson." *Black Perspectives*, March 18, 2017. https://www.aaihs.org/ramp-your-voice-an-interview-with-vilissa-thompson/.

Meyer, Doris. *Speaking for Themselves: Neomexicano Cultural Identity and the Spanish-Language Press, 1880–1920.* Albuquerque: University of New Mexico Press, 1996.

Meyerowitz, Joanne. *How Sex Changed: A History of Transsexuality in the United States.* Cambridge, MA: Harvard University Press, 2004.

Michaeli, Ethan. "'Bound for the Promised Land.'" *Atlantic*, January 11, 2016. https://www.theatlantic.com/politics/archive/2016/01/chicago-defender/422583/.

Milan, Stefania. "When Algorithms Shape Collective Action: Social Media and the Dynamics of Cloud Protesting." *Social Media + Society* 1, no. 2 (July–December 2015): 1–10.

Minian, Ana Raquel. "'Indiscriminate and Shameless Sex': The Strategic Use of Sexuality by the United Farm Workers." *American Quarterly* 65, no. 1 (March 2014): 63–90.

Moodie, Megan. "Handmade Feminism: Irene Lusztig's 'Yours in Sisterhood.'" *Los Angeles Review of Books*, May 11, 2018. https://lareviewofbooks.org/article/handmade-feminism-irene-lusztigs-yours-in-sisterhood/#!.

Morris, James McGrath. *Eye on the Struggle: Ethel Payne, the First Lady of the Black Press*. New York: Armistad, 2015.

Mullin, Benjamin. "Despite Its Blind Spots, the Media Is Getting Better at Telling LGBT Stories." *Poynter.org*, March 24, 2016. https://www.poynter.org/news/despite-its-blind-spots-media-getting-better-telling-lgbt-stories.

Munoz, Lorenza. "An Activist's Vision." *Los Angeles Times*, April 29, 2000. http://articles.latimes.com/2000/apr/29/entertainment/ca-24552.

Nash, Roderick Frazier. *Wilderness and the American Mind*. 4th ed. New Haven, CT: Yale University Press, 2001.

Nelson, Jacob L., and Dan A. Lewis. "Training Social Justice Journalists: A Case Study." *Journalism & Mass Communication Educator* 70, no. 4 (2015): 394–406.

"New Masses, New Media." *New Left Review* 90 (November–December 2014). https://newleftreview.org/II/90/bhaskar-sunkara-project-jacobin.

Newman, Louise Michell.e *White Women's Rights: The Racial Origins of Feminism in the United States*. New York: Oxford University Press, 1999.

Nord, David Paul. "Tocqueville, Garrison, and the Perfection of Journalism." In *Communities of Journalism: A History of American Newspapers and Their Readers*, reprint ed., 92–107. Urbana: University of Illinois Press, 2001.

Oakes, James. *The Scorpion's Sting: Antislavery and the Coming of the Civil War*. New York: W. W. Norton, 2014.

O'Donovan,Caroline. "*Jacobin*: A Marxist Rag Run on a Lot of Petty-Bourgeois Hustle." *Nieman Lab*, September 16, 2014. http://www.niemanlab.org/2014/09/jacobin-a-marxist-rag-run-on-a-lot-of-petty-bourgeois-hustle/.

Oliver, Mary Beth, James Price Dillard, Keunmin Bae, and Daniel J. Tamul. "The Effect of Narrative News Format on Empathy for Stigmatized Groups." *Journalism & Mass Communication Quarterly* 89, no. 2 (June 2012): 205–24.

Ontiveros, Randy. *In the Spirit of a New People: The Cultural Politics of the Chicano Movement*. New York: New York University Press, 2013.

Orentlicher, Diane. "Bearing Witness: The Art and Science of Human Rights Fact-Finding." *Harvard Human Rights Journal* 3 (1990): 83–135.

Ostertag, Bob. *People's Movements, People's Press: The Journalism of Social Justice Movements*. Boston: Beacon Press, 2006.

Patterson, Brandon E. "Police Spied on New York Black Lives Matter Group, Internal Police Documents Show." *Mother Jones*, October 19, 2017. https://www.motherjones.com/crime-justice/2017/10/police-spied-on-new-york-black-

Phelan, James. *Narrative as Rhetoric: Technique, Audiences, Ethics, Ideology*. Columbus: Ohio State University Press, 1996.

Phillips, Barbara E. "Magazine Heroines: Is Ms. Just Another Member of the *Family Circle*?" In *Hearth and Home: Images of Women in the Mass Media*, edited by Gaye Tuchman, Arlene Kaplan Daniels, and James Benet, 116–29. New York: Oxford University Press, 1978.

Pogrebin, Abigail. "How Do You Spell Ms.?" *New York*, October 30, 2011. http://nymag.com/news/features/ms-magazine-2011-11/.

Polletta, Francesca. "Contending Stories: Narrative in Social Movements." *Qualitative Sociology* 21, no. 4 (December 1998): 419–46.

———, and Pang Ching Bobby Chen. "Narrative and Social Movements." In *The Oxford Handbook of Cultural Sociology*, edited by Jeffrey C. Alexander, Ronald Jacobs, and Philip Smith, 487–506. New York: Oxford University Press, 2012.

———, and James M. Jasper. "Collective Identity and Social Movements." *Annual Review of Sociology* 27 (August 2011): 283–305.

Politi, Daniel. "March for Our Lives Put Sarah Chadwick's Spoof NRA Ad on the Big Screen and It Was Glorious." *Slate*, March 24, 2018. https://slate.com/news-and-politics/2018/03/march-for-our-lives-watch-sarah-chadwicks-spoof-nra-ad.html.

Polkinghorne, Donald. *Narrative Knowing and the Human Sciences.* Albany, NY: SUNY Press, 1988.

Powers, Matthew. "The New Boots on the Ground: NGOs in the Changing Landscape of International News." *Journalism: Theory, Practice & Criticism* 17, no. 4 (2016): 401–16.

Quinn, Sally. "Christine: Explaining Transsexualism." *Washington Post*, July 8, 1970, B3.

Rawson, K. J. "Transgender Worldmaking in Cyberspace: Historical Activism on the Internet." *QED: A Journal in GLBTQ Worldmaking* 1, no. 2 (Summer 2014): 38–60.

Rheingold, Howard. *Smart Mobs: The Next Social Revolution.* New York: Perseus Publishing, 2002.

Risley, Ford. *Abolition and the Press: The Moral Struggle Against Slavery.* Chicago: Northwestern University Press, 2008.

Roberts, Gene, and Hank Klibanoff. *The Race Beat: The Press, the Civil Rights Struggle, and the Awakening of a Nation.* New York: Alfred A. Knopf, 2006.

Rosen, Ruth. *The World Split Open: How the Modern Women's Movement Changed America.* New York: Viking, 2000.

Ruff, Allen. *"We Called Each Other Comrade": Charles H. Kerr & Company, Radical Publisher.* Champaign: University of Illinois Press, 1997.

Russell, Adrienne. *Journalism as Activism: Recoding Media Power.* Cambridge: Polity Press, 2016.

———. *Networked: A Contemporary History of News in Transition.* Cambridge: Polity Press, 2011.

Sagarin, Edward. "Transsexualism: Legitimation, Amplification, and Exploitation of Deviance by Scientists and Mass Media." In *Deviance and Mass Media*, edited by Charles Winick. Beverly Hills, CA: Sage Publications, 1978.

Savage, David. "Supreme Court Faced Gay Rights Decision in 1958 Over 'Obscene' Magazine." *Los Angeles Times*, January 11, 2015. http://www.latimes.com/nation/la-na-court-gay-magazine-20150111-story.html.

Savchuk, Katia. "Journalist Sonia Nazario on Coming Out as an Activist." *California Magazine*, April 6, 2017. https://alumni.berkeley.edu/california-magazine/just-in/2017-04-06/journalist-sonia-nazario-coming-out-activist.

Schiller, Herbert. *Culture Incorporated: The Corporate Takeover of Public Expression.* New York: Oxford University Press, 1989.

Schilt, Kristen. *Just One of the Guys? Transgender Men and the Persistence of Gender Inequality.* Chicago: University of Chicago Press, 2010.

Schneirov, Matthew. *The Dream of a New Social Order: Popular Magazines in America 1893–1914.* New York: Columbia University Press, 1997.

Schrepfer, Susan R. *The Fight to Save the Redwoods: A History of Environmental Reform, 1917–1978.* Madison: University of Wisconsin Press, 1983.

Schudson, Michael. *Why Democracies Need an Unlovable Press.* Cambridge: Polity Press, 2008.

Schuessler, Jennifer. "A Young Publisher Takes Marx into the Mainstream." *New York Times*, January 20, 2013. http://www.nytimes.com/2013/01/21/books/bhaskar-sunkara-editor-of-jacobin-magazine.html.

Scotch, Richard K. "Politics and Policy in the History of the Disability Rights Movement." *Milbank Quarterly* 67, Supp. 2 (October 2, 1989): 380–400.

Seldon, Horace. "Garrison's Political Activity, Moral Vision, Public Opinion and Lincoln." *The Liberator Files.* Accessed November 10, 2018. http://theliberatorfiles.com/4-garrisons-political-activity-moral-vision-public-opinion-and-lincoln/.

Severo, Richard. "David Brower, an Aggressive Champion of U.S. Environmentalism, Is Dead at 88." *New York Times*, November 7, 2000. http://www.nytimes.com/2000/11/07/national/07BROW.html?pagewanted=all.

Shapiro, Eve. "'Trans' cending Barriers: Transgender Organizing on the Internet." *Journal of Gay & Lesbian Social Services* 16, no. 3–4 (2004): 165–79.

Shapiro, Joseph. *No Pity: People with Disabilities Forging a New Civil Rights Movement.* New York: Three Rivers Press, 1993.

Sheppard, Alice. *Cartooning for Suffrage.* Albuquerque: University of New Mexico Press, 1994.

Shore, Elliott. *Talkin' Socialism: J. A. Wayland and the Role of the Press in American Radicalism, 1890–1912.* Lawrence, KS: University Press of Kansas, 1988.

Sillesen, Lene Bech, Chris Ip, and David Uberti. "Journalism and the Power of Emotions." *Columbia Journalism Review*, May/June 2015. https://www.cjr.org/analysis/journalism_and_the_power_of_emotions.php.

Silverstone, Roger. "The Sociology of Mediation and Communication." In *The SAGE Handbook of Sociology*, edited by Craig Calhoun, Chris Rojek, and Bryan S. Turner, 188–207. London: Sage, 2005.

Simmons, Ann M., and Jaweed Kaleem. "A Founder of Black Lives Matter Answers a Question on Many Minds: Where Did It Go?" *Los Angeles Times*, August 25, 2017. http://www.latimes.com/nation/la-na-patrisse-cullors-black-lives-matter-2017-htmlstory.html.

Smith, Brice. *Lou Sullivan: Daring to Be a Man Among Men.* Oakland, CA: Transgress Press, 2017.

Smith, C. Calvin. "From 'Separate but Equal to Desegregation': The Changing Philosophy of L. C. Bates." *Arkansas Historical Quarterly* 42, no. 3 (Autumn 1983): 254–70.

Smith, S. E. "Why Disability Rights Activists Stormed Mitch McConnell's Office." *Rolling Stone*, June 23, 2017. https://www.rollingstone.com/politics/news/why-disability-rights-activists-stormed-mitch-mcconnells-office-w489441.

Snow, David A., and Robert D. Benford. "Ideology, Framing Resonance, and Participant Mobilization." *International Social Movement Research* 1, no. 1 (1988): 197–217.

Steiner, Linda. "Finding Community in Nineteenth Century Suffrage Periodicals." *American Journalism* 1, no. 1 (Summer 1983): 1–15.

———. "The History and Structure of Women's Alternative Media." In *Women Making Meaning: New Feminist Directions in Communication*, edited by Lana F. Rakow, 121–43. New York: Routledge, 1992.

Stelter, Brian. "Journalism and Activism: This 'Reliable Sources' Segment Sparked a Debate." *CNN Media*, March 27, 2018. http://money.cnn.com/2018/03/27/media/journalism-activism-reliable-sources/index.html.

Stephen, Bijan. "Get Up, STAND UP: Social Media Helps Black Lives Matter Fight the Power." *WIRED*, November 2015. https://www.wired.com/2015/10/how-black-lives-matter-uses-social-media-to-fight-the-power/.

Stephens, Mitchell. *A History of News: From the Drum to the Satellite*. New York: Penguin, 1988.

Stevenson, Bryan. Introduction to *Lynching in America: Confronting the Legacy of Racial Terror*. 3rd ed. Equal Justice Initiative. Accessed November 10, 2018. https://lynchinginamerica.eji.org/report/.

Stineman, Esther. "Women's Magazines: Serving up the 'New Woman' in the Same Old Ways." *Serials Review* 5, no. 4 (October/December 1979): 25–29.

Stockley, Grif. *Ruled by Race: Black/White Relations in Arkansas From Slavery to the Present*. Fayetteville: University of Arkansas Press, 2012.

Street, Richard Steven. "Delano Diary: The Visual Adventure and Social Documentary Work of Jon Lewis, Photographer of the Delano, California Grape Strike, 1966–1970." *Southern California Quarterly* 91, no. 2 (Summer 2009): 191–235.

Streitfeld, David. "Puncturing the Pathos for the Disabled: Instead, the Gadfly 'Rag' Seeks the Removal of Barriers." *Washington Post*, November 6, 1986, D5.

Streitmatter, Rodger. "*Vice Versa*: America's First Lesbian Magazine." *American Periodicals* 8 (1998): 78–95.

Stryker, Susan. "Portrait of a Transfag Drag Hag as a Young Man." In *Reclaiming Genders: Transsexual Grammars at the Fin de Siecle*, edited by Kate More and Stephen Whittle, 62–82. New York: Bloomsbury Academic, 1989.

———. *Transgender History: The Roots of Today's Revolution*. 2nd ed. New York: Hachette, 2017.

Tarrow, Sidney. *Power in Movement: Social Movements and Contentious Politics*. Cambridge: Cambridge University Press, 1998.

Tcholakian, Danielle. "Is Journalism a Form of Activism?" *Longreads*, March 2018. https://longreads.com/2018/03/29/is-journalism-a-form-of-activism/.

Tichi, Cecelia. *Exposés and Excess: Muckraking in America, 1900/2000*. Philadelphia: University of Pennsylvania Press, 2013.

Tilly, Charles, and Lesley J. Wood. *Social Movements, 1768–2008*. Boulder, CO: Paradigm, 2009.

Timberg, Craig. "In Trump's America, Black Lives Matter Activists Grow Wary of Their Smartphones." *Washington Post*, June 1, 2017. https://www.washingtonpost.com/business/technology/fearing-surveillance-in-the-age-of-trump-activists-study-up-on-digital-anonymity/2017/05/20/186e8ba0-359d-11e7-b4ee-434b6d506b37_story.html?utm_term=.3bd2359f94d5.

Tofel, Richard J. "Non-profit Journalism: Issues Around Impact." *ProPublica*. Accessed October 22, 2018. https://www.propublica.org/impact/.

Tomkins, Stephen. *The Clapham Sect: How Wilberforce's Circle Transformed Britain*. Oxford: Lion Books, 2012.

Turner, Tom. *David Brower: The Making of the Environmental Movement*. Berkeley: University of California Press, 2015.

"Using Social Media to Promote Human Rights." Office of the High Commissioner for Human Rights, United Nations. August 10, 2011. http://www.ohchr.org/EN/NewsEvents/Pages/InternetFreedom.aspx.

van Zoonen, Liesbet. "Spectatorship and the Gaze." In *Feminist Media Studies*, 87–104. London: Sage Publications, 1994.

Vanderbilt, Tom. "Hold the Mayo." *Los Angeles Times*, March 11, 2001. http://articles.latimes.com/2001/mar/11/books/bk-36064/2.

Vongkiatkajorn, Kanyakrit. "How Russia Exploited Black Lives Matter, Sean Hannity, and Mass Shootings." *Mother Jones*, February 17, 2018. https://www.motherjones.com/politics/2018/02/how-russia-exploited-black-lives-matter-sean-hannity-and-mass-shootings/.

Waddell, Kaveh. "The Exhausting Work of Tallying America's Largest Protest." *Atlantic*, January 23, 2017. https://www.theatlantic.com/technology/archive/2017/01/womens-march-protest-count/514166/.

Wan, William. "Postcards from the Left: Resistance Groups Take Aim at Trump, One Letter at a Time." *Washington Post*, November 2, 2018. https://www.washingtonpost.com/national/postcards-from-the-left-resistance-groups-take-aim-at-trump-one-letter-at-a-time/2018/11/02/699df7e0-c1ba-11e8-a1f0-a4051b6ad114_story.html?utm_term=.8ddd0f086e6b.

Washburn, Patrick S. *The African American Newspaper: Voice of Freedom*. Evanston, IL: Northwestern University Press, 2006.

———. *A Question of Sedition: The Federal Government's Investigation of the Black Press During World War II*. New York: New York University Press, 1986.

Wells, Jonathan. "Tyler Oakley: How the Internet Revolutionised LGBT Life." *Telegraph*, November 12, 2015. https://www.telegraph.co.uk/men/thinking-man/tyler-oakley-how-the-internet-revolutionised-lgbt-life/.

Welter, Barbara. *Dimity Convictions: The American Woman in the Nineteenth Century*. Athens, OH: Ohio University Press, 1976.

"What's Your Ms. Story?" *Ms. Magazine* Blog, September 26, 2017. http://msmagazine.com/blog/2017/09/26/whats-ms-story/.

Whyte, Iain. *Zachary Macaulay, 1768–1838: The Steadfast Scot in the British Anti-Slavery Movement*. Liverpool: Liverpool University Press, 2011.

Winter, Jana, and Sharon Weinberger. "The FBI's New U.S. Terrorist Threat: 'Black Identity Extremists.'" *Foreign Policy*, October 6, 2017. http://foreignpolicy.com/2017/10/06/the-fbi-has-identified-a-new-domestic-terrorist-threat-and-its-black-identity-extremists/.

Wolff, Eli A., and Mary Hums. "'Nothing About Us Without Us'—Mantra for a Movement." *Huffington Post*, September 5, 2017. https://www.huffingtonpost.com/entry/nothing-about-us-without-us-mantra-for-a-movement_us_59aea450e4b0c50640cd61cf.

Woloch, Nancy. *Women and the American Experience: A Concise History*. New York: McGraw-Hill Education, 2001.

Wolseley, Roland Edgar. *The Black Press, U.S.A.* 2nd ed. Ames: Iowa State University Press/ Ames, 1990.

"Women's March 2018: Protesters Take to the Streets for the Second Straight Year." *New York Times*, January 20, 2018. https://www.nytimes.com/2018/01/20/us/womens-march.html.

Zelizer, Barbie. "How Communication, Culture, and Critique Intersect in the Study of Journalism." *Communication, Culture & Critique* 1, no. 1 (March 2008): 86–91.

———. *Taking Journalism Seriously: News and the Academy*. Thousand Oaks, CA: Sage Publications, 2004.

Zerbisias, Antonia. "Feminism's Fourth Wave Is the Shitlist." *NOW*, September 16, 2015. https://nowtoronto.com/news/feminisms-fourth-wave-is-the-shitlist/.

Court Cases

Bates v. State of Arkansas. 197 S.W.2d 45 (Ark. 1946), 210 Ark. 652.

Brown v. Board of Education of Topeka. 349 v. U.S. 294 (1955).

Burleson v. U.S. Workingmen's Co-operative Publishing Association. 274 Fed. 749 (1921).

Pitts v. Board of Trustees of the DeWitt Special School District. 84 F. Supp. 975 (E.D. Ark., 1949).

Oral Histories

Douglass Adair. Interview by Greg Turex, March 10, 1995. Farmworker Movement Oral History Project—1995, Part 1. Accessed November 1, 2018. https://libraries.ucsd.edu/ farmworkermovement/media/oral_history/swf/csun/adair01.swf.

"Daisy Bates." Interview by Elizabeth Jacoway, October 11, 1976. Series G. Southern Women. Southern Oral History Program Collection (G–0009). Accessed August 5, 2017. http:// docsouth.unc.edu/sohp/G-0009/G-0009.html.

"David R. Brower: Environmental Activist, Publicist, and Prophet." Interviewed by Susan Schrepfer, 1974–1978. Regional Oral History Office, University of California, Berkeley, 1980.

"David Ross Brower: Reflections on the Sierra Club, Friends of the Earth, and Earth Island Institute." Interviews conducted by Ann Lage, 1999. Regional Oral History Office, University of California, Berkeley, 2012. http://digitalassets.lib.berkeley.edu/roho/ucb/text/ brower_david.pdf.

"Francis Farquhar on Accounting, Mountaineering, and the National Parks." Interview by Willa K. Baum, 1958. Regional Cultural History Project, University of California, Berkeley, 1960.

"Cynthia Jones, Editor and Publisher for *Mainstream Magazine*." Interviewed by Mary Lou Breslin, 1999. *Mainstream Magazine*: Chronicling National Disability Politics, Regional Oral History Office, Bancroft Library, University of California, Berkeley, 2000.

Richard M. Leonard, "Mountaineer, Lawyer, Environmentalist, vol. 2." Interviews by Susan R. Schrepfer, 1972–1975. Regional Oral History Office, University of California, Berkeley, 1975.

"A Publisher's Career with the University of California Press, the Sierra Club, and the California Native Plant Society: August Frugé." Interviews by Suzanne B. Riess 1997–1998. Regional Oral History Office, University of California, Berkeley, 2001.

"Reminiscences of William Edward Colby." Interviews by Corinne Gilb, 1953–1954. Regional Oral History Office, University of California, Berkeley, 2001.

"William Stothers, Journalist and Managing Editor for *Mainstream Magazine*." Interviewed by Susan O'Hara, 1999. *Mainstream Magazine*: Chronicling National Disability Politics, Regional Oral History Office, University of California, Berkeley, 2000.

Dissertations and Theses

Adams, John Lewis. "Time for a Showdown: The Partnership of Daisy and L. C. Bates, and the Politics of Gender, Protest and Marriage." PhD diss., Rutgers University, 2014.

Guerrero, Carlos Reyes. "Silent No More: The Voice of a Farm Worker Press, 1964–1975." PhD diss., Claremont Graduate University, 2003.

Martinek, Jason. "'Mental Dynamite': Radical Literacy and American Socialists' Print Culture of Dissent, 1897–1917." PhD diss., Carnegie Mellon University, 2005.

Nelson, Marjory. "Ladies in the Street: A Sociological Analysis of the National Woman's Party, 1910–1930." PhD diss., State University of New York at Buffalo, 1976.

Purvis, Hoyt Hughes. "Little Rock and the Press." MA thesis, University of Texas, 1963.

Ransom, Lillie Sharon. "Disability Magazine and Newsletter Editors: Perceptions of the Disability Press, Community, Advocacy, Mainstreaming and Diversity." PhD diss., University of Maryland, 1996.

Terborg-Penn, Rosalyn. "Afro-Americans in the Struggle for Woman Suffrage." PhD diss., Howard University, 1977.

Terry, Emylia N. "An Exclusionary Revolution: Marginalization and Representation of Trans Women in Print Media (1969–1979)." Honors Thesis, University of Nevada, Las Vegas, 2014.

Wassell, Irene. "L.C. Bates: Editor of the *Arkansas State Press*." MA thesis, University of Arkansas–Little Rock, 1983.

Interviews

Adamski-Smith, Marilee. Telephone interview by author. May 8, 2018.

Balton, Tom. Interview by author. Sierra Club, San Francisco. April 13, 2016.

Mark, Jason. Interview by author. Sierra Club, San Francisco. April 13, 2016.

Raub, Paul. Interview by author. Sierra Club, San Francisco. April 13, 2016.

Rios, Carmen. Telephone interview by author. June 4, 2018.

Sobik, Jakub. Interview by author. Anti–Slavery International, London. June 16, 2016.

Websites

"Birth Control Organizations: The Brownsville Clinic and Committee of 100." The Margaret Sanger Papers Project. Accessed October 26, 2018. http://www.nyu.edu/projects/sanger/aboutms/organization_brownsville_clinic.php.

Brown, Steven E. "Disability Culture Beginnings: A Fact Sheet." Institute on Disability Culture. Accessed October 12, 2017. http://www.instituteondisabilityculture.org/disability-culture-beginnings-a-fact-sheet.html.

"Code of Ethics." Society of Professional Journalists. Accessed November 10, 2018. https://www.spj.org/ethicscode.asp.

"Decade of Dissent—Andy Zermeño." Center for the Study of Political Graphics, Los Angeles. YouTube video, 10:10. Accessed June 10, 2017. https://www.youtube.com/watch?v=ht7HG68Vwdk.

Ernst, Rhys. "Dear Lou Sullivan, 2014." Vimeo video, 6:34, posted by Visual AIDS. Accessed November 3, 2018. https://vimeo.com/112424796.

Farmworker Movement Documentation Project. University of San Diego Library. https://libraries.ucsd.edu/farmworkermovement/archives/.

Gallo, Marcia. "Introduction." The Ladder: An Interpretation and Document Archive. University of Nevada, Las Vegas, September 2010. http://womhist.alexanderstreet.com/mgallo/intro.htm.

"Gateway: FTM Mentoring Through Newsletters." OutHistory.org. Accessed November 3, 2018. http://www.outhistory.org/exhibits/show/man-i-fest/exhibit/gateway.

"Man-i-fest: FTM Mentorship in San Francisco from 1976–2009." OutHistory.org. Accessed November 3, 2018. http://www.outhistory.org/exhibits/show/man-i-fest.

"Results: Women Candidates in the 2018 Elections." Center for American Women and Politics, November 16, 2018. Updated November 29, 2018. http://www.cawp.rutgers.edu/sites/default/files/resources/results_release_5bletterhead5d_1.pdf.

"Sean Dorsey Dance: 'Lou' (from Uncovered: The Diary Project)." YouTube video, 4:06, FreshMeatSF. Accessed November 10, 2018. https://www.youtube.com/watch?v=zW8__oZ9E1o&list=PL986A71A2937F6259&feature=share&index=9.

"Social Justice and Investigative Reporting." Medill School of Journalism, Media, Integrated Marketing Communications, Northwestern University, Evanston, Illinois. Accessed November 10, 2018. http://www.medill.northwestern.edu/journalism/graduate-journalism/specializations/social-justice-and-investigative-reporting/index.html.

"This Is the American Earth, 1955 Exhibit and 1960 Book." Sierra Club. Accessed November 10, 2018. http://vault.sierraclub.org/education/leconte/history/this_is_the_american_earth.asp.

"We Are the Leaders We Have Been Waiting For." Power to the Polls. Accessed October 2, 2018. http://www.powertothepolls.com/.

"What Is Modern Slavery?" *Anti-Slavery International*. Accessed November 23, 2018. https://www.antislavery.org/slavery-today/modern-slavery/.

"Welcome to ADAPT!" *ADAPT: Free Our People*. Accessed November10, 2018. http://adapt.org/.

Wong, Alice. "Storytelling and the Disability Visibility Project." YouTube video, 4:24. Posted July 11, 2015. https://www.youtube.com/watch?v=8bgBOX42WyE.

INDEX

AEJMC–PETER LANG SCHOLARSOURCING SERIES

Launched in 2014, Scholarsourcing is a joint book publishing venture of the Association for Education in Journalism and Mass Communication (AEJMC) and Peter Lang Publishing that has redefined how scholarly books are proposed, peer-reviewed, and approved for contract. An initiative of 2013–2014 AEJMC President Paula Poindexter, Scholarsourcing is based on the concept of crowdsourcing, with AEJMC members proposing books which are then voted on by the association's membership. Authors of top proposals are invited to write full book proposals that are then reviewed by the Scholarsourcing Series editorial board, with the goal of offering at least one book contract annually.

A very special thanks goes to all who have contributed to the success of Scholarsourcing. These include AEJMC Executive Director Jennifer McGill; Peter Lang Publishing, particularly editor Kathryn Harrison and founding editor Mary Savigar; Founding Series Editor Jane B. Singer; founding editorial board members Carolyn Bronstein, David Perlmutter, Paula Poindexter and Richard Waters; and the hundreds of AEJMC members who have contributed ideas and input, along with a rich supply of wonderful book proposals.

To order books, please contact our Customer Service Department at:

(800) 770-LANG (within the U.S.)
(212) 647-7706 (outside the U.S.)
(212) 647-7707 FAX

Or browse online by series at www.peterlang.com

CPSIA information can be obtained
at www.ICGtesting.com
Printed in the USA
LVHW021257021222
734417LV00002B/134

9 781433 165061